THE *DECAMERON* THIRD DAY IN PERSPECTIVE

The *Decameron* Third Day in Perspective

Volume Three of the *Lectura Boccaccii*

EDITED BY FRANCESCO CIABATTONI
AND PIER MASSIMO FORNI

UNIVERSITY OF TORONTO PRESS
Toronto Buffalo London

Toronto Buffalo London
www.utppublishing.com

ISBN 978-1-4426-4824-1

Toronto Italian Studies

Library and Archives Canada Cataloguing in Publication

The Decameron third day in perspective : volume three of the Lectura Boccaccii/edited by Francesco Ciabattoni and Pier Massimo Forni.

(Toronto Italian studies)

Includes bibliographical references and index.
ISBN 978-1-4426-4824-1 (bound)

1. Boccaccio, Giovanni, 1313–1375. – Decamerone. I. Ciabattoni, Francesco, editor of compilation II. Forni, Pier Massimo, editor of compilation III. Series: Toronto Italian studies

PQ4287.D4255 2014 853'.1 C2013-908319-7

University of Toronto Press acknowledges the financial assistance to its publishing program of the Canada Council for the Arts and the Ontario Arts Council.

Canada Council for the Arts Conseil des Arts du Canada

University of Toronto Press acknowledges the financial support of the Government of Canada through the Canada Book Fund for its publishing activities.

In memory of Ron Schoeffel, who dedicated his professional life to fostering literary criticism and Italian studies at University of Toronto Press

Contents

Acknowledgments

The publication of this volume was made possible by many individuals and institutions. We wish to thank the Johns Hopkins University Faculty of Arts and Sciences, Betty Jean Craige and the Willson Center for Humanities and Arts (University of Georgia), Fabian Alfie, Luisella Bovio Arnold, Susanna Barsella, Dino Cervigni, Brandon Essary, Elsa Filosa, Pier Massimo Forni, Chris Geekie, Warren Ginsberg, Eugenio Giusti, Steven Grossvogel, Christopher Kleinhenz, Marilyn Migiel, Valerie Mirshak, Christopher Nissen, Kristina M. Olson, Michael Papio, Judy Serafini-Sauli, Michael Sherberg, Janet Smarr, Anna Strowe, Lorenzo Valterza, Elissa B. Weaver, Elizabeth Welles, Judith Williams, and the American Boccaccio Association.

THE *DECAMERON* THIRD DAY IN PERSPECTIVE

Introduction

PIER MASSIMO FORNI AND FRANCESCO CIABATTONI

The third day of the *Decameron* marks a new beginning in the structure of the book. The second day ends on a Thursday night. The storytelling resumes on Sunday under the reign of Neifile, after the observances of Friday and the baths of Saturday, which constitute a two-day break leading to the relocation to a new estate. This change of set-up has been interpreted as a necessary shift to re-establish the foundations of the *brigata*'s new society. The new estate, with its *hortus conclusus*, lush garden, warbling birds, clear fountain, and Edenic surroundings, represents the ideal location for this new civic beginning. The theme of Day Three is "people who by dint of their own efforts have achieved an object they greatly desired, or recovered a thing previously lost," and the connection to the lost, and then found again, Eden of civic values is clearly marked by the circular structure of the day's tales. In fact, in the tenth novella, Alibech and Rustico seem to re-enact a travesty of earthly paradise, as Steven Grossvogel's reading astutely points out. This is the day in which human ingenuity dominates, after the incertitudes of Day Two's ups and downs of fortune.

In addition to the day's explicit subject matter, another overarching theme superimposed on the narrative section encompassing Days Three to Five is that the pursuit of adulterous love which characterizes the third day ends in the fulfilment of desire thanks to human ingenuity. A unique feature of this day is that two songs are performed at its end: Fiammetta and Dioneo sing "la dama del Vergiù," an adulterous story with tragic consequences, and Lauretta's own song ends the day with the account of a young woman who is forced to marry a man she does not love. These texts prepare the ground for the transition to the unhappy loves of Filostrato's fourth day, casting a shadow on the successful erotic encounters of the third day. Then in the fifth day, the social order is restored with marriages that sanction and grant social legitimacy to the romances' happy endings.

The novellas of the third day present a particularly rich network of intertextual links, which each *lectura* in this volume helps to illuminate. A plurality of methodological approaches is employed in this volume – and indeed each text invites us to adopt a different perspective – including readings based on allegory, historicist perception, structuralism, and economic history. The most evident innovation of this volume consists in demonstrating the unifying patterns and thematic consistency of Day Three. These *lecturae* also greatly advance the body of scholarly work done on each individual novella, as is the case with Alessandro Vettori's reading of III.5, which relies in part on P.M. Forni's 1986 essay "Zima sermocinante (*Decameron*, III, 5)," which accurately identified the story's rhetorical make-up. Vettori, however, also looks at the story from the points of view of both women's studies and psychoanalysis, taking his reading of the tale in an important and under-explored direction. Elsa Filosa explores III.2, one of the least studied novellas of the *Decameron*. Although Stassi, Ferroni, Alicata, and Muscetta all offer interpretations of this story, before Filosa's essay in this volume, the only scholarly article dedicated solely to this tale was Emma Grimaldi's 1982 publication. In her essay, Filosa, taking a cue from Alberto Moravia, opens a window on the construction of the action to reveal its hidden mechanisms, laying bare its bipartite, symmetrical structure. In addition, Filosa links this novella to other stories (VI.2, X.7, and X.10) that treat the issue of nobility of heart prevailing over nobility of class. Grossvogel develops the critical discourse on III.10 and proposes a moral reading of the novella against the backdrop of the rich scholarship on it. He brings to his study compelling evidence from intertexts such as the lives of saints, the *Life of Maria the Harlot*, and Augustine's *City of God* to address the still debated issue of the novella's moral message.

Massimo Ciavolella places his discussion within certain existing critical contours (Forni, Mazzotta, Marcus, Picone) that define the parodic value of *Decameron* III.1. He then examines sources from Andreas Cappellanus's *De amore* to medieval lyrics and *fabliaux* to Francesco da Barberino's *Reggimento e costumi di donna*. The nuns' carnal desire appears as one aspect of the Catholic Church's battle against the clergy's sexual degradation in the eleventh century. Ciavolella distinguishes, on the basis of Thomistic theology, between two types of passion in the novella: concupiscent love and love of nobility. One of this discussion's key points is the notion that seduction for Masetto is made possible exactly by his muteness: the nuns, encouraged by his alleged inability to use verbal deception or to retell their sexual encounters, lower their defences and give in to their sexual desire. This is the first in a group of *lecturae* that centre on the silencing of speech, which includes King Agilulf's choice of not accusing the groom and the groom's quietness as he seduces the queen (III.2), the silence that Francesco Vergellesi imposes on his wife in the face of Zima's wooing (III.5), and Ricciardo Minutolo's use of his hand to muffle Catella's protestations after he has tricked her into making love with him (III.6).

Elsa Filosa's discussion of *Decameron* III.2 moves away from Alberto Moravia's reading, focusing on action, which, in this novella, fills in the gap left by the above-mentioned silencing of speech. In III.2 action is the real language of the tale. Here, action speaks in a wiser fashion than rash words for both King Agilulf and the groom, as the former refrains from openly accusing his rival and the latter from telling the queen about his feelings for her. It is precisely this wisdom on the part of both men that allows them to retain their reputation. It also allows this tale to challenge the boundaries of a traditional prank-tale while bringing to the fore the two primary themes of the novella: silence as a form of wisdom and a critique of the traditional courtly connection between social rank and a noble heart. This perspective allows Filosa to illuminate the social import of Boccaccio's critique of courtly love as codified by tradition in Boccaccio's day.

Stefano Gulizia's reading of III.3 explores the relationship between rhetoric and genre, with particular attention to the device of the trick that the wool merchant's wife plays on the dim-witted friar as a form of topsy-turvy exemplum. Gulizia outlines the mechanism of a new economy of desire and interweaves it with a discourse on literacy and social status. This chapter illustrates the way in which Boccaccio skilfully plays with the similarities between the two crafts of wool making and storytelling. As a result, this tale effectively highlights the civic values of Florentine merchants, especially their ability and desire to "civanzarsi," or improve one's social and economic position. Gulizia's reading of III.3 addresses the multi-layered substance of the novella, unpacking its gendered treatment of the trick (a woman tricking a friar) as well as its critiques of the clergy and of town gossip. Gulizia also demonstrates how the mercantile language employed in III.3 sets up various layers of reading, adding to the tale's social critique and satirical outcome.

Jelena Todorović revisits the role of the tale of Fra Puccio (III.4) in the macrotextual context of the third day, which retraces in reverse order the three realms of the afterlife. Open references to Dante's *Comedy*, with Paradise, Purgatory, and Hell strategically ordered in between, urge the reader to reconsider the meaning of the afterlife and to take a critical distance from the clergy's manipulative representations of it. Boccaccio's disparagement of bigots and preachers climaxes in Day Three, with the fourth story featuring the unique instance of an encounter of two *homines religiosi* at direct odds with one another. From a parody of the sacraments of the Church, to the critique of Fra Puccio's failure as a husband, to a complete reversal of the beliefs of common people, in Day Three – enclosed within the description of a *locus amoenus* of the Earthly Paradise, but purposely reversing the order of the three realms of the afterlife we find in Dante – Boccaccio clearly paints a caricature of that ideal world, where sin is punished and virtue rewarded, in order to point to the shortcomings of the world around him.

In the fifth story of Day Three, Francesco Vergellesi shares in the destiny of those who, "thinking to beguile others, are themselves beguiled" and ends up unwittingly giving his rival Zima the greatest gift: access to carnal pleasure with his wife. Alessandro Vettori's reading of this tale lays bare the structural mechanism of Zima's *beffa* by showing the underlying dynamic of power and manipulation, and outlines the elements for a "morphology of the prank." The horse that Zima trades to Francesco Vergellesi in exchange for a private conversation with Francesco's wife becomes the metonym of Zima's genitals and the symbol of Francesco's cuckoldry. Vettori suggests that, for all the earnestness of Zima's passionate declaration of love, the courtly love topoi of III.5 may appear parodic in light of the novella's comedic tone, which is kindled by Francesco's prohibition against speaking imposed on his wife. Ironically, the wife's forced silence (even her name remains unspoken and thus we must refer to her as "Francesco Vergellesi's wife") prevents her from giving Zima an honest and stern rejection, as she would no doubt have done, being a "very fair and no less virtuous" woman who had already resisted all previous attempts at courtship.

Myriam Swennen Ruthenberg's reading of III.6 hinges on the dynamics between truth/deception, speech/silence, and envy/jealousy, highlighting a web of intertexts, including Dante's *Commedia*. Viewing III.6 within a framework of courtly references, Swennen Ruthenberg shows how Catella's excessive jealousy and lack of reason could have potentially led to blame or death, were it not for Ricciardo's caution and strength. Uncritical readers who accept situations at face value are destined to suffer the consequences of their superficiality. This principle, laid out in several of Day Three's texts (Eremellina who believes the friar's preaches, Francesco Vergellesi who thinks that silencing his wife will prevent Zima from seducing her, Frate Puccio's extreme naïveté), causes the courtly code structure that apparently supports the day's architecture to crumble.

The crisis of medieval thought and the break in the relation between divine and human are the starting points of Susanna Barsella's analysis of III.7, following scholarship by Eugenio Garin and Kurt Flasch. The impossibility for human knowledge of what is beyond earthly experience appears from the very first novella of the *Decameron*, and III.7 (and really the entire third day) explores the relationship between the courtly secular doctrine of love and religious moral teachings, both of which fail to provide helpful advice on marriage and faithfulness. In particular, Boccaccio's invective concerns the failure of the religious to show consistency between words and action. Tedaldo's preaching to Ermellina while in disguise uncovers the real reason for which Ermellina has distanced herself from her lover: an "accursed" friar had terrorized her with visions of the eternal damnation that would have resulted had she continued loving Tedaldo. Thus, the pedagogical intention underlying Tedaldo's sermon is to educate women as well as the clergy about the risks of an inconsiderate moral terrorism. Boccaccio aims to moralize the moralizers.

Martin Eisner investigates the web of Dantean references in III.8, and links this novella to a series of other tales of the *Decameron* (I.1; III.1; III.10) that deal with the Christian other world. Eisner points out the epistemological import of Boccaccio's discourse on the afterlife, noting the impossibility for the living to attain a true knowledge of the beyond, as well as the liable gullibility of the sanctimonious and the superstitious. Such epistemological critique also extends to the sphere of textual truth, especially when Boccaccio explicitly links the truth of his tale, which has the semblance of a lie ("di menzogna sembianza"), to Dante's figure of Geryon ("quel ver c'ha faccia di menzogna").

First published in 2006 in *MLN*, Anthony Cassell's reading of III.9 parses the controversial judgments this novella received from critics, and proposes a reassessment of it, maintaining that Boccaccio deliberately muffles the verve and genius of III.9 to cause the surrounding tales to shine brighter. The tale's narrative plot – revolving around the thematic threads of Giletta falling in love and her triumph over the medical challenge – incorporates a critique of Christian asceticism and eroticism, whose origin may be traced back to the tradition of the *fabliaux*. Boccaccio's smirking narrative assesses the role of matrimony and childbearing in the complex balance of medieval social dynamics. Basing his reading on the medical and psychological motives behind Boccaccio's depiction of a female physician, Cassell then construes Giletta as a "wandering womb," a tradition that Platonic and Hippocratic philosophies brought to the medical school of Salerno. A mobile uterus allegorizes and parodies Giletta's vicissitudes in her attempt to fulfil motherhood. By escaping her courtly, chauvinistic milieu and by healing the King of France, Giletta exerts her dead father's intellectual and social function, thus succeeding in marrying her beloved Beltramo. She proves able to carry out her absent husband's governing duties, and eventually tricks him into sleeping with her. She then begets two children, fulfilling Beltramo's nearly impossible requests. Thus, by virtue of an errant life, Giletta "gains manipulative and even sadistic mastery over what has made her abject to herself and to others."

The final tale of Day Three conveys the moral message that sexual instincts are a natural drive, a good one indeed, if one that must be managed rather than frustrated. Drawing from a constellation of texts, including the *Life of Maria the Harlot* by the Archdeacon Ephraim, Steven Grossvogel compares Alibech's insatiable but innocent sexual appetite with that of Ephraim's Maria. He concludes that Alibech remains innocent exactly because she is ignorant of the sinful implications of her acts, just like Filippo Balducci's son in the story appearing at the beginning of Day Four. Grossvogel compares Alibech's innocence and Rustico's very self-aware approach to sex to the Augustinian discourse on Adam and Eve's prelapsarian innocence. The Edenic representation of Alibech's life, however, is destined to yield to the constructs and moral strictures imposed by civilization. With Rustico and Alibech's novella about "how the Devil is put back in hell," the *Decameron*'s discourses on the afterlife and the recovery of lost innocence in Day Three have come full circle.

The Tale of Masetto da Lamporecchio (III.1)

MASSIMO CIAVOLELLA

1. Critical Literature

The novella of Masetto da Lamporecchio has not garnered widespread critical attention, despite the strategic position it occupies in the book (it is, after all, the first novella of the third day), its clear connections with the first novella of the first day (Ser Ciappelletto) and the first novella of the second day (Martellino and St Arrigo), and its subject matter dealing with the role of erotic instinct and female sexuality in Christian society, applied in this particular instance to the category of nuns. With certain noteworthy exceptions to be discussed below, the secondary literature has largely dealt with this novella only in passing, either to denounce its obscenity or exalt its free and natural sensuality. In fact, the novella has been regularly expurgated, together with the story of Alatiel (II.7), from the time of Luigi Groto to the beginning of the 1960s, when critics began to celebrate the "natural power of sex [that] is asserted against any superstructure" (Baratto, *Realtà*, 302) and argue that "the desires of the flesh are stronger than any moral or social law, and affect everyone indiscriminately" (Almansi, *The Writer*, 77). Such freedom, as Carlo Muscetta put it, shows Boccaccio aligned "against the silly class prejudices inherited from the feudal era" and "giving back [to the peasant] the capacity to understand and yearn for his own *desires* and those of others, to escape the position of wage-earner and accumulate riches, using all of his *power* to his advantage: an axe, arms, a *tail*, but above all knowing how to *think* and to *imagine* a real world." Referring to Francesco da Barberino (whose *Reggimento e costumi di donna* is purportedly parodied and capsized ideologically in this novella), Muscetta adds, "the workers of the sanctimonious Guelf moralist flay the nuns and their offspring with superstitious ferociousness. Masetto happily propagates young *monks* and deliberately desacralizes their mystical marriage with Christ" (Muscetta, *Giovanni Boccaccio*, 211). The canonical interpretation of the novella, alluded to in the few examples given here, stands between two extremes. On the one hand, there is a moral condemnation of a perverse and corrupting story. On the other hand, there is a blind acceptance of the story based almost exclusively on its presumed defence of the sexual instinct – a defence that purportedly shows the author to be a new man standing at the threshold of a new world.

More recent studies have been more measured in their interpretations and more aware of methodological questions. They have been more inclined to examine the novella within the context of the book itself, as well as with regard to the culture that gave rise to it and to which it belongs. I will mention here only three such studies: those of Pier Massimo Forni, Giuseppe Mazzotta, and Millicent Marcus. In examining the way in which the work is organized "as a collection of complex connections that are made possible by a continual violation of the principle of unity and of the autonomy of the single novella, as well as of the 'natural' and 'obligatory' criterion for aggregation represented by the single day," Pier Massimo Forni devotes a few rigorous and interesting paragraphs to the relationship between the first novellas of the first three days in order to highlight the "concatenated progression" of the narrative discourse, centred in all three instances on "Catholic topics" and on the imposture of individuals who have presumably been saved (*Forme complesse*, 18–20).

For Giuseppe Mazzotta, the novella of Masetto opens as a parody of the allegory of Earthly Paradise. In this story, the author "clearly reverses the conventional exegesis of the *Canticle of Canticles*" (*The World at Play*, 112). And revisiting the relationship between the novella and Andreas Cappellanus's *De amore* – a relationship first suggested by Howard Limoli in an article published in 1965 – he observes that "as Boccaccio casts Masetto cuckolding Christ, he signals that this story is to be read within the bounds of the courtly love system" (ibid., 113). For Millicent Marcus, too, the novella starts from the exclusionary principles of Cappellanus:

> the primacy of language in Andreas' code is overturned in this tale of Masetto, whose feigned muteness endears him to all eight nuns and the abbess ... In fact, Andreas is indirectly responsible for Masetto's success, since it is the widely held misconception that language seduces which allows Masetto to enter the convent at all. ("Seduction," 2–3)

Mazzotta and Marcus privilege the relationship between the novella of Masetto and Cappellanus's *De amore* inasmuch as they see Boccaccio's first story of the third day as a programmatic reversal of the work of his illustrious predecessor and his moralistic, anti-natural, didactic, and anti-erotic positions. Cappellanus's work is thus taken as the true and only source for the novella, and in the process of being capsized, *De amore* is thereby rendered passé.

2. The Sources

The possible antecedents of the novella of Masetto have been identified by Vittore Branca in his edition of *The Decameron*: the *fabliaux* "De l'abesse qui fut grosse," which among all the sources seems to me the most remote; story XIII of the *Alphabetum narrationum*; the story of the count of Poitou; the fourteenth-century ballad "Kyrie, kyrie, the nuns are pregnant"; the prose of the *Novellino* (LXII); the prose that accompanies the ninth part of Francesco da Barberino's *Reggimento e costumi di donna* regarding the behaviour of nuns; and, lastly, Cappellanus's *De amore*, with respect to the two central themes of the novella, namely, the rejection of the notion that nuns are not subject to erotic passions and the appreciation that a man of lower social standing such as a farm-worker can act in ways other than purely animal when tempted by pleasures of the flesh. Leaving aside for a moment *De amore*, the other sources are antecedents that represent themes running throughout medieval culture. Revisiting the sources, to see what Boccaccio takes from them or leaves behind, and to see how he reworks and transforms specific elements, helps us to catch a glimmer of his creative process.

The lyric "Farai un vers, pos mi sonelh" tells of William IX, the count of Poitou, who while travelling encounters two gentlewomen who are going in the same direction. To the two women's greetings, he responds with incomprehensible sounds, leading them to believe he is mute. They find it hard to believe that they have come across a man at once mute and so vigorous, who cannot tell anyone what they plan to do. The two women know altogether too well that the principle of secrecy in love is the stuff of fiction rather than reality. We have found what we've been after, says one to the other; we can certainly trust this man, so let's take advantage of the situation, for opportunities like this don't come around every day: let's take him to the inn. At the inn, after having enjoyed some refreshments, the two gentlewomen lead the poet, who continues to feign stupidity and silence, to their bed. But at this point the two women begin to have doubts: what if this unknown man is not as silent or as stupid as he seems? How can we know? Why not put a cat in the bed where he lies? This is done quickly enough, but the poet, despite being tormented and scratched everywhere, does not speak; he emits only confused and incoherent sounds, like those of a mute. Unconvinced, the two gentlewomen put the cat in the bed again, whereupon he is scratched anew, but emits only confused sounds and never a word. At this point, the two women know that they can trust him and they abandon themselves to sensual pleasure, fearless of being discovered (Jeanroy, *Poésies*, 32–7). The similarities between this story and the novella of Masetto are clear: passing oneself off as mute and stupid as an instrument of seduction, and seducing more than one woman. But the differences are also pronounced: William is a noble, Masetto a yokel; the two women are both of high social status, while the women in the tale of Masetto are nuns; the episode of the count of Poitou begins in an open place and moves to the bedroom of an inn, while the story of Masetto takes place entirely within the walls of a convent.

The subject of the ballad of "Kyrie, kyrie, the nuns are pregnant" is the licentious life of the nuns in a convent, an all-too-common theme of popular medieval literature.[1] The nuns become pregnant through their licentious behaviour – an element this ballad shares with the novella of Masetto. Another echo of this ballad will be heard as well in the second novella of the ninth day, in which "an abbess rises hurriedly from her bed in the dark when it is reported to her that one of her nuns is abed with a lover. But being with a priest at the time, the Abbess claps his breeches on her head, mistaking them for her veil" (IX.2.1).[2]

Francesco da Barberino's prose is set in a Spanish convent. The twelve nuns of the convent founded by a saintly woman are expelled by the notables of the town, and in their place they put twelve of their own daughters – "all eighteen years of age or younger and incredibly beautiful" – in order to protect them from the temptations of daily life. But the life these twelve young women led is hardly exemplary. It is true that they all have "famously holy and wholesome reputations," "and yet secretly among themselves they focused on eating and drinking well, primping themselves and making themselves beautiful, and they devoted little time to

1 See Casini, "Notizie," 1.

2 All quotations from the *Decameron* are from Vittore Branca's Einaudi edition (1992); English translations are by G.H. McWilliam (London: Penguin, 1995). This translated passage is at 655.

prayers or to God, except in the presence of someone from the outside." Observing their behaviour and remembering the wrongs suffered by the twelve poor nuns who have been expelled from the convent, God decides to test the young women's faith by sending Satan to tempt them: "So Satan took one of his devils, which he knew for a long time was very cunning, and gave him this commission. And this devil was named Rasis." Rasis convinces the abbess to take into the convent three new girls, who in reality are three boys aged thirteen, fourteen, and fifteen years, "very beautiful and blonde," and dressed in women's clothing. In the convent, Rasis becomes invisible and "tempts everyone inside with carnal vices," which turns out to be easy in light of the style of life the young women have been living inside, where they have enjoyed a bounty of food, drinks, and idleness. "Within six months they were all pregnant," the text relates. In the end, even the abbess falls into the trap laid by the demon and allows herself to be seduced by one of the young men. When the people found out what was happening in the convent,

> they entered by force, found women with pregnant bodies; they start throwing stones and stoned to death both their kin and everyone else; they burned the abbess and buried their servants alive ... and they went to bring back those twelve poor nuns who were there before and they gave back to them the abbey and chose an abbess; and they lived a very saintly life for a long time. (Francesco da Barberino, *Reggimento*, 137 ff.)

The women accused of consorting with the devil are given the same punishments as those inflicted on the nuns, the abbess, and their servants: the death of the young purifies the convent from misdeeds and placates the ire of the Lord. Even in this case, the similarities – but more importantly the differences – between the two texts are plain to see: the nuns in both cases are young and predisposed to love, but in Barberino's text the catalyst is the devil who tempts them with "carnal vice," while the nuns in the tale of Masetto possess the devil in their bodies. Moreover, the story told by Barberino spreads beyond the confines of the convent, while the novella of the *Decameron* unfolds and is contained within the walls of the convent without any outsider ever becoming aware of what is happening inside.

Prose LXII of the *Novellino* seems instead to have offered Boccaccio some precise elements that he uses directly in the novella we are analysing here, as well as the ninth novella of the fourth day, in which "Messer Guiglielmo Rossiglione dà a mangiare alla moglie sua il cuore di messer

Guiglielmo Guardastagno ucciso da lui e amato da lei" [Messer Guillaume de Roussillon causes his wife to eat the heart of her lover, Guillaume de Cabestanh, whom he has secretly murdered (IV.9.1)].

Pier Massimo Forni analyses the way in which Boccaccio draws upon and recombines elements of this story from the *Novellino*, noting that here too there is a worker – "a dim-witted and very large janitor, whose name was Baligante." Here too there is a community of women: some female servants that choose to lie with him and the "old" countess, who, "hearing ... that he was very well endowed," decides to follow their example (*Novellino*, LXII). Baligante is dim-witted; Masetto, on the other hand, acts as if he were mute and is wrongly believed to be a "giovinaccio sciocco, cresciuto innanzi al senno" [mentally retarded, dim-witted hulk of a youth (III.1.24)]. In the *Decameron* a nun, rather than the abbess who holds authority, spies on the illicit encounters between Masetto and the two nuns who are the first to seduce him. This fact, in turn, leads not to an end to the amusements, but to their diffusion. The "old" countess *feels* that Baligante is "well endowed" and immediately wants him. In Boccaccio, by contrast, the abbess falls into temptation when she happens to see Masetto sleeping naked. The short story of the *Novellino* concludes with the countess and the chambermaids taking the veil. The novella of Masetto opens with the nuns as protagonists. Boccaccio, Forni concludes, "takes the convent setting of the second part of the *Novellino* LXII and combines it with a version of the storyline of the first part" (*Forme complesse*, 52–3).

But what these sources contribute, whether directly or indirectly, is exhausted at a structural level. The relationship that is established with *De amore* appears to consist in something more substantial: Boccaccio seems to draw upon some fundamental principles of Andreas Cappellanus's work in order to subvert the moral structure of the book and the way in which it conceives of love. Moreover, this subversion occurs with a view to establishing a new freedom of thinking, and especially of narrating. In the chapter dealing with love and members of the clergy, the author of *De amore* maintains that it is natural that they feel amorous stimuli, given that they live a sedentary and solitary life. In Boccaccio's novella, however, those receiving stimuli of the flesh are the nuns. As Limoli writes,

> To the medieval writer, and to Andreas in particular, it was one thing to justify a monk's service to love, but quite another to extend the same privilege to nuns. Andreas recognizes a sexual appetite in nuns but hardly approves or justifies it. Thus we have in Filostrato's opening paragraph an important departure from Andreas. ("Boccaccio's Masetto," 285)

In the chapter on "de amore rusticorum," the narrator of *De amore* says to his disciple that "rustic people" can feel only stimuli of the flesh, not of love, given the nature of the work that they do. But, Mazzotta writes,

> Andreas vetoes their love and as the Italian version has it: *"adunque basti loro continua fatica di lavorare i campi e gli sollazzi della zappa e del marrone"*. The proposition is given a pointed refutation by the very experience of Masetto and, more precisely, by a phrase that seems to be a calculated polemic against Andreas' veto and those who believe that *"la zappa et la vanga ... tolgano del tutto a' lavoratori della terra i concupiscibili appetiti."* ... it would appear from this sustained parody of *De arte honeste amandi* either that Boccaccio writes against the subtle ironies that punctuate Andreas' handbook of love or that, blind to these ironies, he mistakes the chaplain's pornographic text for a moralistic construction which he sets out to dismantle. (*The World at Play*, 114)

3. The Language of Desire

I would like to make an attempt at verifying these interpretations by reading the text through other social and cultural filters. I will take for granted everything that has been said so far, but I will privilege ecclesiastical and medical-philosophical texts, rather than those texts that lie specifically within the literary tradition, like those that we have hitherto examined.

Let us begin with Boccaccio's first paragraph:

> Bellissime donne, assai sono di quegli uomini e di quelle femine che sí sono stolti, che credono troppo bene che, come ad una giovane è sopra il capo posta la benda bianca e indosso messale la nera cocolla, che ella piú non sia femina né piú senta de' feminili appetiti se non come se di pietra l'avesse fatta divenire il farla monaca: e se forse alcuna cosa contra questa lor credenza n'odono, cosí si turbano come se contra natura un grandissimo e scelerato male fosse stato commesso, non pensando né volendo aver rispetto a se medesimi, li quali la piena licenzia di poter far quel che vogliono non può saziare, né ancora alle gran forze dell'ozio e della sollecitudine. E similmente sono ancora di quegli assai che credono troppo bene che la zappa e la vanga e le grosse vivande e i disagi tolgano del tutto a' lavoratori della terra i concupiscibili appetiti e rendan loro d'intelletto e d'avedimento grossissimi. Ma quanto tutti coloro che cosí credono sieno ingannati, mi piace, poi che la reina comandato me l'ha, non uscendo della proposta fattaci da lei, di farvene piú chiare con una piccola novelletta. (III.1.2–5)

[Fairest ladies, there are a great many men and women who are so dense as to be firmly convinced that when a girl takes the white veil and dons the black cowl, she ceases to be a woman or to experience feminine longings, as though the very act of making her a nun had caused her to turn into stone. And if they should happen to hear of anything to suggest that their conviction is ill-founded, they become quite distressed, as though some enormous and diabolical evil had been perpetrated against Nature. It never enters their heads for a moment, possibly because they have no wish to face facts, that they themselves are continually dissatisfied even though they enjoy full liberty to do as they please, or that idleness and solitude are such powerful stimulants. Again, there are likewise many people who are firmly convinced that digging and hoeing and coarse food and hardy living remove all lustful desires from those who work on the land, and greatly impair their intelligence and powers of perception. But, since the queen has bidden me to speak, I would like to tell you a little tale, relevant to the topic she has prescribed me, which will show you quite clearly that all these people are sadly mistaken in their convictions.]

Just who are these "great many men and women" who believe that once a woman has donned a nun's habit she no longer feels "feminine longings"? The answer can only be simple-minded people, who are bigoted and ignorant both of human nature and of what science and the Catholic Church say about human nature. Indeed, the Church has long fought a merciless public battle against temptations of the flesh from which no one is free – neither man nor woman, priest nor nun. It is a battle, to be sure, that extends from the writings of the Church fathers and ecclesiastical legislation, from St Jerome and St Augustine to the penitentials, from the Canonical collections of the eighth and ninth centuries to Canon law of the eleventh and twelfth century up to the decretists, from Gratian onward. The problem, as Mazzotta notes, is inherent in the concept of original sin, that is to say, what was and would have been obtained for humankind in the Earthly Paradise in the absence of Adam and Eve's transgression, and what in effect was lost in the wake of their defiance against the divine command. The human being clearly did not change: it still consists of a body and a soul, humours, *pneuma*, and spirits. In the Earthly Paradise, however, the soul was in perfect harmony with the body, and the soul and body were in perfect tune with the external world, with nature, and hence with God. Eternal happiness consisted precisely in this. Original sin, thus, destroys this basic equilibrium and introduces an imbalance between the qualities of the body, and between body and soul, and hence produces sickness. In the world after the fall, sickness is a predominant element of human nature – a genetic element, we might say today – and the life of the Christian is a continual struggle to find order, equilibrium, and harmony in the body and spirit in an effort to become closer to God. The most serious affliction is erotic desire, for it entails not only a great physiological imbalance but one of the soul, too, since by focusing an individual's attention on an object he so ardently desired, it fatally destroys his spirit as well. This does not mean, to be sure, that sex as such did not exist in the Earthly Paradise: procreation would have happened through sexual union, but this union would not have been accompanied by any pleasure of the senses, for passion itself is an illness provoked by the overheating of the genital organs – a physiological imbalance. In his *Historia scholastica*, the authoritative ecclesiastic writer Petrus Comestor maintained that in the Garden of Eden, contact between genital organs provoked the same sensations as when one hand touches another. And because sexual pleasure is the strongest and most destructive of all the *passiones*, it is the gateway by which the devil can take possession of an individual with greatest ease (*Historia scholastica*, 1081).

In Francesco da Barberino, the demon Rasis damns the young nuns, tempting them, as the text says, "with carnal vice." The Church's attention was devoted to the clergy in general and to nuns in particular. The problem of the clergy was exacerbated by the fact that idleness and indulging in food and drink augmented sexual stimuli. Clergymen and nuns were not subject to the strains of manual labour and the hardships of poverty. Beginning in the eleventh century the clergy was enjoined not to marry or keep concubines in the home or monastery – a prohibition that raised many protests among the clergy in various parts of Europe. They were ordered not to keep young women at home or in the monasteries and not to consort with members of the opposite sex except in the presence of other clergymen. The Dominican constitution prohibited monks from looking at women or speaking to them outside of the confessional booth. Ecclesiastical history is replete with injunctions against monasteries in which monks lived happily with their women and children.

The problem concerning the nuns was different and potentially more destructive for a couple of reasons. First, taking vows meant becoming *sponsa Christi*, thereby dedicating oneself bodily and mentally to Christ. Virginity is a heavenly gift, as the *Glossa palatina* of the twelfth century states: "Non ideo hoc dicit ut sole uirgines habeant paradisum, sed quia facilius ... uel quia uirginitas soror est angelorum"[3] [Thus he does not say this so that only the virgins may gain paradise, but more easily ... or because virginity is the sister of the angels]. Moreover, women were not only considered intellectually and physically inferior to men, but also naturally more susceptible to physical and emotional disorders stemming from erotic passion. It was a widespread opinion that female inferiority derived from the fact that women's basal temperature – their innate heat – was lower than men's, and that for this reason nutrients tended naturally to sediment in the lowest parts of the body; from the hips and below, women were supposedly heavier than men (this apparently explained why women had wider hips than men), while from the waist and above they were more slender and colder. Since heat refines the intellect, inasmuch as it is a perfecting element of the universe, men, who are naturally warmer, will be more robust in their upper body and intellectually superior. Equally widespread was the notion that women, despite being colder, suffered more uncontrollably from stimuli of the flesh. This apparent contradiction was resolved by explaining that feminine appetites depended on particular humours that were different from men's; they were connected to the uterus and to its erratic and sudden movements (hysteria). All of this could provoke intense heat in the genital region, as well as sudden and uncontrollable erotic *raptus*. This anatomic argument justified the notion that women in general – and virgins in particular – found sensual stimuli irresistible. Cardinal Ostiense, bishop of Ostia (d. 1271), said in a widely disseminated *Lectura* that women are always ready and willing to have sexual encounters and that they have no need for any preparation. He concluded that a priest who travelled with two women – one in front of him and another behind – could never guarantee that the one sitting behind him was still a virgin.[4] It is for this reason that ecclesiastical legislation was much more severe with regard to nuns than with priests or monks. Nuns are always able and inclined to betray their "husband," and for this reason they need to be controlled continually – in their gestures, in what they read, and in what they see. If a priest is discovered to have sinned with a woman, he must be reprimanded, but he does not lose his ecclesiastical position, because the fault lies unquestionably with the woman. Nuns who allow themselves to be overcome by carnal desires will be accused of *moechnia*, that

3 Cited in Brundage, *Law, Sex*, 350–1 and note 133.

4 Cited in ibid., 557.

is, of marital infidelity, placed under trial, expelled from the convent, and perennially branded as *infames*.

Boccaccio's nuns are young, virgin, and firmly in possession of those "feminine appetites" that make them more frenzied and aggressive than men. It is a universally known biological truth that ought not surprise us. Hence Nuto says to Masetto that the nuns of the convent from which he has just escaped "are all young and they seem to me to have the devil in them, because whatever you do, it is impossible to please them" (III.1.9; translation 193). The expression "to have the devil in them" is traditionally connected to erotic hysteria and implicitly means sexually possessed.

The medieval reader would not have missed the subtle irony in the antiphrastic trope that opens the novella stirred by hyperbole (as Delcorno says, "almost mirrored in a second antiphrasis hidden in a brazen parenthetic [digression]" ["Ironia/parodia," 164]): "In queste nostre contrade fu, e è ancora, un munistero di donne assai famoso di santità (il quale io non nomerò per non diminuire in parte alcuna la fama sua)" [In this rural region of ours, there was and still is a nunnery, greatly renowned for its holiness, which I shall refrain from naming for fear of doing the slightest harm to its reputation (III.1.6)]. The narrator's voice, disavowing the reputation of the nunnery and the nuns who live in it, unveils the brand of infamy hidden in their soul.

Let us return to the second part of the first paragraph of the novella:

> Again, there are likewise many people who are firmly convinced that digging and hoeing and coarse food and hardy living remove all lustful desires from those who work on the land, and greatly impair their intelligence and powers of perception.

Like the sentence pertaining to the nuns, this too is suffused with subtle irony; it is the opening, together with what precedes it, to a fun and provocative joke with the reader. There is no one who does not know that even farm workers can experience "lustful desires" and that not all of them have great "powers of perception." Rarely, however, is their relationship with the opposite sex dictated by anything other than "lustful desires." And while they may not have "great" powers of perception, they are certainly intellectually inferior to those who belong to the ruling class. It is a truth that everyone knows, including the author of *De amore*, who distinguishes clearly between this sort of untamed love – what Thomas Aquinas called *amor concupiscentiae* – and the love of the nobility, which is sustained by idleness, food, reading, and discussion, and goes by the name of *amor heros* or *hereos*, that is to say, noble or heroic love. To explain the differences between these two types of erotic passion, I will draw once again on texts that are not specifically literary.

Among the many texts at our disposal, I will focus on the gloss that Gerard of Berry (a contemporary of Andreas Cappellanus) wrote on the chapter on love in one of the most widely diffused books in Europe prior to the fifteenth century, the *Viaticum* by the monk Constantine the African, a book plagiarized from an Arabic original in the medical school of Salerno. At the word *heros* the gloss explains, "noble men are called heroes insofar as they suffer most from this malady, given their wealth and the ease of the life they lead" (*Notule*, 199–205). For Gerard, whose gloss has been handed down to us in numerous manuscripts throughout Europe, the relationship is firmly based on considerations of a medical variety. Constantine himself wrote in his treatise *De coitu* that "an idle heart and daily pleasure augment lustfulness."[5] This sort of love was considered different from the kind that afflicted the lower class precisely because it was fostered by the easy life. If delicious foods and superior digestion create more refined spirits, this also enables intellectual life: stories of exploits and loves, conversations and debates on the pleasures of life, and so on. *Amor heros* is thus, in part, the product of physiological processes, and, in part, the product of cultural processes. An individual who works the land all day and eats "coarse food" will have more volatile humours and will be wilder in his passions – passions that certainly are not refined by reading and all the other activities of the noble classes. Refined eroticism becomes a distinctive sign of the upper class, together with wealth and idleness. Indeed *amor heros* is what distinguishes a noble man from a commoner. It is interesting to note that this sort of love does not appear in the treatises that were addressed specifically to the have-nots, such as the *Thesaurus pauperum*. But neither does it appear, for that matter, in the treatises on the maladies of women, which discuss instead melancholy, mania, and frenzy. We have already seen why: since women are intellectually inferior to men and dominated by their own instincts, their sensuality is not so different from the peasant's: the intensity of women's passions and their sexual readiness are in fact greater.

Read through these filters, Masetto's acting mute in order to seduce young nuns has the same social and cultural weight as the nuns who want to take advantage of his muteness in order to do to him what he wants to do to them. At this level, it is a game among equals; at a

5 Constantine the African, *De coitu*, cited in Brundage, *Law, Sex*, 187.

physiological level, it is a battle between unequals, inasmuch as women's desire and sexual capacity are far superior to men's: to recall Cardinal Ostiense, women are always ready and willing to have sexual encounters and they have no need for any preparation.

It is for this reason that all the nuns suddenly want to follow the example of the first two nuns (and later the abbess herself) upon seeing Masetto's member exposed while he sleeps. Their behaviour is entirely natural within the context of medieval culture.

4. Desire and Morality

Boccaccio knew perfectly well that this is nothing but a model of erotic behaviour, one of the most prominent indeed, although certainly not the only one. The same can be said for the role of feigning muteness as an instrument of seduction or the sexual voraciousness of nuns and their resulting pregnancies, which repeat well-known and tested literary models. Moreover, the subtle irony that permeates the novella from the very beginning establishes immediately a privileged relationship between the narrator and reader, a relationship of complicity not unlike what in pre-modern theatre is the premise of the *vis comica*. The tale deals with "Catholic topics" in an irreverent and scandalous key, but it unfolds entirely on a stage surrounded by the impenetrable walls of a convent, within the garden inside. It is a *hortus conclusus* that is impermeable to the external world and a *hortus deliciarum* in which everything is permitted: nuns can abandon themselves to their own feminine nature, betraying their "husband" with any man, have children, and live happily ever after. Masetto can cuckold Christ and become a "rich father." We readers know the nature of "feminine appetites"; we are aware of the brand of *infames* that marks the nuns who have sinned of *moechnia*, and we know likewise that peasants are largely coarse and dominated by their "lustful desires." The space within which the tale unfolds reproduces in its essential traits the state of human beings when they are left to their own devices in a postlapsarian world. But it is a space that is enclosed within another garden, namely, one in which a group of ten young people take refuge after having abandoned the first country estate and which reproduces the harmony of the Earthly Paradise. It is this garden that allows the young individuals in the group and us as readers to continue "quella festa, quella allegrezza, quello piacere che noi potessimo, senza trapassare in alcuno atto il segno della ragione" [feasting and merrymaking as best we may without in any way overstepping the bounds of what is reasonable (I.Intro.65)].

The Tale of the King and the Groom (III.2)

ELSA FILOSA

1. The Action (I)

One of the most attentive and exceptional readers of the tale of King Agilulf and his groom was Alberto Moravia, who, as a writer himself, focused his attention on Boccaccio's need to write and tell stories.[1] He claims that "what Boccaccio needed was action pure and simple" (*Man as an End*, 137). Moravia goes into III.2 in length, as he considers this tale to be "one of the best in the *Decameron* and one in which the passion for action seems to attain the highest level of articulation and depth" (151).

It is precisely in the action that we find one of the most distinctive features of the novella: the moves and countermoves of the king and the groom, the repetition of acts, the rapid change of scene, the serial tonsures at the end, and, last but not least, the silencing of speech, all of which contribute a sense of theatre, if not cinematography, to the tale. If we do think of the tale in terms of film, it would have to be a black-and-white one (which would play up the *chiaroscuro* of the many scenes with candles, lamps, and lanterns). And it would be a silent film, too, with very few intertitles, and those would be concentrated in the scene in Queen Teudelinga's bedchamber and the scene in which Agilulf confronts the servants at the end of the story. One imagines a film from

1 Although Moravia thought this novella was one of the best in the *Decameron*, III.2 has not attracted many commentators: only Emma Grimaldi has written an essay specifically focused on Agilulf and his groom. Nevertheless, other scholars writing about Day Three give a close look at the second novella: see Stassi, "Amore e industria," 46–50; Ferroni, "Eros," 240–3; Alicata, "La terza giornata," 250; Muscetta, *Giovanni Boccaccio*, 212–23; Usher, "Industria."

the early days of cinema, in which the projection would speed up the movements slightly. One could picture Buster Keaton as the groom, barely able to restrain his yearning for Teudelinga when he helps her go riding; an unabashed suitor who, after considering and rejecting several possible alternatives, decides to impersonate the king. From a hiding place in a large hall between the chambers of the king and queen, where the groom has been going night after night to spy on the king's movements, on "one night among others" ("intra l'altre una notte" [III.2.12]),[2] he sees the king knock and enter Teudelinga's chamber and, after a while, leave. The groom inserts himself into this sequence, entering and leaving just like the king. But soon after he has left, we see the king enter the queen's bedchamber – intertitles tell us what he and Teudelinga say to each other – and leave, but this time the king does not take his customary route. Instead of going back to his own chamber, he makes his way rapidly to the servants' quarters above the stables. The scene changes: we find ourselves in a long dormitory, with a line of cots in which the servants are sleeping. The king enters the room and goes from cot to cot, feeling the chest of each person. Starting with the first bed, he places his hand on the sleeper's chest; he proceeds to the second, then the third, and the fourth, and so on, until he reaches the groom. There is a pause while he draws something from his garments. It is – a pair of scissors. The king cuts off a hank of the groom's hair and departs. At that point, the groom sits up, rummages around until he finds a pair of horse-grooming scissors, and he too goes from bed to bed, cutting hanks of hair off the first sleeper, then the second, and the third, and so on, until he has finished. Then he goes back to bed and falls asleep. And so we cut to the final scene: early the next morning, in front of the doors of the palace, all the servants are lined up. Most have their hair cut in exactly the same way, and the king is inspecting them. He is, for a moment, astonished. But then he recovers his regal bearing. He speaks to the assembled servants. Below his intent and expressionless face appears the title: "Chi 'l fece nol faccia mai piú, e andatevi con Dio" [Whoever it was who did it, he'd better not do it again. And now be off with you (III.2.31)].

---

2 All quotations from the *Decameron* are from Vittore Branca's Einaudi edition (1992) and the English translations from J.M. Rigg (1903), unless stated otherwise.

I wanted to start with these images from the story because they demonstrate clearly the action – above all, the game-like repetition of acts and movements and their comic connotations, which abound in this story.

But let me introduce the characters more fully. On the one side, we have Agilulf, king of the Lombards, who is presented by the story's narrator, Pampinea, as a strong and wise man, under whose rule the people have enjoyed peace and prosperity for many years.[3] This characterization most likely comes from Paul the Deacon, who in his *Historia Langobardorum* describes Agilulf as "vir strenuus et bellicosus et tam forma quam animo ad regni gubernacula coaptatus" [a man energetic and warlike and fitted as well in body as in mind for the government of the kingdom (III.35)]. All of Agilulf's fine abilities, including, above all, his good sense, are evident in each of his actions.[4]

---

3 Agilulf reigned as king of the Lombards between 590 and 616, and rose to the throne thanks to his marriage with Theodelinda, queen of the Lombards and widow of his cousin Authari (540–90). Following Boccaccio's orthography, I use the spelling Teudelinga when talking about the character in the Decameron; I use the common spelling Theodelinda when talking about the historical character.

4 Books III–IV of *Historia Langobardorum* by Paul the Deacon might have served as an inspiration for Boccaccio in describing the historical background of this novella, the only one in the *Decameron* to take place in the early Middle Ages. It is useful to recall here that, as Vittore Branca has pointed out (*Boccaccio medievale*, 386), pages from the *Historia* were the basis of the initial description of the plague in the *Decameron*'s Introduction. And Boccaccio's primary source for a curious description of the Lombards in his *De casibus virorum illustrium* (IX.48–9) also comes from Paul the Deacon: "Post hanc longus ordo sequebatur hominum, oris habitu a ceteris adverso, ut, dum primo inspicerem, potius ludentes larvatos quam flentes miseros extimarem. Erant enim eis a cervice in occipitium capita depilata, et a lateribus in ora diffusa vertebatur cesaries, et a semitecta crinibus facie barba unicuique prolixa declinabat in pectus; vestes illis large atque fluxe, variis contexte coloribus, albisque fasceolis infra suras, fere omnibus, ligata crura; his insuper calciamenta aperta fere ad pollicis usque summum, hinc inde alternis corrigiarum alligata laqueis. Quos ego postquam paululum mirabundus aspexi, Langobardos esse cognovi" [After her followed a big crowd of men, so different in facial expression from the others that, when I saw first them, I thought they were playing in masks instead of crying grief-stricken. In fact, their heads were shaved from the neck to the forehead, and from the sides the hair was turned streaming in toward the mouth. And from the face half-hidden by the hair, each man's beard spread forward thickly over the chest; their garments were large and long, woven from different colors, and almost everybody's legs were bound up with white straps on the calf; their shoes were almost completely open to the top of their big toe, and from there bound with shoelaces with alternate lacing. After looking at them astonished for a while, I knew they were Lombards] (Boccaccio, *De casibus virorum illustrium*, IX.4; translation mine) Laura Pani has recently recognized in the codex Harley 5383 the *Historia Langobardorum* transcribed, owned, and glossed by Boccaccio himself.

The groom, the other hero of the novella, is the one who sets things in motion: he is described as "uomo quanto a nazione di vilissima condizione, ma per altro da troppo piú che da cosí vil mestiere, e della persona bello e grande cosí come il re fosse" [a man of exceedingly low birth, gifted out of all proportion to his very humble calling, who was as tall and handsome as the King himself (III.2.5)]. The comparison, appearing right at the beginning of the tale, immediately sets up a direct equivalence between king and groom, which anticipates the development of the plot. In addition, the two characters are introduced together in a single sentence, thus linking them grammatically and placing them on the same level of worth, as human beings. In the presentation of this very humbly born groom, the reader also learns something about the king: that he is as tall and handsome as the groom. But although the two characters are equals in intelligence, physicality, and character, they occupy opposite ends of the social spectrum.

The closing phrase of the sentence that introduces Agilulf and the groom to the reader gives us the prime motive for the story. The descriptions of king and groom lead straight to the sentence's main verb "adivenne che": "adivenne che un pallafreniere della detta reina … senza misura della reina s'innamorò" [It happened that the groom … fell hopelessly in love with his royal mistress (III.2.5–6)]. The groom's love for the queen is what drives the story, like a spring that is wound tighter and tighter until it finally releases tension, setting off all the events of the novella. Moravia observes that this pattern occurs throughout the *Decameron*: "The role of love here [in the *Decameron*], as in reality, is as a mainspring of human action and once the spring has been released Boccaccio turns his attention exclusively to action" (*Man as an End*, 138).

The groom is consumed by his hopeless love for Teudelinga and makes his decision. Spurred by inextinguishable ardour, he is ready to die for love of the queen – not by simply pining away, but by gambling his life for one delicious night with her. The only possibility open to him is to become someone else: that is, to pretend to be the king. And to realize his plan, he studies, secretively and in minute detail, the king's characteristics and movements. It is precisely this study and his continual watchfulness that allow the groom to keep always one step ahead of Agilulf, an advantage that he does not lose until the very end of the tale.

At the point when the groom makes this decision, there is a crucial change of context: from the outdoors, in daylight – where we have the description of the groom in love, happy just to brush against the queen's clothing – we pass to nocturnal interior spaces, where the locations of the action are dark and secretive, qualities synonymous with deceit and illicit amorous adventures. The hero is mute, wrapped in silence and shadows, and hides quietly in out-of-the-way corners of the Lombard palace night after night while everyone else is asleep, in order to spy how the king is dressed and what he does when he goes to lie with the queen. This action, repeated "piú volte di notte" [several nights], Boccaccio tells us, underlines the single-mindedness and constancy of the groom, but also his shrewdness in obtaining what he desires. Finally, one night "amongst others" he has his chance:

> e intra l'altre una notte vide il re uscire della sua camera inviluppato in un gran mantello e aver dall'una mano un torchietto acceso e dall'altra una bacchetta, e andare alla camera della reina e senza dire alcuna cosa percuotere una volta o due l'uscio della camera con quella bacchetta, e incontanente essergli aperto e toltogli di mano il torchietto. (III.2.12)

> [one night, amongst others, he saw the king emerge from his room in an enormous cloak, with a flaming torch in one hand and a stick in the other. Walking over to the Queen's room, the King knocked once or twice on the door with his stick, whereupon he was instantly admitted and the torch was removed from his hand.]

This is what the groom saw, and this is what he would do: he would repeat exactly the same sequence of actions. Repetition of the action has enormous value in this case, because it creates an exact parallel between the king and his physical double, and because it creates the conditions for the comic dimensions of the tale. This parallelism was foreshadowed in the initial description of the two men, when the groom is described as being "della persona bello e grande cosí come il re fosse" [as tall and handsome as the King himself]. The nocturnal scene described earlier is recreated exactly by Agilulf's doppelganger, with the same props, costume, and gestures. To transform from one character into another, he needs to construct a new mask. The entire account of these preparations resembles the description of the work of an artisan: to recreate the perfect image of the king with the limited means at his disposal. The tale's narrator, Pampinea, describes the tools and materials that he uses in terms that poke a little fun at the groom's endeavours: "e trovato modo" [he found means] to procure "un mantello simile a quello del re" [a mantle like that which he had seen the king wear], who himself was wrapped in "un gran mantello" [a great mantle]. He finds "un torchietto" [a taper] and "una mazzuola" [a small rod], in place of the "bacchetta" [the regal wand] that the king uses.[5] He also thinks to provide himself with a flint and steel so he can light the taper. But the most striking proof of the groom's refinement and intelligence is that he thinks to take a hot bath so he does not smell of the stable. The bath is not only a very useful idea (the queen must not suspect that he is not the king), but also a considerate one, for he will not then disturb the queen's sensibility. His attention to hygiene demonstrates the groom's noble spirit, and takes on all the characteristics of the courteous homage of a lover to his beloved. Cleanliness thus becomes an element of mindful love and respect for the lady (Baratto, *Realtà*, 229). To this can be added the idea that the bath is also a symbolic moment of rebirth, which effectively cancels the original identity of the groom (Grimaldi, "Il silenzio di Agilulf," 21). But the groom's mimesis does not stop at visual and olfactory camouflage: he also manages to mimic the psychology of the king, and it is in this last quality that he truly shows his greatness. Once he has entered the queen's bedchamber – dressed like the king, following the same ritual of entry as the king – has pulled aside the bed curtains, and has climbed into bed alongside the queen, he acts as if he were "turbato" [angry], and thus is able to conceal his voice:

> Egli disiderosamente in braccio recatalasi, mostrandosi turbato (per ciò che costume del re esser sapea che quando turbato era niuna cosa voleva udire), senza dire alcuna cosa o senza essere a lui detta, piú volte carnalmente la reina cognobbe. (III.2.16)

> [Knowing that the King, whenever he was angry about anything, was in the habit of refusing all discourse, he drew the Queen lustfully into his arms with a show of gruff impatience, and without a single word passing between them, he repeatedly made her carnal acquaintance.]

To avoid further risk, the groom decides at that point to leave the queen: taking the taper and the mantle with him, he promptly returns to his own bed.

At this point in the novella, in the sophisticated contest between the king and the groom, the groom (as in a game of chess) has made the first move: a slow, precise, premeditated move, which is answered by

5 The translations of this passage are mine.

an equally precise (though rapid) move by the king, who realizes he has been checked. The parallel between groom and king, which had been established by the groom, is now broken. The narrative point of view, which up to this point has focused on the groom, now passes to the king. Finally, we accompany him into Teudelinga's bedchamber and hear the first exchange of words to occur between any of the novella's characters. This is the moment of stasis between the actions of the two male protagonists, a pause, in the form of speech, which is prologue to a new series of actions – characterized, as we shall see, by the same kind of repetition we saw in earlier scenes – and which forms the second part of the novella, not to mention the line of demarcation between the actors.

2. In the Bedchamber

Malice in various forms creeps into all parts of the scene that now play out in the bedchamber. In a reverse image of the groom, who entered the room looking grim and preoccupied (in order to avoid the need to talk), the king is cheerful; so cheerful, in fact, that the queen is emboldened to ask:

> O signor mio, questa che novità è stanotte? Voi vi partite pur testé da me; e oltre l'usato modo di me avete preso piacere, e cosí tosto da capo ritornate? Guardate ciò che voi fate. (III.2.17)

> [Heavens! Whatever has come over you tonight, my lord? You no sooner leave me, after enjoying me more passionately than usual, than you come back and start all over again! Do take care of your health!][6]

6 The queen's words, the first to be spoken by any character in the novella, are in a central position in III.2, and are also the turning point of the action that shifts from the groom to the king. They are known to have been inspired by novella 100 of the *Novellino*: "Lo 'mperatore medesimo volle provare la moglie però k'elli era detto k'uno suo barone giacieva con lei. Levossi una notte et andò allei nella camera. E quella disse, voi ci foste pur ora un'altra volta" [This same emperor (Federico II) wished to test his wife, for he had been told that one of his barons was lying with her. One night he arose and went to her in her chamber. And she said, "What, back again; but you were just here"]. *Il Novellino*, ed. Conte; translation by Consoli, *The Novellino or One Hundred Ancient Tales*. We should, however, remember that there is not one unique or primary source for *Decameron* III.2. Instead, Boccaccio mixed themes and situations from many different texts, thereby creating a new literary

From her exclamation, Agilulf immediately understands that the queen has been the victim of a switch – of "bed tricks"[7] – and that he has been tricked as well. The king's acuity and ingeniousness are conveyed by the adverb "subitamente" [immediately], used twice and in close proximity, a positioning that implies the king's nearly simultaneous realization of what had happened ("subitamente presunse") and decision about his next course of action ("subitamente pensò"). The swift and sound resolution of the problem that comes to him in that moment is to say nothing of the deceit to Teudelinga, given that she is unaware of the trick, and to keep the facts – and her, literally – "in the dark." The tale's narrator, Pampinea, voices her approval, not just by praising the king but by commenting:

> il che molti sciocchi non avrebbon fatto ma avrebbon detto: "Io non ci fui io: chi fu colui che ci fu? come andò? chi ci venne?" Di che molte cose nate sarebbono, per le quali egli avrebbe a torto contristata la donna e datale materia di disiderare altra volta quello che già sentito avea: e quello che tacendo niuna vergogna gli poteva tornare, parlando s'arebbe vitupero recato. (III.2.18)

> [Many a stupid man would have reacted differently, and exclaimed: "It was not I. Who was the man who was here? What happened? Who was it who came?" But this would only have led to complications, upsetting the

---

work. Amongst the works that inspired Boccaccio, it is possible to cite *Il Novellino* for Teudelinga's question; Paul the Deacon for the historical setting and the regal characters; Capellanus's *De amore* for the description of the groom in love; and, finally, an ancient Asian text, *Kalila and Dimna*, which Boccaccio probably knew through Johannes de Capua's Latin translation: *Directorium humanae vitae alias parabolae antiquorum sapientum* (in particular, see the story of the painter told by Dimna in chapter III: *De fine illius qui delectatur in malo alterius*). Also in this tale, as in *Decameron* III.2, the servant pretends to be his master by using a disguise (he steals and wears the master's mantle) in order to have a carnal relationship with the woman. Moreover, this woman reacts in a similar manner to Teudelinga and the empress of the *Novellino*. When she meets her usual lover, she is surprised and says: "Quid tibi nocte ista et quare rediisti ad me iterum festinanter, ex quo adimplevisti tuam volutatem?" [What happened to you tonight!? Why did you come back to me so quickly, when you had already fulfilled your desire? (translation mine)]. Both the painter and the king, Agilulf, understand immediately what has happened, and they immediately react.

7 See Anthony Cassell, "The Tale of Giletta di Narbona (III.9)," below 170, for an in-depth discussion of the bed-trick as a topos in literature. Cassell also provides an ample bibliography.

lady, when she was blameless, and sowing the seeds of desire, on her part, to repeat the experience. And besides, by holding his tongue his honor remained unimpaired, whereas if he were to talk he would make himself look ridiculous.]

Thus, by wisely keeping silent, Agilulf preserves a double honour: private honour and public honour.

It is from Teudelinga's famous remark that the reader first learns that the ardour displayed by the groom was something of a surprise in this marriage bed, but the words of Pampinea confirm it: the queen is not used to such experiences, and the king does not want her to desire a repetition of them. This detail will immediately put the reader in mind of the highly polysemic phrase "male avventurata in amadore" [unfortunate in her lover] that was used to describe the queen at the start of the tale.[8] The phrase can be interpreted in at least three ways. First, in the literal and historic sense, Theodelinda was unlucky in love: she would be twice widowed, losing her first husband, King Autari, and then her second, King Agilulf.[9] The second sense in which she is unfortunate in

8 Theodelinda (c. 570–628) is a magnificent historical female character; in the novella she is the desired woman whose presence is able to turn a man into a perfect courtly lover. Retaining the Latin spelling of her name, Boccaccio describes "Teudelinga" at the beginning of the novella through the narrator Pampinea by means of a *tricolon* of adjectives: "bellissima donna, savia e onesta, ma male avventurata in amatore" [beautiful, very intelligent and virtuous, but unfortunate in her lover]. It is likely that this brief, yet effective, description comes from Paul the Deacon, who says in his *Historia* that Theodelinda is "satis eleganti forma" [a very beautiful figure (III.30)]. Paul also describes Theodelinda as very wise and intelligent: in Monza she oversaw the construction of the cathedral and a palace, she reigned over the Lombards after Agilulf's death, corresponded with Pope Gregory the Great, and above all converted her people to Christianity. Paul the Deacon also describes Theodelinda's exemplary honesty during her first meeting with Authari (III.30) and then again in her first meeting with Agilulf (III.35). He narrates both episodes in a manner reminiscent of fairy-tales, probably to add a bit of love interest to a work whose primary purpose is to relate a historical account of the Lombards. In both meetings with her future husbands, Theodelinda blushes: a sure sign of her humility and discretion.

9 As Vittore Branca suggests in the notes to his 1992 edition of the *Decameron*, the legendary female figure of Theodelinda would very likely have impressed Boccaccio, since Paul the Deacon tells, in detail, the curious matrimonial facts regarding the queen. In 589, Authari, king of the Lombards, chose as his wife Theodelinda, daughter of the Bavarian duke Garibaldo, in order to cement an alliance between the Lombards and Bavarians against the French. Authari died a little more than a

love emerges from a careful interpretation of the events within the text. The fictional character, the Queen Teudelinga of the *Decameron*, is a passive protagonist, the object of the contest between the male protagonists of the novella; she is, above all, completely unaware that she has been sexually abused by an "amadore" whose social rank – by ill fortune – is far below hers.[10] To these two interpretations we can add a third: the apparently inferior quality of her marital relations with Agilulf. This series of misfortune adds her to the long list of the "malmaritate" [ill-married] characters of the *Decameron*.[11]

In the face of such a challenge, Agilulf seems to feel that he has a duty to affirm his own virility in the eyes of his consort, who is doubly surprised: first, by the passion of the earlier lovemaking and, second, by his apparent return for more. He asks, in the same light tone: "Donna, non vi sembro io uomo da poterci altra volta essere stato e ancora appresso questa tornarci?" [Do you not think, my dear, that I am capable of returning to you a second time after being here once already? (III.2.20)] The question may in fact be a serious one, centred on that verb "sembrare" [to seem]: Does his wife consider him a poor lover? Does she in fact know that it was not he who was there with her? Her quick answer, "Signor mio, sí" [Yes, my lord (III.2.21)], presumably reassures him. With this question the king makes his first gamble, sacrificing his pride in his own virility in order to maintain his reputation in the eyes of others. That is, the king prefers Teudelinga to believe that the erotic energy shown by his antagonist is in fact his own, rather than be perceived as a weak lover. Furthermore, he gives up personal honour in

---

year after the wedding (he was probably poisoned), in the fall of 590. Theodelinda subsequently married Agilulf in the fall of the same year, thereby making him king. In 616, after a reign of twenty-five years, Agilulf died, leaving Theodelinda to rule through their son Adaloaldo for another ten years, until her own death in 627. She was buried in the cathedral of Monza, next to Agilulf.

10 Readers are generally astonished by Teudelinga's naïveté. It is hard to believe that she was both completely unaware of the change of person and also unable to distinguish her husband from someone else. As readers, we must accept the fictional world created for us by the author; moreover, Boccaccio creates many different strategies to lend credibility to the groom's "bed-trick": the groom takes a hot bath to rid his body of the reek of the stable, he dresses and acts like Agilulf, he refrains from speaking, and, above all, the groom is "as tall and handsome as the king himself," almost Agilulf's twin brother!

11 "Malmaritate" are numerous in the *Decameron*: we have, for example, Bartolomea (II.10), monna Isabetta (III.4), Mazzeo's wife (IV.10), Pietro's wife (V.10), and many other women in Day Seven.

order to retain public honour, for "tacendo niuna vergogna gli poteva tornare, parlando s'arebbe vitupero recato" [by holding his tongue his honor remained unimpaired, whereas if he were to talk he would make himself look ridiculous (III.2.19)]. The groom too has made a gamble: his life for the chance to make love to the queen.

But personal honour demands vengeance. Just as the groom left the queen without saying anything, pretending still to be preoccupied, so the king dissimulates his true emotions, saying he will take Teudelinga's advice to leave.

3. The Action (II)

Full of anger and vindictiveness, the king makes his countermove in this rapid game. He understands that he has been checked by a pawn. The only clue he has, though it is enough for him to act on "subitamente" [immediately], is that this person must have left the bedchamber very recently, for the queen remarks, "Voi vi partite pur testé da me" [You only just left me (III.2.17)]. Besides, as the narrator tells us, Agilulf surmises that the traitor is a member of the royal household – that is, a servant – and thus could not have escaped from the palace; and that whoever it was, his heart must still be pounding as a result of his energetic and lengthy lovemaking.

At this point, we enter what may be considered the second phase of this famously bipartite novella. While the first part is dedicated to the groom, the second focuses on the king. But the two parts should be seen not so much as two consecutive periods of the story, but as parallel or, better, as mirror images of each other, with the second bedchamber scene functioning as the mirror. In fact, even though there is a marked physical and intellectual similarity between Agilulf and the groom, the two protagonists are not only at opposite ends of the social spectrum, but they also act in opposing – though similar – ways. In the second part of the novella, the action proceeds as in the first part, but in a reverse image. We have already seen that the groom enters Teudelinga's chamber in the same way that he leaves it, in a manner that seems troubled, and he does not speak to her, nor she to him. When the king enters, the roles are reversed: he is cheerful; he and the queen talk to each other, and he leaves, apparently still in his cheerful mood. In the first part of the novella, the groom goes secretively at night to a large antechamber of the king's palace, effectively invading the royal space. In the second, the king goes, also secretively and at night, to the long and narrow room over the stables, entering thus the domain of the servants. In the first part, the groom uses tools and instruments to effect his plan (a flint and steel, a taper, and a rod); in the second, the king has a "picciolissimo lume in una lanternetta" [small light in a little lantern (III.2.24)] and a pair of "forficette" [scissors (III.2.28)]. The groom's scheme is premeditated and planned down to the last detail over a long period; the king's is conceived and enacted in haste. The groom spies on the king from a distance across a large room; the king pursues his investigation close up, feeling for the heartbeat in order to identify the perpetrator of the act.

In the second part of the novella, as in the first, the repetition of movements is essential to the blocking of the scenes. Recall that the groom hid himself in the antechamber "più volte" [more than once (III.2.9, 12, 16)], while the king in the servants' dormitory goes to more than one bed, touching more than one person, before he arrives at the bed of the groom. The groom, who of course is not asleep, because he has only just got into bed, sees the king and thinks that he will be found out and killed on the spot – a thought that makes his heart race even faster. In this tense situation, the groom manages to stay enough in control to notice that the king seems unarmed and decides to pretend to be asleep. Agilulf, as we expect, finds his man, and cuts off a hank of his hair, so he will recognize him the following day and proceed with the rest of his private vendetta, without creating a disturbance.[12]

The groom, however, saves himself, because he is a step ahead of the king, constantly observant (ever the spy), and most of all because he again acts like the king. The wily groom's reaction is swift: he finds a

12 Vladimir Propp (*Le radici storiche*, 475–83) points out how cutting off a hank of hair is a stereotypical way to mark the hero in fairy-tales, in order to recognize him later in the story. Generally, in fairy-tales, it is the princess who cuts the hair of the male protagonist, so she can recognize him and finally marry him; but it could also be in order to take vengeance on him. This trick has therefore been previously canonized in storytelling, and Boccaccio uses it twice in the *Decameron*: here in III.2, and again in VII.8. In VII.8 Arriguccio, betrayed by his wife, monna Sismonda, wants to take revenge by cutting off her braids; but the smart Sismonda places a maidservant in her bedchamber and Arriguccio beats the unfortunate girl black and blue, cutting off her braid. Both Agilulf and Arriguccio want to avenge themselves by cutting hair, but both will be disappointed when they are unable to recognize the guilty person. Monna Sismonda, in fact, will have all her hair in order, while the groom will have the hank of the hair cut, as will all the servants. In both cases, Boccaccio recasts this "old" trick in an elegant and comical way; far from succeeding, it frustrates the efforts of those protagonists who still try to employ it.

pair of scissors used for grooming horses and cuts a hank of hair off every man sleeping in the dormitory, from the same place on the head, just above the ear. Once again, we find the same move repeated; the pawn has responded to the countermove of the king and has put him back in check, something that Agilulf discovers only the following morning, when he is obliged to declare the game a draw. Seeing his servants lined up in front of him, the king realizes that he will not be able to identify his rival, and he says to himself, "Costui, il quale io vo cercando, quantunque di bassa condizion sia, assai ben mostra d'essere d'alto senno" [This fellow I'm looking for may be low-born, but he clearly has all his wits about him (III.2.29)]. Agilulf understands, with the rapidity of thought that we already know him capable of, that he cannot pursue his vendetta without causing a public uproar. But he wants to ensure that the episode does not occur again and to warn the guilty party that the king knows what has happened. So he says: "Chi 'l fece nol faccia mai piú, e andatevi con Dio" [Whoever it was who did it, he'd better not do it again. And now be off with you (III.2.30)]. The king thus acts like the wise man he is: as Pampinea is at pains to stress, he doesn't ruin his honour in order to pursue a vendetta, and at the same time, without losing his regal dignity, he serves notice to his adversary not to attempt in the future what he managed to do once.

Most of all, Agilulf restores the social order threatened by the groom's act of adultery. The groom – "sì come savio" [like the wise man he is (III.2.31)] – returns to his lowly rank. Alone among the listening servants, he knows what the king is referring to and learns the lesson: the game is over and will not be repeated. We are told that "mai, vivente il re ... piú la sua vita in sí fatto atto commise alla fortuna" [not while the king was still alive ... did he ever again risk his life by performing any deed of similar nature (III.2.31)]. This last sentence of the novella establishes a tacit complicity between the king and the groom, and confirms the intelligence of both protagonists.

In many ways, the story of Agilulf and his groom looks like a "novella di beffa," in which trickery is the basis of the plot, like the novellas in Days Seven and Eight. The groom sets up the first trick, by sleeping with the queen and cuckolding the king. The king counters with the "controbeffa," the countertrick, by cutting the groom's hair so he can exact his revenge. The last trick, the "beffa della controbeffa" [trick of the countertrick], is executed by the groom, cutting everyone's hair, so that the king has no way to recognize him. It is the king who stops this series of tricks with his last words, which establish complicity with his antagonist. He does this by recognizing his servant's intelligence and accepting him as a rival with whom he can play a game and share a secret – even if this rival is at the other end of the social spectrum. The distance between this novella and the "novella di beffa" is nevertheless huge. In fact, the intelligence and wisdom of both protagonists are clear from the plot and are also praised by the narrators at the beginning of the next novella, whereas in the "novella di beffa" there is always one character who demonstrates his or her cleverness in contrast to another's stupidity. Moreover, in III.2, the moves and countermoves are the results of trickery with no comic intent or hilarity. Agilulf and the groom do not do what they do out of a sense of play, as happens in many other stories in the *Decameron*, but instead out of a real and vital necessity: the groom is so desperately in love with the queen that he may die, and the king must not lose his regal honour.

4. The Explicit Message: Silence

As we have seen from the plot, the novella fulfils perfectly the theme of the third day, which is to talk "di chi alcuna cosa molto da lui disiderata con industria acquistasse o la perduta ricoverasse" [of people who by dint of their own efforts have achieved an object they greatly desired, or recovered a thing previously lost (III.2.29)]: the groom, by dint of diligence, acquires a much-desired thing (making love to the queen), and the king, by dint of diligence, recovers a lost good (his honour).

Moreover, the novella closes with a precise and circular demonstration of the lesson, which Pampinea gives us in her prefatory remarks:

> Sono alcuni sí poco discreti nel voler pur mostrare di conoscere e di sentire quello che per lor non fa di sapere, che alcuna volta per questo riprendendo i disavveduti difetti in altrui, si credono la loro vergogna scemare, dove essi l'accrescono in infinito. (III.2.3)
>
> [Some people, having discovered or heard a thing of which they were better left in ignorance, are so foolishly anxious to publish the fact that sometimes, in censuring the inadvertent failings of others with the object of lessening their own dishonour, they increase it out of all proportion.]

The readers (and Pampinea's listeners) are set up therefore to expect a story that illustrates this point. But Pampinea is not going to take a direct route. She declares: "e che ciò sia vero, nel suo contrario ... vaghe donne, intendo che per me vi sia dimostrato" [And I now propose, fair ladies, to illustrate the truth of this assertion by describing a contrary state of affairs (III.2.3)].

The novella therefore starts off with a declared moral, stated with authority by the narrator, and the moral is indeed demonstrated by the characters in the development of the plot: it is better to maintain a discreet silence and not accuse others, because you risk exposing faults in yourself that will ruin your reputation. Pampinea guides us to see this lesson play out at critical points throughout the tale – at its beginning and end, and, as we have seen, in the crucial bedchamber scene that is at the centre of the action and the pivotal point of the story, where the groom first starts to yield ground to the king.

All of Pampinea's interventions praise silence and discretion as characteristics of the wise. The king and groom are in fact bound by silence, becoming involuntary accomplices in maintaining the secret of what happened that night. Both protagonists know something that is unknown to the public and that if brought into the open would result in loss of life for one and loss of dignity for the other.

The first great secret is the one that sets the action rolling: the passion of the groom who has the nerve to fall in love with the queen. He realizes that his love is inappropriate:

> E per ciò che il suo basso stato non gli avea tolto che egli non conoscesse questo suo amore esser fuor d'ogni convenienza, sí come savio, a niuna persona il palesava, né eziandio a lei con gli occhi ardiva di scoprirlo. (III.2.6)
>
> [Since his low station in life had not blinded him to the fact that this passion of his was thoroughly improper, he had the good sense not to breathe a word about it to anyone, nor did he even dare to cast tell-tale glances in the lady's direction.]

The judicious groom makes a pact with himself: to reveal his passion to no one, for otherwise everyone would think him out of his mind. Later, after the night of lovemaking, this habit of discretion serves him well: if he says anything, his life is at risk.

In Agilulf's case, secretiveness is allied to silence, discretion, the ability to hide, and above all to the wise ability to control his instincts for revenge, which, if left unchecked, could lead to enduring and damaging public scandal for both him and his queen.

In both cases, therefore, silence is not just necessary; it is also a sign of wisdom, and in this both protagonists gain the approval of Pampinea's audience. In fact, at the start of the third novella of the third day, the author comments: "e l'ardire e la cautela del pallafreniere era da' piú di loro stata lodata, e similmente il senno del re" [the bravery and prudence of the groom were praised by most of her listeners, who likewise applauded the wisdom of the King (III.3.2)]. The two protagonists therefore are equivalent in the eyes of the *Decameron*'s internal audience: the one's qualities are praised, and, "similmente" [likewise (III.3.2)], so are the other's, a judgment that sets the two protagonists once more on the same level, their extreme social differences notwithstanding.

5. The Implicit Message: "il vil mestiere"

The adverb "similmente" in that last citation leads us to the implicit moral of the novella, which has to do with social distinctions. The phrase "vil mestiere" (lowly occupation, or "very humble calling" in the translation I have been quoting) occurs in the *Decameron* not only in relation to the groom in III.2, but also in the second tale of Day Six, in reference to the character Cisti, the baker, to whom Nature has allotted "ad un corpo dotato d'anima nobile, vil mestiere" [an inferior calling to a body endowed with a noble spirit (VI.2.3)]. This second occurrence of "vil mestiere" immediately creates an intratextual reference between the two novellas. Moreover, it bears some relevance to our tale, especially in light of the elaborate philosophical preamble to the tale of Cisti, which is delivered, not by accident, by the same Pampinea who gives us the tale of the groom and King Agilulf. She, in fact, narrates both tales, a fact that draws the two lowly men even closer together. The tale of Cisti, like the tale featuring the groom, is the second tale of the day, and in it, Pampinea observes:

> Belle donne, io non so da me medesima vedere che piú in questo si pecchi, o la natura apparecchiando a una nobile anima un vil corpo, o la fortuna apparecchiando a un corpo dotato d'anima nobile vil mestiero, sí come in Cisti nostro cittadino e in molti ancora abbiamo potuto vedere avvenire; il qual Cisti, d'altissimo animo fornito, la fortuna fece fornaio. E certo io maladicerei e la natura parimente e la fortuna, se io non conoscessi la natura esser discretissima e la fortuna aver mille occhi, come che gli sciocchi lei cieca figurino. Le quali io avviso che, sí come molto avvedute, fanno quello che i mortali spesse volte fanno, li quali, incerti de' futuri casi, per le loro

> oportunità le loro piú care cose ne' piú vili luoghi delle lor case, sí come meno sospetti, sepelliscono, e quindi ne' maggior bisogni le traggono, avendole il vil luogo piú sicuramente servate che la bella camera non avrebbe. E cosí le due ministre del mondo spesso le lor cose piú care nascondono sotto l'ombra dell'arti reputate piú vili, acciò che di quelle alle necessità traendole piú chiaro appaia il loro splendore. (VI.2.3–6)
>
> [Fair ladies, I cannot myself determine whether Nature or Fortune be the more at fault, the one in furnishing a noble soul with a vile body, or the other in allotting a base occupation to a body endowed with a noble soul, whereof we may have seen an example, among others, in our fellow-citizen, Cisti; whom, furnished though he was with a most lofty soul, Fortune made a baker. And verily I should curse Nature and Fortune alike, did I not know that Nature is most discreet, and that Fortune, albeit the foolish imagine her blind, has a thousand eyes. For 'tis, I suppose, that, being wise above a little, they do as mortals often times do, who, being uncertain as to their future, provide against contingencies by burying their most precious treasures in the basest places in their houses, as being the least likely to be suspected; whence, in the hour of their greatest need, they bring them forth, the base place having kept them more safe than the dainty chamber would have done. And so these two arbitresses of the world not seldom hide their most precious commodities in the obscurity of the crafts that are reputed most base, that thence being brought to light they may shine with a brighter splendor.]

In an important article on the presence of Seneca in the *Decameron*, Giuseppe Velli ("Seneca nel *Decameron*"; reprinted in *Petrarca e Boccaccio*) demonstrates how this passage has its philosophical roots in letters 44 and 46 of Seneca's *Ad Lucilium epistulae morales*. Letter 44 is especially pertinent because it is copied partially in the *Zibaldone Magliabechiano*, under the title *De nobilitate generis* (Costantini, "Studi," 118), and thus may have been known by Boccaccio. In this letter, Seneca writes: "animus facit nobilem, cui ex quacumque condicione supra fortunam licet surgere" [the soul alone renders us noble and it may rise superior to Fortune, no matter what that condition has been (44.5)]. As Velli points out, the characteristic of nobility as something absolutely related to the person and not to his or her social status is realized in a narrative way in the tale of Cisti the baker. In the same way, the groom in III.2, who has in common with Cisti a "vil mestiere," is representative of the same philosophy: through his spirit and intelligence he is able to rise from the place given him by Fortune, and to arrive at the level of the king himself.

Cisti, in contrast to the groom, is introduced clearly as having "un altissimo animo" [a lofty spirit], while the groom's spirit is defined with the periphrasis "per altro da troppo più che da così vil mestiere" [gifted out of all proportion to his very humble calling]. What, we may ask, is meant by that "altro"? An annotation by Branca in one of his earlier editions of the *Decameron* may help us here; he paraphrases the Italian as: "ma per tutto il resto d'animo piú alto, piú generoso che a cosí vil mestiere non convenisse" [but otherwise more noble and generous of soul than his humble condition would imply].[13] The reading of this eminent Boccaccio scholar is amply borne out by the development of the action, in which we see that the groom has a remarkably refined intelligence.

It is probably, then, in that preamble to VI.2 that we should seek the underlying meanings of the story of the groom and Agilulf. In this tale of cleverness and diligence (the theme of the third day), we see represented the new man, the modern man, whose worth lies not in his social class but in his internal characteristics – in short, the novella presents us with a victory of natural ability over the social structures that restrict it, even within the rigidly hierarchized structures of the early Middle Ages.

The *Decameron* abounds with lower-class characters who are endowed with noble souls, as Pampinea stresses in the tale of VI.2, citing the case of "Cisti nostro cittadino e in molti ancora" [Cisti, our fellow citizen, and many other people of our acquaintance (VI.2.3)]. Pampinea knows these townspeople well, for she narrates two more tales about such people, though the theme is less prominent in those tales. In II.3, the daughter of the king of England (disguised as an abbess) falls in love with a Florentine by the name of Alessandro. She deems him a gentleman, even though his profession is a lowly one ("mestiere ... servile" [II.3.22]). In X.7, we have Lisa, the daughter of an apothecary from Florence living in Palermo, who falls in love with King Piero when she sees him jousting in a tournament. Pampinea tells her audience that Lisa's speech and bearing lead the king to have a high regard for her; we are told that the king "piú volte seco stesso maladisse la fortuna che di tale uomo l'aveva fatta figliuola" [several times inwardly swore at Fortune for making her the daughter of such a man (X.7.35)]. There are also other tales with similar themes which are not narrated by Pampinea. In IV.1, for example, Fiammetta gives us the story of Guiscardo, the object of Ghismonda's love: "uom di nazione assai umile ma per vertú e per costumi nobile" [a man of exceedingly humble birth, but noble in character and bearing

13 G. Boccaccio, *Decameron*, 6th ed., ed. Vittore Branca (Turin: Einaudi, 1987), 339.

(IV.1.6)]. This is, in short, clearly a theme dear to Boccaccio. As Pier Massimo Forni writes:

> I would like to suggest that these stories ... represent another step: that of the author himself from one social sphere (the one allotted to him by virtue of his birth) into a more privileged one. They are stories about access, about the holes in the fabric of destiny that allowed the illegitimate offspring of a Florentine merchant to breathe the rarefied and gentle air of the aristocratic Neapolitan circles. ("The Tale of the King," 214)

6. Love and Its Discontents: The Groom as Courtly Lover

In this context, in which nobility of spirit is held in contrast to inferiority of social rank, the importance of another detail of the narrative comes to light: that is, the description of the groom in love, which occurs early in the tale. Right after he is first described, in fact (in few words, but incisively), we are told that this groom, graced with so many good qualities, is in love with the queen. What is interesting about the description of how he fell in love and how he feels and acts is that it so closely conforms to the refined thirteenth-century precepts of courtly love. Boccaccio, who certainly knew Andreas Capellanus's *De amore* (and probably knew it very well),[14] describes the groom as a classic courtly lover, who obeys everything, down to the most punctilious injunctions given in that treatise. He must, for instance, choose a lady of higher rank than he, the nobler the better – no woman can be nobler

---

14 Critics have often pointed out the influences of the treatise *On Love* by Andreas Capellanus on Boccaccio's works (Grabher, "Particolari influssi"; Branca, *The Man and His Works*, 210–11; Marcozzi, "*Passio e ratio*"; Porcelli, "L'*Amorosa Visione*"). Recently, the identification of the manuscript (Riccardiano 2317) by Beatrice Barbiellini Amidei ("Un nuovo codice attribuibile a Boccaccio?") as a possible Boccaccio autograph and possibly also as a translation from Latin into Italian made by Boccaccio himself of *De Amore*, leads us to think that he knew this text extremely well and that it was very important for him. Riccardiano 2317 must have been written before 1372, in the same years in which Boccaccio was working on Hamilton 90, the final copy of the *Decameron* now in Berlin. Riccardiano 2317 contains the first two books translated into vulgar of Capellanus's *On Love*; two letters about love; four sonnets; a *laude* addressed to a woman; and a conclusion, in which the compiler and author of the manuscripts explains to the readers how the book is a single organism. The codex is a sum of erotic and love themes, a vademecum on love. For more information, see Beatrice Barbiellini Amedei, *Libro d'Amore*.

than a queen. The situation could appear deliberately comic as the groom prides himself of being in love with a queen: "pur seco si gloriava che in alta parte avesse allogati i suoi pensieri" [inwardly he gloried that he had bestowed his thoughts on so high a place (III.2.7)]. All the same, the comedy is tempered by bitter irony: the groom is too intelligent not to realize that his love is inappropriate. Capellanus had made the point that "no matter how worthy a commoner is known to be, it is considered too incongruous, and the common folk themselves regard it as the greatest drop of humiliation, if a countess or a marchioness or a woman of this rank associates herself in love with a commoner" (*On Love*, 1.119). The only circumstances in which such a love could succeed is when nobody of greater or equal worth can be found; only in this case may a social inferior be acceptable (1.120). We know from the beginning of the novella, when the narrator Pampinea introduces us to the characters, that Agilulf and the groom are of equal worth – remember how the two are depicted through a comparison of equality and are described in the same sentence – but they are also widely separated in social rank. Teudelinga already has a husband, and of the highest rank. The groom, therefore, has no hope of realizing his desire. So, being a wise man ("sì come savio"), he keeps his sentiments under lock and key, living without hope of any change of circumstances, and consoling himself by trying to please the queen in modest ways, thinking himself blessed if he has so much as an indirect contact with her – holding her horse or brushing against her garments (III.2.8).[15] But his desire and desperation bring him to a point at which he can no longer bear to live, and he decides to gamble his life for a night of love with the queen.

The progress of the groom's love, his discreet and sublime vassalage, is described lyrically and in minute detail at a point in the narrative that is still the preamble to the tale proper. The account serves several purposes. One is to make the situation even more comical, and at the same time, increasingly pathetic: here is the lowly worker following the refined codes of behaviour of the court. But his vassalage is literal, and his desire for death real – this is not the role play of the noble-born courtly lover that Capellanus was talking about; the groom is in fact the real-life role model for a player playing the role of a groom or similar

15 This is another characteristic of the perfect courtly love: the humility and a complete *libido serviendi*, the eagerness to serve the beloved one in every way possible (Mancini, "Antitesi e deviazione").

humble servant. It is possible to visualize through novella III.2 the literal enactment of one of Capellanus's rules: the lover has to become the servant of the beloved woman. So, here we have a real servant, a groom, a humble man, who falls in love with his queen. These social incongruities will sooner or later lead to a breakdown in the situation.

The account also makes the reader aware how deeply possessed the groom is by his desire. The passage building up to his momentous decision is full of words relating to his desire and will: "disio," "disidero," and (four times) "voler" (III.2.9–11). Boccaccio seems to take Capellanus's courtly love precepts to their extreme limits, perhaps even to exceed them, and manages thereby not only to make the story comic, but also to pose some searching questions about those precepts (if not to point out their absurdity): how should a man of low rank, a groom for example, comport himself if he falls in love with someone of higher social status, say, a queen? Should he be ready to commit suicide, to risk all, if it is no longer possible for him to bear such intense desire? The extremities of the situation bring to mind the tale of Griselda, the last novella of the *Decameron*. Here also, there is a main character who is of very low birth but possessing a noble soul: "anche nelle povere case piovono dal cielo de' divini spiriti" [even into the cots of the poor the heavens let fall at times spirits divine (X.10.68)].[16] Again, we have two characters at opposite ends of the social spectrum: Griselda is a young shepherdess, whereas Gualtieri is a marquis. Griselda and the groom risk everything for their beloveds. In the context of Griselda's tale, several scholars[17] have pointed out how Boccaccio seems to parody courtly love and society, bringing to light the absurdity of their principles. In this sense, also, the detailed description of the groom's love, presented as comical, is very critical towards such regulations of love. According to *De amore*, a noble man in love has to behave like a servant towards the beloved; in the novella of Agilulf and the groom, we find out what happens in the reverse situation, in which a servant falls in love with his queen: he must behave like a king – pretend to be a king! – thus jeopardizing his

16 Another sentence that originates, as Giuseppe Velli shows ("Seneca nel Decameron"), in Seneca's *Letters to Lucilius*: "Potest ex casa vir magnus exire" [A great man can come from a hut].

17 See Pernicone ("La novella"), Rossi ("Ironia e parodia"), Russo ("Griselda"); see in particular Barbiellini Amidei, whose article "La novella di Gualtieri e Griselda" focuses on how *De amore* can be seen as the primary source for the novella.

own life.[18] The groom seems to love as a lover presented in Capellanus's treatise again: he is not afraid to die for love.

> Ad hoc totus tendit conatus amantis, et de hoc illius assidua est cogitatio, ut eius quam amat fruatur amplexibus; optat enim ut cum ea compleat amoris mandata … In amantis ergo conspectus nil valet amoris actui comparari … Quid enim homo posset possidere vel habere sub coelo, pro quo vellet tot subiacere periculis quot assidue videmus amantes ex libero arbitrio se subiugare? Videmus enim ipsos mortem contemnere nullasque timere minas … (I.2.3–4)

> [The whole impetus of the lover is towards enjoying the embraces of his beloved, and this is what he thinks of continually, longing to fulfil with her all the commands of love … So in the eyes of the lover, nothing can be comparable to the act of love … What is there on this earth which a man could possess or hold for which he would consent to undergo all the dangers which we see lovers constantly shouldering of their own free will? We see them making light of death and fearing no threats.]

7. Conclusion

I have endeavoured to show that this short novella of the king and the groom turns on two important themes: the declared moral of the novella, that discretion is a form of wisdom; and one undeclared position, that there is no direct connection between nobility of spirit and social rank. These positions are perfectly fused in the action of the narrative, beginning with Pampinea's introduction and interventions (which are very much part of the action) and continuing through the events of the tale. The tale, as we saw, is constructed with great care: an elegant binary structure with two preternaturally similar protagonists, who are constantly and intimately linked through the device of the queen and the mirroring acts and gestures of each. Once again, Boccaccio manages to astonish us with his ability to stage characters and action. The action seems effortlessly and pleasantly presented, but the understanding of human psychology and society that informs it is both wide-ranging and profound.

---

18 Whereas Griselda, in order to be loved by the marquis, has to behave like a saint!

The Tale of the Gentlewoman, the Gallant Man, and the Friar (III.3)

STEFANO GULIZIA

Boccaccio stages the humorous obsolescence and inadequacy of three wool trade utensils at the very end of Filomena's retelling of a trick by a young wife, the third tale of the third day of storytelling by the *brigata*. The plot is well known: a lusty lady tricks a friar, who becomes the unwilling instrument of an illicit extramarital affair. After the woman has put her confessor in the position to procure just what he believes he is preventing, her triumph over the gullible friar is complete. She celebrates by exchanging giggles about the holy man's stupidity as well as rude comments on "slubs, combs, and cards,"[1] all objects related to her husband's work as a wool maker. This remarkable conclusion comments on the lady's rhetorical virtuosity and offers a surprising insight on social mobility. It also points back to the third day's general themes: the search for a new organization of desire – proven by Masetto's appointment as a bursar and his parcelling of sexual duties within the convent in III.1 – the witty laugh at the expense of the clergy, and the overarching "reasoning" of pleasure, which is also presented by the arduous short-cuts to heaven of the layman Puccio's tale (III.4).

This essay assumes the traditional view that the young lady's tale is essentially an inversion of a pious exemplum, as seems explicitly suggested by the friar's pedagogical pretence. If Boccaccio's use of the rhetoric of persuasion is essentially aimed at comedy, ironic effects are

1 G. Boccaccio, *Decameron*, ed. Vittore Branca (Turin: Einaudi, 1992), III.3.54, p. 358: "biasimando i lucignoli e' pettini e gli scardassi." All the quotations are taken from this edition and indicated in the text with paragraph numbers. The translation is by Guido Waldman (Oxford University Press, 1993).

especially associated with the prominence of the *suasoria*, a technique borrowed from Ovid's elegiac poetry.[2] In the erotic context of the third day, Boccaccio's interest in declamation and his continuity with Ovid's elegiac poetry is strongest; formal attempts at persuasion are consistently successful. In III.3, on the contrary, we have an ironic portrayal of the friar as an *inops rhetor*. The gross disparity of scale between the lady's speech and the friar's response places still more stress on the former. Boccaccio masters the art of shifting the ground in a way that makes nonsense of the carefully constructed case: the most exceptional scenes of erotic success described in the third day unfold without a single word being spoken on either side. For an Ovidian poet to fail to get his way is of course nothing new; indeed, an inability to control events is a set feature of the love-elegist's persona. Boccaccio's innovation in III.3 is to reverse the typical lack of success of such an elegiac lover. Irrepressible verbal fluency is no longer a sign of failure; on the contrary, the lady's insistence on speech, underlined throughout the tale and evident especially in its conclusion, where consuming love and reasoning about it are conflated, is instrumental in getting her sexual satisfaction. Apart from rhetoric, this essay is also interested in redefining the mercantile ethos as a double movement away from the ethereal love of the courtly code and towards an area of close proximity with trading and the practice of everyday life. My interpretation of Boccaccio's handling of the theme of desire, in this respect, is influenced by the praise of cosmopolitanism in the Proem of *Genealogie* X, where forms of friendships, rituals of economic exchange, and foreign languages are fused in exuberant harmony ("the distance of whose lands had rendered strangers, are united and joined in concord by navigation" [X.1–3; Osgood translation, *Boccaccio on Poetry*]).

Understood by James Wheelock – in the only fully fledged treatment of the novella to date – as a synergistic embodiment of Boccaccio's refinements at storytelling, III.3 has been studied primarily in a comparative context, usually with the goal of envisioning and charting structural

2 Namely, the *Ars amatoria*, where a large degree of scepticism and the same interest in the capacity of speech to persuade are shown; the *Amores*, where failed effort at dissuasion is given the fullest treatment; finally the *Heroides*, a female counterpart to the male-centred *Amores*. The information about Boccaccio's youthful study of Ovid is a staple in any account of the writer's life; it has also provided a factual basis for the constantly repeated characterization of his writing as "rhetorical." On these themes, cf. Smarr, "Ovid and Boccaccio"; Forni, "Realtà/verità"; Battistini, "Retorica"; Baldassarri, "*Adfluit incautis insidiosus amor.*"

symmetries and patterns of narrative.[3] In this line of inquiry, although with caution, Franco Fido noted how in Day Three the coupling of 3 with 4 emphasizes the role of the word in achieving erotic satisfaction, whereas the two initial tales 1 and 2 accentuate the role of silence;[4] without directly mentioning the tale, Marina Scordilis Brownlee observed that in the amorous discourse of Day Three a progression is achieved, even through deceit and bestial excess, and it is defined by a downward moral topography, where "the 'human sheep' are revealed to be rapacious 'wolves' in reality" ("Wolves and Sheep"). Tackling the coexistence of mimetic and fantastic registers in the *Decameron* and the (often Purgatorial) effects of such dualism for the topic of desire, Marga Cottino-Jones focuses especially on the confessional space in III.3 as a symbolic location, offering a precise summary of the tale's plot that is worth quoting here at length:

> The confessional is used by the lady in order to stage a play of deception where she enacts the role of the victim and her would-be lover is cast as sexual harasser who torments her with a series of actions which, if offensive to a virtuous lady, are actually the fantasized projections of what the particular lady desires. This play is carried on for the benefit of a "tondo e grosso … frate bestia" who … becomes her choice as "ottimo mezzano tra lei e 'l suo amante" (III.3.8). In three consecutive sessions in the confessional, the lady is able to convince *frate bestia* of the sexual harassment to which the "valente uomo" has been subjecting her, first by following her everywhere she goes and pacing in front of her home at all times of day and night, and then by sending her rich presents; and eventually, by trying

3 For the comparative studies, cf. Baxmann, *Middletons Lustspiel;* Brunnemann, *Decameron III, 3 in englischen Drama;* Mathes, "*Decameron*, III, 3, and a *Canzone* a ballo of Lorenzo de' Medici." The reading of the novella is that of Wheelock, "The Rhetoric of Polarity in *Decameron* III, 3." Although my project approaches the problem of the rhetorical and socio-economical value of the lady's tale from an entirely different perspective, I am indebted to Wheelock's structuralist discussion of the "trick." Contrary to Wheelock's understanding of the characters in III.3 as mere chess pieces in the woman's intricate scheme is the opinion of Cottino-Jones, "Desire and the Fantastic in the *Decameron*," who considers the social world of III.3 much more carefully detailed.

4 Fido, "Silenzi e cavalli nell'eros del *Decameron*," 80. Ferroni, "Eros e obliquità nella terza giornata del *Decameron*," 246 signals a line of continuity due to the theme of confession between III.3 and III.8.

> to enter her bedroom through a window over the garden when her husband is away from home. ("Desire and the Fantastic," 11)

The playful representation within a religious space, analogous, as Cottino-Jones writes, to the role of the garden during the adventures of Masetto in III.1, sets up a tone of parody of Christian values; Filomena keeps undermining the established view of society in her last comments on the two lovers' successful nights of pleasure, "alle quali io prego Idio … che tosto conduca me e tutte le anime cristiane che voglia n'hanno" [And I pray the Lord in His mercy that He might soon bring me and all other Christian souls that way inclined to enjoy nights such as those (III.3.55)]. This sequence of events could be followed in Boccaccio's tale as follows: Filomena's introduction (III.3.1–5); presentation of the lady and her plan (III.3.6–8); first confession and friar's initial response (III.3.9–16), followed by an encounter between the friar and the young man (III.3.17–21); second confession and rage of the friar (III.3.22–32), who searches for the man and reproaches him (III.3.33–8); third confession (III.3.39–46), and dialogue between the would-be lover and the friar (III.3.47–52); conclusion (III.3.53–5).

1. Staging Wool Utensils

From the point of view of the tale's genre, the mechanics of a "trick" provide the backbone of incident in the comic fiction of III.3. Boccaccio's trick results both in sexual triumph and material gain for the tricksters; during the climactic visit organized by the lady, where the man climbs a tree, steps into the bedroom, and, in a quick embrace, is greeted by her "lietamente" [gladly (III.3.54)], it is explicitly said that the two lovers:

> prendendo l'un dell'altro piacere, ragionando e ridendo molto della semplicità di frate bestia, biasimando i lucignoli e' pettini e gli scardassi, insieme con gran diletto si sollazzarono. (III.3.54)

> [made love, affording each other boundless pleasure, chatting all the time and having a good giggle at that gullible oaf of a friar, and passing rude comments on such objects and utensils of the wool trade as slubs, combs, and cards.]

The passage's structure is ruled by a sequence of gerunds: four in total, combined in three *cola*; by commenting upon the reciprocity of the scene ("l'un dell'altro piacere," "insieme"), these verbs finally lead, through a descending *climax*, to the woman's pleasure, inscribed between the ideas of "diletto" and "sollazzo." With this chain of gerunds, Boccaccio emphasizes that the woman, at the end of the deceit, is left with the advantage in bed, while her liberation from the husband is underlined by the blame cast on the instruments of the wool trade. This sinister touch complicates the simple opposition between a mercantile and a courtly society. Similarly, Filomena insists on the successful outcome and execution of the trick. It is why the narration pairs reasoning with laughter, a sensual *voluptas* with a taste for plotting: the two lovers spend some joyful time "ragionando e ridendo," and their encounter, although eagerly awaited, is far from being a mere, rapturous welcome.

In this respect, tricks in the *Decameron* are a form of reading, writing, and literary criticism. As has been perceptively noted elsewhere, friars in the *Decameron* also seem to be a "distorted image of the story-teller" (Havely, "Chaucer, Boccaccio and the Friars"). This is particularly true of the friar in III.3, who is characterized by a popular and folkloric colour. He is chosen by the lady, "quantunque fosse tondo e grasso" [a fat fellow and thick as two planks (III.3.8)], to act as a go-between, and he is later defined as "frate montone" [blockhead friar (III.3.37)]. With him the crafty woman uses an inventory of downgraded sacred oratory, whose centrepieces are her reference to the "quaranta messe di San Grigoro" [the forty Masses of St Gregory (III.3.32)], the related hope that the friar's prayers could be effective "acciò che Idio gli tragga di quel fuoco pennace" [that God may deliver them from this purging fire (ibid.)], and especially the repeated, discursive association of her worthy friend with a "diavolo del Ninferno" [devil, more like (III.3.39)]. Even the graphic choice of *Ninferno* for *Inferno* degrades the rhetorical capacities of the simple-minded holy man to the level of Calandrino's literalism and Maestro Simone's abecedarian literacy. Ever since Vittore Branca's seminal monograph *Boccaccio medievale,* many scholars have alerted us to Boccaccio's mimetic skill and to the anthology's self-conscious display of literacy;[5] beyond Boccaccio's ability to achieve realistic character portrayal in direct dialogue, a tale such as III.3 also offers insights into the relationship between rhetoric and genre.

5 Cf., among others, Branca, *Boccaccio medievale;* Mazzotta, *The World at Play;* and Marchesi, *Stratigrafie decameroniane.*

Let us continue by sampling the discursive possibilities that are presented in *Decameron* III.3, and mostly associated with the figure of the friar. The tale displays Filomena's retelling of several scenes of confession. The lying and crafty woman of III.3, used by Filomena, transports us back to Panfilo's account of Cepperello's confession.[6] In the narrative territory of Day One, Boccaccio sets one story within another to unfold in calculated succession a false confession (I.1), a tale that describes linguistic entrapment (I.3), and an anecdote told by a professional raconteur, Bergamino (I.7). The numbers 3 seem to join and to reiterate, between Day One and Day Three, a narrative line organized by Boccaccio; yet an evident variation lies in the fact that I.3 is a story of a linguistic entrapment eluded, as Melchisedech the Jew answers Saladino's tricky question on true religion by resorting to his own novella. In III.3 no tale within the tale is present; instead the friar *grossa pasta* is distinguished by his limited understanding, which is played to humorous and aesthetic effect against the woman's clever use of language.

The dim-witted friar is incapable of reproaching the young man other than with insults and is unable to see in his "risposte perplesse" [bewildered response (III.3.47)] anything more than cautionary ambiguity. A little earlier, the religious man is dazzled by the woman's anecdotal punchlines, and to this effect is directed III.3.42: "Il frate, udendo questo, fu il piú turbato uomo del mondo e non sapeva che dirsi, se non che piú volte la domandò se ella aveva ben conosciuto che egli non fosse stato altri" [This story put the friar into a towering rage, and he was at a loss for words. He kept asking her whether it couldn't just possibly have been someone else]. The friar's stumbling reaction has conversely been calculated by the *lanaiuolo*'s wife, who, after counterfeiting the posture of a supplicant woman ("postaglisi nella chiesa a sedere a' piedi" [she sat down at his feet in church, III.3.22]), tactfully tailors to her victim – and for the benefit of the *Decameron*'s "internal audience" – an image of resentment ("quasi turbata" [in a pretended huff, III.3.46]).

This sophisticated fabrication of anger, propelled by the same theatre-oriented vocabulary, is here exploited by the woman to propel the friar's nonsensically confused reaction into a higher ranking of speech pattern. Boccaccio is careful to construct a verbal correspondence when the friar,

6 I am thinking about the episodes in which Ciappelletto declares he wants to erase the "abominevole guadagno" and act "senza alcuna ruggine d'animo" (I.1.43–5), and especially the moment when he shows self-consciousness as a manipulative storyteller: "fermamente io acconcerò i fatti vostri" (I.1.29).

during that very exchange, swears he will try to restrain "questo diavolo scatenato, che io credeva che fosse un santo" [this unbridled devil – and I thought he was a saint (III.3.45)]. The friar's language has been manipulated by the woman's false confession: they both assume, from diametrically opposed points of view, the fictional identity of the young man as a devil of Hell.[7] The mockery of Jesus' crucifixion by the lady's would-be lover ("Perché questo cruccio, messere? ho io crocifisso Cristo?" [Why so cross, my friend? Have I crucified Christ?, III.3.47]) voices an equally preposterous pseudo-Christian discourse. Such convergence, and Boccaccio's talent for sustained parodies of a conventional sermon, should also suggest that we see the purse and the girdle that the woman throws into the friar's lap (III.3.29) as symbols counterfeiting the sacred discourse: like relics, they are precious objects that strike the friar's mind materially, without the possibility of further articulation.

In a similar vein, the friar's loss for words is tellingly displayed when he is confronted with the lady's virtuosity in sacred rhetoric (the "quaranta messe di San Grigoro" of III.3.32), accompanied by the final touch of a coin, a *fiorino*, tossed into his hand at the end of her speech. A transitional paragraph describes the friar's reaction:

> Il santo frate lietamente il prese e con buone parole e con molti essempli confermò la divozion di costei: e datale la sua benedizione la lasciò andare. E partita la donna, non accorgendosi che egli era uccellato, mandò per l'amico suo. (III.3.33)
>
> [The holy friar accepted it gladly; he strengthened her good resolution with improving words and many edifying stories, then sent her on her way with his blessing. After she had gone he sent for his friend, little realizing that the lady had been pulling the wool over his eyes.]

Boccaccio frames the friar's disposition towards the woman's money with the same adverb, "lietamente," that marks the memorable first embrace between the two lovers (III.3.54). Just when the holy man is deceived, "uccellato," the text couples the lady's sexual satisfaction,

7 Similar to this association is "Ferondo's stumbling tongue," which in III.8 "downgrades the divine messenger into a spiderish thing, *Ragnolo Braghiello*"; my quotation is from Kirkham, *The Sign of Reason in Boccaccio's Fiction*, 176.

which is as of now imminent, with a brief satire on the friar's greedy acceptance of the coin; when "lietamente" comes back, it recapitulates the two angles of material gain and sensual achievement from the perspective of the woman's pleasure.

The deceived friar, in other words, fails to understand that the *lanaiuolo*'s wife is exchanging her *fiorino* as a token for a demand dictated by illicit desire, and his failure is conflated by Boccaccio with a broader generic dimension as well. The author juxtaposes "uccellato" to "molti essempli," suggesting that the friar's zealous application of a conventional narrative strategy has been brought to a standstill. Thus the price for happy sex is unsuccessful exempla. By associating the practice of exempla with the simple-minded friar, Boccaccio arrests the hermeneutical profligacy of his tale with a reference to a codified genre of literature of his time: he interrogates how the characters of III.3 have evaded the ethical coordinates of the exemplum, a formidable fourteenth-century rhetorical matrix.

Still, this carnivalesque topsy-turvydom of the exemplum must be measured against the character of the friar, who, by what Filomena tells of him, is a clumsy orator, an irascible fellow, and perhaps even a dubious holy man. The success of the plot of III.3 shows how genre boundaries are *both* breached *and* reinforced.[8] Boccaccio turns attention to the lady's performance of confession with a nod to the literary, generic, and mythico-ritual basis of that Florentine civic experience. In this way the proximity of III.3 to its surrounding tales is equally reinforced, for the novelle of Day Three are situated where the line between *polis* and *oikos* disappears. These tales are interested in the way political policy and comic ingenuity blend. As the plot itself seems to reach a low point of degradation, with a characteristically Boccaccian twist, the city of Florence faces love and joy, instead of chaos and violence. Far from taking the behaviour of the woman and the friar as both a satire on and a symptom of the lamentable disarray in Florentine church and public policies, Boccaccio decides to concentrate on the effects of the joyous, and often economic, hyper-egalitarianism that rounds out many of the

8 This is why, even as a counter-exemplum, the reference to the genre is still a paradigmatic reading for III.3; see Delcorno, *Exemplum e letteratura*, 266: "nell'intenzione del Boccaccio il *Decameron* si presenta come una vasta e complessa registrazioni di voci."

tales in Day Three. His decision parallels the pattern of rejuvenation that earlier in Roman new comedy and later in Renaissance *commedia erudita* – including Ariosto's and Machiavelli's comedies – closes the plot, often enacted in the form of a marriage.[9]

Various scenes of III.3 come very close to a personification of wool utensils and clothing accessories that punctuate the controlling momentum of the woman and that function as collective symbols at the same time. The lady's scorn towards the "artefice lanaiuolo" leads her to put down her husband's knowledge:

> veggendo lui ancora con tutte le sue ricchezze da niuna altra cosa essere piú avanti che da sapere divisare un mescolato o fare ordire una tela o con una filatrice disputar del filato, propose di non voler de' suoi abbracciamenti in alcuna maniera. (III.3.6)

> [He might be as rich as rich could be, but the fact was that his capabilities did not extend beyond creating a textile pattern or setting up a loom or arguing with a spinning-woman about her yarn; she concluded, therefore, that his embraces were something she could very well do without.]

This statement, preceded by a flamboyant sequence of nothing less than four single *novenari*, tangles the clash of a different social origin between husband and wife with a discourse about desire, literacy, and economy – given that the prominent textile metaphors are too obvious a choice for the *téchne* of storytelling to be passed over inadvertently. Once Filomena's narration settles into a comfortable rhythm, this concatenation of monetary value, sexual desire, and linguistic control is carried through the first appearance of the purse and the girdle:

> ma egli è stato sí ardito e sí sfacciato, che pure ieri mi mandò una femina in casa con sue novelle e con sue frasche, e quasi come se io non avessi delle borse e delle cintole mi mandò una borsa e una cintola: il che io ho avuta e ho sí forte per male, che io credo, se io non avessi guardato al peccato, e poscia per vostro amore, io avrei fatto il diavolo. (III.3.26)

> [but he's grown so brazen and barefaced, why, only yesterday he sent me a woman with some inane message and, as if purses and girdles were a

9 Cf. Baratto, *La commedia del Cinquecento*, 57–63.

> thing I'm short of, he sent me a purse and a girdle. This upset me so much, if I had not considered the scandal, and my devotion to you, I do believe I'd have raised merry hell.]

It is a brief mention, somewhat neutral and deprived of further adjectives, but it comes in a densely significant paragraph. The man's boldness, openly criticized and pursued secretly by the woman, literally breaks off the sentence's patterning in two halves: he is "sí ardito e sí sfacciato," he brings "sue novelle e sue frasche" and offers "una borsa e una cintola," as if the lady did not already possess "delle borse e delle cintole." We learn, in fact, that the *lanaiuolo*'s wife, thanks to the Lord's mercy and her husband's proficiency at the market, has so many purses and girdles that she could even drown in them ("per ciò che, la mercé di Dio e del marito mio, io ho tante borse e tante cintole che io ve l'afogherei entro" [because, thanks to the Good Lord and my husband, I've got purses and girdles coming out of my ears, III.3.27]). By overstating her richness with this hyperbole, the woman raises the capital of storytelling in the present exchange between her and the *frate montone*.[10]

But for now, the dual coupling originated by the fictional man's pursuit should give us pause. For along with purses and girdles, he brings *novelle* and *frasche*: this very terminology is defended by Boccaccio in the important Introduction to Day Four, when he tries to find out more wisely "donde io dovessi aver del pane che dietro a queste frasche andarmi pascendo di vento" [if I had any sense I'd see to earning my crust instead of tightening my belt as I attend to so much nonsense (IV. Intro.7)]. The economic value of purse and girdle, thus, is at the core of storytelling itself as a craft; those who enjoy success in the former relish also the elegance and refinement of the latter. In its ambiguity between token of affection and fashion accessory, a richly decorated girdle from the Fletcher Fund of the Metropolitan Museum of Art in New York could serve here as a example of how Boccaccio's storytelling is perfectly calibrated against the value of commodities and the function, both actual and symbolic, of weaving. In this girdle, which is edged in silver galloon and may once have been completed with a buckle, a lively green ground sustains a series of diagonal cartouches inscribing a love poem: the effects dictated by the words of the poem are

10 A consonant note, in Day Three, is that of Masetto, who begins his adventures by stating "non contentandosi del salario" (III.1.6).

incorporated in the graphic execution of the green silk backing, which in fourteenth-century Florence is a typical motif of expensive gifts, often as a part of dowries.[11]

So intensely is this clever interplay of text and object felt by the woman in III.3 that Boccaccio makes her stumble across the duality of her desire: she treats the man's objects as a text ("pien di stizza gliele tolsi di mano e holla recata a voi" [I snatched them angrily out of her hands, and I've brought them along to you, III.3.27]), despite the careful syntactic distance underlined before. Moreover, the woman overlaps the singular and feminine gender of purse and girdle in a subsequent participle that refer to both ("mi mandò una borsa e una cintola: il che io ho avuta" [he sent me a purse and a girdle: which I took, III.3.26]).[12]

These momentary lapses reflect how much is at stake in this part of the novella. The woman knows that a smart handling of the purse and the girdle will have a shattering effect on the friar's psychological reaction to the story, so he will believe that somebody is set up to "raise hell." The readers and the internal audience of the *Decameron* also remember what a crucial role was already played by a purse and a girdle in the controversial tale of Bernabò and Ambruogiuolo, at II.9, similarly told by Filomena.[13] In a nocturnal scene, Ambruogiuolo tries to test the faithfulness of his friend's wife, but he has to resort to other tricks, for

11 This girdle was shown in conjunction with the exhibition Art and Love in Renaissance Italy, whose catalogue is edited by A. Bayer (New Haven and London: Yale University Press, 2008). Entry no. 55, written by Deborah L. Krohn (128–9), mentions *Decameron* III.3, underlying the symbolic transformation of the girdle in the novella, which comes to embody the adulteress's illicit desire, just as it had once served to manifest a legitimate marital love. This transformation, however, is not limited to this type of inversion, but more deeply implicated with the technology of storytelling as a whole.

12 To cite Branca's note, "l'oggetto femminile che precede (*borsa, cintola*) si è sovrapposto evidentemente all'astratto *il che* determinando questo participio femminile" [The previous feminine object (*purse, girdle*) has evidently replaced the abstract pronoun, thus causing the feminine participle] (*Decameron*, 352; translation mine).

13 An interesting account on the tensions within the *brigata* concerning this episode of mercantile reading is offered by De Coste, "Filomena, Dioneo, and an Ass." Further links between Days Two and Three are mediated by the rhetoric of nudity: in III.3 the woman confesses to have been "ignuda com'io nacqui" (III.3.40) during the man's nocturnal aggression, while in II.7 another woman is praised for being "oltre a ogni comparazione ignuda" (III.3.56).

avendo udito lei essere cosí cruda e alpestra intorno a quelle novelle, non s'arrischiò. E statosi la maggior parte della notte per la camera a suo agio, una borsa e una guarnacca d'un suo forzier trasse e alcuno anello e alcuna cintura, e ogni cosa nella cassa sua messa, egli altressí vi si ritornò e cosí la serrò come prima stava. (II.9.28)

[in view of her reputation for craggy untouchability when it came to dalliance, he did not risk it, but merely lingered in the bedroom for most of the night; he went to her chest and abstracted a purse, a tunic, a ring or two, and the odd belt, laid them all in his own chest, then climbed back inside and locked himself in as before.]

It comes as no surprise that Filomena would want to cluster novelle, purses, and girdles around the same juncture of narrative – paragraph 28 – in III.3 as well.[14] It is to be expected, then, that ultimately the friar, moved to an extreme by this phantasmal representation, would aggressively instruct the man, holding the purse and the girdle in his hands (III.3.37). It is a sequence where Boccaccio chooses not to report the actual lectures of the friar, dispatched with an evasive "Ora le parole fur molte" [a great deal of discussion took place (III.3.37)], but focuses instead on the sense of security that the man feels at the sight of the woman's indirect gift (III.3.37). This security springs from knowing that the engine of the plot is running smoothly for the two lovers, and Boccaccio only has to make up a voyage to Genoa ("convenne al marito andare infino a Genova" [the husband had reason to make a visit to Genoa, III.3.38]) to allow the action to culminate and that final, gleeful look over the husband's wool utensils – synonymous with an older system of desire and narrative compensation – to take place.

Purses and girdles are no match for combs and cards; among the symbols that refer to the collectivity of Florence, these are the objects most beaten back into the materiality of consumable goods. The differentiation between the two economies of which they are metonymic markers happens in a literary *tour de force*: the wool trade disappears, deserted in the last scene of Filomena's tale, while the other accessories receive a full mention before turning into a physical (and generic)

14 One could profitably add another sequence from II.9.48: "Ora avvenne tra l'altre volte che, essendo egli a un fondaco di mercatanti viniziani smontato, gli vennero vendute tra altre gioie una borsa e una cintura le quali egli prestamente riconobbe essere state sue, e maravigliossi."

burden for the friar's lap, who does not quite know how to deal exempla for novelle of the recent, expensive kind:

> E detto questo, tuttavia piagnendo forte, si trasse di sotto alla guarnacca una bellissima e ricca borsa con una leggiadra e cara cinturetta e gittole in grembo al frate; il quale, pienamente credendo ciò che la donna dicea, turbato oltre misura le prese. (III.3.29)

> [This said, she drew out from beneath her long cloak the most beautiful and expensive purse and the dearest, daintiest little girdle and, sobbing her eyes out, threw them into the friar's lap. He believed every word she said and took them both, seething with indignation.]

It is a vertiginous mix of sexual and economic fantasies on the part of the woman; behind the engineering of her transgressive scheming lies a long-lived scenario of social mobility that finds its fullest and, for the friar, its most self-defeating exemplar in the spectacle of the purse and the girdle. This section also unpacks the tale's literary background, without ever mentioning directly the *physis* of storytelling.[15] Filomena records a myth of female predominance, offering at the same time a "social charter" of fourteenth-century Florence: the city's blocked reproductive power is embodied in the male figure of the husband, who accumulates wealth but is too vulgar to enjoy sex with his spouse. The point of his wife's shift of sexual entrepreneurship is to provide a new economic model of desire, which becomes the index of fecundity of *Decameron* III.3, and to place a distinctive Florentine stamp on the strategy of story-making and mercantile-reading.

---

15 Here I would like to point out that the momentary and symbolic "occultation" of the wool utensils is similar to the heliotrope, for in both resonates a conversion to the invisible from the palpable. The disappearance of the wool combs, in particular, is analogous to the first of Calandrino's tales (VIII.3), where the heliotrope makes Calandrino become socially invisible: see Martinez, "Calandrino and the Powers of the Stone," a crucial reading of how proportional exchange and literal *contrapasso* are filled by and distributed through economics. Boccaccio's use of trade objects finds at least two important comparative echoes in Shakespeare: first, in *The Winter's Tale*, where the roguish peddler Autolycus declares: "I have sold all my trumpery; not a counterfeit stone, not a ribbon, glass, pomander, brooch, table book, ballad, knife, tape, glove, shoe, tie, bracelet, horn ring, to keep my pack from fasting"; secondly, in *Cymbeline*, which is based on *Decameron* II.9, in turn intertextually associated with III.3. In general, on relics and objects as vestigial origins of narrative, see also Valesio, "Sacro."

2. "Intender alla melanese": Floundering in the Waters of Literalism

"di meno avria macinato un mulino."

[sufficient to turn a mill-wheel (III.Intro.9)]

Assuming at this point that the woman's pranks at the expense of the gullible friar are a meta-linguistic form of literary criticism – one in which rhetorical and economic discourse converge – I propose now to study the range of intertextual implications that locks III.3 in the grid of its day and in the larger frame of narrative. Boccaccio repeatedly refers to the collective participation of the *brigata*, signals the various reactions of its components, and effectively chronicles the diffusion of his own storytelling within the general anthology.[16] These episodes are paradigmatic examples of theatricality in the *Decameron*; in them culminates a collision course of page and stage that breaks Boccaccio's authorial intention into several agents, intentions, and efforts to materialize, embody, and even handle early modern storytelling as a commodity. It is against the frame and its internal tensions that Boccaccio can invoke the lawless trickster god of eloquence, Mercury, as a master of shifting identities, a stage performer of a polymorphic social representation.[17] Each tale is framed by a sort of utopian communicative framework, where a fundamentally dual rhetoric of praise and blame – probably available to Boccaccio thanks to the humanistic revival of Cicero – allows the circulation of social energy among the ten Florentine frame characters.

According to this principle, Filomena's tale in the third day merits "honeyed words" from Dioneo, who praises the lady's wit, "con dolci parole molto lo 'ngegno della donna commendato" [in honeyed words much commended the woman's wit (III.4.2)], and conforms to the

16 Boccaccio's strategy is similar to Cervantes' use of *burlas*, stemming out of the novella-tradition, in *Don Quijote* (part II, chs. 34–5), where the popularity of Cervantes' novel and its two heroes is celebrated. Cf. Close, "Seemly Pranks."

17 Cf. Kirkham, "The Word, the Flesh, and the *Decameron*," 173–4: "Calendrically mated, the Wednesdays of Days One and Six are architectural portals leading into both the anthology as a whole and its second half. Their shared theme, implicit the first time around and explicit the second, is symbolically appropriate to the day 'mercoledì,' because for medieval mythographers and astrologers alike Mercury was the god of eloquence. Mercury's rule at the threshold of each narrative week raises the medium of language itself to high-ranking status in the system of values that informs the Author's message."

general subject of the day. Time and again, in the texts that surround this tale, the stress is on wit and speech. The fact that rhetoric functions as a social software is visible also in the queen's proposal, which wins universal approval during the conclusion of the second day of storytelling. This is a crucial moment in which the subject of the upcoming tales is set up, by somehow restricting the limits of choice. Dioneo's last tale of Paganino and Ricciardo (II.10) left the women of the *brigata* with their jaws aching from laughter; Boccaccio places a considerable emphasis on Neifile's blushing on account of the honour conferred on her, "di questo piccol popolo il governo sia tuo" [let this little realm be in your charge (II.Concl.2)], and on how she supervises seating arrangements, almost as if she were aware of anthropological themes of hospitality:[18] the young queen primarily wants to avoid the threat represented by Dioneo's de-centring narratives.

Her restoration of "order" is offered with the belief that the *brigata* should turn to some Christian practice, "piú tosto a orazioni che a novelle vacassimo" [by attending to prayer rather than to story-telling (II. Concl.1)], and the concomitant consciousness of an upcoming Purgatorial atmosphere that pervades the surroundings. The first belief explains the proximity of orations and storytelling, and the prominence of *suasoriae* in Day Three; the Purgatorial idea brings to the idealized landscape that is about to be described in the Introduction to the following day a further generic dimension, enhanced by the "sucidume" [dust and dirt (II.Concl.6)] that the Florentine frame characters have to wash away. This is the same term for what Dante the pilgrim dutifully washes off in the *Divine Comedy* at the start of his climb up the mountain of Purgatory.[19] But Neifile's advice in the Conclusion to Day Two contains more than a Dantesque typology of narrative:

---

18 In literature, one could think of Homer's emphasis on the hostile nature of the Phaeacians' treatment of Odysseus; for a study of anthropological themes in the *Decameron* see Falvo, "Ritual and Ceremony in Boccaccio's *Decameron*," who turns attention to female resourcefulness as ironic reminder of the Fall narrative (147) and studies episodes of religious prepostery as a sign of a larger semiotic crisis. This is true of the story of Ser Ciappelletto, at I.1, but also of III.3, where, as Falvo remarks, "the language of confession is transformed into a supernatural power that is able to convey sacramental efficacy" (151).

19 In other words, the pastoral state of affairs described by the lush nature of the Introduction to Day Three, which contains "una fonte di marmo bianchissimo," "un prato di minutissima erba," and "tutta la spezieria che mai nacque in Oriente"

> se noi vogliam tor via che gente nuova non ci sopravenga, reputo opportuno di mutarci di qui e andarne altrove … Quivi quando noi saremo domenica appresso dormire adunati, avendo noi oggi avuto assai largo spazio da discorrere ragionando, sí perché piú tempo da pensare avrete e sí perché sarà ancora piú bello che un poco si ristringa del novellare la licenzia e che sopra uno de' molti fatti della fortuna si dica, e ho pensato che questo sarà: di chi alcuna cosa molto disiderata con industria acquistasse o la perduta recuperasse. (II.Concl.6–8)

> [if we want to avoid strangers calling on us, I think we might do well to change our residence … When we foregather there next Sunday after our siesta, as we've been given plenty of scope today in choosing a story to tell, and you'll have ample time to think up the next one, and as, besides, somewhat restricting the limits of choice can only be for the good, here's what I propose: the topic will be a single aspect of the hand of Fate and, specifically, about the way a person uses his wits to acquire something greatly prized, or to recover something lost.]

The notion of contempt that the Florentine frame characters feel for the *gente nuova* is at the core of a slightly restrictive reformation within their storytelling: the paradigm is now one of geographical relocation, rhetorical constraint about the spatial (and moral) limits of "ragionare," and the heavy economics inscribed into tales that have to demonstrate the stubborn industry of how one can either *acquistare* or *recuperare* an object of desire.

Neifile's discourse promotes her reformation of storytelling in association with the trade of commodities: without necessarily repudiating that the *brigata* is amused by linguistic trifles – a claim that rests on a vigorous assertion of leisure present in the Introduction to Day Three, when she walks "per una vietta non troppo usata ma piena di verdi erbette e di fiori … e cianciando e motteggiando e ridendo" [along a fairly unfrequented grassy path strewn with flowers … laughing and jesting (III.Intro.3)],[20] the queen's narrative developments are a central feature

(III.Intro.6–9), becomes also a Purgatorial state of affairs thanks to the "sucidume," taken from *Purg*. I, 96, which in Dante's narrative is a rite of passage and a powerful example of the doctrine of legal "restitution" (*restitutio iuris*).

20 Branca observes in his note that "la vaga descrizione prende un ritmo quasi di canzone" (*Decameron*, p. 323).

of merchant ethics. A substantial portion of tales in Day Three are organized around Florence and the Florentine *contado*; through numerous intertextual links between Day Three and the conclusive cluster of Day Two, especially tales 9 and 10, and through the memory of the clash on morality between Dioneo and Filomena, a cultural ambiguity emerges. The sensation is that the storytelling of Day Three is surrounded by a type of mercantile reading that the *brigata* tries to dismiss as a form of credulous idolatry, while retaining from it – for the sake of a better narration – a certain degree of trumpery. The tales of Day Three retain from II.9 the way merchants gloat over their ability to pass off their shabby merchandise to an undiscriminating public, and Boccaccio insists that the voice of Filomena is associated with merchandise, as when the character of Ambrogiuolo from Piacenza is presented along with the trade commodities stocked on his Venetian ship. The tale of III.3, in particular, while treating the friar's limited wisdom as a version of idolatrous worship, adopts a specific representativeness of the purse and the girdle that goes far beyond the semiotic opacity traditionally associated with the fetish.

In Day Three Boccaccio recasts both Florence's odd inventory and the Tuscan motley collection of municipal tales as catalogues of human folly. If we look at the way Neifile's argument is outlined and enacted in the succession of each story, it is clear that the exchange of narration derives most of its power from a tension between different levels of rhetoric. The presence of the wool trade utensils at the end of III.3 is ambiguously symbolic. It is one of the moments in the novella in which the materiality or immateriality of storytelling becomes itself an issue, and in which the sexual pleasure of the two lovers turns into an almost transubstantial experience.

Strikingly, that triumph is a literal duplication of the Introduction to Day Three (III.3.13–15): as the lady of Filomena's tale enjoys "diletto" and "sollazzo," so do the members of the *brigata*:

> altre piú maniere di non nocivi animali, ciascuno a suo diletto, quasi dimestichi andare a sollazzo: le quali cose, oltre agli altri piaceri, un vie maggior piacere aggiunsero ... De' quali chi v'andò e chi, vinto dalla bellezza del luogo, andar non vi volle, ma quivi dimoratisi, chi a legger romanzi, chi a giucare a scacchi e chi a tavole ... si diede. (III.Intro.13)

> [and young fawns browsing, all manner of harmless animals going about their business for all the world as if they were tame. All of this added

> immeasurably to their pleasure ... while the rest found the place too enchanting and preferred not to: they stayed where they were and read romances or played chess or backgammon while the others were resting.]

The scene is dominated by an atmosphere of happy agitation or, to put it in economic terms, by a fervour of naïve consumers among the young Florentine frame characters. The *romanzi* consumed here belong to the courtly tradition of Boccaccio's *Amorosa Visione* or *Caccia di Diana*, and also to the dangerous readings of Paolo and Francesca in Dante.

It is against this background that Day Three constructs its rhetoric. In III.1 the "piccola novelletta" [little story] of Masetto immediately raises up "la zappa e la vanga e le grosse vivande" [the most basic of diets and of hard toil with mattock and spade (III.1.4)]; later the story presents an interesting short-circuit internal to the logic of the *beffa*, "le monache incominciarono a dargli noia e a metterlo in novelle" [the nuns began to make a nuisance of themselves and tease him (III.1.20)], and a folkloric proverb is then used to seal the narration: "affermando che cosí trattava Cristo chi gli poneva le corna sopra 'l cappello" [this is the way Christ treats the man who makes a cuckold of Him by making free with His brides (III.1.43)].

As often in Boccaccio, the "frame" serves to reorganize different types and levels of literacy. Thus the *locus amoenus* of the device corresponds to the fine touch of Filomena, who, in III.3, "vezzosamente cosí incominciò a parlare" [gracefully began to speak (III.3.2; translation mine)]; right after, however, the narrator is explicit about her understanding of the tale's genre: "Io intendo di raccontarvi una beffa" [I'm going to tell you a true story about a trick (III.3.3)]. With this declaration, the discursive machinery of the trick is set in motion, but Boccaccio complicates the situation by adding a tirade against religious fraud. Humanity is divided between those who know how to "civanzarsi" [prosper (III.3.3)] and those who "si rifuggono dover aver possano da mangiar, come 'l porco" [have to take refuge in a place that will feed them, like pigs (III.3.3)]. This pig is another proverbial element that looks back, through Masetto's tale, to Dioneo's conclusive remarks at II.10: "mi pare che ser Bernabò disputando con Ambruogiuolo cavalcasse la capra inverso il chino" [it seems to me that when Bernabò was arguing with Ambruogiuolo, he did not know his arse from his elbow (III.3.43)]. It becomes clear that the trick, for all its neutral narrative, is also surrounded by other types of literacy, such as exempla (at which the friar *grossa pasta* fails), folkloric proverbs that are particularly suited to mercantile readings – and in fact play a role, as we just saw, in Dioneo's reinterpretation of the dispute among the two merchants of II.9 – and finally municipal gossip. In this way the trick in III.3 is rewritten by Boccaccio according to a complex social and even geographical strategy. This is why Filomena protests:

> io racconterò non solamente per seguire l'ordine imposto, ma ancora per farvi accorte che eziandio che i religiosi, a' quali noi oltre modo credule troppa fede prestiamo, possono essere e sono alcuna volta, non che dagli uomini, ma da alcuna di noi cautamente beffati. (III.3.4)
>
> [I'll tell you about this trick not only to do as I am bidden, but also to wake you up to the fact that even monks and friars (whom we women tend to trust too blindly, gullible creatures that we are) can be and occasionally will be slyly hoodwinked, and not only by men but by one of our own sex.]

At this point in her presentation, Boccaccio inserts a decidedly geographic move that brings the tale to the closest proximity with Florence:

> Nella nostra città, piú d'inganni piena che d'amore o di fede, non sono ancora molti anni passati, fu una gentil donna di bellezze ornata e di costumi, d'altezza d'animo e di sottili avvedimenti quanto alcuna altra dalla natura dotata, il cui nome, né ancora alcuno altro che alla presente novella appartenga come che io lo sappia, non intendo di palesare, per ciò che ancora vivon di quegli che per questo si caricherebber di sdegno, dove di ciò sarebbe con risa da trapassare. (III.3.5)
>
> [Our city is a place for knavery rather than for love and trust. That is where, not so many years ago, there lived a lady of beauty and breeding; she possessed an innate nobility of spirit and a sharpness of wit to match that of any woman, and her name – that I shall not tell you (any more than the names of anyone else who comes into this story, for all that I know what they are) because it would give offence to certain people who are still alive, whereas it ought to be shrugged off with a smile.]

Filomena observes Neifile's order of narration, and ranges a variety of impulses that go from gender, with the female version of a trick, to religious critique and to municipal gossip. The decision not to reveal the protagonist's name is parallel to the presentation of Masetto in III.1: "In queste nostre contrade fu e è ancora un munistero di donne assai famoso di santità (il quale non nomerò per non diminuire in parte alcuna la fama sua)" [there was once upon a time in these parts a convent with a great name for holiness – it still exists and I shall not identify it so as not to detract in the slightest measure from its reputation (III.1.6)]. The laughter's possibility to transcend the tale's local coordinates, "con risa da trapassare," looks beyond the traditional narrator's excuse for the lack of narrative predecessors and the consequent reuse of civic material.

Florence is implicitly brought to centre stage and put on trial, in what Branca considers a "tenue riflesso, nell'atmosfera pacata e fiabesca del *Decameron*, di giudizi non rari nell'opera del Boccaccio" [subtle echo, in the soft and eerie atmosphere of the *Decameron*, of a type of judgment that is not infrequent in Boccaccio's work (Branca, ed., *Decameron*, 347)]. However, while Filomena's narration is firmly set on its forward trajectory in III.3.5, Boccaccio also moves the tale back into a productive comparison with the Conclusion of II.9 – once again a crucial crossroads of thematic issues with III.3:

> Ambruogiuolo il dí medesimo che legato fu al palo e unto di mele, con sua grandissima angoscia dalle mosche e dalle vespe e da' tafani, de' quali quel paese è copioso molto, fu non solamente ucciso ma infino all'ossa divorato: le quali bianche rimase e a' nervi appiccate, poi lungo tempo, senza essere mosse, della sua malvagità, fecero a chiunque le vide testimonianza. E cosí rimase lo 'ngannatore a piè dello 'ngannato. (II.9.75)
>
> [As for Ambrogiuolo, the very day on which he was bound to the stake and smeared with honey, which left him in agony from the horse-flies, wasps, and bluebottles in which the place abounded, he was left not merely dead but eaten down to the bone. Indeed, his bones were allowed to remain there for ages untouched, all bleached and held together by the sinews, as a testimony to his wickedness for whoever set eyes on them. "He who laughs last laughs best." So it proved.]

This final scene of II.9, told by Filomena, who at the time is also serving as a queen for the day, is visually stunning. Boccaccio remarks on Ambruogiuolo's ruthless cruelty, transforming his agony into a powerful *memento mori* and a symbol of Florence's misdeeds. Boccaccio is also capitalizing on a little note of ethnology about the gadflies that come to pillage the evil merchant's nerves and white bones; following the same logic, at the foot of the torture lies a proverb which, in turn, marks a circular link with the initial set-up of the story: "Suolsi tra' volgari spesse volte dire un cotal proverbio: che lo 'ngannatore rimane a' piè dello 'ngannato" [there's a proverb that folk are forever coming out with: "He who laughs last laughs best" (II.9.3)].

Filomena's version of the same proverb in III.3, inserted before the novella descends into the scorn for the husband's expertise, suggests that Boccaccio is touching here a malleable territory of merchant hermeneutics. It is the type of writing (and plotting) that tries to assess verifiable information, to convince with facts, or, as III.3.22 puts it, "certificare dell'amore" [convince him of her love]; it is conversely the type of reading in which the simple-minded friar gets too much involved, since the woman's story has made him warm and attentive, "per sí fatta maniera riscaldar gli orecchi" [I'm going to give him such a dressing down (III.3.30)]. This malleable mercantile hermeneutics reflects an earlier approach taken by Filomena in II.9, when Bernabò appears "turbato" [upset] and wants to downplay too subtle a "quistionar con parole" [quibble with words] at Ambruogiuolo's contention that female instability is such that all women "sono cosí pieghevoli" [are so malleable (III.3.21)]. Immediately after, the narrator catches Ambruogiuolo dangerously trying to increase the capital of narration: he asks his colleague to bet "cinquemila fiorin d'oro," and he is shown to be "già in su la novella riscaldato" [thoroughly roused (III.9.22)].

The municipal turn impressed by Boccaccio on III.3 discovers a literalist, mercantile technology of reading that proves fallible, synonymous with the civic *inganni* of Florence, and doomed to founder on the bedrock of language. Further parallels with this effective return to Tuscan material in Day Three are offered by III.4, one of Panfilo's tales. Its rhetorical strategy is downplayed at the very beginning, as Panfilo contents himself with adding "alcuna piacevole cosetta" [some trifle] to the preceding tale, whereas its contiguous nature is evidently derived from the reoccurrence of similar Florentine themes: "il che a una nostra vicina, non ha ancor lungo tempo … intervenne" [what happened not all that long ago to one of our Florentine ladies (III.4.3)]. To the low circle of civic chronicles also refer a "uomo idiota … e di grossa pasta" [being of obtuse and plodding disposition] (III.4.5), and the young Isabetta, who is described with a fourteenth-century *ribobolo*,[21] tinged with nostalgic scratches from the Valdelsa: "fresca e bella e ritondetta che pareva una mela casolana" [fresh as a daisy, plump as an orchard-grown apple

21 Cf. Brambilla Ageno, "Riboboli trecenteschi," 422.

(III.4.6)].[22] In the same tale, the Tuscan context goes along with another key feature of Day Three, the importance of speech: the layman Puccio, who is already burning with desire at a fairly early stage of the novella, does not let the matter sit for long and openly "ragionò il suo piacere" [speaks to her of what he had in mind (III.4.10)]. When the Florentine thread seems to get lost, due to Boccaccio's careful observance of variety rules, the *brigata* commits III.7 to Emilia, who strikes a programmatic municipal statement, "A me piace nella nostra città ritornare" [I should like to return to our own city (III.7.1)], loyally echoing also Neifile's wording of the day's subject. Even in III.5, despite Zima's crafty display of courtly lyric,[23] what is really at stake is the juxtaposition of high rhetoric and proverbial immediacy, for here the friar *uccellato* of III.3 corresponds to a realistic declination of the day's wisdom: "mentre altrui si credono uccellare, dopo il fatto sé da altrui essere stati uccellati conoscono" [how often do they lay a trap for another party only to discover that it is they themselves who have fallen into it! (III.5.3)].

This mercantile reasoning, incapable of allegorizing beyond the surface of literalism and forced to act "come 'l porco," lends to III.3 a rich intertextuality. Its dual understanding leaves traces in Boccaccio's polysemic use of *intendere*. In the lady's first confession, the man's dubious actions are ascribed to a cognitive breakdown, "forse non avvisandosi che io cosí fatta intenzione abbia come io ho" [he doesn't appreciate what my feelings are (III.3.11)], soon to be suffered by the holy friar himself. The slippery presence of *intendere*, in fact, is the key idea behind III.3.17:

> Al santo frate ... venne il valente uomo; col quale poi che d'una cosa e d'altra ebbero insieme alquanto ragionato, tiratol da parte, per assai cortese modo il riprese dello intendere e del guardare che egli credeva che esso facesse a quella donna, sí come ella gli aveva dato a intendere.
>
> [It was not long before the gentleman paid the good friar one of his customary visits and, after they had chatted a while about this and that, the

22 On the tale see Ferreri, "La novella di frate Pucci." Forni ("Realtà/verità," 316), signals another realistic configuration: "Fu adunque in Toscana una badia, e ancora è, posta, sì come noi ne veggiam molte, in luogo non troppo frequentato dagli uomini" (III.8.4).

23 Zima's literary exploits are parallel to Filomena's Provencal "vezzeggiare"; on III.5 see Forni, "Zima sermocinante," an extraordinary reading of Pygmalion's relationships between the word and the *res muta*.

> friar drew him aside and very tactfully admonished him for paying his addresses (so he believed) and ogling the lady, as she had given him to understand.]

The double-crossed friar is prisoner of a hermeneutics that Boccaccio is eager to repeat in the Conclusion to Day Three (III.3.18), during a memorable scene that seems to recapitulate most of recent storytelling from the vantage point of the themes debated through III.3:

> Qui fece fine la Lauretta alla sua canzone, la quale notata da tutti, diversamente da diversi fu intesa: e ebbevi di quegli che intender vollono alla melanese, che fosse meglio un buon porco che una bella tosa; altri furono di piú sublime e migliore e piú vero intelletto, del quale al presente recitar non accade. (III.Concl.18)
>
> [Lauretta ended her song; everyone had followed it closely, but not all had understood it the same way. Some were inclined to a rather down-to-earth interpretation, that the bird in hand is (for all its faults) worth two in the bush; others took a more uplifting view, which was closer to the truth – but this is not the place to discuss it.]

This extraordinary page of Boccaccio is nothing less than a miniature of Dante's *Vita nova*, including a nod to the mechanism of its transcription. A multiple layer of understanding as an aesthetic response to lyric poetry (in this case, to Lauretta's *canzone*) is suggested to Boccaccio by *Vita nova* III.14: "A questo sonetto fue risposto da molti e di diverse sentenzie" [this sonnet elicited many different verse interpretations]; here, though, on one side of *intendere* there is a "melanese" way, a mercantile reading according to which a pig is better than a young girl. On the other side lies a more accomplished strategy of meaning that Boccaccio decides not to report, echoing Dante's notorious reluctance in the *Vita nova* to transcribe responsive material and the occasional omission of his own lyrics.[24]

---

24 Boccaccio transcribed Dante's *libellus* and gave his own textual solution to the tangle of scribal and literary metaphors of the *Vita Nova*; cf. on this Boli, "Boccaccio's *Trattatello in laude di Dante*," and Usher, "Boccaccio, Cavalcanti's Canzone *Donna me prega* and Dino's Glosses." Although the Ovidian nature of Dante's *Vita Nova* is a much-debated issue, we can assume that Boccaccio was influenced by "the medieval tendency to combine the *Ars* and *Remedia* into one work" (Smarr, "Ovid

Filomena's cautionary note against those who live (and read) "come 'l porco" suggests in III.3 a similar division between those who practise a mercantile reading "alla melanese" – the husband with his dispossessed wool combs would definitely be among these ranks – and those who actually enjoy a more refined understanding of literature. This elusive version of *intendere* could be grasped through Branca's characterization of a "Filostrato femminile" behind Lauretta's insistence on the idea of "lassa inamorata" (III.Concl.12), or by how the crafty woman of III.3 constructs a female and Ovidian version of a trick, otherwise of a differently popular taste, which is fuelled by Boccaccio's intuition of a new social structure of desire.

---

and Boccaccio," 252), responsive to Dante's multiple use of *intendere* in the *libellus*, and finally encouraged to promote his own version through the promiscuous reading "alla melanese" that closes Day Three. F. Bruni, "Prove di arcaismo cortese," analyses a suggestive example of a "lyric miniature," a private *divertissement* taken from the *Vita Nova*.

The Tale of Fra Puccio (III.4)

JELENA TODOROVIĆ

The fourth tale of the third day of the *Decameron* tells the story of Puccio di Rinieri, a good and old, but not so brilliant man of Florence, who becomes a pious tertiary of the order of St Francis, thus becoming henceforth known as Fra Puccio. Overcome by a fervent sense of religion and obsessed with the idea of salvation and achieving Paradise, Puccio loses interest in his much younger wife, Monna Isabetta. Dom Felice, a young priest just arrived from Paris, seizes the opportunity to spend time alone with the neglected wife by teaching the poor old man how to pay penance and consequently earn an ardently desired place in Paradise. Dom Felice creates a situation in which the bedroom is liberated from its usual occupant so that he can use it freely and consequently gain "Paradise" himself with Fra Puccio's wife.

Scholars have approached this novella from different points of view. Rosario Ferreri's analysis ("La novella") historically contextualizes the novella, interpreting some parts of the tale of Fra Puccio as a parody of *Lo specchio della vera penitenza* [*Mirror of True Penitence*] by Iacopo Passavanti, who, like Dom Felice, returned to Florence from Paris where he had studied, and who taught penance to Florentines beginning in 1345. Paolo Valesio ("Sacro") approaches III.4 as a representation of the sacred in the *Decameron*. He views this novella as different from the others, in which friars are usually attacked by Boccaccio for abusing laymen's superstitions. In this tale, according to Valesio, we find ourselves before "un'immagine sacra desacralizzata, 'profanata', resa grottesca" [a desacralized, "profaned" sacred image, rendered grotesque] which "definisce un'esperienza sacrale proprio nel momento in cui sembra far da ostacolo a tale esperienza" [defines a sacred experience in the very moment in which it seems to represent an obstacle to such experience

(395)]. Michael Calabrese's understanding of III.4 from the point of view of the study of medieval masculinities suggests that the dynamics between Fra Puccio and Dom Felice depend on their understanding of their own masculinities, with which they deal in different ways ("Male Piety and Sexuality"). Calabrese's conclusion, valid for all the characters he analyses in the *Decameron*, is applicable to our two protagonists as well: they are both at a loss in the end, for "whether the clerics are punished or not, they have nonetheless failed in their holiness, and whether the husbands learn of their folly, they have still failed in their masculinity" (270). My approach to this novella is based on its role in the macrotext of the third day, which as a whole is organized as a reversal of the three realms of the afterlife from Dante's *Comedy*. The day's tales move from Paradise to Purgatory to Hell, all of which are carefully distributed within the frame of the *giornata*. Day Three's setting recalls the Earthly Paradise and ends with an explicit citation of the final verse from the *Comedy*. Moreover, under the sign of the number three that is the building block of the entire *Comedy*, Day Three parodies the Church as an institution, its representatives (who appear in the majority of the novelle), and common superstitions among people created and encouraged by their spiritual "shepherds."

Boccaccio's own presence in III.4 is evident from the very opening, where a careful reader must recognize the author who makes an appearance within Panfilo's remarks. In the spirit of the thematic task of the third day, that of recounting tales in which something is gained or regained through one's wit and genius, Panfilo decides to tell a story of a fellow citizen, playing with the familiarity of the places, names, and, above all, context for the *brigata* listeners. After prefacing the events with a moralizing remark that "assai persone sono che, mentre che essi si sforzano d'andarne in Paradiso, senza avvedersene vi mandano altrui" [not a few there are that, while they use their best endeavours to get themselves places in Paradise, do, by inadvertence, send others thither], the narrator introduces the topic of his story.[1] He claims:

> *Secondo che io udi' già dire*, vicino di San Brancazio stette un buono uomo e ricco, il quale fu chiamato Puccio di Rinieri, che poi essendo tutto dato allo

1 Unless otherwise noted, the citations are taken from Giovanni Boccaccio, *Decameron*, ed. Vittore Branca (Milan: Mondadori, 2008). English translations are from *Decameron*, trans. J.M. Rigg (London, 1903).

spirito si fece bizzoco di quegli di san Francesco e fu chiamato frate Puccio. (III.4.4; emphasis mine)

[Hard by San Pancrazio there used to live, *as I have heard tell*, a worthy man and wealthy, Puccio di Rinieri by name, who in later life, under an overpowering sense of religion, became a tertiary of the order of St. Francis, and was thus known as Fra Puccio.]

Instead of simply beginning the narration by stating that a certain event happened, with perhaps brief references to place and time, or to a moral of the story, and then continuing with the story itself, Panfilo insists that he has *heard* about the events that he is going to retell. The storyteller, and through him the author himself, thus insists on the familiarity of the social and geographical context (Florence), as he is beginning to capture everyone's attention. Not only the other members of the *brigata* but also Boccaccio's intended audience are thus immediately involved in the story and interested in its protagonists, whose identities they are eager to discover. This rhetorical device of providing veracity for one's claims by stating that the story was heard and consequently must be true is not an uncommon way of capturing the reader's attention in Boccaccio. It is found not only in the *cornice* of the *Decameron*, but also in other instances in Boccaccio's works, both within his texts and in the glosses copied in the margins of his manuscripts.[2] The attention of Panfilo's listener and of

2 On similar uses of this formula, see my article "Nota sulla *Vita Nova*." A longer discussion of some of these issues will be available in "How to Satisfy the Desire of the Author: The Case of Giovanni Boccaccio," in *Boccaccio filologo-filosofo*, ed. T. Barolini and H.W. Storey (Indiana University Press, forthcoming). We find perhaps the most important and most influential instance of Boccaccio's use of this rhetorical device in the margins of his two copies of the *Vita Nova*, in the editorial note known as *Maraviglierannosi molti* (*Many will be amazed*). In order to add credibility to his claim that Dante would himself have wanted to have changed his *Vita Nova* and to have taken out the *divisiones* from the text of his *libello*, Boccaccio underpins his statement by adding that he, Boccaccio, had *heard* so from the "persone degne di fede" [trustworthy people]. His editorial interference within the text of the *Vita Nova*, which influenced the *libello*'s reception until the twentieth century, is thus justified by the supposed claims of trustworthy people, and we are to take Boccaccio's word on that. In the *Trattatello in laude di Dante*, we find a similar formula on several occasions. At the beginning of Dante's life as told by Boccaccio, the reader is informed about how the Florentine poet became Love's subject at a very young age. Boccaccio is actually retelling the story of the *Vita Nova* told by Dante himself: how and when he fell in love with Beatrice, how he was so blinded by love for her as to wander around

Boccaccio's reader is thus assured, and the author can continue to build the narration with greater ease. We read and hear Boccaccio himself in the words pronounced by Panfilo that introduce an episode from what Rosario Ferreri defines as "cronaca cittadina," which he connects with the context of Florence in the years of Iacopo Passavanti's preachings ("La novella," 78). This chapter will remain within the boundaries of fourteenth-century Florence, and it is concerned primarily with Dante's importance for Boccaccio as an author and as a literary editor.

As has already been observed, from the very beginning of Boccaccio's collection of tales, the reader encounters Dante:

> Comincia il libro chiamato *Decameron* cognominato Prencipe Galeotto. Nel quale si contengono cento novelle in diece dì dette da sette donne e da tre giovani uomini. (I.Intro.1)
>
> [Beginneth here the book called *Decameron*, otherwise Prince Galeotto, wherein are contained one hundred novels told in ten days by seven ladies and three young men.]

The entire title of the work is under the sign of Dante: from its nickname, Prencipe Galeotto, which recalls immediately the fifth canto of the *Inferno* and the tragic love story of Francesca and Paolo, to Boccaccio's explanation of his work's structure, where we cannot but recognize the characteristics of Dante's work. Boccaccio's *Decameron* indeed contains one hundred novelle that numerically correspond to the

---

Florence hoping to see her and thus feel the blessings he desired. At this point, eager to convey the truth about the greatest love story in Italian literature at the time, Boccaccio informs his reader that Dante's love was sincere and most honest, which we know from Dante himself and from what other people said ("secondo che egli [Dante] scrive *e che per altrui*" [emphasis mine]). Moreover, later in the text Boccaccio tells an anecdote about how much Dante was dedicated to his studies and how deeply he would immerse himself in the readings. The story, told by "alcuni degni di fede," was reported by Boccaccio in detail. Yet again, in lesson VIII of the *Esposizioni sopra la Commedia di Dante,* Boccaccio repeats the same rhetorical formula to support information about Beatrice's origins. He knows "*secondo la relazione di fededegna persona,* la quale la conobbe e fu per consanguinità strettissima a lei" (emphasis mine) that Beatrice was a real person, not just a product of Dante's imagination, who came from an old Florentine family. In the *Decameron,* Boccaccio uses the same expressions: "da fededegna [persona] *udito l'avevo*" (I Intro.16) and "da persona degna di fede *sentii*" (I.Intro.49, emphasis mine).

one hundred *canti* of the *Comedy*. This similarity and many other striking parallels between Dante's and Boccaccio's works have been explored in a series of studies based on intertextuality between Dante and Boccaccio, which remain invaluable to every student of our Certaldese.[3] The main question among scholars has been whether Boccaccio had such a profound knowledge and understanding of Dante as early in his career as when he was composing the *Decameron*. The conclusion has been unanimous: analyses of Boccaccio's youthful texts, written before the *Decameron*, and of the *Decameron* itself demonstrate that Dante is woven deeply into their structures. Millicent Marcus, on the other hand, disagrees that Dante was the primary source for Boccaccio's *Decameron*. Instead, Marcus suggests that while Boccaccio uses the syntagm "montagna aspra ed erta" (in which he overtly alludes to the opening of the *Comedy*) as early as the Introduction to the First Day, he does so in order to be able to depart from the text of his predecessor and start looking for a new model, which he finds in Boethius's *Consolatio Philosophiae* (Marcus, *An Allegory*, 112). However, Marcus sees in the *Esposizioni sopra la Commedia di Dante* reasons to believe that Boccaccio's interest in Dante is more complicated and in fact twofold: "Dante is at once *auctoritas*, deserving an exegesis worthy of Holy Writ; and colleague, inviting the aesthetic judgments of a fellow poet" (111). A look at Boccaccio's activity as editor and scribe of Dante's texts would support such a claim. Extant codices help us understand the extent to which the Certaldese was involved in building what we refer to today as the cult of Dante. Boccaccio did not just read and absorb Dante for his own use, but by carefully expunging, editing, and copying Dante's texts, he also started a discipline still very alive in our own times – Dante criticism. From the Zibaldone Laurenziano (MS Pluteo XXIX.8), copied as early as 1338–9, where the correspondence between Dante and Giovanni del Virgilio is copied alongside some of Dante's epistles, to MS Toledo 104.6 and MS Chigi L V 176, to the composition of the *Trattatello in laude di Dante* and public exegesis of the *Commedia* – to name but a few major episodes from Boccaccio's dedicated work on Dante – the Certaldese combines his reverence for his predecessor with

3 For essential bibliographical references, see Fido, "Dante personaggio"; Bettinzoli, "Per una definizione delle presenze dantesche nel Decameron I" and "Per una definizione delle presenze dantesche nel Decameron II"; Cassell and Kirkham, *Diana's Hunt*; Branca, *Boccaccio medievale*; Kirkham, *The Sign of Reason*; Delcorno, "La 'predica'"; Hollander, "*Decameron*: The Sun"; Picone, "The Tale."

superb mastery and independence in all things literary, codifying in the process Dante's literature within the Italian tradition, but, even more, establishing himself within that literary canon as an *auctoritas*.[4]

Let us return now to Day Three of the *Decameron*. Neifile, the queen of the third day, whose name translates as "new lover," is often understood either as a symbol of courtly and stilnovist love or, as Victoria Kirkham suggests, as Christian love or Charity.[5] If we were to interpret Neifile's name in the former way, that is as a representative of courtly and stilnovist love, then the author's intentions would be directed towards creating a concept of successful "earthly" love, which we encounter from the very benning of the *giornata*: from the first novella, in which Masetto devises a plan to gain access to a convent and is subsequently rewarded in ways he could not have remotely imagined, to the witty dame in the third novella, who achieves her long-desired bliss through manipulating a priest, to Dom Felice and Monna Isabetta's earthly paradise, to Zima's "gli ultimi termini d'amore" with Francesco Vergellesi's wife, to Ricciardo Minutolo's fulfilled desire for Catella, to Tedaldo's reconquered love of Monna Ermellina, to Rustico's bliss with Alibech. If, on the other hand, we are to accept that Neifile indeed represents Charity, then in the case of Day Three we can interpret the author's choice as a parodic take on the ways in which core Christian concepts are (mis)understood among people, and, above all, intentionally neglected among clergy, given that we can hardly find Charity in the stories told and their protagonists. In accordance with this interpretation, Boccaccio's reversal of the ordering of the three realms of the afterlife would then fit his intention to parody (mis)conceptions about Church doctrine and the abuse of the Church's institutions by those very men who should instead guard and ennoble them through their devotion and lead their flock by their own example.

4 Boccaccio's independence and editorial entrepreneurship are evident in his rewritings of the *Vita Nova* as well as in his constant correcting of the *Comedy*. In the introduction to *La Commedia secondo l'antica vulgata*, Giorgio Petrocchi points out that there were two traditions of the *Divine Comedy*: the "prima tradizione" (1321–55) and the "seconda tradizione," which starts with Boccaccio's edition of Dante's text (Petrocchi, *La Commedia*, 17). When Petrocchi defines Boccaccio's intervention in the text's editing as contaminatio, he states that Boccaccio contaminates more than he corrects (Petrocchi, *La Commedia*, 45–6). The same can be said of his work on the *Vita Nova* in MSS Toledo 104.6 and Chigi L V 176, for which see my "Nota sulla *Vita Nova*."

5 In Kirkham's interpretation, Elissa represents Hope and Emilia stands for Faith. See Kirkham, *The Sign of Reason*, 161.

On the contrary, as Tedaldo will utter in his speech, they ask people to do as they say, not as they do.[6] In his discussion of irony and parody in the *Decameron*, Carlo Delcorno states that Boccaccio's recalling the dawn in the Introduction to the third day is a "parodic desecration" of Dante's *Comedy* ("La 'predica,'" 174). In addition to these remarks, I would argue that Boccaccio nonetheless follows in Dante's footsteps where Dante's treatment of clerical corruption is concerned: we shall remember that Dante spares not even popes who have betrayed the mission of the Church and have failed themselves in the values they should represent and inspire in people. When Boccaccio, in one of the most central episodes of Day Three, has Tedaldo pronounce in his invective that the priests "non le cappe de' frati hanno costoro, ma solamente i colori delle cappe" [have nought of the habit of the friar save only the colour thereof (III.4.35)], through the use of "cappe" and the reference to their deceiving appearance, he recalls to the reader's memory the infernal episode of the hypocrites, where Dante has two friars (sic!) serve as the exemplum of a sinner in this category:

Là giù trovammo una gente dipinta
che giva intorno assai con lenti passi,
piangendo e nel sembiante stanca e vinta.
Elli avean cappe con cappucci bassi
dinanzi a li occhi, fatte de la taglia
che in Clugnì per li monaci fassi.
Di fuor dorate son, sì ch'elli abbaglia;
ma dentro tutte piombo, e gravi tanto,
che Federigo le mettea di paglia. (*Inf.* XXIII.58–66)

[Below that point we found a painted people,
who moved about with lagging steps, in circles,
weeping, with features tired and defeated.

6 Tedaldo says, among other things: "E quando di queste cose e di molte altre che sconce fanno ripresi sono, l'avere risposto: 'Fate quello che noi diciamo e non quello che noi facciamo' estimano che sia degno scaricamento d'ogni grave peso, quasi piú alle pecore sia possibile l'esser costanti e di ferro che a' pastori." [And when they are taxed with these and many other discreditable practices, they deem that there is no censure, however grave, of which they may not be quit by their glib formula: "Follow our precepts, not our practice:" as if 'twere possible that the sheep should be of a more austere and rigid virtue than the shepherds.]

And they were dressed in cloaks with cowls so low
they fell before their eyes, of that same cut
that's used to make the clothes for Cluny's monks.
Outside, these cloaks were gilded and they dazzled;
but inside they were all of lead, so heavy
that Frederick's capes were straw compared to them.][7]

Moreover, the opening of the third day – which begins in a sort of Edenic scene at a new villa where the *brigata* arrives after having decided to change lodging in fear that they were not safe in the first house – is construed in such a way as to recall the beginning of Dante's *Purgatory* (Hollander, "*Decameron*: The Sun Rises," 58–9). The *locus amoenus* of the *brigata*'s second refuge, contrasted to the dreadful atmosphere in plague-infested Florence from the beginning of the *Decameron*, is thus even more beautiful and charming than the first one. A detailed description provided by the author recalls the Earthly Paradise in the protagonists', and therefore in the reader's, imagination:

> Il veder questo giardino, il suo bello ordine, le piante e la fontana co' ruscelletti procedenti da quella tanto piacque a ciascuna donna e a' tre giovani, che tutti cominciarono a affermare che, se Paradiso si potesse in terra fare, non sapevano conoscere che altra forma che quella di quel giardino gli si potesse dare, né pensare, oltre a questo, qual bellezza gli si potesse agiugnere. (III.Intro.11)

> [The aspect of this garden, its fair order, the plants and the fountain and the rivulets that flowed from it, so charmed the ladies and the three young men that with one accord they affirmed that they knew not how it could receive any accession of beauty, or what other form could be given to Paradise, if it were to be planted on earth.]

Furthermore, the sun rising on a Sunday morning is a clear reference to the opening of Dante's *Purgatory*:

> L'*aurora* già di *vermiglia* cominciava, appressandosi il sole, a divenir *rancia*, quando la domenica, la reina levata e fatta tutta la sua compagnia levare e

7 Translations of Dante are from Allen Mandelbaum, *The Divine Comedy of Dante Alighieri*.

avendo già il siniscalco gran pezzo davanti mandato al luogo dove andar doveano assai delle cose oportune e chi quivi preparasse quello che bisognava, veggendo già la reina in cammino, prestamente fatta ogni altra cosa caricare, quasi quindi il campo levato, con la salmeria n'andò e con la famiglia rimasa appresso delle donne e de' signori. (III.Intro.2, emphasis mine)

[The *dawn* of Sunday was already changing from *vermilion* to *orange*, as the sun hasted to the horizon, when the queen rose and roused all the company. The seneschal had early sent forward to their next place of sojourn ample store of things meet with folk to make all things ready, and now seeing the queen on the road, and the decampment, as it were, begun, he hastily completed the equipment of the baggage-train, and set off therewith, attended by the rest of the servants, in rear of the ladies and gentlemen.]

Boccaccio's choice of vocabulary in these lines clearly comes from the following passage in *Purgatory*:

Sì che le bianche e *vermiglie* guance
là dov'era de la bella *Aurora*
per troppa etate divenivan *rance*. (*Purg*. II.7–9, emphasis mine)

[So that, above the shore that I had reached,
the fair Aurora's white and *scarlet* cheeks
were, as *Aurora* aged, becoming *orange*.]

In addition to these references to the second *cantica*, the closing *ballata* sung by Lauretta recalls the very last verse of the *Comedy*: Boccaccio's "Colui che move il cielo e ogni stella" is an overt rewriting of Dante's "L'Amor che move il sole e l'atre stelle" (*Par*. XXXIII.145). Direct references to *Purgatory*, as well as the circumstance of Sunday morning in the opening of Day Three, and a clear citation of the very last verse from *Paradise*, are without a doubt intentional. Quotations are strategic, and nothing is coincidental. And finally, the closing of Day Three refers to Boccaccio's greatest *auctoritas*, around whom he conceived the structural skeleton of this day. And while the rising sun is encountered at the beginning of several other days as well, its connection to *Purgatory* II through direct citation serves an additional purpose on the macro-level of Day Three. Thus an Edenic atmosphere determined by Dante's *Comedy* encloses stories that reverse the order of Dante's afterworld. In a series of novelle that punctuate the *giornata*, in which the three realms of the afterlife are explicitly named (Paradise in the fourth, Purgatory in the eighth, and Inferno in the tenth), the tenth tale represents a category of its own.[8] Around tales 4 and 8 we find two structural clusters, the first featuring the idea of Paradise and the second the concept of Purgatory. In the group of the first six stories, the protagonists achieve bliss more or less simply through the proper use of their wit. As one of this *giornata*'s primary interests is indeed courtly love, it is only appropriate that the first six of the day's novelle recount a joyous fulfilment of the ideals of courtliness, and are connected with the idea of earthly paradise. In the second group, consisting of novelle 7, 8, and 9, the happy ending is reached through some long and trying process in which the characters' perseverance in regaining the component of happiness lost at the beginning of the story is tested and challenged.[9]

From Fra Puccio's Paradise to Ferondo's Purgatory to Alibech's Inferno, Boccaccio's narrators tell stories which, while celebrating courtliness, also parody the intended values of the Christian (after)life in the form presented by the Church and its dignitaries. Franco Fido, referring to the anthropological analysis of the *Decameron* by Joy Hambuechen Potter, has noted that Boccaccio (often ruthlessly) criticizes the Roman Church not because he lacks faith or religiosity, but because of "his awareness of a crisis in these institutions, which have lost their power to certify and sanctify."[10] Boccaccio begins his criticism of the Church from the first novella of the first day, that of Ser Cepparello, and continues it throughout the collection. In the second novella of the first day, he has Abraham notice that in the Roman Church there is "niuna santità, niuna divozione, niuna buona

8 For a discussion on the perversion of the concept of hell and its representation as a travesty of earthly paradise in III.10, see Steven Grossvogel's chapter in this volume.

9 The case of the central novella in this cluster is rather unique and more complicated. Its primary purpose is to ridicule the belief in Purgatory and afterlife as a concept. However, it should be noted that in this tale, Ferondo does achieve a happy ending of a sort – although only in his own view, not in the view of the reader, of his wife, or of the abbot. After returning from Purgatory, he accepts with pleasure his new role as the messenger from the other world and rather enjoys the attention he is getting from his compatriots. Even though in the meanwhile his wife and the abbot enjoy the bliss of their carnal relationship, and even conceive a child together in the parallel plot concerned with the earthly concept of love, Ferondo is ignorant of these circumstances and continues to believe that he is the blessed one with a wonderful child, faithful wife, and a new gift of "bridging" the two worlds.

10 Fido, "The Tale of Ser Ciappelletto," in Weaver, ed., *The "Decameron" First Day in Perspective*, 63–4. The reference is to Joy Hambuechen Potter, *Five Frames for the Decameron: Communication and Social Systems in the "Cornice."*

opera o essemplo di vita o d'altro" [[no] holiness, devotion, good works or exemplary living of any kind (I.2.24)], and that the only things he found there were "lussuria, avarizia e gulosità, fraude, invidia e superbia e simili cose e piggiori, se piggiori esser possono" [lewdness, avarice, gluttony, and the like, and worse, if worse may be (I.2.24)]. He continues to state that "mi vi pare in tanta grazia di tutti vedere, che io ho più tosto quella per una fucina di diaboliche operazioni che di divine" [to my thinking the place is a centre of diabolical rather than of divine activities (I.2.24)]. This view will be elaborated in a much harsher manner in Day Three.

As H. Wayne Storey has noted in his article on III.10, one of the primary sources for the parody in Day Three's last tale is "the most unifying sentiment among the people in medieval western Europe: the dislike of the clergy" ("Parodic Structure," 173). The reader is not to be surprised, then, to find that friars, often overtly accused by Boccaccio of being contrary to the values they are meant to represent and embody, are frequent subjects of, or participants in, the tales, especially in this *giornata*. Jonathan Usher has established that the word "frate" appears sixty-six times in the third day – far more frequently than in the first day (thirty-one times), the fourth day (twenty-seven times), the seventh day (twenty-six times), the sixth day (twenty-one times), or the eighth day (three times) ("Industria e acquisto erotico," 107n35). The fourth tale, however, is a unique occurrence in the *Decameron* and differs from the other novelle in this day as well. Only in this story do we have two representatives of Church life directly at odds and in direct opposition with one another; we are not confronted with a conflict between a religious person and a layman, "but [one] between two different types from the category of *homo religiosus*" (Valesio, "Sacro," 393). One of these men is "[un] uomo idiota e di grossa pasta" [a simple soul and slow of wit] and as such he becomes the easy prey of the other, who is "d'aguto ingegno e di profonda scienza" [keen-witted, and profoundly learned] and has just returned from his studies in Paris. Boccaccio's way of building the narrative from the opening of this novella anticipates the ending: the reader does not even have to read the rest of the story to know that the good and rich but not so bright husband, whose one and only concern is his salvation, is going to end as a victim of the young and learned priest's wit.

Within the third day, Boccaccio's harsh invective against priests culminates in the words uttered by Tedaldo of the seventh novella. Whereas the invective is implicit in the novella of Fra Puccio, Tedaldo's monologue is as explicit as it can be. In a detailed analysis of Boccaccio's approach to immoral friars, Delcorno offers a vast array of possible sources that the author used, among which Matthew 23 is dominant ("La 'predica'"). Delcorno also notices that the three main vices of the priests are identified as John's three capital sins:

> La superbia dei frati moderni, manifestata dalle loro vesti, non va disgiunta dagli altri due vizi, la "concupiscentia carnis" e la "concupiscentia oculorum": "E dove gli antichi la salute disideravan degli uomini, quegli d' oggi disiderano le femine e le ricchezze." (70)

> [Priests' arrogance, manifest in their clothes, is not to be separated from the other two vices, "concupiscentia carnis" and "concupiscentia oculorum": "And, whereas the friars of old time sought to win men to their salvation, those of today seek to win their women and their wealth."]

From a long series of defects, we encounter at least one in Dom Felice: that of "concupiscentia carnis." In the fourth novella Boccaccio concentrates on penance, which, as people are led to believe, if performed properly, can bring salvation and even blessedness, as Fra Puccio hopes. The reader of this tale is witness to the way in which Dom Felice, whose official task is to care for the spiritual well-being of his flock, creates and supports a mechanism whose outcome is the foundation and perpetuation of nothing more than a mere superstition.

The third protagonist, Fra Puccio's wife Isabetta, is young and beautiful, and tragically neglected by her husband:

> E quando ella si sarebbe voluta dormire o forse scherzar con lui, e egli le raccontava la vita di Cristo e le prediche di frate Nastagio o il lamento della Magdalena o così fatte cose. (III.4.6)

> [And when she was sleepy, or, maybe, riggish, he would repeat to her the life of Christ, and the sermons of Fra Nastagio, or the lament of the Magdalen, or the like.]

She is in the most disadvantageous position of all the protagonists at the beginning of the novella: as "giovane ancora di ventotto in trenta anni, fresca e bella e ritondetta che pareva una mela casolana" [a woman of from twenty-eight to thirty summers, still young for her age, lusty, comely and plump as a casolan apple (III.4.6)], she cannot obtain marital satisfaction "per la santità del marito, e forse per la vecchiezza" [by reason of her husband's devoutness, if not also of his age (III.4.6)]. The legal means available to her to resolve her marital problem are rather limited. Her marriage is obviously fulfilling all the requirements of the time: consents have been exchanged, and, more importantly, the marriage has been consummated. These two steps, according to canon law, guarantee the validity of a marriage. She could ask for a divorce and a revocation of the consent, but that would involve troublesome court procedure and having to prove that her husband is impotent. She could ask that he return her the favour by performing his marital duties, but what good would that do her, when Fra Puccio is primarily interested in God and in his own salvation?[11] On the other hand, Isabetta does not react with indifference to the new presence in their house, Dom Felice:

> Continuando adunque il monaco a casa di fra Puccio e veggendo la moglie così fresca e rotondetta, s'avvisò qual dovesse essere quella cosa della quale ella patisse maggior difetto; e pensossi, se egli potesse, per torre fatica a fra Puccio, di volerla supplire. E postole l'occhio adosso e una volta e altra bene astutamente, tanto fece che egli l'accese nella mente quello medesimo disidero che aveva egli: di che accortosi il monaco, come prima destro gli venne, con lei ragionò il suo piacere. (III.4.9–10)

> [So the monk, being a constant visitor at Fra Puccio's house, and seeing the lady so lusty and plump, surmised that of which she must have most lack, and made up his mind to afford, if he could, at once relief to Fra Puccio and contentment to the lady. So cautiously, now and again, he cast an admiring glance in her direction with such effect that he kindled in her the same desire with which he burned, and marking his success, took the first opportunity to declare his passion to her.]

Although one of the two direct beneficiaries of the outcome of the situation, Monna Isabetta does not participate actively in the organization of Fra Puccio's elaborate penance. Rather, instead of going through a painful and uncertain court process, she opts to accept this opportunity newly created by another, but not without stipulating some terms of her own:

11 For a more detailed study of the legal implications of marriage, see Makowski, "The Conjugal Debt."

> Ma quantunque bene la trovasse disposta a dover dare all'opera compimento, non si poteva trovar modo, per ciò che costei in niun luogo del mondo si voleva fidare a esser col monaco se non in casa sua; e in casa sua non si potea però che fra Puccio non andava mai fuor della terra; di che il monaco avea gran malinconia. (III.4.11)

> [He [Dom Felice] found her fully disposed to gratify it [his passion]; but how this might be, he was at a loss to discover, for she would not trust herself with him in any place whatever except her own house, and there it could not be, because Fra Puccio never travelled; whereby the monk was greatly dejected.]

Dom Felice is thus faced with a seemingly impossible situation. But, as Boccaccio informs us at the beginning, the young priest has just returned from Paris, a city known for its schools and universities. This detail creates a sort of readerly expectation about this friar. Indeed, he does not fail to confirm these expectations, and soon comes up with a solution: he teaches Fra Puccio how to attain Paradise through acts of penance. This particular penitential procedure, purportedly known only by the most powerful men in the Church, who keep the secret jealously, should help Fra Puccio attain eternal blessedness. In his simple-mindedness, Fra Puccio believes his new friend because, after all, he has just returned from Paris and must be acquainted with the secret ways of the Church dignitaries. Fra Puccio's religious zeal overpowers and even cancels out his ability to think rationally; therefore, he readily accepts Dom Felice's lies at face value. For this gullibility, in the logic of the *Decameron*, he deserves to be tricked.

The penance that he must undertake involves a rather complicated process and an even more complicated setting, as Dom Felice explains:

> Conviensi adunque l'uomo principalmente con gran diligenzia confessare de' suoi peccati quando viene a cominciar la penitenzia; e appresso questo gli conviene cominciare un digiuno e una abstinenzia grandissima, la qual convien che duri quaranta dì, ne' quali, non che da altra femina, ma da toccare la propria tua moglie ti conviene astenere. E oltre a questo si conviene avere nella tua propria casa alcun luogo donde tu possi la notte vedere il cielo; e in su l'ora della compieta andare in questo luogo e quivi avere una tavola molto larga ordinata in guisa che, stando tu in piè, vi possi le reni appoggiare, e tenendo i piedi in terra, distender le braccia a guisa di crocifisso: e se tu quelle volessi appoggiare ad alcun cavigliuolo, puoil fare;

e in questa maniera guardando il cielo star senza muoverti punto infino a matutino. E se tu fossi letterato, ti converrebbe in questo mezzo dire certe orazioni che io ti darei: ma, perché non se', ti converrà dire trecento paternostri con trecento avemarie a reverenzia della Trinità; e riguardando il cielo, sempre aver nella memoria Idio essere stato creatore del cielo e della terra, e la passion di Cristo, stando in quella maniera che stette Egli in su la croce.

Poi, come matutin suona, te ne puoi, se tu vuogli, andare e così vestito gittarti sopra il letto tuo e dormire: e la mattina appresso si vuole andare alla chiesa e quivi udire almeno tre messe e dire cinquanta paternostri con altrettante avemarie; e appresso questo con simplicità fare alcuni tuoi fatti, se a far n'hai alcuno, e poi desinare e essere appresso al vespro nella chiesa e quivi dire certe orazioni che io ti darò scritte, senza le quali non si può fare; e poi in su la compieta ritornare al modo detto. E faccendo questo, sì come io feci già, spero che anzi che la fine della penitenzia venga tu sentirai maravigliosa cosa della beatitudine eterna, se con divozione fatta l'avrai. (III.4.16–20)

[First of all then the penitent must with great exactitude confess his sins when he comes to begin the penance. Then follows a period of fasting and very strict abstinence which must last for forty days, during which time he is to touch no woman whomsoever, not even his wife. Moreover, thou must have in thy house some place whence thou mayst see the sky by night, whither thou must resort at compline; and there thou must have a beam, very broad, and placed in such a way, that, standing, thou canst rest thy nether part upon it, and so, not raising thy feet from the ground, thou must extend thy arms, so as to make a sort of crucifix, and if thou wouldst have pegs to rest them on thou mayst; and on this manner, thy gaze fixed on the sky, and never moving a jot, thou must stand until matins. And wert thou lettered, it were proper for thee to say meanwhile certain prayers that I would give thee; but as thou art not so, thou must say three hundred paternosters and as many avemarias in honour of the Trinity; and thus contemplating the sky, be ever mindful that God was the creator of the heaven and the earth, and being set even as Christ was upon the cross, meditate on His passion.

Then, when the matin-bell sounds, thou mayst, if thou please, go to bed – but see that thou undress not – and sleep; but in the morning thou must go to church, and hear at least three masses, and say fifty paternosters and as many avemarias; after which thou mayst with a pure heart do aught that thou hast to do, and breakfast; but at vespers thou must be again at church, and say there certain prayers, which I shall give thee in writing and which are indispensable, and after compline thou must repeat thy former exercise. Do this, and I, who have done it before thee, have good hope that even before thou shalt have reached the end of the penance, thou wilt, if thou shalt do it in a devout spirit, have already a marvelous foretaste of the eternal blessedness.]

Dom Felice instructs Fra Puccio very convincingly, and in minute detail, on how to organize his penance. In order to make it more believable, he even claims to have done it himself. Apart from a false relationship with his supposed friend, Dom Felice is also in a false relationship with God, whom he should serve and respect. Once again, as in many other instances within the *Decameron*, Boccaccio points to the shortcomings of the ways of the Church. The critique in this particular case is directed towards some of the principal pillars of the medieval Church – the sacrament of confession and the practice of penance – and to the two sides involved in the process – the priest and the believer. At the centre of the story is Fra Puccio's penance and the lengths to which he will go in order to achieve blessedness. At an extradiagetic or historical level, also central is Boccaccio's interest in the culture of penance as a way to attain personal salvation.[12] As we find out early in the story, Fra Puccio belongs to a group of religious zealots who practise rigorous self-discipline in the form of self-flagellation. In addition, he attends church regularly, goes to the mass and other services, and even sings hymns of praise.[13] Boccaccio attributes these activities to Fra Puccio's being "[un] uomo idiota e di grossa pasta." And while Dom Felice, who supposedly has a secret knowledge of salvation, is at fault for abusing Fra Puccio's faith and honesty, Fra Puccio is well deserving of such a treatment, for in his simple-mindedness he is too ready to accept a ritual and believe in its positive outcome. His religiosity is based on a complete belief in ready-to-use recipes for attaining salvation, which consequently makes him susceptible to Dom Felice's offer.

Dom Felice's idea of penance will fulfil its one and only purpose: it will keep Fra Puccio away from his wife and his bedroom every night for forty days, and thus make it possible for Dom Felice to enjoy Isabetta's

12 The author probably witnessed first-hand the public mania of self-flagellation as an act of penance following the plague, and his sensitivity to the subject was most likely affected also by these mass scenes of futile self-infliction of pain in the streets of Florence.

13 On Fra Puccio's "terrible musical taste," see Ciabattoni, "Musica sacra."

company. When Fra Puccio notices unusual sounds coming from his bedroom, where Isabetta spends her nights with Dom Felice during the husband's penance, he is mocked again. In a playful and comical dialogue based on a series of double entendres, the woman – who is, as we learn, *motteggevole* [[she] dearly loved a jest (III.4.24)] – humiliates the poor husband even more: she tells him that the noise and her tossing and turning in bed are due to her hunger from fasting. Another element of his penance, the fast, is turned upside-down and challenged. While he is depriving himself of food and reciting his prayers with only one goal in mind, that of being saved in the afterlife, she is enjoying herself with Dom Felice by breaking her maritally imposed sexual starvation in this one. In this case as well, "Boccaccio is not afraid to suggest that due obeisance to the nature of this world should come before aspirations to the next" (Thompson, *Chaucer, Boccaccio*, 188). Moreover, the act of penance, which by definition is considered solemn and heavy with *gravitas* (and is in fact, for Fra Puccio, even in these circumstances to which he remains oblivious), is interrupted by the subversive, "comic," and "humble" register of his wife's answers, resulting in a complete undercutting of the sacrament through the use of parody. Her perversion of fast as part of his penance in the end transforms into a joke for everyone's amusement, and at Fra Puccio's expense. However, the reader should remember that Fra Puccio is deserving of such a treatment because (as we know from the beginning of the tale) he constantly fails to meet his marital obligations. Like many other husbands in the *Decameron*, he, too, is being punished for not satisfying his wife. In the marital economy of the collection, Fra Puccio deserves to be cuckolded, and Boccaccio adds insult to injury in the verbal exchange between the husband and the wife, who further humiliates him by stating that her tossing and turning are his own doing.

As Panfilo notes at the very beginning of his storytelling, "assai persone sono che, mentre che essi si sforzano di andarne in Paradiso, senza avvedersene vi mandano altrui" [not a few there are that, while they use their best endeavours to get themselves places in Paradise, do, by inadvertence, send others thither (III.4.3)]. Believing that the penance will indeed earn him a place in Paradise, Fra Puccio sends his wife and his new friend, Dom Felice, to their version of heaven. In a circular motion, from the opening to the closing statements made by Panfilo, Boccaccio insists on the idea of Paradise. The two conceptions, however, are diametrically opposed: while Fra Puccio's Paradise should bring him salvation and blessedness and is of a deeply religious nature, Paradise at the end of the novella – that of Dom Felice and Isabetta – is a parodic version of the spiritual one, and the only one actually achieved. By the same token, the concept of love from the beginning of the novella, that of Charity – however flawed – mirrored in Fra Puccio's dedication to attaining blessedness, is parodied through the act of the fulfilment of courtly love between the two young protagonists.

The narrator finishes the story with a pun that not only subverts once more the true values of the Christian faith and the conception of salvation cherished by Fra Puccio, but also seals Boccaccio's negative portrayal of the clergy, be it narrow-minded Fra Puccio or deceiving Dom Felice:

> Di che, acciò che l'ultime parole non sieno discordanti alle prime, avvenne che dove frate Puccio faccendo penitenzia si credette mettere in Paradiso, egli vi mise il monaco, che da andarvi tosto gli avea mostrata la via, e la moglie, che con lui in gran necessità vivea di ciò che messer lo monaco, come *misericordioso*, gran divizia le fece. (III.4.33; emphasis mine)

> [Whereby (that my story may end as it began) it came to pass that Fra Puccio, hoping by his penance to win a place for himself in Paradise, did in fact translate thither the monk who had shown him the way, and the wife who lived with him in great dearth of that of which the monk in his *charity* gave her superabundant largess.]

Dom Felice, according to the narrator, gives to Isabetta, out of his "mercy," what she lacked in her married life. In these last lines of the novella, Panfilo attributes *misericordia* (mercy, charity) – a supreme Christian virtue entailing compassion, empathy, and piety – to Dom Felice, who is anything but virtuous in the Christian sense. Moreover, with this use of *misericordia* in such a strategic place and context, Boccaccio's parody reaches its apex. Earlier in the story, when Dom Felice instructs Fra Puccio on how to carry out his penance, he finishes the description of the actions to be taken by stating that if everything is done as prescribed, Fra Puccio will feel "maravigliosa cosa della *beatitudine* eterna" [a marvellous foretaste of eternal *blessedness* (III.4.20; emphasis mine)]. But, here and now, before Fra Puccio has finished his penance, it is Dom Felice, and not the husband, who attains bliss with the wife. The aftermath of the attempted penance, and the outcome of the situation in the bedroom, seem to be an intended pun on Matthew 5:7: "Beati misericordes quia ipsi misericordiam consequentur" [Blessed are the merciful, for they will receive mercy].

The idea of achieving blessedness is here reversed: while Fra Puccio should be the one rewarded with it, it is his adversary who enjoys it in the end. Instant "blessedness" and "Paradise" are immediate rewards for Dom Felice, who has used his *industria* in order to fulfil his desire, swindling the ingenuous old Fra Puccio. Thus, the imminent, worldly victory in erotic matters is his. Meanwhile, Fra Puccio is blissfully repeating his prayers posing in the form of the crucifix, looking forward to eternal blessedness and salvation. In Boccaccio's story, it is thus a person who is anything but deserving of blessedness and *misericordia* in the Christian sense who most readily obtains them.[14] In the narrative economy of the third day, the concept of Paradise as well is thus turned upside-down and parodied, within a broader ironic representation of the Church itself and of the clergy as her ministers.

Moreover, the climax of this novella is strengthened by the comic effect produced by the author's overt corroboration of the truth the reader has already discovered and enjoyed: Panfilo's closing remarks to the story confirm what Pier Massimo Forni (*Adventures in Speech*) describes and defines as "the poetics of realization" in the *Decameron*. While Boccaccio shifts between the literal and the metaphorical meanings of Paradise, he achieves a comic effect through insisting on these two diametrically opposed concepts.

The multifold irony of the pun which closes the story of Fra Puccio's "penance" acquires yet another dimension when taken into consideration alongside Boccaccio's previous comment, made through Panfilo, that Dom Felice is actually doing Fra Puccio a favour:

> Continuando adunque il monaco a casa di fra Puccio e veggendo la moglie così fresca e ritondetta, s'avvisò qual dovesse essere quella cosa della quale ella patisse maggior difetto; e pensossi, se egli potesse, per torre fatica a fra Puccio, di volerla supplire. (III.4.9)

---

14 I find Paolo Valesio's interpretation of the moral of this novella rather interesting. In his chapter on the sacred, he asks his reader: is Dom Felice really the winner? Valesio suggests that Dom Felice challenges God by using "un esercizio spirituale (da lui stesso consigliato) come sfondo piccante della sua piccola avventura erotica" [a spiritual exercise – suggested by him – as a bawdy background of his little erotic adventure]. Valesio, therefore, poses the question: who will laugh last? ("Sacro," 396).

> [So the monk, being a constant visitor at Fra Puccio's house, and seeing the lady so lusty and plump, surmised that of which she must have most lack, and made up his mind to afford, if he could, at once relief to Fra Puccio and contentment to the lady.]

The "favour" is completed in the end: Fra Puccio is relieved of his duty, while Monna Isabetta is well content with the outcome. The novella's extremely cynical tone is consequently rounded and confirmed by its end, in the distorted image of mercy attributed to Dom Felice.

In the end, one man's religious ideals are confronted and defeated, at least for the moment, by another man's purely carnal exigencies; one man's dim-wittedness is overpowered by the other man's brightness of mind, in the fulfilment of the *Decameron*'s celebration of wit. As Hollander has noted, "in the *Decameron* we hear nothing true of the world to come, only lies about it (often purveyed by friars)" (*Boccaccio's Dante*, 4). Dom Felice's suggestions for the expressway to Paradise parody true penance and its significance for the Church, and more importantly for those who truly place their faith in it. Boccaccio's treatment of the act of penance thus suggests its futility. His critique of devotional practices as proclaimed, divulged, and counselled by the clergy is captured yet again in the grotesque image of Fra Puccio lying in the form of the crucifix and reciting prayers for forty days and nights.

The events in this tale are narrated in a theatrical fashion, with very little static description and with dynamic dialogues between the protagonists. Especially theatrical is the central scene, written in the style of stage directions, in which Fra Puccio "a guisa di crocifisso" [as a sort of crucifix] is doing his penance, designed and perfected in such detail by Dom Felice. Fra Puccio's vain act of penance, which is bound to fail from its beginning, thus ends in a rather comic sense: from Fra Puccio's serious intentions to Dom Felice's instructions (uttered in holy tones suitable only for such a solemn act), to the complete subversion of the sacrifice that enables redemption in the Christ-like figure of Fra Puccio. Penance, which, by Boccaccio's times, had already progressed to become a private act between only a priest and a sinner, is here restored to its original form – it becomes public. As in the first centuries of Christianity, when sinners were entitled to one penance in their lifetime or in the course of one year, which would then be enacted publicly as a sign of true repentance, Fra Puccio's penance becomes public, for everyone to read, and, thanks to Boccaccio's vividly detailed description of the ritual, to "see." On the micro-level of the novella, Fra Puccio's penance is semi-public, known only to his wife and Dom Felice. Nevertheless, it is humiliating even in that small world. Fra Puccio is derided before his wife and his confessor, before the *Decameron*'s audience, and before God.

If we now take a step back and look at the macro-text of the third day, we can connect the tales of Fra Puccio and of Ferondo, about two not-so-intelligent men and their ingenuous credulity in Paradise and Purgatory as described by the clergy.[15] Just as Fra Puccio is "uomo idiota e di grossa pasta" [a simple soul and slow of wit], Ferondo in III.8, who believes he is in Purgatory, is "uomo materiale e grosso senza modo" [a man coarse and gross beyond measure]. Although Ferondo is not a clergyman, it is important to note that both he and Fra Puccio fall victim to monks. Moreover, in the tenth novella we have on the one side a candid and naïve Alibech, and on the other a monk, Rustico, who fools her into believing that she is punishing the devil by showing him the way to hell.[16] Boccaccio's interest in the first two victims' stupidity and simple-mindedness, and in Alibech's ingenuousness, is surpassed by his fascination with the other side: men of the Church who deceive in various ways in order to obtain illicit goals. If the pope and the cardinals in the first day's second novella are behaving contrary to their mission and duties, then what are we to expect from the simple clergy of lower ranks in the Church?

It is not by chance that Boccaccio constructs the storytelling of Day Three around a playfully reversed ordering of the three parts of Dante's *Comedy*. Whereas Dante's text, which culminates with Paradise, is based on and inspired by a sincere sense of faith, in the *Decameron* we are presented with a situation in which the Church and its representatives have turned that world upside-down. In the *Comedy*, the misbehaving and unruly clergy is punished in Hell, but Boccaccio's Florence and his world are still full of examples of ungodly attitudes towards the people and the values of Christian life. As Delcorno writes, in late medieval Italy, "abbandonati i temi più impegnativi e più alti della dottrina teologica, i predicatori sviluppano una pastorale della paura, che insiste sul pensiero della morte e dell' oltretomba" [having abandoned the most demanding and the highest themes of the theological doctrine, preachers develop a pastoral of fear, which insists on the thought of death and

15 On III.7 see Martin Eisner's chapter in this volume.
16 On III.10 see Steven Grossvogel's chapter in this volume.

of the afterlife ("La 'predica,'" 70)]. It is this concept of twisted ethical and moral values proposed by the clergy that Boccaccio criticizes and consequently parodies, and he chooses to do so through a series of references to one of the most widely read works of literature in his time, whose moral message is well known to his readers. Whereas the other stories that criticize the clergy serve to create a general context of the third day by treating different instances of the Church's failed mission as an institution, novelle 4, 8, and 10 represent the structural skeleton of Day Three, based on the reversal of Dante's Hell, Purgatory, and Paradise. In Day Three, enclosed within the description of a *locus amoenus* of the Earthly Paradise, and reversing the order of the three realms of the afterlife we find in Dante, Boccaccio clearly creates a reversal of that ideal world in which sin is punished and virtue rewarded, in order to point to the shortcomings of his own epoch.

The Tale of Zima (III.5)

ALESSANDRO VETTORI

The fifth novella of the third day strikes even a first-time reader for its simplicity and clarity. A linear and straightforward Introduction preparing the terrain for the protagonist's action and a felicitous Conclusion featuring the attainment of his much-desired goal flank a long speech by the protagonist, which constitutes the bulk of the plot. The storyline can be reduced to the main character's oration in the central part of the novella.[1]

Zima loves Francesco Vergellesi's wife. Francesco needs a palfrey before he leaves Pistoia and sets out on a trip to fulfil his newly appointed role as *podestà* of Milan, but he is too avaricious to spend any money on one.[2] He decides to exploit Zima's love for his wife and obtain Zima's beautiful palfrey for free. As a condition for granting Francesco the horse, Zima requests a private conversation with Francesco's wife. Francesco will be able to watch the conversation, but not hear it. In the course of this encounter, Zima manages to win Francesco's wife's love. After

1 The text of the original is Giovanni Boccaccio, *Decameron*, ed. Vittore Branca (Florence: Accademia della Crusca, 1976). The English version is Giovanni Boccaccio, *The Decameron*, trans. G.K. McWilliam (London: Penguin Books, 1972). The English translations of critical materials originally in Italian are mine.

2 The clear, realistic Pistoiese mark on this novella is given by the presence of Francesco Vergellesi. The Vergellesi or Vergiolesi were a notable and powerful Ghibelline family from Pistoia. The jealous husband in the novella could be drawn from one of the family members, Francesco de' Vergellesi, who went to Lombardy as *podestà* in 1326. Selvaggia, the beloved of Cino da Pistoia, the famous stilnovist poet and Dante's contemporary, supposedly belonged to this Pistoiese family; Cino devotes part of his poetic production to Selvaggia. See Giovanni Boccaccio, *Decameron*, ed. Vittore Branca (Turin: Einaudi, 1992), 369n2.

Francesco's departure for Milan with the palfrey, Zima and his lover enjoy their time together – and they continue their love story even after her jealous husband comes back home. The prank Francesco tried to play on Zima has been reversed. Francesco obtains his palfrey, but is cuckolded as a punishment for his avarice.[3] Zima gets Francesco's wife in exchange for his palfrey.

The story could not be more linear and more typical of the third day, in which "the discussion turns upon people who by dint of their own efforts have achieved an object they greatly desired, or recovered a thing previously lost," as the editorial introduction reads. Like most of the stories in this day, III.5 thematizes the achievement of illicit love by means of intellect and complete dedication. Crucial elements of this recipe for the successful acquisition of one's goal are secrecy, the use of silence, and the power of rhetoric.

The story is a *beffa* and displays all the typical qualities of this subgenre of novella writing. The *beffa* exerts a dynamic of power, in which the *beffatore* subjugates and torments the *beffato* in an abusive display of bullying tricks and authoritarian manipulation.[4] But the story's eventual reversal is aimed at demonstrating the unpredictable workings of an industrious and skilful would-be *beffato*, whose reaction forcefully transforms the course of his destiny, thereby overturning the roles and changing the *beffatore* into a *beffato* and vice versa.[5] The novella exudes, moreover, a tension between social classes, which could contain an encrypted authorial message on class relations, given that Francesco Vergellesi belongs to the aristocracy and Zima is a wealthy bourgeois, or a *nouveau riche*.

3 It might be interesting to note that, in the popular tradition, the *podestà* was notoriously considered a cuckold, possibly because he spent long periods of time away from his native land and his wife. The fact is reported, without further references to medieval sources, by Carlo Muscetta, *Giovanni Boccaccio*, 214.

4 Michel Plaisance's study, "La structure de la *beffa* dans les *Cene* d'Antonfrancesco Grazzini," is particularly useful for an investigation of *beffa* as instrument of power.

5 The reference to *beffa* is in the text itself: "Il cavaliere, da avarizia tirato e sperando di dover beffar costui, rispose" [Prompted by his avarice, and hoping to make a fool of the other fellow, the nobleman agreed (III.5.8)]. The reversal of fortune is already contained in the narrator's introduction to the story: "Credonsi molti, molto sappiendo, che altri non sappi nulla, li quali spesse volte, mentre altrui si credono uccellare, dopo il fatto sé da altrui essere stati uccellati conoscono" [Many people imagine, because they know a great deal, that other people know nothing; and it frequently happens that when they think they are hoodwinking others, they later discover that they have themselves been outwitted by their intended victims (III.5.3)].

After the situation has been set up by illustrating Francesco's notorious avariciousness, his wife's beauty and honesty, and Zima's passion for her, the story evolves entirely around Zima's articulated speech. It is the power of Zima's speech that conquers the woman and makes her begin to fall in love with him; she had previously resisted all his love propositions. She succumbs only to his incendiary rhetoric, as the text itself underscores:

> La donna, la quale il lungo vagheggiare, l'armeggiare, le mattinate e l'altre cose simili a queste, per amor di lei fatte dal Zima, muovere non avean potuto, mossero le affettuose parole dette dal ferventissimo amante: e cominciò a sentire ciò che prima mai non avea sentito, cioè che amor si fosse. (III.5.17)
>
> [Though she had previously remained unmoved by Zima's protracted courtship, his tilting of the jousts, his *aubades*, and all the other ways in which he had demonstrated his devotion, the lady was certainly stirred now by the tender words of affection addressed to her by her passionate suitor, so that, for the first time in her life, she began to understand what it meant to be in love.]

The woman did not perceive Zima's previous attempts as seductive. She found it easy to resist his "courting," his jousting, and his "*aubades*," which had no effect on her as the traditional, customary means to conquer a woman's attention and win her love in the medieval cultural milieu. It is only at the moment Zima begins to display his rhetorical skills and speaks to her so convincingly about his passion that her moral rectitude and virtuous resolve begin to crumble. Zima's words make her realize that she has never been in love before. She experiences love for the first time.

What is so overwhelming about this first portion of Zima's speech is not so much its content as the eloquence and forcefulness of his oration. He speaks of the "flames of love," he beseeches her to use "mercy," he hopes for her "compassion," and awaits the "guiderdone" [reward] of her love. He uses all the clichés of amorous exchange, including the loss of his life as a consequence of her refusal to reciprocate his love (III.5.15). He even goes a step further to announce his endless and unrelenting devotion to her "mentre la mia misera vita sosterrà questi membri" [as long as life sustains this poor, suffering body (III.5.11)] and even beyond, in the eternity of "the life hereafter," if people are allowed to love there "as they do on earth" (III.5.11). This tactic is similar to Ricciardo Minutolo's convincing words in III.6, when he placates Catella's anger after he tricks her into making love with him. In Riccardo Minutolo's case, however, the readers only have the "telling" of his speech and can only speculate about the power his words have over Catella, since these are given as reported speech and not "shown" directly. Zima, on the other hand, employs all the topoi of courtly love rhetoric in his declaration of unending love for the woman, but what is especially convincing is the elegance of his style and the sophistication of his language.[6] Zima's speech is a work of art. He manages to articulate his passion, which is rather ordinary in itself, in an irresistible fashion. It is the power of his speech that conquers the woman, not simply his feelings for her.[7] Zima shows his confidence in the convincing abilities of his language; when he requests a meeting with the woman, he reckons he will be able to attain his goal by simply having a dialogue with her – since wanting a private conversation with her is aimed at conquering her love through words. He formulates his love in such a way that she truly believes she has never felt such an emotion before. The beauty of his language and the artistry of his turns of phrase begin to transform her feelings for him. In line with the narrative quality of the third day, Zima's artistic abilities as rhetorician allow him to obtain what he most desires.[8]

---

6 Given that this character seems to be hopeful in the face of insurmountable obstacles, one could see the validity of Victoria Kirkham's theory that Elissa, the narrator of this story, allegorically represents "Hope" and transmits this virtue to the protagonist of her novella. Kirkham, *The Sign of Reason*, 164–8.

7 Vittore Branca connects Zima's speech to the noble tradition of love treatises, such as Andreas Capellanus's *De amore* or the poetry of Guittone d'Arezzo (*Boccaccio medievale*, 113–15), and, even more so, to the poetry of Zima's fellow-citizen, the Pistoiese poet Cino. Branca shows how at least one section of Zima's love proposition could be turned into the verses of a song: "Così il Zima, il cortese concittadino di Cino, [compone] l'alto tessuto del suo discorso amoroso quasi nella classica misura di una stanza di canzone, che porta all'acme l'empito stilnovistico della sua appassionata dichiarazione" [And so Zima, Cino's courtly fellow-citizen, puts together the high-sounding texture of his amorous speech almost in the classical measure of a poetic stanza, which culminates in the stilnovistic vehemence of his passionate proposition]. See Branca, *Boccaccio medievale e nuovi studi sul Decamerone*, 80.

8 His rhetorical elegance can be said to belong to a tradition of linguistic sophistication in the genre of novella that begins with the *Novellino*, also known as *Libro di novelle e di bel parlare gentile*.

The high-sounding tone of Zima's oration leaves ample space for critical debate on its imitation of literary courtly love conventions, which Boccaccio clearly bears in mind while crafting the prose he has flow from Zima's mouth. In light of the explicitly comedic tone, combined with the sexual references at the conclusion of the novella, the deployment of courtly love stylistic conventions might be interpreted as parodic on the author's part, even though it appears to be literal from Zima's perspective.[9] The comic ending reverses the tone of the entire story and transforms the speech into an ironic remake of lyrical topoi.

This speech is simply the beginning of Zima's action. The following course of events will prove even more decisive for his conquest. Since the woman has been relegated to total silence by her husband's command, Zima is left with an unresponsive interlocutor, whose passive role is underlined in the story by her anonymity. The woman is Francesco Vergellesi's wife and Zima's would-be lover. She has no other identity and no name. She sits and listens, unable to respond except by making imperceptible sighs, which will be understood by Zima as possible signifiers for her acceptance of his offer:

> E quantunque, per seguire il comandamento fattole dal marito, tacesse, non poté per ciò alcun sospiretto nascondere quello che volentieri, rispondendo al Zima, avrebbe fatto manifesto. (III.5.17)

> [And despite the fact that, in obedience to her husband's instructions, she said nothing, she was unable to restrain herself from uttering one or two barely perceptible sighs, thus betraying what she would willingly have made clear to Zima, had she been able to reply.]

This is the determining moment for Zima's action. Initially perplexed by her verbal unresponsiveness, he quickly realizes the trick played on

9 In his extensive research on this novella, Pier Massimo Forni has convincingly elaborated on the theory that the stilnovistic imprint of Zima's speech has its source in the stilnovist poet Cino da Pistoia. Forni remarks that, in the novella, "there may be more of Cino da Pistoia than has been realized. It should not come as a surprise … that in his amatory plea the young fop from Pistoia should be using the love poetry of his fellow citizen Cino. If indeed Cino is reflected in Zima's speech, it may be due to an intentional move on Boccaccio's part. This seems a typically Boccaccian game of covert reference. Let us not forget that Cino's muse, Selvaggia, is a Vergellesi; Boccaccio's choice of a Francesco Vergellesi and his wife as co-protagonists of this story is probably connected to Cino's lyric autobiography." Forni, *Adventures in Speech*, 97.

him by Francesco Vergellesi. But he is also very attentive to interpret the woman's silent signs. He realizes she approves of his love, as "alcun lampeggiare d'occhi di lei verso di lui alcuna volta" [every so often her eyes would dart a gleam in his direction (III.5.18)], and he also reads approval in her repeated sighs, which she is unable to contain, and which to him represent her reciprocation of his proffered feeling. It is at this point that Zima's enterprising resolve presents him with an original and winning idea. He plays the woman's part and answers in her stead. He puts on a theatrical act that involves "in forma della donna" [mimicking the lady's voice (III.5.18)] and formulating a response that will serve his purpose.[10]

This impersonation will prove to be a winning tactic for the lover.[11] I would argue that, even more than the elegant courtly love rhetoric Zima employs in the first portion of his speech, it is the novelty and originality of this comical act that wins the woman's love. She is impressed by his intelligent reaction to an impasse created by her husband's trick and she is amused by his humorous impersonation of her own character.

Zima thinks quickly and proactively, but also shows laudable acting abilities, when he plays the woman's part and mimics her voice.[12] His speech complacently reveals and argues in favour of his own heart's desire. He has the woman admit that she has been "aware of the intensity and completeness" (III.5.19) of his devotion and that her reticence to express her true feelings for him has been motivated by her desire to retain her moral reputation and her good name. But the time has come when, her husband being on his way to Milan, they will be able to bring their "love to its total and pleasurable consummation" (III.5.22). Zima

---

10 The original text has an ambiguous "in forma della donna," which is subject to the reader's interpretation, whether as voice and manners, or simply as manners, or more generally as "acting her part." The two translations consulted have two different ways of rendering the original: McWilliam translates it as "mimicking the lady's voice," while Payne has an inexact "after the following fashion." See *The Decameron of Giovanni Boccaccio*, trans. John Payne (New York: Random House, 1931), 238.

11 Numerous critics consider this the turning point of the novella. See, for example, Forni, *Adventures in Speech*, 92: "This is certainly the turning point of the story. In fact, it is the point without which there would be no story."

12 Forni identified this rhetorical move as *sermocinatio* and traces it back to the *Rhetorica ad Herennium*, which Boccaccio knew well. *Sermocinatio* is "a detachment of the speaker from himself ... even though the words are the speaker's, he puts them in the mouth of another person" (*Adventures in Speech*, 93); the definition of *sermocinatio* quoted by Forni is by Heinrich Lausberg, *Elementi di retorica*, 240–1.

then devotes the last portion of his impersonating speech to devising the details of a planned secret meeting between them: two towels hanging in the window of her room will be the signal for him to come to her in the evening. The signifier for the woman's acceptance of his offer is relegated to these lowly objects of housekeeping and, together with the "open garden gate" – which resonates with sexual connotations in the transposition of the woman's own body as open to fulfil his desires – it creates the Boccaccesque atmosphere, which is typical of the majority of novelle in the third day, from its inception with Masetto da Lamporecchio to its conclusion with Alibech and Rustico.

But it is once again the modality of Zima's speech, more than its content, which is irresistibly effective. This is an improvised action. When Zima had requested an encounter to speak with the woman as compensation for giving up his horse to Francesco Vergellesi, he had envisioned a dialogue, a *tête-à-tête*, whose outcome was difficult to predict, since Zima had no indication of the woman's disposition towards him. He would simply offer his love and hope that it was reciprocated. Francesco Vergellesi's intended trick turns out to be a very useful instrument that Zima uses to his own advantage. The comical quality of Zima's self-reply is granted by his impersonating the woman's part and voice, but also by the wide discrepancy and sharp contrast between the elevated rhetorical style of his speech and the lowly subject matter of organizing their illicit amorous encounters in her house by means of two rags hanging from a window.[13]

A similar contrast is enacted in the interaction between the *cornice* and the single stories of this particular section of the *Decameron*. The third day falls on a Sunday, when the *brigata* walks to a palace on a high elevation, where they enter a garden surrounded by high walls – an idyllic place resembling an earthly paradise. The *locus amoenus* bears a striking resemblance to the Garden of Eden, the biblical location of human innocence and happiness, but, from a literary point of view, it also brings to mind Dante's Limbo in the Fourth Canto of *Inferno*, and specifically the place of the magnanimous souls, isolated from the rest of the circle, a privileged locality reserved for the great intellectuals. The purity elicited by the location in which the stories are told creates an

---

13 The implicit irony in combining an overtly sexual encounter with courtly love rhetoric can be expressed critically with Erich Auerbach's words: "The stylistic device which Boccaccio employs was highly esteemed by the ancients, who called it 'irony.'" See Auerbach, *Mimesis*, 221.

interesting tension with the erotic and sexual contents of the stories themselves, which are among the most openly or metaphorically licentious of the whole *Decameron*.[14]

In III.5, a similar rhetorical tension is enacted through the juxtaposition of the two portions of Zima's dialogue with himself.[15] The rhetoric of courtly love and sweet new style he employs when he speaks as himself clashes stridently with the comic impersonation of the woman's part in the self-reply, which inevitably changes the interpretation of Zima's own first speech. It transforms the entire story into a comical act.[16] The seriousness and earnestness of Vergellesi's initial pact with his wife and with Zima change into the playful atmosphere of the novella's second half. Its comical quality derives, moreover, from the contrast itself between the seriousness of Zima's stilnovistic rhetoric (or, at least, what appears as such initially) and the risible scene of emulation in the second part of his dialogue/monologue.[17] The sublime rhetoric of love for a woman precedes an improvised cross-gendered reply aimed at orchestrating a sexual encounter; this succession of histrionic scenes on the part of one single character gives rise to that contrast of modes and styles that is considered the origin of the comic and laughter. Femininity is elevated and placed on a pedestal in order to be worshipped, according to courtly love paradigms.[18] But femininity is

---

14 For a commentary on the echo of the Garden of Eden and the moral implications connected to the location in which the stories of the third day are told, see David Wallace, *Giovanni Boccaccio: Decameron*, 41–2.

15 Paolo Valesio's definition of Zima's impersonating speech as "mimesi dialogica," "dialogic mimesis," seems particularly fitting. See "Sacro," 374.

16 More than an opposition between two types of love, one purely mental, one physically sexual, Auerbach considers Boccaccio's conception of love as a transformation of courtly love into a more lowly sentiment: "His ethics of love is a recasting of courtly love, tuned several degrees lower in the scale of style, and concerned exclusively with the sensual and the real" (Auerbach, *Mimesis*, 226). The definition appears particularly fitting in this story.

17 In Muscetta's comment on this novella: "lo stile comico sale a uno dei più alti gradi di finezza raggiunti dal Boccaccio" [The comic style rises to one of the highest degrees of refinement that Boccaccio ever reached (*Giovanni Boccaccio*, 214)].

18 The pertinent texts inspiring Zima's words for the woman have been quoted by previous critics of this novella. His praise of Vergellesi's wife may derive from Andreas Capellanus, Provençal poets, Dante Alighieri, and other stilnovo poets. I would like to point out that a comprehensive understanding of *Frauendienst* and *religio amoris* in the Middle Ages can be gained through the reading of a classic study on the topic, such as Lewis, *The Allegory of Love*.

subsequently (directly or indirectly) derided, when Zima mocks the woman in his cross-gendering skit. The carnivalesque reversal of situations, roles, and modalities results in the comical quality of the entire story.[19]

The moral tenor of the novella undergoes an interesting shift that matches the transformative pattern of its narratological structure. The modification from serious to jocose bears a correspondence with the change from the morality of Zima's love proposal (to be intended within the standards of courtly love parameters) to the openly adulterous and explicitly sexual proposition he makes at the end. The shift validates the theory that Zima's speech is biased and ironic from the beginning; his expressions of refined amorous feelings appear to be simply the covert rhetoric of less noble instincts and more physical sexual appetites.

Despite the high-sounding rhetoric employed in Zima's speech, the narration is structured around its erotic outcome. Impersonation originates much of the novella's comical characteristics. Zima performing the woman's voice is in itself irresistibly humorous, and it is plausible that her decision to surrender to his insistent requests may be caused as much by his ability to make her laugh in the second part of his speech as it is by his composed rhetorical skills in the first part. Humour and laughter are strictly related to sexuality, particularly in the medieval context, where laughter is often considered synonymous with coitus.[20] But in this particular text, Zima's comic reaction and his humorous solution prepare for and allude to his sexual encounter with Vergellesi's wife at the end of the story.

---

19 More than the definition of irony as a "clashing of styles," as developed by Booth, *A Rhetoric of Irony*, especially 67–9, this analysis has profited from Bakhtin, *Rabelais and His World*.

20 See, for example, Valesio, *Ascoltare il silenzio*, 322–3: "l'atto del ridere è (fra altre cose) anche una diffusa rappresentazione eufemistica dell'atto sessuale … la natura eufemistico-sessuale del riso era come tale riconosciuta ab antiquo … nella retorica della fiaba la principessa che non ride è una giovane donna che rifiuta l'esperienza del sesso … Con la sua risata, la fanciulla si dichiara pronta all'esperienza del sesso" [The laughing act is (among other things) also a widespread euphemistic representation of the sexual act … the euphemistic-sexual nature of laughing was acknowledged as such in ancient times … in the rhetoric of fairy-tales the princess who does not laugh is a young woman who rejects the sexual experience … With her laughter the maiden declares her readiness for the experience of sex]. See also Vladimir Propp, *Theory and History of Folklore*, 124–46.

The horse at the origin of the situation is itself an additional erotic element, which remains ambiguously placed between woman and lover, lover and husband, husband and wife. It clearly has a phallic referent, coming as it does between husband and lover as bartering merchandise. However, it also replaces the woman's body. While it is traditionally the symbol of sexual prowess and male potency, in the story the palfrey also figures as a substitute for the woman's sexual favours. In the course of the narration it bears all metaphorical connotations of Zima's genitalia – and the announcement of his sexual encounter with Francesco Vergellesi's wife at the conclusion of the novella literally sanctions such a substitution. Zima gave up his horse, but has gained sexual pleasure. In addition, the palfrey also replaces the woman next to Vergellesi. If the husband cherishes the illusion that he has obtained the horse for free, he has in fact exchanged it for his wife's body. This exchange grants Vergellesi possession of the horse and ensures Zima's possession of the woman. The horse metonymically represents the cuckoldry of Vergellesi.

The symbolic value of the horse in III.5 parallels the metaphorical significance of the falcon in VI.6, when Federigo degli Alberighi manages to win Monna Giovanna's love at the cost of the falcon, which was his last remaining possession. While the two novelle have been compared on the basis of their lyricism and sophisticated love rhetoric, I would argue that there are further fundamental similarities between them in plot and symbolism.[21] The donation of an animal to win a woman's love leaves ample space for critical argumentation over the sexual nature of the exchange, also in consideration of the openly erotic nature of the two animals in question. In Federigo's story, the bird that is fed to the woman, when in fact she had wished to possess it alive, creates an interesting narratological suspense and a convoluted ethical pattern aimed at displaying Federigo's devotion to Giovanna and her eventual acceptance of his love. In III.5, it is not so much the highly sensual nature of the equine species as it is the role assigned to the beautiful palfrey that establishes a connection with the wife's sexual favours. Zima gives the horse to Vergellesi in order to obtain sexual pleasure from the other man's wife in compensation. The horse also implicitly represents Zima's own sexual desire. The transfer of the palfrey from Zima to Francesco Vergellesi, at a symbolic level, signifies Zima's physical encounter with Vergellesi's wife. Within

21 For an association of the two stories, which is based solely on their lyrical beauty, see Branca, *Boccaccio medievale e nuovi studi sul Decameron*, 80.

the narrow context of the story, while the donated horse appears to cement the matrimonial ties within the couple, it in fact contributes to their eventual adulterous separation.

However, on a purely literal level, in this story the horse serves fundamentally as a means of transportation. As such it evokes thoughts and dreams of travel as a distraction from the tedious routine of steady and sedentary daily life, especially for women, confined as they are within the restricted space of the family home, as Boccaccio points out in the Preface to the *Decameron*. The horse will take the husband to a faraway place, thereby allowing Zima and Francesco Vergellesi's wife to bring their love story to fruition. The fantasy of journey elicited by this important occurrence in the plot bears the connotation of an image for storytelling itself as a distraction and a form of mental travelling. The tale of Madonna Oretta (VI.1), which resembles III.5 in other ways (to be investigated further on), clarifies how horse-riding can metaphorize storytelling.[22] Madonna Oretta finds herself in the countryside and has to move on foot from place to place in the company of knights and ladies. In order to alleviate the fatigue of walking long distances, one of the knights offers to take her "gran parte della via che andare dobbiamo, a cavallo con una delle belle novelle del mondo" [riding along a good stretch on one of the beautiful tales of the world (VI.1.7)].[23] Besides being an erotic image, travelling by horse is part of the subframe in which the tale within the tale is inserted – which is what this novella is all about. Telling stories while travelling brings to mind echoes of the future Chaucerian pilgrimage to Canterbury, when narration happens en route and the diversion produced by the stories serves as a pastime for the pilgrims while at the same time mirroring their own journey. In III.5, the necessity of travelling by horse constitutes the source and origin of the entire narrative.

---

22 Guido Almansi's lucid analysis of Boccaccio's narratological techniques, and especially of this novella, inspired this connection between III.5 and Madonna Oretta's tale (VI.1). See his *The Writer as Liar*, 19–24. I would like to point out, however, that Almansi's interpretation of a literal horse Madonna Oretta would be riding, while the knight very poorly recounts her a story, does not find confirmation in Boccaccio's text, in which horse riding is a pure metaphor for the act of telling the story itself.

23 This translation is mine. McWilliam's translation remains ambivalent about the metaphorical significance of riding a horse as representing storytelling, which is a crucial element in the original; it reads: "I shall take you riding along a goodly stretch of our journey by telling you one of the finest tales in the world" (484).

Even in the brevity of this tale, there are multiple reasons why the woman falls prey to Zima's seduction. One might argue, already in the first portion of Zima's speech, that Francesco's wife lets herself be seduced by Zima mainly because of his passion: she finds in him the passion her husband has never displayed for her. Francesco's chief quality is his avariciousness, and one is inclined to think that his inability to give and his lack of generosity may extend to his amorous disposition. Avarice and jealousy are synonymous with a more general lack of self-giving, which seems to characterize Francesco Vergellesi's personality. Zima, on the contrary, feels an irresistible love for the woman and expresses it in the most ardent fashion, since "no man ever loved any woman more deeply and more ardently" and "shall continue to do so unfailingly" (III.5.11).[24] Then Zima declares his undying love: He will love her for all his life and "if, in the life hereafter, people love as they do on earth," he shall love her forever.

The second part of Zima's speech, in which he pretends to be the woman, bears the crucial characteristics of a speech act – and, as such, it is radically different from the first part, which is inspired by love rhetoric.[25] The first portion is essentially descriptive, while the second portion is factual. What Zima says on behalf of the woman is alluring and accomplishes what the impersonator wishes. It achieves seduction, in the true etymological sense of the Latin *seducere*, as "leading somebody astray, or on a misleading path." The woman's stern resolve not to betray her husband starts to crumble under the pressure of Zima's amorous rhetoric, but it is only after he puts on his impersonating act that she makes the decisive move to become his lover. When Zima openly declares the woman's love for him in his self-reply, he no longer describes

24 For avariciousness as a character flaw for the lover and eloquent speech as one of the qualities of the perfect lover, see Forni, *Adventures in Speech*, 96, who quotes Andreas Capellanus on the subject.

25 Eduardo Saccone interestingly opposes Zima's "rhetoric of words" to Francesco Vergellesi's "rhetoric of facts." But he also points out the shift in Zima's rhetoric in the second portion of his speech, when the protagonist combines his word rhetoric with actions: "il Zima non [abbandona] la retorica delle parole, ma [la combina] accortamente a quella degli atti. Reitererà le parole, ma teatralmente: recitando due parti, quella della donna e la sua: proponendo, e in certo modo mimando, lo scenario del desiderio soddisfatto" [Zima does not abandon the rhetoric of words, but carefully combines it with the rhetoric of actions. He reiterates words, but in a theatrical manner, by playing two parts, the woman's and his own, proposing and in a certain way miming the scene of satisfied desire] See "Azione," 65.

his own feelings or hers. His rhetoric achieves what it promises; it acts and accomplishes results, instead of simply describing or narrating.[26]

Boccaccio's ambivalent attitude towards women finds an exemplary expression in this novella.[27] The female protagonist, the object of Zima's attention, the reason for tension between the two men, and the origin of all plot complications, fulfils an utterly passive role in the story, as do most women in the other novelle of the third day. Seven of the female characters in an equal number of novelle are impassive to the events unfolding around them, which are entirely orchestrated by their male counterparts. The women are either seduced by the skilful art of their lovers or induced by means of a *beffa* to have sexual encounters they have not desired or anticipated.[28] There is a harmonious confluence of the Garden of Delights, the location of the *cornice*, and the enjoyment of sexual pleasure in the stories, since they all implicitly or explicitly recount a plot that leads to a physical union between two characters.[29] In III.5 the woman is simply the *casus belli* for a diatribe between Zima and Francesco Vergellesi: she has no other role than being the passive object of her lover's attention; her husband uses her to gain a horse for free; her silence, while being a symbolic referent for her imposed sexual unavailability, contributes to her general passivity. The woman never utters a word. She initially obeys her husband, keeps silent, and earns the palfrey for him. She subsequently listens to her lover, silently agrees to his requests, and obtains pleasure for herself. Her only decision-making

26 The following studies on speech acts have been important for the development of this argument in *Decameron* III.5: Briggs, *Words in Action;* Loxley, *Performativity;* Petrey, *Speech Acts;* Tsohatzidis, ed., *Foundations of Speech Act Theory*.

27 Marilyn Migiel's book, *A Rhetoric of the Decameron*, brilliantly problematizes the concept of Boccaccio's relation to women in the *Decameron;* her Introduction is especially illuminating on the ambiguities and complexities of Boccaccio's attitude towards female characters.

28 In the third day, seduction through rhetoric or action occurs in novellas 4, 5, 7, 8, and 10; the woman is tricked into having a sexual encounter with a male protagonist in 2 and 6; women actively pursue their lovers in the remaining three novelle (1, 3, and 9). Often, as is the case in III.5, female characters retain an anonymous identity, which further enhances their passivity in the narrative.

29 Giuseppe Mazzotta convincingly demonstrates how the Introduction to the third day represents the "point of departure for a critical-textual analysis" of Boccaccio's belief in sexuality as an irrepressible natural instinct, but also his more profound awareness that all love literature can turn into a "galeotto" with powers to give and arouse erotic pleasures. See Mazzotta, *The World at Play*, 106–10.

power consists of accepting Zima's proposition and following his instructions. She does not seek an adulterous affair; instead, she simply takes the opportunity when it presents itself, and her faulty wisdom induces her to act for fear now that she might regret her inaction later. Her silence functions at once as a symptom of her subjugation to male authority and as her empowerment to rebel against her husband's imposition. She has no voice. Since she never speaks in the story, the only words readers hear from her are reported as her thoughts:

> Che fo io? Perché perdo io la mia giovanezza? Questi se ne è andato a Melano e non tornerà di questi sei mesi; e quando me gli ristorerà egli giammai? quando io sarò vecchia? E oltre a questo, quando troverò io mai un così fatto amante come è il Zima? Io son sola, né ho d'alcuna persona paura: io non so perché io non mi prendo questo buon tempo mentre che io posso. Io non avrò sempre spazio come io ho al presente: questa cosa non saprà mai persona: e, se egli pur si dovesse risapere, sì è meglio fare e pentere, che starsi e pentersi. (III.5.30)

> [What am I doing? Why am I throwing away my youth? This husband of mine has gone off to Milan and won't be returning for six whole months. When is he ever going to make up for lost time? When I'm an old woman? Besides, when will I ever find such a lover as Zima? I'm all by myself, and there's nobody to be afraid of. I don't see why I shouldn't enjoy myself whilst I have the chance. I won't always have such a good opportunity as I have at present. Nobody will ever know about it, and even if he were to find out, it's better to do a thing and repent of it than do nothing and regret it.]

Aware that this may be her one chance in a lifetime to exercise her freedom, she contravenes her matrimonial vows and chooses adulterous sex, thereby aligning this plot with the rest of the stories of the third day, which all deal with illicit sexual relations.

If Boccaccio holds true to the promise made in his Preface to console women with his text, in III.5 he depicts a cathartic portrait that will liberate his female readers from the yoke of male domination and will instruct them on how silent obedience can lead to independent thinking. The tale of a woman who is subjected to her husband's jealousy and avariciousness, yet unexpectedly manages to win her freedom, will undoubtedly show the surprising turns of fortune reserved as a reward to obedient, silent wives. While not exemplary, Francesco Vergellesi's wife seizes the opportunity to follow her desire and become sexually liberated. Her ambiguity and disloyalty may appear morally objectionable; her empowerment by means of being obliged to be speechless is equally controversial. But the story emphasizes more the punishment of a jealous and greedy husband, who uses his wife's submission in order to achieve his despicable goal and save money. In the more general economy of the story, her sexual enjoyment paradoxically represents the reward for complying with her husband's command, while her betrayal of him serves as a punishment for Francesco Vergellesi's own dishonesty. The woman mostly concentrates on seizing the opportunity to enjoy sex. Only indirectly and unintentionally does she punish him for his abusive behaviour towards her and also towards Zima, of whom Vergellesi has taken advantage by exploiting his deep feelings and his vulnerable condition.

The woman's impassivity finds compensation in her illusion to betray her spouse freely. More than an investigation into the reality of her freedom – whether it is real or apparent, chosen personally or imposed by circumstances – the novella deserves an attentive study of the role of silence, which displays an overpowering ambiguity. The woman's silence is the pivot around which the entire plot revolves. It is at the root of the whole counter-*beffa*. Because of his wife's silence, Francesco Vergellesi thinks he has won the horse without paying any money and without suffering any consequences. The woman's silence is also instrumental for Zima's achieving sexual union with her.

There is a pattern of silence that pervades the novelle of the third day. The phenomenology of silence in this *Giornata* becomes alternately amalgamated with the obscuring of facts, the clouding of truth, and the veiling of facts, which help to structure several of the ten plots. Every single novella of this day contains at least one ambiguous use of silence, which determines the development of the narrative. Silence often facilitates the concealment of truth. Whether the women assume an active role in seducing their lovers, as in novelle 1, 3, and 9, or remain the passive agents of male suitors, as in the other seven novelle, an untold fact, a quieted piece of information, or the occurrence of silence *tout court* intervenes to transform the course of events. The phenomenon of silence manifests itself narratologically through secrecy, confession, or wordplay – at other times simply through lying as an alternative to or silencing of the truth. The presence of silence, concealment, and betrayal is so pervasive as to structure the entire third day, perhaps to reflect the deceitfulness enacted in the Garden of Delights of the *cornice*, which might constitute a parody of the Fall out of the Garden of Eden. The biblical account of Genesis tells of disobedience, lying, and the deceitful appropriation of the "illicit fruit," much the same as the novella about Zima and Francesco Vergellesi's wife.

The silence imposed on the woman by her husband semiotically (but also quite literally, in this particular story) represents the sexual passivity Francesco Vergellesi expects from her. If she does not reply to Zima's solicitation, from her husband's perspective, she also denies him her availability to love him. Quite on the contrary, Zima's loquacity implies his ardent erotic desire and fiery sexual propensity. In this sense, the metaphorical correspondence of verbosity and sexuality in Zima contrasts with the direct and literal parallel of mutism and lustfulness in Masetto da Lamporecchio in III.1. By pretending to be dumb, Masetto gains access to the convent and earns the trust of the nuns, since speechlessness is associated with celibate or impotent behaviour. Believing him unable to speak, the nuns exploit him sexually, as they are confident he will not be able to reveal their sexual misconduct to the world. The whole story is orchestrated around the apparent and commonsensical incongruity of speechlessness and sexual potency. In III.5, the woman's silence inspires Zima's further eloquence and instigates his additional second speech, which is instrumental to the two protagonists' love affair at the end of the story. The fluidity of Zima's rhetoric hermeneutically points in the direction of his erotic power. The potency of his eloquent oration is a metonym for his sexual prowess.[30]

The endemic ambiguity of silence constitutes the real protagonist of the counter-*beffa* enacted in this novella. I would argue that silence represents the chief interaction between the two lovers and greatly contributes to bringing them together, at least in the initial stages of their love story. As the fundamental seductive agent in the story, silence has the important role of erotic mediator. If Francesco Vergellesi's wife had been permitted to speak, she presumably would have declined Zima's propositions at the very beginning of his talk. Her passive acceptance is the result of being silenced and being made unable to formulate her rejection in words. In III.5, silence is the Galahalt that interjects between Zima and Francesco Vergellesi's wife and brings them together. All qualities of silence fit the description of Galahalt in the literary tradition of Arthurian romances, particularly his status as vehicle between two adulterous

30 For a theoretical articulation of a connection between *rhetorica* and *erotica*, I am indebted to Valesio, *Ascoltare il silenzio*, especially 5.2, pp. 316–41.

lovers. The role of go-between Boccaccio assigns to the *Decameron* in the inscription and conclusion of the book can be identified rhetorically in the silence of this particular novella.[31]

Decameron III.5 possesses all the chief qualities of a meta-text, or rather a *mise-en-abîme* for the *Centonovelle*. Its hermeneutics casts light on the interpretation of the entire *Decameron*. The reading strategies that are applicable to this short piece highlight possible interpretations of the whole collection. The novella mirrors the literary work in its entirety – or, more precisely, speaks to the interpretation of it. Zima's story centres on seduction through rhetoric. The first part of his speech aims at conquering his listener's love by means of his passionate feelings, as articulated through elegant words and eloquent turns of phrase. The silent interlude serves as ambiguous mediation and offers him the opportunity to begin the actual seductive piece of his oration. The passive role of the woman inspires him to formulate his self-reply, which completes the act successfully for him. This dynamic of seduction resembles critical interpretation in reader response theory. When the text elicits no active response on the reader's part, the author manages to catch the reader in his own interpretive web. The danger of textual seduction is not implicit in the text itself; rather, it emanates from the reader's impassive role.[32]

Boccaccio's own self-reflective strategies on the interactive dynamic between text and readers appear in this story under the metaphorical veil of narrative. Zima conquers the woman as a result of her unresponsiveness, which ironically was imposed on her by her jealous husband in order to protect her integrity. The self-reflective quality of this silent scene bears interesting resemblances to the seduction of reading as Boccaccio conceives of it. The danger of its attractiveness is in the beauty of its formulation, in the defeating power of its language. Zima's alluring abilities consist of his stylish manner, neat demeanour, handsome

---

31 The concept of the book of the *Decameron* as metaphorical Galahalt has been investigated by Hollander in the chapter entitled "The Book as Galeotto," in *Boccaccio's Two Venuses*, especially 105–7.

32 The meta-textual qualities of this novella bring to mind Almansi's analysis of VI.1, the story of Madonna Oretta. On the basis of its strategic position within the collection (as the central novella at number 51), Almansi reads it as a meta-novella, a story about telling stories (Almansi, *The Writer as Liar*, 19–24). In her assessment of the story within the story she is being told, Madonna Oretta confirms that the beauty of narration rests on the signified more than the signifier or, to put it in Almansi's words, "art is the enjoyment of forms, not of things" (23).

countenance, and trim appearance – after all, his name is an abbreviation of "azzimato," dapper. He makes the woman fall for him by means of the beauty of his language and the skilful formulation of his speech. More than the content of his talk, it is the fascinating manner in which he expresses himself that seduces her. In response to her silence, he picks up her cryptic signals and enwraps her in his own interpretation of her sighs and looks. The defeat of her loyalty and uprightness results in the joy and satisfaction of both.

Zima's humorous technique dispels the woman's melancholy and instils merriment in her life, much in the same way that Boccaccio's *Decameron* serves the purpose of bringing consolation to women. Zima's story fits the description Boccaccio himself gives of storytelling at the conclusion of the collection. "Stories ... were told in a garden, in a place designed for pleasure," and, "like all other things in the world, stories ... may be harmful or useful, depending upon the listener" (III.Concl.7–8). Silence is the woman's Galahalt, her facilitator. Silence is the lovers' erotic mediator, the means through which they can come to the full expression of their love.[33]

33 Mazzotta highlights the role assigned by Boccaccio himself to the *Decameron*: "Boccaccio seems intent on assigning to this text the role of erotic mediator, and thus unmasking the threats and seductions of his own artifact." See "The *Decameron*: The Marginality of Literature," 68–9.

The Tale of Ricciardo and Catella (III.6)

MYRIAM SWENNEN RUTHENBERG

If "reason is one of the key words in the *Decameron*," as Janet Levarie Smarr has it (*Boccaccio and Fiammetta*, 165), lack of reason equally asserts its presence in the one hundred novellas, where the tension between reason and desire – but not as mutually exclusive entities – constitutes the very dynamic of the *Decameron*. This tension already lies at the heart of the courtly love tradition, from Arthurian legend to the troubadours, from Tristan and Isolde, Lancelot and Guinevere to Dante's Paolo and Francesca.[1] In approaching the "Centonovelle" we cannot fail to recognize the importance of these canonical courtly love protagonists, especially the doomed lovers of *Inferno* V in view of the subtitle Boccaccio affixes to his *Decameron*: "Prencipe Galeotto." This subtitle, or better, nickname – we remember the Certaldese's novella collection is "cognominato" – fixes the semantic boundaries within which the novellas must be read, i.e. as ten times ten tales that are subject to misreading.[2] In other words, from Paolo and Francesca's interpretation of courtly love fiction in Dante's *Inferno* V we learn that the "franceschi romanzi"

1 For a reading of the ambiguity in the courtly love code and its relationship to Andreas Capellanus's failure to grasp the notion of "Mezura" in his condemnation of that code, see Cherchi, Andreas; for a study of the importance of the subtitle of the *Decameron*, "Prencipe Galeotto," see Hollander's "Boccaccio's Dante."

2 The term "nickname" rather than subtitle was inspired by Potter in *Five Frames*: "I have deliberately translated 'cognominato' as 'also called' even though its more usual meaning is 'nicknamed.' It is a *hapax legomenon* or word used only once (actually it is used twice) in the *Decameron* (usually Boccaccio uses the less latinized 'detto'), and may well serve not only to embed the *Decameron* in formal latinisms but to reflect the medieval opposition between name (given at baptism, as an auspice) and nickname (given later, as a judgment based on experience)" (92).

are susceptible to misinterpretation. Earlier Andreas Capellanus in *De amore* had juxtaposed fictional, imaginary love and, in the third book of his famous treatise, real, earthly love resulting directly from a lack of reason and unwarranted for the sake of the soul's health.[3] While Dante's tragic lovers are condemned to the circle of the lustful for their amorous excess by mistaking fiction for reality, Boccaccio allows humans to behave in human ways. For the Certaldese, misinterpretation results from the absence of reason, from excess, or *dismizura*, to use courtly love terminology.[4] By the same token, both *dismizura* and misinterpretation as a result of lack of *mizura* are also human. Without the tempering quality of reason, excessive passions, erotic or other, obfuscate the mind; they blur vision; they hamper perception beyond the physical world and prevent the arrival at a higher form of knowledge. Misinterpretation and misreading, while ingredients of the courtly code – and the lovers of the fifth canto of Dante's *Inferno* attest to that – characterize the reception of that code by its readers, who, after all, react to it in a human way: "Umana cosa è aver compassione degli afflitti" is the axiom with which Boccaccio inaugurates his *Decameron*.

What I am arguing is that Boccaccio in the *Decameron* plays a balancing act between different levels of interpretation and perception, while signalling that some conventional, "common" ways of understanding are not necessarily true, that misinterpretation is a "common," human vice.[5] The way the courtly code has been read is an example of this. The highly moral and religious restrictions that were placed upon the medieval reader might have blinded the interpreter of a code that has misinterpretation built into its very configuration, i.e. the code of courtly love.[6]

---

3 Allen in *The Art of Love* shows how this ambiguity between fictional and real love was Andreas Capellanus's adaptation of the *Ars amatoria* by Ovid, who taught his readers "that literary love ... is a conventional and constructed fiction, which poet and reader create together, and which can exist only within the clearly designated bounds of the textual world." Allen continues: "the *Remedia* ... dissolve these illusions and reveal that the fantasy is only a fantasy – one person's solitary creation, rather than a love that can last between two people. Both *De Amore* and the *Roman de la Rose* offer this twofold lesson, creating an imaginary love and then dismantling it. Andreas's work re-creates Ovid's twofold text in the literary context of the late twelfth century" (12).

4 For the notion of *dismizura* and *mezura* see Wettstein, *Mezura*.

5 For a study of Boccaccio's use of axioms and colloquialisms and his frequent recurrence to common experience, see Forni in "Retorica del reale."

6 For the distinctions between Courtliness, Chivalry, and Courtesy see Scaglione's *Knights at Court*; see also note 1.

What follows, then, rests upon my suspicion that Boccaccio scrutinizes conventional interpretation in general, especially when such forces as reason and desire are at play.[7] The warning signals emitted by that courtly code, where reason and desire, according to generally accepted interpretative guidelines, must be delicately balanced, are misread by its very agents. The novella of Ricciardo and Catella (III.6), centred on the theme that "what seems to be, is not; and what seems not to be, is" (Cottino-Jones, *Order*, 66), can be read as a novellistic admonition against the dangers of conventional interpretation in general and that of the courtly love code in particular.

The novella of Ricciardo and Catella is told by Fiammetta, whose name is associated with both excessive passion and the inability to read, and, because of her literary prehistory, calls to mind the courtly tradition, in particular the "franceschi romanzi" she refers to in the *Elegia di Madonna Fiammetta*.[8] This sixth story of the third day, over which Neifile reigns as queen, juxtaposes reason and desire, allowing the latter either to be tamed by the former or to dominate over it. It is, moreover, a tale about appearance and reality, about decoding and encoding, about the power of things said and the power of things not said, much like the *Decameron* itself. Finally, like the *Decameron*, the tale of Ricciardo and Catella is subtly inscribed in a courtly context. Following the tale's summary, I will start from this last concept first, both inside the novella and in the *cornice*. From there I shall place the novella in a context of excess, again inside and outside the textual contours of the tale, and make a detour through Dante's *Commedia* and Boccaccio's Introduction to the fourth day of the *Decameron*. I will subsequently link this novella to the overall frame of the *Decameron*, more specifically its title and nickname.

1. The Tale

Boccaccio's sixth novella of the third day tells the story of Ricciardo Minutolo and Catella, he a young nobleman who, for love of Catella, would be capable of anything; she the virtuous but extremely jealous

---

7 For support of this thesis, see the introduction to Janet Levarie Smarr's *Boccaccio and Fiammetta*, where the author states: "I find in him [Boccaccio] … a growing sense of the difficulties of both moral and literary pursuits, a growing distrust of the power of reason and thus an increasing wariness of love's potential to lead to good, and a concomitant need to speak more clearly or directly" (2).

8 *Elegia di Madonna Fiammetta*, from here on abbreviated as *Elegia*.

wife of Filippello, of whom she claims the exclusive right. In order to have his heart's desire, Ricciardo devises a shrewd scheme: he pretends to be in love with another woman (Boccaccio's version of a *donna schermo* or screen lady) and plays his part so well that soon everyone assumes he has forgotten Catella. One afternoon Ricciardo and his party follow Catella and her entourage to a beach resort near Naples where the two *brigate* have ample opportunity to mingle socially, as is a Neapolitan custom, so Boccaccio informs us. At an opportune moment Ricciardo drops the rumour that Filippello has a mistress. The distressing tiding instantly triggers the jealousy of Catella, who decides to investigate her husband's liaison. Ricciardo pledges his cooperation in return for her silence and promises to find out where and how she can catch Filippello *in flagrante*. He convinces her to meet her husband in a dark and windowless room inside a beach house and to pretend that she is Filippello's mistress. It is, however, Ricciardo who goes to meet Catella there and takes Filippello's place in bed. After their lovemaking, which occurs in silence, Catella, convinced that she is framing her husband, reveals her true identity in an avalanche of curses and hot-tempered rhetoric. This only fuels the sexual appetite of Ricciardo, who silences her with kisses and embraces. For fear of repercussions if Catella is left with the illusion of having caught her husband in the act, he determines to break the silence. Catella, recognizing him by his voice, reacts by attempting to escape and scream. But both the escape and the scream are suppressed by Ricciardo's strong arms and convincing rhetoric. Relying on the axiom that "la gente è piu acconcia a credere il male che il bene" [folk are more prone to believe evil than good (III.6.44)],[9] he blackmails her into never revealing their secret and reminds her of the possible consequences: she will lose her honour and reputation, and there will be such enmity between husband and lover that one of them will almost certainly kill the other. She accepts her unfortunate fate, swearing revenge. Ricciardo reacts to that threat with flattery in words and deeds, to which she gives in a second time, only now conquered by the sweet kisses of a lover, and turning her "durezza" in "dolce amore," for so much sweeter are the kisses of a lover than those of a husband [quanto più saporiti fossero i basci dell' amante che del marito].

9 From here on, all translated quotations are from J.M. Rigg, *The Decameron* (London: Bullen, 1903). Quotations of the original are from *Decameron*, ed. Vittore Branca (Milan: Mondadori – I Meridiani, 1985).

2. "Cortesia" and the Reversal of the Courtly Love Code

The textual contours of this novella are at first sight no different from those of any other tale of the *Decameron*: in the Introduction to Day Three, Neifile, who rules that day, is described as adorned with courtly manners and beauty, while the *locus amoenus* is not just any pleasant garden but the estate of a "bellissimo e ricco palagio" [a palace most fair and sumptuous (III.Intro.3)] with many lavishly decorated rooms and a splendid loggia where the *brigata* stops for some "preziosissimi confetti e ottimi vini" [comfits and wines most choice and excellent (III.Intro.4)]. The group also engages in typically courtly activities such as chess playing and the "gioco delle tavole." As such the description of the *locus amoenus* and of the *brigata*'s activities is almost an exact replica of that of the Introduction to the first day (106–15), as has often been noticed. However, the description of this particular *locus amoenus* in the Introduction to Day Three conceals several significant aberrations from the norm: after dinner the *brigata* not only engages in playing chess and "tavole," but is offered, for the first and only time in the *cornice*, the option of reading "romanzi," a nobility-enhancing activity, according to courtly love tenets.[10] Moreover, this novella is told by Fiammetta, a storyteller with a literary past: in the *Elegia* Boccaccio has his eponymous female protagonist read "franceschi romanzi," or rather, *mis*read the French romances.[11] Boccaccio also takes his audience back to the place of Fiammetta's excessive amorous desires, the Naples of the *Elegia*. Finally, "on day III, a day full of illicit sexual adventures, they [Fiammetta and Dioneo] sing 'la dama del Vergiu', the story of an adultery with tragic consequences, which leads from III into the tragic topic of IV" (Smarr, "Symmetry," 183) and thus thematically echoes the plight of Paolo and Francesca. At the end of Day Three Lauretta sings a

10 The Branca edition of the *Decameron* mentions in a footnote that the *brigata* engages in leisurely activities that are a repetition of those described in the introduction to Day One. However, upon rereading this part of the *Decameron*, I noticed that all the ingredients are indeed there, except this one of "legger romanzi" (15). For a reading of the Decameron as a retrieval of courtly and chivalric values, see also Franco Cardini's *Le cento novelle*.

11 Smarr points at the gradual decline of Fiammetta throughout Boccaccio's work: in the *Filocolo* she is queen and elevated above her entourage "by special associations with the divine, in the *Commedia delle Ninfe fiorentine* she is no longer above the others, in the *Decameron* she has faded even further" (Boccaccio and Fiammetta, 174); in the *Decameron*'s *cornice* Fiammetta is a middle-class Florentine and not a noble Neapolitan.

"canzonetta" that is similar in content and is, according to its singer, understood in different ways by different people: "diversamente da diversi fu intesa." And Lauretta adds: "e ebbevi di quegli che intender vollono alla melanese, che fosse meglio un buon porco che una bella tosa, altri furono di più sublime e migliore e più vero intelletto, del quale al presente recitar non accade" [some were inclined to give it a moral after the Milanese fashion, to wit, that a good porker was better than a pretty quean. Others construed it in a higher, better and truer sense, which 'tis not to the present purpose to unfold (III.Concl.18)]. In other words, the content of this song is open to interpretation. For interpretation one can either depend on general popular belief or look for a "higher" meaning.[12] The textual contours of Day Three thus establish a clear connection between courtly love and interpretation. Let us, therefore, reread novella III.6 with this in mind.

At first the tale of Catella and Ricciardo resembles any other story of adulterous love in the *Decameron*. What seems a cliché is not, as the courtly love code is alluded to through textual indices: the most obvious one is the presence of the *donna schermo*, an expedient typical of the Provençal troubadour poets, and one that Dante also calls upon in the *Vita Nova*. Furthermore, for love of the screen lady, Ricciardo engages in typically courtly behaviour: as a valiant knight he fences and participates in jousts ("cominciò a mostrar d'armeggiare e di giostrare e di fare tutte quelle cose le quali per Catella soleva fare" [he accordingly began to tilt and joust and do all that he had been wont to do in honour of Catella, III.7.6]).[13] Catella too lives up to the expectations of the courtly code: she remains distant, literally, and allows herself only to greet him discreetly in passing just as she would any other man, and only after ascertaining that she is no longer the object of his amorous pursuit: "sì per fermo da tutti si teneva [i.e. Ricciardo, in his love for the other woman], che, non ch'altri, ma Catella lasciò una salvatichezza che con lui avea dell'amor che portarle solea, e dimesticamente, come vicino, andando e vegnendo il salutava come faceva gli altri" [the opinion was so firmly rooted in the minds of all that even Catella laid aside a

---

12 In his edition, Branca explains *tosa* as Lombard for young girl. "Come dire: meglio avere un bene materiale, piuttosto che cosa che diletti ma di dubbia possibilità. Cioè meglio un cattivo marito vivo che un buon marito defunto" [As if to say: it is better to own a material good, rather than something pleasant but with dubious possibilities. That is, better a bad husband than a good, but dead husband] (999).

13 Cf. the novella of Federigo degli Alberighi, V.9.

certain reserve which she had used towards him while she deemed him her lover, and, coming and going, greeted him in friendly, neighbourly fashion, like the rest (III.6.8)]. Moreover, while at the seaside resort she enjoys the exclusive company of other women; even when Ricciardo throws a "certo motto" about her husband's infedelity in her direction, she ensures female companionship: "essendo Catella *con poche* rimasa quivi dove Ricciardo era" (emphasis mine) [Catella and a few others with Ricciardo (III.6.10)]. We can conclude that, at first, Catella behaves according to the rules that the courtly code prescribes to women, and apply to her, at least for now, what Claude Perrus writes on the subject of the "dame secourable": "La Dame se trouve comme enfermée à l'avance dans un réseau de conduites obligatoires, nécessaires, que dessine la logique chevaleresque. Son comportement effectif était sagesse, son indifférence, une mise à l'épreuve, tous ses actes une observance rigoureuse du code de courtoisie" [The woman finds herself trapped in a web of prescribed and necessary rules of conduct drawn by chivalric logic. Her actual comportment was wisdom, her indifference a way of testing herself, her actions a rigorous observance of the courtly code ("Le Décameron," 73; translation mine)]. The virtuous wife of Filippello fits the profile of the "dame" encapsulated inside a rigorous "code de courtoisie." However, Catella's only vice, her excessive jealousy, is what triggers the reversal of the entire code and catapults the protagonists into the second part of the novella.

Upon hearing from Catella's female relatives about the jealous nature of his object of desire, Ricciardo, weary of loving from a distance, ignores all women's talk and decides to follow the voice of passion ("prese consiglio ai suoi piaceri"). It is knowledge about Catella's jealousy that turns Ricciardo into an agent of deception.[14] As for Catella, once her suspicions are raised about a possible contender to her husband's love, she undergoes an instant metamorphosis: she becomes "di subita ira accesa" [suddenly kindling with wrath (III.6.21)] and from here on physically isolated from her female companions. She can no longer contain her curiosity and anger and loses all ability to reason. In addition, it is not until Catella has substituted blind rage for reason, the result of her jealousy, that she rejects and starts breaking all courtly conventions: she trades modesty and

14 "The final song is Fiammetta's, happy in love except for her jealous fear of rivals" (Smarr, *Boccaccio and Fiammetta*, 180). Catella shares this characteristic with Fiammetta.

discreta retorica or silence altogether for outright rage and loquacity.[15] In fact, during her performance in the role of Filippello's lover in which Ricciardo has cast her, Catella verbally parodies male courtship: "volevi giugnere molto fresco cavaliere alla battaglia" [wast minded to shew thyself a lusty knight when thou shouldst join battle (III.6.37)]. Subsequently, after knowing the true identity of the man who has just enjoyed her, she rejects Ricciardo's advances with the words "non mi toccare, che tu hai troppo fatto d'arme per oggi" [touch me not; thou hast done feats of arms more than enough for to-day (III.6.40)]. Catella's double referral to chivalric imagery underlines her recognition of false male chivalry in a parodic way. In short, within the institutionalized forms of the courtly love tradition, Ricciardo and Catella are the antagonists of the courtly love structure from the moment jealousy arouses excessive passions. Both protagonists step outside these institutionalized forms, she unconsciously, driven by excessive jealousy, he consciously, by tenaciously and deliberately following the voice of passion.

3. Appearance versus Reality

The combination of Ricciardo's sexual desire and Catella's lack of reason sets the stage for easy deception through rhetoric. In a long and eloquent verbal display of his discovery of Filippello's relationship to the *donna schermo*, Ricciardo insists on the necessity of giving Catella visible and tactile proof of her husband's infidelity: "E acciò che voi non credeste queste essere *parole e favole*, ma il poteste, quando voglia ve ne venisse, *apertamente e vedere e toccare*" (emphasis mine) [And that you may not suppose that these are but *empty words* and idle tales, but may be able, should you so desire, to *verify them by sight and touch* (III.6.19)]. Ricciardo's lengthy, improvised rhetorical *tour de force* sets Catella up for her downfall and his triumph as his good use of reason starkly contrasts with hers, conditioned by jealousy. It is jealousy that morphs Catella into a credulous, impulsive victim: "senza alcuna considerazione a chi era colui che gliele dicea o a' suoi inganni, secondo il costume de' gelosi subitamente diede fede alle parole" [without so much as giving a thought to the speaker or his wiles, inclined at once to credit his story (III.6.21)]. Catella believes what seems to be true from what she heard. At play are Ricciardo's rejection of what is generally known

15 For the concept of *discreta retorica* see Minghelli, "Il ritorno."

(that Catella cannot be conquered) and Catella's acceptance of what is not known, of "parole o favole" which exist only in her mind (that Filippello has a lover). In other words, he who is driven by love can employ reason to go against the current; she who is ruled by jealousy is entirely swept away by that current, as can be expected "secondo il costume dei gelosi." From the moment Ricciardo is driven by reasoned passion for Catella, that which generally passes for true, i.e. that Catella shall never love another man besides her husband, Ricciardo dismisses as fiction. Ricciardo does not rely on rumours, least of all when their source is female: "avvenne che da donne, che sue parenti erano, [Ricciardo] fu un dì assai confortato che di tale amore si dovesse rimanere, perciò che in van si faticava" [it befell one day that some ladies that were of kin to him counseled him earnestly to be quit of such a love, whereby he could but fret himself to no purpose (III.6.6)]. Instead he prefers to ignore the women's advice altogether and "prese consiglio a' suoi piaceri" [forthwith began to ponder how he might make it subserve his end (III.6.7)]. What is obvious to no one is true, i.e. that Ricciardo hungers for Catella; on the other hand, what is general knowledge, namely that Ricciardo is in love with the *donna schermo*, is not true, and what is not true is subject to talk, women's talk, that is: "Quivi [at the "bagni"] le donne, e Catella insieme con loro, incominciarono con lui a motteggiare del suo novello amore, del quale egli mostrandosi acceso forte *più loro di ragionare dava materia*" [When the ladies received him, they all with one accord, including Catella, began to rally him on his new love, and *he furnished them with more matter for talk* by feigning a most ardent passion (emphasis mine) (III.6.10)]. Truth imposes silence and results in isolation. This brings us back to Catella.

4. Silence versus Rhetoric

In believing gossip, Catella is on equal footing with her female companions, but with this difference: what she perceives as true, a rumour planted in her ear by Ricciardo, conditions her behaviour, verbally and physically: the desire to know more leads her further away from the truth and deeper into the metaphorical realm of silence, a space in which she first isolates herself and then becomes trapped. The baths where Ricciardo has schemed an encounter with the object of his erotic desire (a scheme devised with the help of a woman who knows the truth and promises to be silent) consist of a dark room without windows in which she locks herself up with him. Not a word is uttered between the two protagonists. The amorous encounter is literally veiled in darkness and secrecy:

> Catella, che cercando andava quello che ella non avrebbe voluto trovare, fattasi alla camera menare dove Ricciardo era, *col capo coperto*, in quella entro e *dentro serrossi* … Catella, per mostrarsi bene d'essere altra che ella non era, abbracciò e basciò lui e fecegli la festa grande *senza dire alcuna parola* … La camera era *oscurissima*, di che ciascuna delle parti era contenta … *senza favellare, in guisa* che scorger si potesse la voce, per grandissimo spazio con maggior diletto e piacere dell'una parte che dell'altra stettero. (III.6.31–2; emphasis mine)

> And so Catella, in quest of that which she would gladly not have found, was shewn to the chamber where Ricciardo was, and having entered *without uncovering her head, closed the door behind her*. Catella, dissembling, for she was minded at first to counterfeit another woman, returned his embrace, kissed him, and lavished endearments upon him; *saying, the while, not a word* … The *darkness* of the room, which was profound, was equally welcome to both … *with no word said* on either side in a voice that might be recognized, they lay a long while, much more to the solace and satisfaction of the one than of the other party.

Silence and darkness are required in order not to compromise truth and deception.[16] Catella, assuming she is having intercourse with her husband, is actually fulfilling Ricciardo's sexual desire; hence "what seems to be, is not, and what seems not to be, is" (Cottino-Jones, *Order*, 60). This game of appearance and reality, which, as Cottino-Jones pointed out, exists for most of the novelle of Day Three (we think especially of the novella of Zima in III.5), is given a more dramatic twist when Catella reveals her true identity, or believes she does, to the man whom

16 About eloquence and silence and their relation to erotic expression in III.5 and III.6, see Franco Fido, "Silenzi." Marilyn Migiel in *A Rhetoric of the "Decameron"* provides an illuminating gendered reading of Day Three's novelle and storytellers, highlighting the female characters' explicit sexually charged rhetoric (72–3). Catella is associated with the "idea of sexual economy in terms of loading and unloading" (Foster Gittes, *Boccaccio's Naked Muse*, 181–2).

she mistakes for her husband.[17] The game of appearance and reality now takes on the sound of Catella's rage and the silence of Ricciardo: what is really not true makes Catella loquacious; what is really true silences Ricciardo. The reversal of this situation is noticeable as soon as Ricciardo identifies himself: she wants to scream, but is silenced by Ricciardo; she wants to run away, but cannot: "Catella ... subitamente si volle gittare del letto ma non potè; ond'ella volle gridare ma Ricciardo le chiuse con l'una delle mani la bocca" [Catella ... would have sprung out of the bed; which being impossible, she essayed a cry; but Ricciardo laid a hand upon her mouth (III.6.43)]. It is now her turn to be silent and his turn to talk. Only this time rhetoric employs truth rather than deception. And the truth is, according to Ricciardo, that people, to quote Boccaccio, have more often the tendency to believe in evil than in good: "voi sapete che la gente è più acconcia a credere il male che il bene" [folk are more prone to believe evil than good (III.6.43)]. Ricciardo relies on this general popular wisdom, which Catella is prone to believe, so as to convince his beloved that silence is her only option if she is not to lose her honour and her husband. Now that she has come to her senses, the voice of reason suggests to her that it is best to follow his advice: "Catella ... piagneva forte; e come che molto turbata fosse e molto si ramaricasse, nondimeno *diede tanto luogo la ragione alle vere parole* di Ricciardo, che ella cognobbe esser possibile a avvenire ciò che Ricciardo diceva" [Ricciardo's admonitions were received by Catella with many a bitter tear; but though she was very wroth and very sad at heart, yet Ricciardo's *true words so far commanded the assent of her reason*, that she acknowledged that 'twas possible they might be verified by the event (emphasis mine) (III.6.47)]. Reason also suggests to her that shouting is to no avail and that her simplicity and jealousy are the cause of her ill fate. Truth must be muffled and contained.

Just as we are approaching the novella's conclusion and expecting that Catella has learned her lesson not to take appearances for reality – and fiction too is a textual/verbal appearance – Ricciardo demands forgiveness. He begs for it with "dolcissime parole" [most dulcet phrases] and insists so much as to move her to submission: "e ella vinta, con lui si paceficò" [made his peace with her]. Boccaccio goes as far as to make them equally desirous of each other. Indeed, Catella and Ricciardo now take delight in each other's company "di pari volontà." The carefully

17 For the importance of silence in III.5, see Pier Massimo Forni in "Zima sermocinante."

constructed binary structure along the axis of deception and truth, of appearance and reality, thus reaches its surprising synthesis in this unexpected harmonious union of Catella and Ricciardo.

5. Of Excess, *Ira*, and Dogs

From its outset, the novella of Ricciardo and Catella is inserted in a context of excess. First, the tale is set in Naples, which is described as "città antichissima e forse così dilettevole, o più, come ne sia alcuna altra in Italia" [very ancient city, which for loveliness has not its superior or perhaps its equal in Italy (III.6.4)]; second, Ricciardo Minutolo is introduced as "splendido per molte ricchezze" [renowned for the splendour of his vast wealth (III.6.4)]. Part of his wealth is an exceptionally beautiful wife, "una bellissima giovane e vaga per moglie" [a very fair and loving wife (III.6.4)]; yet in spite of his wife's beauty, he is obsessed with Catella and in the grip of excessive desire for her: "e da amor non sappiendo o non potendo disciogliersi, né morir sapeva né gli giovava di vivere" [powerless to loose himself from his love, [he] found life scarce tolerable, and yet knew not how to die (III.6.5)]. Catella surpasses by far all women of Naples – "di gran lunga passava di bellezza tutte l'altre donne napoletane" [vastly surpassed in beauty every other lady in Naples (III.6.5)] – and she is, furthermore, called "onestissima." Her only obvious defect is her apparent excessive jealousy: "niuno altro bene avesse che Filippello, del quale era in tanta gelosia vivea che ogni uccel che per l'aere volava credeva gliele togliesse" [Catella cared for nought in the world save Filippello, and lived in such a state of jealousy on his account that never a bird flew but she feared lest it should snatch him from her (III.6.6)]. Excessive wealth, extraordinary beauty, boundless desire, extreme jealousy are set against the unsurpassed beautiful background of the city of Naples (the site of – we recall – Fiammetta's excess in love in Boccaccio's *Elegia di Madonna Fiammetta*) and are stylistically evoked through a chain of superlatives and hyperbolic constructions, reminiscent of the ones found in the *Elegia*. While hyperboles and superlatives are a common stylistic device in Boccaccio's novellas, in this tale they take on added connotations, especially with regard to a blatant manifestation of *dismizura* in the form of *ira*, or rage.

At the other textual extreme from this novella, i.e. in the the third tale of Day Four, Boccaccio delegates to a logical and reasonable Lauretta a warning against the dangers of *ira*: "la quale niuna altra cosa è che un movimento subito e inconsiderato, da sentita tristizia sospinto, il quale, ogni ragion cacciata e gli occhi della mente avendo di tenebre offuscati, in ferventissimo furore accende l'anima nostra" [anger is nought but a rash and hasty impulse, prompted by a feeling of pain, which banishes reason, shrouds the eyes of the mind in thick darkness, and sets the soul ablaze with a fierce frenzy (IV.3.4)].[18] It is interesting at this point to carefully read Catella's incensed outburst to the man she mistakes for her husband, for it covers a textual space so long that it cannot go unnoticed. What follows is a summarized version:

> Così di fervente ira cominciò a parlare: "Ahi quanto è misera la fortuna delle donne e come è male impiegato l'amor di molte ne' mariti! ... Io son Catella, non sono la moglie di Ricciardo, traditor disleal che tu se' ... e parmi mille anni che noi siamo al lume, che io ti possa svergognare come tu se' degno, sozzo *cane* vituperato che sei. Oimè, misera me! a cui ho io cotanti anni portato cotanto amore? A questo *can* disleale ... Tu se' bene oggi, *can* rinnegato, stato gagliardo, che a casa ti suogli mostrare così debole e vinto e senza possa! ... Che non rispondi, reo uomo? che non di' qualche cosa? Se' tu divenuto mutolo udendomi? In fe' di Dio io non so a che mi tengo che io non ti ficco le mani negli occhi e traggogliti!" (III.6.33–8) (Emphasis mine)[19]

> [Then, Catella, deeming it high time to vent her harboured resentment, burst forth in a blaze of wrath on this wise: "Alas! how wretched is the lot of women, how misplaced of not a few the love they bear their husbands! ... 'Tis I, Catella, not the wife of Ricciardo, false traitor that thou art ... it

18 We know how *ira* affects the rational mind from other novellas. Ninetta's fury in IV.3, for instance, is what makes her poison Restagnon. In the *Teseida*, *ira* takes a very central place, as Kirkham already pointed out: "the grim allegorical image of a man's irascible appetite" looming at the centre of the Teseida in the Temple of Mars ("il tempio di Marte, cioè, questo appetito irascibile" [VII.30 gl.]); "A cold, rainswept, eternally dark, sterile forest that roars with the noise of 'mille furor' surrounds the edifice, which has steel walls, barred windows, and an adamantine gate to suggest the stubborn obstinacy and coldblooded plotting typical of wrathful temperaments" ("An Allegorically Tempered *Decameron*," 34).

19 The fact that Catella wonders if her husband, Filippello, has become "mutolo" is a wordplay that underscores the identity confusion of both men even further: the enraged Catella turns the man she thinks is Filippello into a "mutolo," while he is, in fact, Ricciardo "Minutolo."

seems to me a thousand years till then – that I might shame thee as thou deservest, vile, pestilent *dog* that thou art! ... A lively spark indeed art thou to-day, renegade *dog*, that shewest thyself so limp and enervate and impotent at home! Where is thy answer, culprit? Hast thou nought to say? Have my words struck thee dumb? God's faith! I know not why I forbear to pluck thine eyes out with my fingers!"]

Catella's irate outburst only fuels the amorous passion of Ricciardo, who remains quiet while incessantly embracing and kissing her as she proceeds:

Sì, tu mi credi ora con tue carezze infinite lusingare, *can* fastidioso che tu se', e rapaceficare e racconsolare; tu se' errato ... Or non sono io, malvagio uomo, così bella come sia la moglie di Ricciardo Minutolo? non sono io così gentil donna? che non rispondi, sozzo *cane*? che ha colei più di me? (III.6.39–40; emphasis mine)

[Ay, thou thinkest to cajole me with thy feigned caresses, wearisome *dog* that thou art, and so to pacify and mollify me; but thou art mistaken ... Am I not, miscreant, as fair as the wife of Ricciardo Minutolo? Am I not as good a lady as she? Why dost not answer, vile *dog*? Wherein has she the advantage of me?]

In the flow of curses that spill from Catella's lips we immediately notice the obstinate repetition of the word "cane." Boccaccio has Catella call her husband "cane" five times, enhancing the canine image with a repertoire of fitting adjectives: "sozzo cane vituperato," "can disleale," "can rinnegato," "can fastidioso," and "sozzo cane." Considering the excessive rage that moves Catella's tongue, the canine image might not be such a surprising choice, if we remember Dante's use of the word. In fact, the association of Catella's rage with the image of a howling, enraged, and voracious dog is very appropriate and inevitably forces a detour through the *Commedia*.

In the *Commedia* Dante employs the word "cane" ten times, eight times in *Inferno* (VI.19 and 18; VIII.42; XVII.49; XXI.68; XXIII.18; XXX.18; XXXIII.78), and only once each in *Purgatorio* (XIV.50) and *Paradiso* (IV.6).

We read in *Inf.* VI.19: "urlar li fa la pioggia come cani" [That downpour makes the sinners howl like dogs], and the greedy in the third circle of *Inferno* are guarded by Cerbero, "con tre gole caninamente latra" [his three throats barking, doglike];[20] the dog image associated with greed, irascible appetite, and *ira* returns in *Inf.* VI.28, where Cerbero is compared to a dog who stops howling and growling only when he tastes food: "qual è quel cane ch' abbaiando agogna, / e si racqueta poi che 'l pasto morde, / che solo a divorarlo intende e pugna, / cotai si fecer quelle facce lorde / de lo demonio Cerbero" [Just as a dog that barks with greedy hunger / will then fall quiet when he gnaws his food, / intent and straining hard to cram it in, / so were the filthy faces of the demon / Cerberus transformed]. In *Inf.* VIII.42, during Dante's meeting with Filippo Argenti, one of the "iracondi," the image of the dog is attached specifically to the concept of *ira*: one of the damned is so enraged that he wants to turn over the boat that holds Virgil and Dante. Virgil chases him with the words: "Via costà con li altri cani!" [Be off there with the other dogs!]. In *Inf.* XVII.49, a canto that abounds with animal imagery, the usurers in the third "girone" of the seventh circle of Hell who are trying to avoid the burning hot vapours rising from the hot soil under their feet are compared to dogs bitten by insects: "non altrimenti fan di state i cani" [not otherwise do dogs in summer]. In *Inf.* XXI.67–8 inside the bolgia dei barattieri, we read: "Con quel furor e con quella tempesta / ch'escono i cani a dosso al poverello" [With the same frenzy, with the brouhaha / of dogs, when they beset a poor wretch]. These verses are part of a simile that repeats the image of the unchained "mastino" chasing after the thief, allowing Dante once more to resort to the dog image to denote uncontrolled rage. In Inf. XXIII.16–18, in the pouch of the hypocrites, we read: "Se l'ira sovra 'l mal voler s'aggueffa, / ei ne verranno dietro più crudeli / che 'l cane a quella lievre ch'elli acceffa" [If anger's to be added to their malice, / they'll hunt us down with more ferocity / than any hound whose teeth have trapped a hare]. In other words, adding rage to the devils' natural inclination to do evil increases their cruelty. In *Inf.* XXX.16–21 Hecuba, the queen of Troy, is described as a dog: after having first found her daughter Polyxena sacrificed on the tomb of Achilles and subsequently her son Polidor dead on a seashore, she loses her mind. Her lament is compared to the howling of a dog (she changes into a dog in the *Metamorphoses*). "Ecuba trista, misera e cattiva, / poscia che vide Polissena morta, / e del suo Polidor in su la riva / del mar

20 All English-language quotations from the *Commedia* are by Alan Mandelbaum in *The Divine Comedy of Dante Alighieri.*

si fu la dolorosa accorta, / forsennata latrò sì come cane; / tanto il dolor le fe' la mente torta" [then Hecuba was wretched, sad, a captive; / and after she had seen Polyxena / dead and, in misery, had recognized / her Polydorus lying on the shore, / she barked, out of her senses, like a dog]. Finally, in *Inf.* XXXIII.76–8 Ugolino, upon finishing the story of his horrifying ordeal, continues chewing on a skull like a dog on a bone: "Quand'ebbe detto ciò, con li occhi torti / riprese 'l teschio misero co' denti, che furo a l'osso, come d'un can, forti" [When he had spoken this, with eyes awry, / again he gripped the sad skull in his teeth, / which, like a dog's, were strong down to the bone]. The image evoked is one of uncontrolled appetite and rage. The word "cane" is in every instance placed within the semantic contours of rage, gluttony, and more often than not both irascibility and painful howling ("latrare").

The only dog occurence in *Purgatorio* is in a context that is only peripherally interesting for our purposes. In *Purg.* XIV, where Dante and his guide walk among the *invidiosi*, we read at v. 46–50: "Botoli trova poi, venendo giuso, / ringhiosi più che non chiede lor possa, / e da lor disdegnosa torce il muso. / Vassi caggendo; e quant ella più 'ngrossa, / tanto più trova di can farsi lupi" [Then, as that stream descends, it comes on curs / that, though their force is feeble, snap and snarl; / scornful of them, it swerves its snout away. / And, downward, it flows on; and when that ditch, / ill fated and accursed, grows wider, it / finds, more and more, the dogs becoming wolves.]

While in the *Inferno* the canine imagery surfaces in a context of voracity and irascibility and while Dante's chart of Florentine corruption on the terrace of Envy in *Purgatorio* XIV has Florentines turn from dogs into wolves, it is the last and for the *Paradiso* only canine reference that captures our attention:

> Intra due cibi, distanti e moventi
> d'un modo, prima si morria di fame,
> che liber' omo l'un recasse ai denti;
> sì si starebbe un agno intra due brame
> di fieri lupi, igualmente temendo;
> sì si starebbe un cane intra due dame. (*Par.* IV.1–6)

> [Before a man bit into one of two / foods equally removed and tempting, he / would die of hunger if his choice were free / so would a lamb stand motionless between / the cravings of two savage wolves, in fear / of both; so would a dog between two deer.]

Dante employs this triple simile to explain how, between two equally pressing questions, the pilgrim does not know which one to ask first. His silence and his facial expression are interpreted by Beatrice, who formulates both questions in his stead.[21] By guessing his thoughts and knowing precisely what his dilemma is, Beatrice does for Dante what Daniel did for Nebuchadnezzar:

> Fè sì Beatrice qual fè Daniello,
> Nabucodonozor levando d'ira,
> che l'aveva fatto ingiustamente fello. (*Par.* IV.15–18)

> [Then Beatrice did just as Daniel did, / when he appeased Nebuchadnezzar's anger, / the rage that made the king unjustly fierce.]

The reference is to the biblical story of Nebuchadnezzar's dream, which none of his advisors was able to interpret. Only Daniel was able to interpret it for his master, thereby tempering the rage of the Babylonian ruler and saving his own life. The simile not only establishes Beatrice as a good interpreter but also alludes to Dante's discontent by implying that Dante the pilgrim is like the irate Babylonian ruler. In other words, Dante has both the likings of a dog and those of an *iracondo*, at first. In a second stage, after his thoughts have been interpreted, his rage is tempered. The correlation between the dog image and *ira* on the one hand and the inability to interpret signs correctly on the other is thus enforced.

The answer which regards the place of the souls in the first heaven is just as interesting, for it relates to what Dante the pilgrim sees, or thinks he sees. Because there are gradations in beatitude, according to the vicinity of the blessed souls to God, the souls of the Empyrean appear to Dante in the stars shining with more or less intensity. They conform to Dante's, the mortal human's, ability to see, or better, inability to see, i.e. they allow themselves (through the will of God, since their will is wanted by God) to be perceived via Dante's human intellect, which has not yet abandoned the world of the senses. Beatrice, paraphrasing Thomas Aquinas in *Summa Theologiae* (I.q.I.a), explains to Dante why it is necessary for him, a mortal, to see the blessed souls in this way:

---

21 Dante's first question – why nuns are shorn of what else had been the full measure of their glory because they were torn against their will from the cloister (19–22) – is answered in the next canto. The second question she reads from Dante's mind is: why, as Plato has it, do the souls return to the stars after the body dies?

Così parlar conviensi al vostro ingegno,
però che solo da sensato apprende
ciò che fa poscia d'intelletto degno.
Per questo la Scrittura condescende
a vostra facultate, e piedi e mano
attribuisce a Dio e altro intende; (*Par.* IV.40–5)

[Such signs are suited to your mind, since from / the senses only can it apprehend / what then becomes fit for the intellect. / And this is why the Bible condescends / to human powers, assigning feet and hands / to God, but meaning something else instead.]

Because Dante is a mortal human, Beatrice must talk to him in a way that he can understand through his human intellect. For this same reason, the language of the Scriptures lowers itself to the level of humans and explains high concepts in ways intelligible to mortals, which is why God is given feet and hands, while these physical attributes point towards a higher meaning. The passage is highly significant, since this time the canine image is located in direct reference to the act of interpreting, as well as to the polysemous nature of the *Commedia*. Dante, unlike Beatrice, must rely on figurative speech, the kind humans depend on, as Beatrice points out to him, in order to understand some of the "high" notions of wisdom by which he is being challenged. In other words, misinterpretation is common without a higher, sublime level of understanding. Misinterpretation is human. Beatrice, on the other hand, is able to interpret Dante's silence and facial expression, since she sees through the eyes of the All-Seeing, which is what Dante the pilgrim, the human, strives for. Beatrice sees the truth; Dante sees only a reflection of it in a format comprehensible to mortals.

When we now return to the *Decameron*, we understand why the canine image should be given more importance than literally "meets the eye." Boccaccio may well deliberately echo Dante's use of it in association with Catella's uncontrolled rage, but he might also allow his reader to recollect a place in the *Commedia* where interpretation and different levels of knowledge constitute *Paradiso* IV's supporting framework. It is indeed noteworthy that precisely an animal that can hardly be disassociated from the vice of *ira* leads us to Beatrice as both decoder of Dante's mind and spokeswoman advocating the necessity of a commonly accessible language that hides great inaccessible concepts. In juxtaposition to Beatrice, Boccaccio's Catella, then, has left reason so far behind that she no longer understands herself. Her jealousy has enraged her so, and reason is so remote a virtue, that she mistakes herself for her husband, so to speak. Indeed, although Catella's rage is certainly associated with that of a mad dog, Boccaccio does not once compare Catella to a dog. Instead, it is Filippello, the person suspected of betraying her, whom she curses as a mad dog. In other words, her rage spurred by jealousy has so clouded her ability to reason and recognize what is appearance and what is reality that she places the name-tag "cane" onto her husband. Catella is howling at her own reflection. She has completely misunderstood a common, conventional metaphor: that rage ("ira") equals dog ("cane"). Catella seems not to be a dog but is one, and the person who is called a dog is not. This discourse is again one of appearance versus reality and makes the last reference in Dante's *Commedia* all the more relevant.

6. *Ira* and *Invidia*: Misinterpretation in the Introduction to Day Four

The echo of Catella's rage carries over into the Introduction to the fourth day. So too do the themes that lie at the heart of the novella: misinterpretation as a result of excessive passsion, including anger and envy.[22] I am here referring to Boccaccio's famous apology for his work against the biting criticism of misinterpreting critics.

In the beginning of the Introduction to Day Four, Boccaccio identifies envy as the source of his critics' biting comments against his *Decameron*, comments that result in misinterpretation of his work as the result of envy:

> Carissime donne, sì per le parole de' savi uomini udite e sì per le cose da me molte volte e vedute e lette, estimava io che *lo impetuoso vento e ardente della 'nvidia* non dovesse percuotere se non l'alte torri o le più levate cime degli alberi: ma io *mi truovo della mia estimazione ingannato*. Per ciò che, fuggendo io e sempre essendomi di fuggire ingegnato *il fiero impeto di questo rabbioso spirito*, non solamente pe' piani ma ancora per le profondissime valli mi sono ingegnato di andare; il che *assai manifesto può apparire* a chi le

22 In Latin the term *invidia* implies ill will, hatred, towards another's possessions; *gelosia*, from *zelosus*, means "full of zeal," in the sense of suspicious, apprehensive of rivalry, resentfully envious. The two terms are semantically related. Both are linked to excess and possession of either a person or a thing or a quality.

presenti novellette *ri*guarda, le quali non solamente in fiorentin volgare e in prosa scritte per me sono *e senza titolo*, ma ancora in istilo umilissimo e rimesso quanto il più si possono. Né per tutto ciò l'essere *da cotal vento fieramente scrollato*, anzi presso che *diradicato* e tutto *dai morsi della invidia esser lacerato*, non ho potuto cessare; per ché *assai manifestamente* posso comprendere quello esser *vero che sogliono i savi dire, che sola la miseria è senza invidia nelle cose presenti* (IV.Intro.1–4; emphasis mine).

[Dearest ladies, as well from what I heard in converse with the wise, as from matters that not seldom fell within my own observation and reading, I formed the opinion that the *vehement and scorching blast of envy* was apt to vent itself only upon lofty towers or the highest tree-tops: but therein *I find that I misjudged*; for, whereas I ever sought and studied how best to elude the buffetings *of that furious hurricane*, and to that end kept a course not merely on the plain, but, by preference, in the depth of the valley; as *should be abundantly clear* to who so looks at these little stories, written as they are not only in the vulgar Florentine, and in prose, and *without dedicatory flourish*, but also in as homely and simple a style as may be; nevertheless all this has not stood me in such stead but that *I have been shrewdly shaken, nay, all but uprooted by the blast*, and altogether *lacerated by the bite of this same envy*. Whereby *I may very well understand* that 'tis true, what the sages aver, that only misery is exempt from envy in the present life.]

The passage is famous enough, and would hardly need to be elaborated on if it did not share two key ingredients with the novella of Catella and Ricciardo, besides the very obvious metaphor of *invidia* as a destructive and biting wind: the first is jealousy and envy as a breeding ground for misconceptions; the second is conventional versus "higher" knowledge. *Invidia* is what has triggered the criticism of Boccaccio's work, in spite of the fact that he has always avoided it. In the same way, *gelosia* is what precipitates rage and is thus the indirect source of Catella's misreading of the false text that is Ricciardo's body. In the above-quoted passage Boccaccio warns us against misinterpretation and laments his having become its victim. Convinced that envy would not attack the humble – hearing, seeing, and reading the word many times – he now understands that his critics' envy has made them do just that. Second, he carefully suggests that it *might seem* very clear ("assai manifesto *può apparire*") from looking again at his novellas ("*ri*-guarda") that there was no reason for the vicious attack of his critics. Again he carefully hints at the mere relative reliability of perception ("assai manifesto" and "può apparire" seem an oxymoric couple). Furthermore, we notice how Boccaccio alludes to his reluctance to giving a title to his novellas. By doing so he does not merely suggest, as Branca does, that "l'estrema varietà della materia ... non consentiva un titolo unitario alla diffusione di varie novelle prima che fosse compiuta l'opera" [the extreme variety of the material ... did not allow for a unifying title under which to divulge the various novellas before the work's completion (Branca, ed., *Decameron*, 460)], but might very well deliberately opt for not preconditioning his reader through a title, thus leaving his audience with the burden of interpretation. Boccaccio was acutely aware of the nature of storytelling as a powerful tool for concealing higher concepts: "Boccaccio was firmly convinced of the serious intent hidden in fable and showed the seriousness of his belief by stating that even the Holy Ghost and Christ himself spoke in fables" (Potter, *Five Frames*, 69).[23] Giving his novellas a title would mean conditioning the reader, forcing that reader into the hidden intent of fable, unless precisely that was the intent. This brings us to the title Boccaccio chose for his one hundred novellas.

Boccaccio gave his collection of tales a name, "Decameron," and a surname, "Prencipe Galeotto." In other words, through inevitable, almost conventional, association of his work with respectively Lancelot and Guinevere and Dante's Paolo and Francesca, Boccaccio places the reader in front of a context of misreading. Let me therefore end with the beginning.

---

23 Potter points out that the very title of Book 14 of the *Genealogia* is self-explanatory: "It is foolish to believe that poets did not hide meanings beneath the bark of fable." According to Potter, Boccaccio further states that poets hid the truth beneath fictions "so that those things which, if openly expressed would have been held to be of little account, when sought after with hard work by the mind and understood in different ways would be held more dear" (*Five Frames*, 70). Boccaccio's contention is that there may be more bread to be had from fables than the rich would have from their treasures and that, in fact, poets who pursued fables "fecero la loro età fiorire" (IV.Intro.37–8). In other words, spiritual food is better than the food that his critics would want to give him by making him do real work rather than write about love. Potter uses this passage to point out how Boccaccio's view can be interpreted through the *Genealogia deorum gentilium* and how, though written later in life, the *Genealogia* sheds light on Boccaccio's views on the role of literature and "may nevertheless be a guide to the *Decameron* because its point of view is the same as that expressed in defense of poetry in the Introduction to the Fourth Day" (*Five Frames*, 69).

7. "Decameron" versus "Prencipe galeotto"

The *Decameron* begins as follows: "Comincia il libro chiamato Decameron cognominato Prencipe Galeotto, nel quale si contengono cento novelle in dieci di dette da sette donne e da tre giovani uomini" [Beginneth here the book called Decameron, otherwise Prince Galeotto, wherein are contained one hundred novels told in ten days by seven ladies and three young men (Proem.1)]. Its *incipit* is echoed at the end of the "Conclusione": "Qui finisce la decima e ultima giornata del libro chiamato Decameron cognominato Prencipe Galeotto" [Endeth here the tenth and last day of the book called Decameron, otherwise Prince Galeotto]. The symmetry between the *Decameron*'s textual extremities is well known, but I would like to draw attention to another factor, inspired by Joy Hambuechen Potter, that the pairing of the title "Decameron" and the courtly love figure of Prince Gallehault "is internal evidence that suggests the opposition between name and nickname" (*Five Frames*, 93). I would add to that, and suggest that the very act of nicknaming the *Decameron* is in turn an indication of Boccaccio's intent to imply a relationship between truth and fiction, as if to say, "I am presenting you a Decameron and am telling you to that you should re-present it to yourselves as mis-re-presentation. In addition, I rely on your being mortal humans and on the conventional associations that you will most likely make with Gallehault." In other words, Boccaccio equips Gallehault with a code that transgresses the dictates of its own code. The *Decameron* is then also about misinterpretation.

If the novella of Ricciardo and Catella seems far removed from these concepts, let us accept Boccaccio's invitation to look back, to "riguardare." Inside the contours of the novella format, Ricciardo and Catella are characters in a fictional representation that hides an internal truth under the bark of the surface: the story is really about appearance and reality, more particularly about how language can be employed as appearance of truth. Depending on how we use or abuse reason or let it be dominated by excessive passions, by *dizmisura*, our ability to decode what Boccaccio has so cleverly encoded can be affected. Catella's misreading of the body of Ricciardo because she is blinded by *ira* is a good example. Ricciardo's independent reading of conventional language, in spite of his being driven by passion, is still guided by reason and thus yields him the hoped-for results. The courtly love code that lies embedded in this tale seems susceptible to its own language, for it transgresses that very language. To conclude then, within the courtly framework of the novella of Ricciardo and Catella, excess, *dismizura*, leads to misinterpretation. Absence of reason makes one an uncritical reader who accepts common knowledge unconditionally and does not distinguish between truth and appearance. It unconsciously makes the entire courtly code structure crumble. When reason tempers excess, such as Ricciardo's erotic passion, it makes one aware of the unreliability of fiction and offers one the possibility of creating one's own fiction, as Ricciardo does through deceptive rhetoric. Reason can be employed to one's advantage and yield the desired results; it is even capable of overthrowing courtly conventions. Within the courtly context of the *Decameron*, then, we can take its content at face value and react to its displaying symptoms of *dismizura* as Boccaccio's critics did, or as Paolo and Francesca did to the story of Lancelot and Guinevere; alternatively, readers can employ reason as a tempering device in order to raise their level of literary consciousness and read the text with the awareness that underneath fiction hides a "higher" truth. Perhaps the *Decameron*'s surname "Prencipe Galeotto" only warns us against the dangers of misinterpretation, i.e. against *dismizura* in our approach to the courtly code that has misinterpretation as a result of *dismizura* at its very centre. For what seems to be is not, and what seems not to be is.

The Tale of Tedaldo degli Elisei (III.7)

SUSANNA BARSELLA

The tragic opening of the *Decameron* on the devastated urban landscape of a plague-ridden Florence illustrates the crisis of communal institutions, of their moral and religious codes, and of the belief that there existed knowledge capable of understanding and controlling natural phenomena.[1] The plague in the Introduction to Day One can be seen as the "correlative objective" of the crisis of medieval thought, which was founded on the premise of an ontological continuity between human and divine worlds, truth and appearance.[2] Panfilo's conclusion on the impossibility of investigating what is beyond experience in the first novella of the *Decameron* reveals how deeply the consciousness of this epistemological crisis informs Boccaccio's work.[3] From this new intellectual perspective, the ascertainment of reality becomes problematic. What appears and what actually is become interchangeable realities in terms of the capacity to convey knowledge and understanding, for reality is no longer perceived as a mere sign of the manifestation of the unknown but acquires a value of truth of its own. Fiction and truth emerge as permeable spheres

A shorter version of this essay appeared in *Humanistica* 1 (2010):1–13.

1 As Flasch observes: "La peste viene descritta come una crisi del sapere umano, soprattutto di quello che si riteneva di sapere a proposito di malattie e salute. Questo sapere non ha certezze ed è inutile; non riesce ad attuare nessuna efficace profilassi; e non consente neanche di fare previsioni" (*Poesia dopo la peste*, 53–4).

2 On the epistemological and ontological crisis of medieval thought as leading to the perception of truth as attainable within the boundaries set by human nature, nature, history, and society, see Garin, *La crisi* and *Poesia e filosofia* (in Garin, *Medioevo e Rinascimento*, 11–47 and 48–65).

3 "secondo quello che ne può apparire ragiono" [I speak according to that which appears (I.1.89)].

linked by an amplified spectrum of metaphorical relations that the rhetoric of the literary text can exploit.[4] On the diegetical level, transformations, disguises, concealments, and metamorphoses of the *Decameron*'s characters dramatize the problematic relation between truth and appearance, allowing for the representation of a reality that would otherwise escape rational discourse. As Boccaccio stages a crisis (the plague) and its consequences as a key to illustrate a broader crisis involving the medieval system of thought and a turn towards a less systematic, more "practical" approach to questions concerning ethical values, the *Decameron* emerges as a work already projected in a humanistic perspective.[5]

Reflecting a turn from theoretical to practical philosophy, the *Decameron* presents a new perspective on the ethical implications of literature. What distinguishes Boccaccio from a medieval author is not just the explicit goal of the moral education of young ladies in love, but also – and most importantly – the modalities through which he articulates such a goal. By offering various "exempla" of *ars vivendi* and – at the same time – *narrandi*, the *Decameron* points at the special role literature plays in addressing ethical questions in view of a renovation of society in the post-plague, epistemological context. This role emerges explicitly in the recognition of the regenerating power of narrative and its constitutive rhetorical principles of "delight" and "usefulness."[6] Neither of these values, Boccaccio

4 Grassi argued that the centrality of cognitive metaphor marked the progressive convergence of rhetoric and philosophy that characterized humanistic thought. This trait was already present in Boccaccio's idea of poetry as theology and theology as a form of poetry, a conception that the poet developed in his *Genealogie*. See "La priorità," 11–30.

5 As Giuseppe Mazzotta argues, the *Decameron* is by its own nature concerned with moral philosophy: "So bound is this text to the concrete world of experience, so rooted are its characters in the realm of the variable and contingent that ethics, the branch of philosophy which is concerned with the practical order of choices and values and which is conventionally defined as the 'ars bene vivendi,' is the appropriate discipline for probing the principles within which ideal social interactions can be envisioned" (*The World at Play*, 248).

6 In the last two decades, the moral aspect of Boccaccio's masterpiece has been investigated with unprecedented vigour against the traditional vision of a secularized *Decameron*. See, among others, Kirkham, *The Sign of Reason*; Flasch, *Poesia dopo la peste*; Morosini, "Per difetto reintegrare." See also Kirkham, "Morale." Overcoming the opposition between "moral" and "secular" readings of the *Decameron* is Mazzotta's interpretation of an ethics of pleasure and "play" that finds its visible realization in the imaginative force of Boccaccio's text: "Pleasure, in short, is one of the main metaphors for the text and it is through this category that we are forced to raise the issue of the moral value of the *Decameron*" (*The World at Play*, 243).

adds, can be realized ("senza passamento di noia" [without enduring pain, Proem 14]). The "passamento di noia" indicates the ethical perspective in which delight and utility should be considered. The expression alludes to the effort one must endure to achieve them, as an effort is necessary in order to attain virtue. In Aristotle, pleasure and utility indeed belong to the definition of the good pursued in view of happiness (defined as the activity of the virtuous soul), and in Cicero one cannot be without the other.[7] These notions are likewise inseparable in the *Decameron*, and their unity constitutes the essence of its moral dimension. Although set within the broad horizon of Christian values, within which any humanist project of reformation of the *polis* lies, this endiadic couple also evidences the necessity of an autonomy of the ethical-literary discourse from a purely religious one in order to reconsider a post-plague society. It is the consciousness of such an autonomy that makes the *Decameron* a "modern" work, and its modernity is visible in the new approach Boccaccio chooses by presenting the novelle as a collection of case-studies offered to privileged readers such as the young ladies so that they may understand moral issues and deliberate upon which actions to avoid and which to pursue.[8] Metaphorically, these young ladies represent all souls affected by passions with no cultural instruments to curb them, remaining therefore unable to achieve a state of virtue. By embracing this perspective, Boccaccio attributes to himself the role of writer-philosopher (i.e. moral philosopher) and educator. Only by virtue of the intrinsic power of literature to combine pleasure and utility does the *Decameron* become a privileged guide for practical moral purposes, an alternative to both religious teaching and the courteous code of behaviour contained in secular treatises such as Andreas Capellanus's *De amore*.

Another element that reveals the presence of an already humanistic educative mentality in the *Decameron* is the fact that, unlike these religious and courtly models, the *Decameron* refrains from a traditional form of explicit moral teaching; indeed, it does not set *a priori* rules of behaviour, but instead presents stories that offer the readers the opportunity to reflect openly on moral issues. The novelle are no longer medieval examples with which the author imposes his judgment upon his

7 For the influence of Aristotelian and Ciceronian ethics on the conceptual nucleus of the *Decameron*, see Barsella, "I marginalia di Boccaccio."

8 *Proem* 14. Unless otherwise indicated, Italian quotations are from Vittore Branca's 1992 edition of Boccaccio's *Decameron*. English translations are from J.M. Rigg, unless otherwise indicated.

readers, but open-ended representations of often verisimilar situations.[9] Boccaccio thus moves away from a precept-based approach to moral issues towards one centred on judgment and choice. A careful reader of the *Nicomachean Ethics* and the *De officiis*, Boccaccio recovers the philosophical inspiration of this tradition, making it serve the needs of the moral re-edification of the mercantile society. In doing so, he does not discover new texts, but a new way of reading and using them.

The novella III.7 can be read as a case-study taken to illustrate the following issue: what is the difference – in terms of practical consequences – between the courtly secular doctrine of love and the religious moral teachings in matters of love? What makes these two institutions – the literary and the sacred – ultimately produce the same results? For one allows adulterous love and the other fails to prevent it. Almost an indirect response to these questions, the story of Tedaldo degli Elisei – who returns to Florence disguised as a pilgrim to win back Ermellina Palermini, who had rejected him because of her confessor's counsel – shows the failure of these prevailing models of moral teaching in the communal society and introduces a different perspective based on the recovery of non-confessional moral teaching.[10]

This novella displays two structural elements: a criticism directed at the preaching orders, and a criticism directed at the courtly code of love represented by Andreas Capellanus's *De amore* (c. 1185).[11] The two codes,

9 To the traditionally studied subtexts of the Boccaccian novelle, such as religious and vernacular literary texts, at least three other sources may be added: the manuals of practical moral philosophy; the *quaestiones disputates* studied in Civil and Canon Law; and the manuals for confessors. All of these genres present collections of "cases." Fredi Chiappelli first formulated the hypothesis of a possible influence of Boccaccio's juridical studies on the structure of the *Decameron*. Paolo Cherchi illustrated the influence of the medieval genre of the "controversy" on medieval storytelling and the "courtly casuistry." Nella Giannetto, based on Cherchi's study, argues for the direct influence, exploited in the forms of parody, of the "controversy" model in Boccaccio's *Decameron*, particularly in the novella VI.7. See Chiappelli, "Discorso o progetto"; Cherchi "From 'controversia'"; Giannetto, "Madonna Filippa." For a reference to the manuals of confessors, see Le Goff, *Pour un autre Moyen Âge*, 62–80.

10 Emilia is the narrator of the story, which, under the reign of Neifile, is dedicated to "those who successfully apply ingenuity to acquire or recover something they desire" [di chi alcuna cosa molto da lui disiderata con industria acquistasse o la perduta ricoverasse (translation mine)].

11 For the general theme of religion in the *Decameron*, see Ó Cuilleanáin, *Religion and the Clergy*; Valesio, "Sacro"; Branca and Degani, "Studi sugli 'Exempla.'" For a

the religious and the secular, are not simply Boccaccio's sources, but also models structurally at work in the texture of the story, which illustrates their parallel weaknesses.

Boccaccio's critique of religious institutions characterizes many novelle of the *Decameron*, and can be seen as an illustration of the flaws in the moral guidance that the Church attempted to provide in secularized communal societies such as Florence in 1300.[12] As Carlo Delcorno remarks, preaching and confession are the two main religious institutions placed under critical revision in the *Decameron*.[13] Novella III.7 presents an explicit reference to the preaching literature of the mendicant orders with which Boccaccio was familiar.[14] Sermons, and particularly the sermons *ad status* addressed to special professional categories, aimed at providing

---

detailed analysis of the exemplary and homiletic subtexts of Decameron III.7, see Carlo Delcorno, "La 'predica,'" and, for the importance of the genre of the exemplum, Delcorno, "L''exemplum' nella predicazione." Ó Cuilleanáin combines formalism and historical critical methods to investigate the ideological meaning of religious presences in the *Decameron*. In his view, Boccaccio pragmatically exploits the narrative possibilities offered by religious institutions, including religious literature and cultural models: "Boccaccio, in making complicated stories out of resources of religion in his day, is opportunistically exploiting the formal possibilities inherent in religious institutions: possibilities which also undergo permutations in the course of religious history" (Ó Cuilleanáin, *Religion and the Clergy*, 35). The way Boccaccio chooses to characterize his clerical characters, however, is also a sign of a renovated, critical view of the Church and its institutional and doctrinal role in the society depicted in the *Decameron*.

12 The importance of religion, and preaching in particular, in Boccaccio's masterpiece can be measured by the number of novelle in which clerics are protagonists or play important roles (thirteen novelle), and by the total number of characters belonging to the Church (forty-three characters).

13 "Alcune delle novelle più famose mettono in scena lo psicodramma della predica e soprattutto della confessione, due momenti complementari della cultura penitenziale diffusa e organizzata dai frati mendicanti" (Delcorno, "La 'predica,'" 55).

14 Boccaccio probably listened to the Dominican preaching at Santa Maria Novella during the years of the activity of Jacopo Passavanti, the leader of the *opera* of the church and one of its most active preachers. Another Dominican friar active in Santa Maria Novella in the years after Boccaccio's return to Florence was Angelo Acciaiuoli, a cousin of Niccolò Acciaiuoli, whom Boccaccio had probably met in Naples. For the thorny relationship between Niccolò Acciaiuoli and Boccaccio, see Branca, *Giovanni Boccaccio: Profilo biografico*, 128–31. Angelo was bishop of Florence between 1340 and 1342. Jacopo Passavanti preached in Florence between September 1340 and spring 1341, before moving to the Dominican convent in 1346. For the dates of preaching activity of the friars in Santa Maria Novella, see Orlandi, "*Necrologio*."

the believers with moral teachings by means of an eloquence modelled on evangelic and apostolic examples.[15] The preachers also made a fundamental contribution to the elaboration of the manuals for confessors, further improving the effective capacity of the Church to reach and regulate the complex reality of civic vices.[16] The doctrinal body that the Dominican *Ordo Predicatorum* in particular developed in the eleventh and twelfth centuries was collected in manuals for preachers and organized in *summae praedicationis*, collections of sermons, manuals for confessors, and inventories of exempla.[17] This body of religious literature testifies to the impact that Dominican pulpits had on medieval popular consciousness.[18] These texts, including the sermons (most sermons were written before being preached), constituted a model of edifying literature expressed in the unmediated and effective form of short stories.[19] The preachers

15 Preachers such as Jacopo Passavanti turned to a penitential reinterpretation of the religious spirituality of the Early Fathers, which betrayed to a certain extent the original nature of the Fathers' vocation. This penitential religiosity became prevalent among the Florentine Dominicans around 1340.

16 See Le Goff, *Pour un autre Moyen Âge*, 162–80.

17 One of the most diffused *Artes praedicandi* was Alan of Lille's, which Boccaccio probably knew. Antonia Mazza, however, disagrees that the codex containing Alan de Lille's *Ars* included in the inventory of Boccaccio's "parva libraria" belonged to him. See Mazza, "L'inventario." The bibliography on medieval exempla is vast. Among the general works, the following should be mentioned: Welter, *L'"Exemplum"*; Tubach, *Index Exemplorum*; Brémond, Le Goff, and Schmitt, *L'Exemplum*; Schneyer, *Repertorium*; Delcorno, *Exemplum e letteratura*; Baldassarri and Varanini, eds. *Racconti esemplari*; Berlioz and Polo de Beaulieu, *Les "Exempla" Médiévaux*; Pellegrini, *I manoscritti*. See also Branca and Degani, "Studi sugli 'Exempla.'"

18 The Dominican convent of Santa Maria Novella in Florence was one of the most important cultural centres of the fourteenth century, together with those of the Franciscans in Santa Croce and the Augustinians in Santo Spirito, with whom Boccaccio had a close relation, especially in the last period of his life. See Branca, *Giovanni Boccaccio: Profilo biografico*, 180–94. The convent of Santa Maria Novella, where the *Decameron*'s narration starts, had a strong tradition of preachers. Remigio dei Girolami, Giordano da Pisa, and Domenico Cavalca at the turn of the thirteenth century and Jacopo Passavanti in Boccaccio's time preached from its pulpit. Remigio dei Girolami introduced the teaching of Thomas Aquinas's *Summa* in Florence around 1303. It is possible that Boccaccio studied Aristotle's *Ethics* and Thomas's commentary under the influence of the Dominicans. See Panella, "Nuova cronologia" and Pellegrini, *I manoscritti*.

19 The sermons also had literary relevance, since they required the use of rhetorical devices. Moreover, since they were destined for a popular audience, they were preached in the vernacular and influenced the development of vernacular literature. See Delcorno, *Giordano da Pisa*, 83–237.

exhorted their audience to behave according to exemplary models presented in the forms of stylized figures of peasants, merchants, and artisans in continuity with the traditional religious literature of the low Middle Ages.[20] In the *Decameron*, Boccaccio turns the sermons' standardized characters into parodic anti-types, as in the cases of Ciappelletto's confession in I.1 or Cipolla's *oratio* in VI.10. The artificial device the author uses to construct his text in a parodic key often relies on the theatralization of deception in the form of disguises, transformations, and concealments of identity that characterize in particular the novelle dedicated to religious themes, such as III.7. Boccaccio's dramatization of moral issues reflects the passage from moral teaching based on models, typical of the exemplary tradition on which preaching had developed, to one in which the "model" either disappears or becomes problematic (such as in the case of the virtuous excesses of the tenth day) and is replaced by verisimilar cases that stage the ambiguities of reality.

The presence of several codices containing religious works in Boccaccio's partially reconstructed library is evidence of the author's acquaintance with the corpus of religious vernacular literature composed of exegetical works, hagiography, homiletic writings, manuals for preachers and confessors, and the collections of exempla that contained a stock of religious figures.[21] An examination of Boccaccio's use of such a repertoire of characters in the *Decameron* indicates the structural importance of the exempla in the

---

20 For a study on work in the *sermones ad status*, see Van Den Hoven, *Work*, 201–43. See Delcorno, *Giordano da Pisa*, 29–80 and especially 37 for the impulse the sermons gave to the development of vernacular literature.

21 Antonia Mazza classifies Ambrose's *Hexaemeron*, Augustine's *Enarrationes in psalmos* (two codices), and Dionigi di Borgo San Sepolcro's commentary to Valerius Maximus among the works certainly belonging to Boccaccio. A relevant piece of data for our analysis is the presence of Basil's homily X, in Rufinus's translation (*PL* 36, 63), which is the preface to the first of the two codices containing Augustine's *Enarrationes*. Among the codices doubtfully attributed to Boccaccio's library are Gregory's *Dialogues*, Alan de Lille's *De arte praedicandi*, and William of Auxerre's *Summa*. Mazza does not specify the reasons for the exclusion of Alan de Lille's volume, which Boccaccio likely knew. The inventory of Santo Spirito's "parva libraria" was compiled only in 1451, so many volumes belonging to Boccaccio were not included in it. Among these there is a very important codex, the MS Ambrosiana Milan, *Ambrosiano* 204 f, containing Boccaccio's autograph of Aristotle's *Ethics* copied together with Aquinas's commentary. Boccaccio's knowledge of ancient *sillogi* of edifying examples can be deduced from the implicit and explicit quotations scattered in his works and highlighted by the studies dedicated to the relation between the Boccaccian novella and the exempla.

economy of the multi-layered narrative of the ten days, and reveals the author's technique of transforming an exemplum into a novella. This transformation is based not only on narrative amplification but also – and principally – on the subversion of the linear relation between example and reality, in which disguise and change of identity play a major role. Nevertheless, it is generally agreed that the novelle retain a certain degree of exemplarity since they are set in the judgmental frame of the narrators' introductions and comments. By focusing on human action, however, the Boccaccian novella loses the eschatological perspective of the exemplum and develops its ethical dimension within the framework of a Christian providential vision, as Vittore Branca and Chiara Degani note:

> Nel *Decameron* al fine spirituale, suasorio ed edificante, metafisico-escatologico dell'*exemplum* si sostituisce una rappresentazione risolutamente narrativa, una visione soprattutto comportamentale – o addirittura utilitaria – sia pure all'interno di una generale visione provvidenziale. (Branca and Degani, "Studi sugli 'Exempla,'" 184–5)
>
> [The *Decameron*'s primarily behavioural, and perhaps even utilitarian, vision replaces the spiritual, suasive, edifying, metaphysical, and eschatological goals of the exemplum, although it accomplishes this within a general vision of Providence. (Translation mine)]

Carlo Delcorno has shown that Boccaccio intentionally structured the rhetoric of Tedaldo's discourse to Monna Ermellina on the prevalent models of medieval preaching, directed at the edification not only of the public but also of the preachers themselves (sermons *ad clerum*).[22] Boccaccio's choice of this preaching model suggests an indirect hint at the intent of the novella: that of moralizing the moralizers. The secularization of the clerics in the urban context had undermined the moral authority of the preachers, thus destabilizing the effectiveness of exemplary teaching.

Criticism of the practical moral theology of the mendicant orders is not, however, the only key element to understanding the narrative and meta-narrative mechanisms of Tedaldo's story. The reference to courtly

22 The exhortation to "concordia actionum" typically introduced the preachers' sermons directed to the clergy ("ad clerum"). For the structure, diffusion, and modalities of this preaching activity developed by the mendicant orders, particularly the Dominicans, see Delcorno, "La 'predica,'" 61–8.

literature is also evident in the novella, and studies such as that of Antonio Franceschetti have evidenced the resonances of Andreas Capellanus's *De amore* in the narrative structure of the story.[23]

I would like to take a step further in this critical tradition by arguing that the parodic interplay of religious and secular elements within Boccaccio's ethical perspective is integral to a full understanding of the novella. These elements are purposely connected to form an internal dialogue that illustrates a problematic aspect of communal customs relative to adultery and, more generally, to love. The dimensions of the sacred and the profane, and their institutional literary counterparts, combine in the language and structure of the novella by hinging on the inverted relation between appearance and reality. Tedaldo impersonates in a parody both the chivalric and the exemplary teaching on adulterous love. His emblematic transformations reveal that, while in the code of courtly love concealment is motivated by the necessity to hide adultery, in religious preaching it results from the discrepancy between preached and pursued values; between exemplum and exemplar. For Tedaldo, religious discourse is nothing but rhetoric employed to hide the vices of its ministers. In both the courtly and the predicatory discourses, language is a means to mask a truth that (for the readers) is contrary to Christian precepts. What can be called the "function of disguise" is therefore crucial to the narrative scheme of the comedy that the characters of the story enact.

The novella moves from one disguise to the other in a climax of successive exemplary transformations. Teldaldo's incessant concealments and changes of identity alert the reader that Boccaccio is narratively exploiting the art of *celare* (hiding) to hint at the dramatized relation between words and actions, appearance and truth, good preaching and bad deeds. It also presents the limits of a penitential form of religiosity, which – with its medieval language and imagery – was not able to interact effectively with the mentality of the communal society. Disguise is thus both the representation of the moral codes being critiqued and the strategic narrative device Boccaccio uses to engineer a story that illustrates the common weaknesses of the doctrines and ideologies of love and, most importantly, of the moral teachings of his contemporary society.

An analysis of the novella shows how the courtly and the religious elements surface and intertwine in its narrative structure. Its complex plot is summarized in the rubric:

---

23 See Franceschetti, "Dall'amore cortese."

Tedaldo, turbato con una sua donna, si parte di Firenze; tornavi in forma di peregrino dopo alcun tempo; parla con la donna e falla del suo error conoscente, e libera il marito di lei da morte, che lui gli era provato che aveva ucciso, e co' fratelli il pacefica; e poi saviamente colla sua donna si gode. (III.7)

[Tedaldo, being in disfavour with his lady, departs from Florence. He returns thither after a while in the guise of a pilgrim, has speech of his lady, and makes her sensible of her fault. He delivers her husband, convicted of slaying him, from peril of death, reconciles him with his brothers, and thereafter discreetly enjoys his lady.]

In communal Florence, the young and gracious Madonna Ermellina, married to Aldobrandino Palermini, rejects without apparent cause her young and noble lover, Tedaldo degli Elisei. Both Palermini and Elisei were ancient Florentine families, but Boccaccio insists on Tedaldo's nobility and Ermellina's virtuous qualities, while leaving Aldobrandino without qualifications in the role of a neutral *maritz* (husband). It is a classical adulterous situation, where the qualities of *midons* (the lady) win the noble heart of the lover ("innamorato oltre misura per li suoi laudevoli costumi"),[24] who in turn gains her mercy. It is not, however, the *fin'amor* of the Occitan lyric tradition, where the ever-postponed conquest of the object of desire acts as a principle of research of moral perfection. It is instead a secularized version of love (the *fol'amor*), so characterized in the environment in which Tedaldo and Ermellina's passion, not diminished or altered by the fulfilment of their desire, is set.

Apparently following the rules of the courtly code, Boccaccio presents a case of a love so well concealed that no one realizes why or for whom Tedaldo suffers when Ermellina suddenly and firmly refuses to further grant him her favours.[25] Desperate, the nobleman decides to hide his pain from Ermellina and secretly leaves Florence for Ancona under the name

24 "beyond measure enamoured ... by reason of *her* admirable qualities richly deserving to have his desire" (III.7.4; emphasis mine). The sense of the passage, however, seems to indicate that the "qualities" of *madonna* are the cause of his immoderate passion.

25 "In tutta questa prima parte della novella, che è soltanto introduttiva, non può sfuggire il tono favoloso e romanzesco che è così comune nelle *vidas* dei trovatori e nelle situazioni dei romanzi cavallereschi medievali ... L'amore ricambiato e poi negato (e tenuto così segreto che nessuno conosce il vero motivo della tristezza di Tedaldo quando Ermellina lo respinge), la partenza in incognito nota ad un solo amico, la lontananza che dura sette anni, la fortuna negli affari come un eroe cavalleresco l'avrebbe avuta nelle guerre e nei tornei, la canzone da lui stesso scritta al momento della felicità e l'irresistibile desiderio di ritornare sono tutte componenti troppo

of Filippo di Sanlodeccio (only one friend knows, *l'amic*). With this act of self-exile, Tedaldo begins the series of transformations that mark his regressive metamorphosis. After leaving the courtly environment, the comedy is set against the backdrop of a mercantile society, staging a sort of *descensus ad inferos* along the social ladder. In Ancona, Tedaldo becomes the servant of a rich merchant, but in a few years, thanks to his entrepreneurial qualities, he is a partner in the company of his previous master and becomes a renowned and esteemed merchant. After seven years of voluntary exile from Florence (a number charged with spiritual meanings), and while he is in Cipri (another topical name of mercantile epics), Tedaldo hears by chance a love song he had composed for Ermellina.[26] Suddenly taken by nostalgia, he decides to return to Florence, again secretly and in disguise. This time, Tedaldo appears in the clothes of a pilgrim on his way back from the sacred *sepulcher* in Jerusalem. The pilgrim is another key figure of troubadour literature: a knight disguised as a false pilgrim to conquer the carnal love of two damsels figures in a famous lyric by William IX of Aquitaine. Although it is conjectural that Boccaccio may have taken suggestions from the poem of the Duke of Poitier, introducing dramatic elements in this comic text, the lyric could be considered to be an antecedent of novella III.7.[27]

---

tipiche ed indicative" [In the first part of this novella, which is just an introduction, one cannot fail to spot the tone of fables so common in the troubadours' *vidas* and in medieval chivalric romances ... Reciprocated and then denied love (and kept so secret that nobody knows the real reason for Tedaldo's sadness when Ermellina rejects him); the concealed departure known to only one friend; the seven-year absence; Tedaldo's success in business, similar to the success a chivalric hero would have won in tournaments or wars; the song he himself wrote in time of happiness; his irresistible longing to return are all too typical and indicative components (Franceschetti, "Dall'amore cortese," 150; translation mine)].

26 In Tedaldo as a poet in exile, Franco Fido sees the indirect presence of Dante in the *Decameron*: "La memoria del passato viene a tentare e a riscuotere Tedaldo in forma di musica e di poesia, anzi *della sua stessa poesia*. Come non pensare ancora a Dante che ascolta Casella nel secondo canto del Purgatorio?" [The memory of the past, in the form of music and poetry – indeed *of his own poetry* – tempts and shakes Tedaldo. How can one not think of Dante listening to Casella in the second Canto of Purgatory? (Fido, "Dante personaggio," 188; translation mine)].

27 William IX of Aquitaine's poem "Farai un vers" tells the story of a knight who, in the disguise of a monk, pretends to be mute and conquers two ladies. The two introductory strophes of the poem seem to anticipate part of the narrative nucleus of III.7: "Domna non fai pechat mortau / que ama cavalier leau; / mas s'ama monge o clergau, / non a raizo: per dreg la deuri'hom cremar / ab un tezo" [Great mortal sin a lady does / if she won't give us knights her love. / To favor priests instead of us / is a mistake; / and monks?, I'd say we ought to burn / her at the stake]. *The Poetry of William VII.*

Accompanied only by his servant, Tedaldo arrives unrecognized in Florence. His changeable identity and his art of disguise are paradoxically a sign of consistency marking the character of Tedaldo, although his material transformations do not seem to correspond to a real process of interior evolution. The nobleman's play with appearances and his real vicissitudes (Tedaldo's fall from aristocrat to merchant, his relocation from Florence to Ancona, then his return in disguise) have made him unrecognizable even to his own brothers:

> e conoscendosi in tanto trasfigurato e d'abito e di persona da quello che esser soleva quando si partí, che di leggieri non potrebbe essere stato riconosciuto, sicuramente s'accostò ad un calzolaio. (III.7.10)
>
> [He knew that he was so changed from his former semblance, both in dress and in person, that he might not readily be recognized and he had therefore no hesitation in going up to a shoemaker.]

At this point the comedy of errors reaches its climax: Tedaldo finds out that Aldobrandino is in jail, accused by Tedaldo's brothers of having murdered Tedaldo out of jealousy. Disguise and errors concur to produce an equivocal and almost surreal representation of what would have been a possible ending to the story, had Tedaldo not escaped and renounced his original identity. When things seem to be at an impasse, chance once again intervenes to help Tedaldo, for he accidentally overhears a conversation that reveals to him the true identity of the assassins.

It is interesting to note that the theme of the day is here indirectly redefined, for the conclusion of the comedy relies on the crucial role that fortune plays, even in a novella dedicated to ingenuity. What seems to matter the most in Boccaccio's view is the capacity of his characters to respond to the accidental events caused by fortune, which is presented as an unpredictable factor that creates opportunities for human ingenuity to shine.

The entrance of chance on stage is underlined by a narrative pause in which Boccaccio introduces Tedaldo's mental soliloquy "on the number and variety of the errors to which men are liable" (III.7.15), accompanied by his invective against the law and the judges, who are sometimes victims of errors, but more often blind executors of them:

> Tedaldo, udito questo, cominciò a riguardare quanti e quali fossero gli errori che potevano cadere nelle menti degli uomini, (prima pensando a'

fratelli che uno strano avevano pianto e sepellito in luogo di lui, e appresso lo innocente per falsa suspizione accusato, e con testimoni non veri averlo condotto a dover morire) e oltre a ciò la cieca severità delle leggi e de' rettori, li quali assai volte, quasi solliciti investigatori del vero, incrudelendo fanno il falso provare, e sé ministri dicono della giustizia e di Dio, dove sono della iniquità e del diavolo esecutori. (III.7.16)

[What he had heard set Tedaldo musing on the number and variety of the errors to which men are liable: as, first, how his brothers had mourned and interred a stranger in his stead, and then charged an innocent man upon false suspicion, and by false witness brought him into imminent peril of death: from which he passed to ponder the blind severity of laws and magistrates, who from misguided zeal to elicit the truth not unfrequently become ruthless, and, adjudging that which is false, forfeit the title which they claim of ministers of God and justice, and do but execute the mandates of iniquity and the Evil One.]

In this sort of hermeneutical passage on the dramatic relationship between reality and appearance, Boccaccio calls attention to a vital fact of social relevance: the imperfect investigation of appearances in the name of a presumed superior knowledge of truth cannot lead to justice. The only reality we can judge is the one we perceive, and appearance can very well be deceptive. The invective reaches, by analogy, the religious idea of "moral" justice and equally condemns its zealous and blind ministers.

Thanks to his knowledge of the facts and to his quick mind, Tedaldo elaborates a plan to free Aldobrandino and restore Ermellina's love for him. He visits the woman, disguised as a pilgrim from Constantinople sent by God to help her and Aldobrandino. Even Ermellina does not recognize her former lover. Impressed by Tedaldo's familiarity with her case, she mistakes him for a prophet. The series of Tedaldo's transformations achieves here its climax not without comic effects:

di che la donna si maravigliò forte, e avendolo per uno profeta gli s'inginocchiò a' piedi, per Dio pregandolo che, se per la salute d'Aldobrandino era venuto, che egli s'avacciasse per ciò che il tempo era brieve. (III.7.21)

[the lady was lost in wonder, and, taking him to be a prophet, threw herself on her knees at his feet, and besought him for God's sake, if he were come to save Aldobrandino, to lose no time, for the matter brooked no delay.]

Boccaccio stresses the good attitude of Ermellina towards her husband, indirectly pointing at another topical idea of troubadour literature, that true love can exist outside marriage, and that it does not necessarily disrupt the marital relation.[28]

Tedaldo's long and elaborate speech to persuade Ermellina to return his love is considered the critical epicentre of this novella and can be divided into two sections. The first one capsizes a common, negative view of adulterous love: the false prophet convinces Ermellina that her misfortunes were her punishment for sinning against love by abandoning Tedaldo. The second one contains an attack on the friars, as Ermellina reveals that it was her confessor's threat of horrible punishments that forced her to interrupt any relation with her lover:

> La cagione del cruccio furono le parole d'un maladetto frate, dal quale io una volta mi confessai; per ciò che, quando io gli dissi l'amore il quale io a costui portava e la dimestichezza che io aveva seco, mi fece un romore in capo che ancor mi spaventa, dicendomi che, se io non me ne rimanessi, io n'andrei in bocca del diavolo nel profondo del Ninferno e sarei messa nel fuoco pennace. (III.7.28)

> [My harshness was prompted by an accursed friar, to whom I once confessed, and who, when I told him of the love I bore Tedaldo, and my intimacy with him, made my ears so tingle and sing that I still shudder to think of it, warning me that, if I gave it not up, I should fall into the jaws of the Devil in the abyss of hell, and be cast into the avenging fire.]

The figure of the friar, suddenly introduced, links together the two worlds at play in the novella – that of lay customs and that of religious morality – and the respective codes of transmission of their conflicting values: the code of courtly love and the code of practical moral theology of the preaching orders.

Crucial to understanding the dynamic of this novella is the link that Boccaccio implicitly establishes to the *De amore* through the friar's threats of infernal punishments to Ermellina. I suggest that these threats hint at the situation modelled in the fifth dialogue of chapter VI of Capellanus's treatise, dedicated to the art a nobleman should use to

---

28 See Andreas Capellanus, *The Art of Courtly Love* VI, dialogue 7.

speak to a noblewoman of lesser nobility.[29] In this dialogue, the knight convinces *madonna* to reciprocate his love by telling her the allegorical story of his vision of the court of Love, where women are rewarded or punished according to whether they refuse, immoderately accept, or wisely consent to open the gates of Love's castle. The knight illustrates the terrible punishments women experience when they refuse to serve the god, and, frightened by the prospect of these chastisements, the woman consents to open her heart to love.[30]

After Ermellina's confession, Tedaldo, with another *coup de théâtre*, reveals to her that he is actually a friar with authority and cognition sufficient to illustrate to her the truth about this degraded category of man. Tedaldo goes on to lament that modern friars are unlike the monks of the early centuries they had taken as examples of holiness. Their customs, although not their doctrine, had become so secularized that they could no longer act as ethical guides for the people.[31] Thus, he subverts the religious perspective by depriving the confessor's words of any real authority, eloquently demonstrating the friar's unreliability, and attributing to him the worst customs of a corrupted clergy.[32] Building on this premise, Tedaldo adopts an argument reminiscent of – though actually

29 Chapter VI of Capellanus's *The Art of Courtly Love* concerns "In what manner love may be acquired, and in how many ways."

30 So the knight describes his vision of the group of women who refuse all lovers: "Then in the third group there followed a mean and abject troop of women. They were certainly very beautiful, but they were dressed in the most filthy clothes, wholly unsuited to the weather, for although they were in the burning heat of the summer, they wore unwillingly garments of fox skins; besides that, they were very dirty and rode unbecomingly upon unsightly horses – that is, very lean ones that trotted heavily and had neither saddles nor bridles and went along with halting steps." When the knight asks one of the ladies why this group of women is so poorly treated and resides in the zone of "Aridity," she answers: "This army which you see is that of the dead ... subjected to so many other kinds of punishments which no one could know about unless he learned by experience, that it would be impossible for me to tell you about them and very difficult for you to listen to the account." Andreas Capellanus, *The Art of Courtly Love* VI, fifth dialogue (75–8).

31 "Furon già i frati santissimi e valenti uomini, ma quegli che oggi frati si chiamano e cosí volgiono essere tenuti, niuna altra cosa hanno di frate se non la cappa" [Time was when the friars were most holy and worthy men, but those who to-day take the name and claim the reputation of friars have nought of the friar save only the habit (III.7.34)].

32 Tedaldo insinuates that the friar had asked Ermellina to stop seeing her lover only because he wanted to take his place in her bed.

the exact contrary of – the warning of the friar, and convinces Ermellina that she has in fact been punished for refusing her lover. Thus Ermellina is placed before a choice between Christian and pagan punishments, where the authority and effectiveness of the first in curbing passion has been neutralized by the argued moral inconsistency of its preacher. The nobleman's refined words argue in favour of adulterous love by fruitfully applying the same logic attributed to the friars, thus implicitly revealing its limit and its fallacy. His elegant speech eventually overcomes Ermellina's resistance; she is now more scared of betraying the god of Love than the supposedly malicious friar.

Tedaldo's sermon gives voice to a prejudice against the clergy that was widespread in Boccaccio's times, and gives a glimpse of the author's own, more complex, views on the issue of the moralization of the communal society, which was the mission of the religious orders engaged in city life. Paradoxically, however, since these orders had become progressively secularized, they had failed in their attempts to enforce morality. The decline of the friars' spiritual authority was a consequence of a considerable degree of commercialization of the religious status, as priesthood and brethrenhood had become a professional alternative to peasantry and penniless aristocratic status.[33] The character

33 This theme, reflecting one of the causes of the lack of coherence between the friars' words and deeds, is also the object of novella VII.3, connected and almost complementary to III.7. Both novelle VII.3 and III.7 deal with the adulterous love of a nobleman for a non-noble woman, the situation depicted in Andreas Capellanus, *The Art of Courtly Love*, VI.4 and 6. In VII.3, Rinaldo is a gentle young man from Siena who falls in love with madonna Agnesa, a rich man's wife. For unknown reasons Rinaldo becomes a friar and perseveres in his "vocation" of finding in it "good pasture" ("la pastura" [VII.3.7]). After the description of Rinaldo's unbecoming mundane conduct, Elissa pronounces a second invective against mendicant friars which is connected, although in an accentuated comic register, to Tedaldo's dramatic speech: "Ma che dico io di frate Rinaldo nostro di cui parliamo? Quali son quegli che cosí non facciano? Ahi vitupero del guasto mondo! Essi non si vergognano d'apparir grassi, d'apparir coloriti nel viso, d'apparir morbidi ne'vestimenti e in tutte le cose loro, e non come colombi ma come galli tronfi con la cresta levata pettoruti procedono" [But why enlarge upon our Fra Rinaldo, of whom we speak? What friars are there that do not the like? Ah! opprobrium of a corrupt world! Sleek-faced and sanguine, daintily clad, dainty in all their accessories, they ruffle it shamelessly before the eyes of all, shewing not as doves but as insolent cocks with raised crest and swelling bosom (VII.3.8–10)]. Like Tedaldo, to convince his lover Rinaldo devises a para-logic reasoning that is a parody of Scholastic dialectics. Rinaldo's comic mimicry reveals the moral fallacy of this dialectics whenever it is not backed by coherence between practice and theory. In VII.3.17–22, Dioneo recalls Rinaldo's instrumental

of Tedaldo, encompassing both nobility and mercantile status, embodies the reactions of men and women in both of these categories to this increasing secularization of the urban church.

Tedaldo's critique, which reflects the pervasive negative opinion of laymen towards the clergy, centres on the main reason for the crisis of credibility of religious morality: the failure of preachers to show coherence between words and action, what they teach and what they do:

> Perché non seguitano quell'altra santa parola dell'Evangelio: "Incominciò Cristo a fare e a insegnare"? Facciano in prima essi, poi ammaestrin gli altri. (III.7.42–3)
>
> [Why follow they not that other holy text of the Gospel: Christ began to do and to teach? Let them practise first, and school us with their precepts afterwards.][34]

Tedaldo's invective against religious hypocrisy, however, is misplaced: in fact, the confessor in the story does not represent a figure of moral corruption, but one of rigorous religiosity.[35] Nonetheless, penitential religiosity is indirectly under Tedaldo's attack, for the friar "rectifies"

---

utilization of Scholastic syllogism for illicit ends in VII.10.30. Also, Elissa's invective against the friars in VII.3 is addressed to Franciscans and Dominicans, whom she specifically names.

34 The quotation is not from the Gospels, but from Acts 1:1, a text read on the Ascension Day, as Hillers has shown in "Two Notes on the 'Decameron.'"

35 As Francesco Bruni observes, Boccaccio "distingue con chiarezza fra ossequio ai principi religiosi (dei quali era osservante) e parodia e critica della società ecclesiastica"; "Tedaldo degli Elisei non si può considerare senz'altro il portavoce delle idee dello scrittore"; "tanta severità degna di un autentico riformatore religioso, è mossa dall'intenzione di riavere la donna e di salvarne il marito, ingiustamente accusato di omicidio: realtà e apparenza non coincidono, perché l'ucciso non è Tedaldo, perché l'assassino non è il marito di Ermellina, ma anche perché Tedaldo è un innamorato travestito da profeta, non è un profeta" [clearly distinguishes among compliance with religious principles (which he observed), and parody and criticism of ecclesiastical society; Tedaldo degli Elisei cannot be considered the spokesman of the author's ideas; such severity, worthy of an authentic religious reformer, originates from Tedaldo's desire to win back the woman and to save her husband, unjustly accused of murder. Reality and appearance do not coincide, not only because the murdered man is not Tedaldo and the assassin is not Ermellina's husband, but also because Tedaldo is a lover disguised as a prophet, he is not a prophet (Bruni, *L'invenzione*, 249, 257; translation mine)].

Ermellina's moral conduct by using fear and superstition to make her respect the principles of the Christian sacrament of marriage. Taking into account both the literal and the implicit meaning of Tedaldo's sermon, it seems evident that, in the aristocrat-merchant's view, both penitential religiosity and the secularization of the clergy, one by allowing and the other by failing to prevent adulterous love, were disrupting factors in the new equilibrium of values that characterized the mercantile society of the time.[36]

In these two causes of religious decadence, and particularly in the gap between the preachers' words and actions, Boccaccio saw a sign of the inadequacy of the Church's moral teaching, which resulted in a general prejudice against the clerics' hypocrisy and a consequent lassitude in the people's customs. The attempt of the Church to moralize its own members, and fight the corruption deriving from their direct involvement with the secular society, resulted in a failure, for the moralizing friars had replaced a lack of good example with fear, and transformed religion into a pagan hellish imagery, thus debasing Christian faith to nothing more than superstition.[37]

Boccaccio had learned from Aristotle that ethics is not about what *is* good, but rather *how to become* good, so that action and the principles of action, word and act, cannot be separated. By returning to an ethics that implied moral knowledge and the responsibility of choice (the "passamento di noia"), the novella indirectly argues for a recovery of the spirit of classical ethics to harmonize the ideal Christian values with the pragmatic reality of mercantile society; that is, a return to those evangelical

36 As Baratto remarks, "a Firenze i *topoi* cortesi della poesia d'amore, ormai scontati, uniti alla libertà dell'avventura erotica propria della tradizione casistica, trovano in Tedaldo una personificazione eloquente: ma calata in una concreta dimensione cittadina, dove si stanno rielaborando i miti di una nuova aristocrazia laica" (Baratto, *Realtà*, 142).

37 Boccaccio's criticism of "good preaching and bad doing" was general and involved all categories of clerics represented in the *Decameron*. The same criticism, confirming the Church's awareness of the magnitude of this problem, was expressed also in the medieval preachers' manuals: "Di fatto l'esortazione a predicare *verbo et exemplo* è già attestata nella *Regula pastoralis* di S. Gregorio, e diventa un luogo comune delle *artes praedicandi* nel secolo XIII, soprattutto in presenza della propaganda ereticale" [In fact the exhortation to preach *verbo et exemplo* was already in Gregory the Great's *Regula pastoralis* and became commonplace in the *artes praedicandi* of the thirteenth century, especially in times of heretical propaganda (Delcorno, "La 'predica,'" 64; translation mine)].

and philosophical guides that Boccaccio as a humanist was already advocating. This seems to be the message conveyed by the exemplary story of Tedaldo and Ermellina, which happily ends with the general reconciliation of all opposing parties and the order ironically restored, with Aldobrandino encouraging his wife and her lover's embraces, and the identity of Tedaldo undetermined until the end. Indeed, recognition comes with an external epilogue, in which the identity of the murdered man – a double of Tedaldo – is revealed. Truth thus symbolically emerges outside the limits of the rhetorical traditions illustrated by the story, in a sort of extra-diegetical domain where (and only there) factual reality eventually reconciles with appearance. The happy ending of the story of Tedaldo, with the triumph of his concealment, illustrates the secular and religious literary discourses' failure to establish the moral ground necessary for the edification of the Christian mercantile society.

The Tale of Ferondo's Purgatory (III.8)

MARTIN EISNER

Boccaccio invites his readers to interpret the *Decameron* in a Dantean context from his first statement of the work's title: "Comincia il libro chiamato *Decameron*, cognominato prencipe Galeotto" [Here begins the book called *Decameron*, surnamed Galeotto].[1] The meaning of Boccaccio's appropriation of the name of Lancelot and Guinevere's go-between, Galeotto, which is used by Francesca in *Inferno* V to characterize the pandering role played by the Arthurian romance and its author in her relationship with Paolo, has been debated by critics (is it a proclamation of intent or a warning?), but its very existence indicates the special nature of Boccaccio's relationship with Dante.[2] Not prey to the "anxiety of influence" that plagued Petrarch's dealings with the older poet, Boccaccio overtly transforms Dante's texts to make new meanings throughout his

1 "Comincia il libro chiamato *Decameron*, cognominato prencipe Galeotto, nel quale si contengono cento novelle in dieci dí dette da sette donne e da tre giovani uomini" (Boccaccio, *Decameron*, Proem 1). All quotations from *Decameron* are from Branca's edition of 1992 (Turin: Einaudi); translations are my own unless otherwise noted. For a stimulating discussion of how this naming functions in the text, see Stillinger, "The Place of the Title." Whereas Boccaccio reduces the members of the *brigata* to emblematic single names "alle qualità di ciascuna convenienti o in tutto o in parte" [suitable wholly or in part to the qualities of each one], he gives the collection itself a surname.

2 Mazzotta, *The World at Play*, 56–7 argues that "Aware of literature as an erotic snare – a commonplace of medieval romances – Boccaccio seems intent on assigning to this text the role of erotic mediator, and thus unmasking the threats and seductions of his own artifact." For a brief survey of interpretations of Boccaccio's use of Galeotto, see Hollander, *Boccaccio's Two Venuses*, 102–6. On Boccaccio's knowledge and use of the Arthurian tradition of which Galeotto is a part, see Delcorno Branca, "Tradizione arturiana in Boccaccio."

career, from his earliest *ars dictaminis* exercises to the editions of Dante's works he makes at the end of his life.[3]

The tale of Ferondo's Purgatory has not yet been examined as part of the Dantean network of the *Decameron*.[4] Critics have considered Boccaccio's invocation of Dante in this story to be simply "generic" (Hollander, *Boccaccio's Dante*, 4). This essay argues instead that the story constitutes one of Boccaccio's most acute challenges to Dante's claims to truth in the *Commedia*. Located at the intersection of two prominent Dantean patterns in the *Decameron* (one involving the storyteller, Lauretta, and the other Day Three as a whole), this tale represents Purgatory as a non-transcendent place variously constructed by different stories about it. Purgatory is an ideal space for Boccaccio's challenge because it is the least defined and most contested of the otherworldly places whose contours "arose as much from imagery as from reasoning, as much from fantastic tales as from authorities," as Jacques Le Goff demonstrates in *The Birth of Purgatory* (259).[5] Building on the scepticism about human knowledge of the other-world announced by Panfilo at the end of the story of

3 Petrarch's complex relationship with Dante can be seen in *Familiares* 21.15. Boccaccio's *ars dictaminis* exercises are *Crepor celsitudinis* (Ep. 1) and *Mavortis milex* (Ep. 2). On these letters, see Billanovich, *Restauri boccacceschi*, 49–78. Boccaccio's transcriptions of Dante are found in three manuscripts that are now four: Toledo 104.6, Riccardiano 1023, and the original configuration of what are now Chigi L V 176 and Chigi VI 213, both in the Vatican Library.

4 Novelle that have been identified by critics as key moments in Boccaccio's relationship with Dante in the *Decameron* include those of Ser Cepperello (I.1: Hollander, "Boccaccio's Dante: Imitative Distance" and Usher, "A 'ser' Cepparello"), Frate Alberto (IV.2: Auerbach, "Frate Alberto," in *Mimesis*; Ascoli, "Boccaccio's Auerbach," and Bettinzoli, "Occasioni dantesche"), Frate Cipolla (VI.10: Hollander, "Boccaccio's Dante: Imitative Distance"), and Tingoccio (VII.10: Bettinzoli, "Occasioni dantesche").

5 Dante has an important role in Le Goff's account: he writes that "The theologian who gave the best account of the history of Purgatory was Dante" (*The Birth of Purgatory*, 13). Many have criticized Le Goff's idea that the "birth" of Purgatory coincided with the development of the word *purgatorium* which, in his view, confirms its existence as a "real place," but "the historical role of the imagination" (13) that he outlines has been developed further. Peter Brown, "The Decline of the Empire of God" (45–6) argues that "what is usually presented as the emergence of a doctrine of purgatory in the Latin West may best be seen in terms of the inconclusive juxtaposition of two such [imaginative] structures." For critiques of Le Goff, see Edwards, "Purgatory," which argues that Le Goff overstates the novelty of the ternary view of the world that Purgatory creates. Jan Bremmer has proposed an alternative interpretation of the birth of Purgatory as related to the Cathar heresy (*The Rise and Fall of the Afterlife*, 64–9).

Cepperello (I.1), Boccaccio uses the story of Ferondo to challenge the epistemological bases of Dante's claim to truth in the *Commedia* by showing the origins of one man's fictional account of his otherworldly experiences.[6] Using his favourite poet as a testing ground, Boccaccio pushes to the limit the etymology of poets as liars that he will later refute in both the *Genealogie deorum gentilium* and his *Esposizioni sopra la Comedia*.[7]

1. Truth

Lauretta's introduction to the story raises the "problem of truthfulness" in an explicitly Dantean context (Forni, *Adventures in Speech*, 24). Describing the story of Ferondo as "una verità che ha, troppo piú di quello che ella fu, di menzogna sembianza" [a truth that has, much more than it was, the appearance of a lie (III.8.3)], she evokes Dante's description of Geryon as "quel ver c'ha faccia di menzogna" [that truth which has the face of a lie (*Inf.* XVI.124)][8] and, with it, "the *locus classicus* for textual self-awareness in the *Commedia*."[9] At the height of his work's incredibility, when the hybrid monster Geryon ("quella sozza imagine di froda" [that dirty image

---

6 Dante is well aware of the dangers of claiming to know divine justice (see *Par.* XIII.139–42, for example), but he clearly claims for himself a privileged position.

7 In his gloss on the word "poeta" (*Inf.* I.73) in his *Esposizioni sopra la Comedia di Dante*, Boccaccio notes that there are two contrasting etymologies of the word. The first etymology derives the term from Greek *poio*, which is equivalent to the Latin *fingo*, on the basis of which some assert "*poeta* e *mentitore* sieno una medesima cosa" [poet and liar are the same thing]. The other etymology of the word, however, which Boccaccio prefers, means "esquisito parlatore" [exquisite speaker]. Even when poets make things up, he argues, there is truth hidden underneath the story's fictitious veil, as in the case of Dante's *Commedia* or Petrarch's *Buccolica* (Boccaccio's preferred title for Petrarch's *Bucolicum carmen*), "la quale chi prenderà e aprirrà, non con invidia, ma con caritevole discrezione, troverrà sotto alle dure cortecce salutevoli e dolcissimi ammaestramenti" [which whoever will take it and open it not with envy but with generous discernment will find healthful and sweet teaching beneath a hard shell]. Even though they may appear to make things up, then, poets are only hiding deeper truths.

8 Quotations from the *Comedy* are from *La Commedia secondo l'antica vulgata*, ed. Giorgio Petrocchi, 4 vols. (Milan: Mondadori, 1966).

9 Barolini, *The Undivine Comedy*, 58. Boccaccio's gloss to this verse in his *Esposizioni* shows that he takes Dante's vow that he is telling the truth quite seriously: "Il giuramento è in sustanza questo: 'Se io non dico il vero, che questo mio libro non duri lungamente nella grazia delle genti'. Il quale è molto maggior giuramento, quanto a colui che il fa, che molti non stimano; per ciò che, qualunque è colui che in fatica si mette di comporre alcuna cosa, il primo suo disiderio è di pervenire per quella

of fraud] with his false "faccia d'uom giusto" [face of a just man]) appears, Dante declares the truth of his poem and names it a "comedia" for the first time (*Inf.* XVI.124–36). Critics have thus interpreted "that truth which has the face of a lie" as Dante's positive definition of his *comedìa*, which therefore stands implicitly in opposition to the term "Galeotto" that he condemns in *Inferno* V. Just as Boccaccio appropriates Dante's word for the kind of work Dante did not want his poem to be in the title of his work (Galeotto), Boccaccio uses Dante's positive definition of his poem and its veracity in the story of Ferondo to proclaim the truth of a story about false tales of the other world.

Lauretta's allusion to Dante is not accidental, but part of a larger pattern to be found in her stories. The subject of her first novella (I.8) is a character from *Inferno* XVI, Guglielmo Borsiere, and her penultimate story (IX.8) offers an elaborate tale of encounters between several Dantean figures, including Ciacco and Filippo Argenti, as well as Corso Donati.[10] The thematic link between these stories is further underlined by a numeric connection: they occur in the eighth position of their respective days, like the story of Ferondo's Purgatory. This pattern that

---

composizione in fama e in notizia delle genti; e, appresso, è che questa fama duri lungamente, né maggior cruccio potrebbe avere che il poter credere la sua gran fatica dover brieve tempo durare" [In substance, the oath is this: "If I don't speak the truth, let my book not last long in the favour of people." That is a much greater oath for the one who swears it than many understand, since the first desire of anyone who begins the labour of composing something is to become famous through that work and known to people; and, after that, that this fame last for a long time, nor could there be greater grief than being able to believe that his labour must last a short time]. The verse, which leads Boccaccio to reflect on the desire of an author for his work to endure and attain lasting fame, may also be read as a gloss on "come l'uom s'etterna" [how man makes himself eternal (*Inf.* XV.85)], to use the Pilgrim's words to Brunetto Latini in the previous canto. This connection may suggest that Boccaccio is aware of Brunetto's *Trésor* as the potential source for the verse "quel ver c'ha faccia di menzogna," as Pasquini notes (*Dante e le figure del vero*, 79).

10 *Inferno* XVI occupies a central place in Lauretta's Dantean imagination. Ciacco's role in the poem, for example, goes beyond his damnation of gluttony in *Inferno* VI, since he also announces the political decline of Florence and indicates to Dante where he will find those who, to the Pilgrim Dante's mind, "a ben far puoser li 'ngegni" (*Inf.* VI.81), two of whom he will encounter in the circle of the sodomites in *Inferno* XVI. The other three worthy ones mentioned by the Pilgrim are Farinata degli Uberti, who appears in *Inferno* X, and Mosca, who is present in *Inferno* XXVIII. The figure of Arrigo mentioned by Dante in his conversation with Ciacco does not appear later in the poem.

Figure 1. Dantean Structures Surrounding *Decameron* III.8

		Lauretta's Stories ↓		
		I.8 (Guglielmo Borsiere)		
References to Dante's Works →	III.1, 4 (Paradise)	III.8 (Purgatory)	III.10 (Hell)	III. Conclusion (*Vita nuova*/Lauretta's *ca*
		IX.8 (Ciacco, Filippo Argenti)		

associates Lauretta, Dante, and the number eight is not accidental: her penultimate story (IX.8) is the eighty-eighth overall and she is queen for the eighth day.[11]

The vertical pattern that associates Lauretta, Dante, and the number eight intersects with a horizontal pattern that critics have found in the third day, which offers an itinerary of otherworldly places that reverses those of Dante's journey, moving from Paradise (III.1 or III.4) to Purgatory (III.8) and Hell (III.10). Critics have mapped this scheme in various ways, but a consideration of the day's Conclusion, which has not yet been incorporated into these analyses, solidifies the Dantean nature of this pattern.[12] When Lauretta sings at the end of the day, her *canzone* "diversamente

---

11 Boccaccio's decision to associate Lauretta and her Dantean stories with the number 8 should be interpreted as further parody of Dante and his association of Beatrice with the number 9. For an interpretation of the number 8 as the numeral of justice, see Kirkham, "Guglielmo Borsiere," in Weaver, ed., *The Decameron: First Day in Perspective*, 297, which repeats her observations in "An Allegorically Tempered *Decameron*," 13.

12 This pattern has been variously mapped by critics. Fido, "Dante personaggio mancato nel *Decameron*," identifies III.4, 8, and 10 as the itinerary. In his reading, Boccaccio's reuse of these otherworldly toponyms is "giochi irriverenti, se non veramente blasfemi." Kirkham, "Love's Labors Rewarded," includes III.1 and III. Introduction in her mapping of these otherworldly spaces and offers an alternative, moralized interpretation of it. Scordilis Brownlee, "Wolves and Sheep," 265 sees a "progression from the Earthly Paradise with which the day begins, passing through the intermediate stage of Purgatory with Ferondo, to its conclusion in Hell, metaphorically exemplified by Alibech." Ascoli, "Boccaccio's Auerbach," 389 reduces the other worlds to III.1, III.8, and III.10: "the 'other world' systematically translated into this world (and in an order which reverses Dante's) – as a series of stories move us from a kind of (terrestrial) Paradise (Masetto) to a false Purgatory (Ferondo) to Alibech's 'ninferno' (the Hell of nymphomania)."

da diversi fu intesa" [was understood differently by different people], just as the first sonnet of Dante's *Vita nuova* "fue risposto da molti e di diverse sentenzie" [was responded to by many with different meanings].[13] The conflicting interpretations of these poems are similarly left unresolved in both texts.[14] This pattern thus reverses the trajectory of Dante's works, from the *Vita nuova* to the *Comedy*, which Boccaccio would later transcribe in their proper order in two of his Dante editions.

These two intersecting structures, which are diagrammed in figure 1, not only encourage a reading of the story of Ferondo in light of Dante but also provide valuable points of comparison that bring into relief

---

13 Lauretta's *canzone* recounts the experiences of a once happily married woman, who is widowed and then marries a jealous second husband. Lauretta makes clear that the poem is one of her own ("delle mie" [III.Concl.9]) and, given the attention that is called to her allegorical name when she is crowned at the end of Day Seven and the invitation to allegorical interpretation with which the scene ends, Aldo Rossi has suggested that Lauretta sings as the laurel crown whose name she emblematically shares. See Rossi, "Dante, Boccaccio e la laurea poetica." Lauretta's being crowned by herself literalizes Virgil's final words to Dante: "io te sovra te corono e mitrio." On the basis of Boccaccio's long-standing concern with the fact that Dante did not receive the laurel crown and his identification of Petrarch's beloved Laura as "Lauretta," which Boccaccio interprets as the laurel crown in his *Life of Petrarch*, Rossi argues that Dante is the first husband and Petrarch the jealous second husband. In his *De vita et moribus Domini Francisci Petracchi de Florentia*, Boccaccio understands Laura, whom he calls Lauretta, to be the laurel crown ("Laurettam illam allegorice pro laurea corona quam postmodum est adeptus accipiendam existimo" [*Vita di Petrarca*, 26]). Petrarch defends himself from accusations that Laura is not real in a letter to Giacomo Colonna (*Familiares* II, 9). The namesake of Petrarch's beloved Lauretta/laurel crown would thus be singing a lament for her relationship to Petrarch while yearning for her former ties to Dante. The idea of the allegorical marriage may recall Poverty's betrothal to Francis following her long widowhood after Jesus' death recounted by Dante's Aquinas in *Paradiso* XI. Whether or not this literary historical fantasy is the meaning of the poem, it might not be entirely out of place in the "mini-Parnaso" that Jonathan Usher detects in the description of the location of the day's storytelling ("Industria e acquisto erotico," 101). Zanni, "La poesia del *Decameron*," 79–85 provides a detailed consideration of the language of *canzone* in the context of Dante's lyrics.

14 Dante writes that "Lo verace giudicio del detto sogno non fue veduto allora per alcuno, ma ora è manifestissimo a li più semplici" [the true meaning of the dream was not understood by anyone at the time, but is now clear to the simplest (*Vita nuova* III.15)], while for Lauretta's song there is an interpretation of those "di piú sublime e migliore e piú vero intelletto, del quale al presente recitar non accade" [of more sublime, better, and true intelligence, which it is not necessary to recite at present (III.Concl.18)], which contrasts with the reading "alla melanese" which takes the song to mean that "fosse meglio un buon porco che una bella tosa" [it was better to have a good pig than a beautiful girl].

its particular concerns with issues of truth and narrative. Whereas Lauretta's other novelle revivify Dantean characters for tales of cleverness and wit (I.8 and IX.8), her allusion to Dante in the story of Ferondo raises the issue of truth telling. Likewise, while the otherworldly places in the other stories of Day Three are ironic names for erotic desires, like Frate Puccio's Paradise of orgasm in III.4 and the Inferno of Alibech's vagina in III.10, Purgatory never acquires the same kind of sexual significance, even though it is created by the abbot of the story to achieve his own sexual desires.[15] Purgatory is not simply resignified in an erotic key but presented as a place of contrasting and competing narratives, defined differently by Ferondo, the monk who does the abbot's bidding, and the other townspeople. Boccaccio even introduces a larger cultural perspective in his discussion of the distinct eschatological imagining of the Old Man of the Mountain. While the story of Ferondo occurs in a richly Dantean context, its dramatization of competing definitions of otherworldly places and concern with truth distinguish it from the stories that surround it.

The Deputati, who were responsible for expurgating the *Decameron* for the Giunti edition of 1573, seem to have been sensitive to these issues of textual truth and their Dantean context. In their transformation of the story, they make the unnamed abbot who engineers Ferondo's departure to an artificial purgatory into a necromancer named Guido Bonatti, after a character mentioned by Dante in *Inferno* XX among the diviners. The Deputati connect the story of Ferondo with the only other naming of the *Comedy* in the poem, where the issue of textual truth once again comes to the fore.[16] In the episode immediately preceding Bonatti's appearance, Dante has Virgil correct his story about the founding of Mantua that he tells in the *Aeneid*, forcefully concluding:

---

15 This ordered pattern of reference not only reverses the narrative and moral order of Dante's presentation in the *Commedia* but also resignifies those places less as metaphysical spaces than as sexualized locales: the nuns' enclosure becomes a garden of sexual delights, while the term Inferno is used to describe Alibech's vagina, which is another kind of enclosure.

16 Such attentiveness to the text should not surprise. The Deputati were concerned that their changes would make them, in their Petrarchan phrase, "favola del volgo," and made their alterations of the text with the unexpurgated work securely in mind. As a modern editor of their works observes, their modifications constitute nothing less than "una lettura del *Decameron*." Giuseppe Chiecchi, "*Dolcemente dissimulando*," 94 and xi. On the identities of the Deputati, who included Vincenzio Borghini, see xix–xxv.

Però t'assenno che, se tu mai odi
originar la mia terra altrimenti,
la verità nulla menzonga frodi.

[Therefore, I admonish you: if you ever hear another tale of my homeland, do not let any lie defraud the truth. (*Inf.* XX.97–9)]

Teodolinda Barolini interprets Virgil's implicit attribution of falsehood to what he calls a few lines later "l'alta mia tragedìa" [my high tragedy (XX.113)] in contrast to Dante's second and final naming of his poem as a *comedìa* at the beginning of the next canto. She argues that Dante "achieves his redefinition of the term *comedìa* by contextualizing it vis-à-vis *tragedìa* in ways that align *comedìa* (Dante) with truth and *tragedìa* (Virgil) with falsehood, *menzogna*."[17] By evoking this episode with their choice of the name Guido Bonatti, the Deputati pick up on the Dantean resonances of Lauretta's introductory description and tie it even more strongly to the Dantean context in which it occurs, while also connecting it to another major episode where Dante asserts the truth of his poem.

2. Lies

While Dante uses the dialectic between truth and lie to emphasize the truthfulness of his *Commedia*, Lauretta's transformation of the Dantean phrase into "di menzogna sembianza" [appearance of a lie] underlines the disjunction between appearance and reality that is one of the main themes of the novella and "uno dei Leitmotive del *Decameron*" as a whole (Rossi, "Ironia e parodia nel *Decameron*," 388). The deceitful abbot embodies this tension between appearance and reality. He is "santissimo fuori che nell'opera delle femmine" [very holy except in his dealings with women (III.8.4)]. When he becomes attracted to the "bellissima"

17 Barolini, *The Undivine Comedy*, 59. In this episode, according to Barolini, *Dante's Poets*, 220, Dante "distinguish[es] between three kinds of prophet: the utterly false, housed in the fourth *bolgia* and exemplified by its inhabitants; the unwitting prophet, who is unknowingly a carrier of both truth and falsehood, a type exemplified by Virgil, whom Dante both accepts and corrects according to his perception of whether he is dealing with *verità* or *menzogna*; and the unconditionally true prophet, whose vision is divinely sanctioned, exemplified by Dante himself." Dante's insistent distancing of himself from lies crops up again in Cacciaguida's commission of him to write the poem: "rimossa ogne menzogna, / tutta tua vision fa manifesta; / e lascia pur grattar dov'è la rogna" (*Par.* XVII.127–9).

wife of the "ricchissimo villano" Ferondo, who is a "uomo materiale e grosso senza modo," he spends time "nel giardino della badia" [in the garden of the abbey] speaking with Ferondo and his wife "della beatitudine di vita etterna e di santissime opere di molti uomini e donne passate" [about the blessedness of the eternal life and of the very holy works of many men and past women] in order to seduce her. The abbot's stories about the other world, which are the first of many in the novella, excite in Ferondo's wife a desire to confess to the abbot, which she never quite gets around to doing. Instead, as a prelude to her confession, she laments that, much as she would like to "entrare nel cammino che ragionato m'avete che mena altrui a vita etterna" [enter the path that you have shown me leads other to eternal life],[18] the jealousy of her husband prevents her from having any other "marito" [husband].

Although her reference appears to be to the prospect of becoming a nun and becoming "married to Christ," her characterization of religious life as a marriage recalls the erotic possibilities of the convent explored in the story of Masetto (III.1). Does her equivocal language and her declaration to be a widow ("mi posso dir vedova") suggest that she is making herself available to the abbot?[19] Medieval analogues to this story give a more prominent role to the wife's desires and deceptions. Some earlier versions of it are even used in a contest among women regarding who had best deceived her husband, but that is not the focus in Boccaccio's tale, where the wife claims to be motivated by a sense of confinement ("in prigione" [III.8.18]) and is not caught *in flagrante delicto*.[20] The mix of the discourses of sexual and spiritual fulfilment throughout the day may arouse suspicion about the wife's motives, but Lauretta's tale does not exploit equivocal language as explicitly as those other tales, so it is difficult to be certain.[21]

---

18 This phrase may echo Panfilo's "assai persone sono che, mentre che essi si sforzano d'andarne in Paradiso, senza avvedersene vi mandano altrui" [there are many people who, while they are trying to go to Paradise themselves, unknowingly send other people (III.4.3)].

19 More might be said about the role of confession in Boccaccio's stories. In an earlier story (III.3), a woman uses the act of confession to make a monk her go-between. In this story, the abbot uses the confessional to express his desires in an extreme demonstration of the dangers of confession already foreseen by penitential manuals.

20 On analogues and their uses in contests, see Lee, *The Decameron*, 98.

21 This resistance to equivocal language may be related to "Lauretta's association with reality," in the *Decameron*, which is noted by Barolini, "The Wheel of the *Decameron*," 536n24.

Although the wife is "the most ambiguous character in the whole story," the abbot's motives are clear.[22] She is seated at his feet ("a piè postagli a sedere" [III.8.7]) and he only needs to secure her confidence before proceeding with his scheme of seduction. He suggests that they can heal Ferondo's jealousy by sending him to Purgatory. Ferondo's wife confirms her compliance in a phrase that once again echoes a moment in Dante's poem that is concerned with the truth of texts. "Padre mio," she responds, "io mi lascierei innanzi morire che io cosa dicessi ad altrui che voi mi diceste che non dicessi" [My father, I would rather let myself die than say something to someone else that you told me not to say (III.8.12)]. Her *variatio verbi* recalls Dante's polyptoton "Cred'io ch'ei credette ch'io credesse" [I believe that he believed that I believed (*Inf.* XIII.25)] in the wood of the suicides. This flagrant fabrication of language, which calls attention to its own rhetorical structure, stands in tension with the claims of textual truth that occupy the episode as a whole, where Dante confirms through his experience with Pier della Vigna the truth of the Virgilian episode of Polydorus: men can metamorphose into trees. Lauretta changes the phrase to relate the problem of speech (*dire*) that underlies the Dantean verse's concern with belief (*credere*). Questions of speech are questions of belief: language constructs other worlds, explains apparitions, recounts otherworldly experiences, and helps to seduce other people's wives.

This rhetorical display may suggest that the wife is a more willing participant than she initially appears, but it is the abbot's language that is the centre of the story. His seduction intensifies when he shifts the tone of his speech from that of the paternal confessor to the courtly lover: "ma che guiderdon debbo io aver da voi di così fatto servigio?" [but what reward should I have from you for such a service? (III.8.19)] he asks. Although Ferondo's wife attempts to maintain their paternal relationship (or simulates a desire to maintain it) by using "padre mio" twice in her responses to his advances (III.8.20, 24), she cannot derail the abbot's amorous discourse. Adopting the rhetoric of the courtly poet, he no longer addresses her as "Figliuola mia" (III.8.10) but as "Madonna" and "Anima mia bella." At the same time that he reveals his desire with rhetorical flair ("io ardo tutto e mi consumo" [I'm burning all over and I'm consumed by my love]), the abbot develops a clever distinction

22 Bramanti, "Il 'Purgatorio' di Ferondo," 182: "[i]l personaggio più ambiguo di tutta quanta la storia."

between body and soul to convince Ferondo's wife that his desires do not besmirch his holiness. "La santità," he explains, "dimora nell'anima" [sanctity lies in the soul], while what he asks of her is only a "peccato del corpo" [sin of the body]. The abbot plays on the contrast between appearance and reality that Lauretta claims for her story as a whole and uses it to his own sophistic advantage. He clinches his argument by flattering his object of desire that her beauty "piaccia a' santi, che sono usi di vedere quelle del cielo" [pleases the saints, who are accustomed to heavenly beauties (III.8.25)] and promising to give her "di belli gioielli e di cari" [some beautiful and expensive jewels]. Although the lady still appears hesitant or feigns such hesitations, the ring that he secretly puts in her hand ("postole celatamente in mano un bellissimo anello" [III.8.29]) seems to seal the agreement. When she returns to her friends, she "maravigliose cose cominciò a raccontare della santità dello abate" [began to recount marvellous things about the holiness of the abbot] in what may be a deceptive use of language that confirms her complicity.[23]

The dualist sophistry of this seduction speech with its hyperbolic praise anticipates the novella of Frate Alberto (IV.2), which also locates the beginning of desire in the confessional.[24] The complex parodic operations of both of these stories caused the Deputati considerable anguish, and they defend them as social critiques targeted at "que' religiosi che si servissino del titolo o della autorità delle cose sacre a sadisfazione de' loro disonesti appetiti e generalmente delle cose di Dio a utile di mondo o cattivo fine" [those religious who use the title and authority of holy things to satisfy their dishonest desires and generally use things of God for some worldly or bad design].[25] For them, the story

23 Migiel, *A Rhetoric of the "Decameron"*, 74 emphasizes the resistance of Ferondo's wife to the abbot's desires, noting that "she becomes more receptive to him when he gives her gifts, and she does not concede herself to him until after her husband has 'died' and gone to Purgatory." While Ferondo's wife initially acquiesces "vergognosamente" (III.8.28), the fact that the gift of "un bellissimo anello" appears to be enough to convince her to tell her friends extraordinary things about the sanctity of the abbot, which she knows to be false, suggests that she may be playing her own game of manipulation and have her own cupidinous, though not necessarily sexual, motives.

24 Both stories also share references to the Angel Gabriel and an appeal to celestial figures who admire the woman's beauty.

25 See Usher, "Discorsi d'oltretomba nel *Decameron*," 52, who echoes the Deputati in his interpretation of Tedaldo's discourse in III.7.37: "L'oggetto della critica del Certaldese non è la dottrina del Purgatorio di per sé, bensì gli abusi commessi sopratutto dai religiosi."

is not heretical or blasphemous, since it is not an accusation against all religious, but only those who deceive others.

This critique of certain religious is, however, connected to a larger investment in the non-transcendent that led De Sanctis to characterize the *Decameron* as a "commedia umana" (*Storia della letteratura italiana*, 340). Erich Auerbach reformulates this idea in his analysis of the story of Frate Alberto, which argues that the *Decameron* lacks the figural dimension that characterizes Dante's *Commedia*. "Of the figural-Christian conception of which pervaded Dante's imitation of the earthly and human world and which gave it power and depth," Auerbach writes, "no trace is to be found in Boccaccio. Boccaccio's characters live on earth and only on earth" (*Mimesis*, 224). In a cogent critique of Auerbach, Albert Ascoli argues that what Auerbach characterizes as a lack is actually Boccaccio's conscious and intentional strategy to take on "the very figural superstructure, and the vision of history which it implies, that Auerbach claims has disappeared from Boccaccio's work."[26] Ferondo could be read as part of a similar project that critiques not the figural superstructure of the *Commedia* but its epistemological bases by providing a demystified and non-transcendent account of the origins of a story about the other world.

Lauretta's lengthy description of the origins of the "polvere di maravigliosa virtù" that will cause Ferondo to appear to be dead presents another challenge to Dante's claim to truth by introducing a wider cultural context and another kind of other world. She explains that the abbot:

> la quale [polvere] nelle parti di Levante avuta avea da un gran principe, il quale affermava quella solersi usare per lo Veglio della Montagna, quando alcun voleva dormendo mandare nel suo Paradiso o trarlone, e che ella, piú e men data, senza alcuna lesione faceva per sí fatta maniera piú e men dormire colui che la prendeva, che, mentre la sua vertú durava, non avrebbe mai detto colui in sé aver vita. (III.8.31)

> [had in his possession a powder of marvellous strength which had been given to him by a great prince of the East who claimed that it was used by the Old Man of the Mountain whenever he wanted to put someone to

26 Ascoli, "Boccaccio's Auerbach," 387. The parodic impulse of the story particularly with respect to Dante is also emphasized by Branca, *Boccaccio medievale*, 342–3, who notes its deformations of Dante's lyric works.

sleep and send him to his Paradise and then bring him back again, and that, according to the quantity of the dosage, the person who took it would sleep for a greater or lesser time without hurting himself, and that while its strength lasted, no one would ever believe the person to be alive.][27]

This detailed description of the drug's derivation constitutes one of the more marvellous elements in the tale, but its meaning has not been explored by critics.[28] Given that the drug's history could just as easily have been left unremarked and undiscussed, what is the purpose of the digression? The story of the Old Man of the Mountain introduces an alternative image of an other world, the Old Man's "Paradiso," which offers a comparative context in which to understand the eschatological imaginings that will be offered in the story and echoes the multicultural perspectivism found in the tale of the three rings (I.3).[29] Where the story of Cepperello (I.1) describes the epistemological difficulty for humans in understanding God's judgment, the Old Man offers another model of a man-made Paradise that parallels the one constructed by the abbot for Ferondo.

The comparative perspective on constructed other worlds introduced by the allusion to the Old Man of the Mountain persists in the description of Ferondo's Purgatory. Ferondo is pulled from his "grave" ("sepoltura"),

27 Revised Musa and Bondanella translation, 221.

28 According to the Deputati, "certi moderni chiosatori, con parole assai sconce et dispettose, ne vanno biasimando l'autore, et dicono che finge cose strane et fuor d'ogni verisimile" [certain modern commentators blame the author in very indecent and spiteful words and say that he makes up strange things that lack all verisimilitude (Chiecchi, *Le annotazioni e i discorsi*, 174)], but they note that Boccaccio is using a literary source so he should not be held accountable for its verisimilitude. While the powder is mentioned in texts like Marco Polo's *Il Milione*, as the Deputati note, it does not have a role in analogous tales of deception, where the collective effort of a group or community, rather than a drug, usually convinces a man that he's dead, which is a device that can also be found in the Calandrino stories. (In many of these stories, the death is usually disrupted by a moment of speech that shows that the person is not in fact dead, which is a topos that goes back to Apuleius.) The story would have been known to Boccaccio from not only Marco Polo but also Paolo Veneto, from whose chronicle he transcribes it in his *Zibaldone Magliabechiano*. It is interesting to note that La Fontaine begins his version of the story with a discussion the Old Man in the Mountain.

29 The Old Man of the Mountain often represents the culturally Other, as he does in Novellino 100, where his power to control his minions without speech contrasts with Emperor Frederick's inability to control even his own wife.

and "in una tomba, nella quale alcun lume non si vedea e che per prigione de' monaci che fallissero era stata fatta, nel portarono" [they brought him into a burial vault which was without light and which was constructed as a prison for monks that failed to keep their vows]. The place of Ferondo's confinement had thus been constructed as a place for penance, and its prison-like qualities make it an appropriate location for him to purge himself of the jealousy that had kept his wife "in prigione" (III.8.18).

Ferondo awakes from his three-day, drug-induced sleep to find himself whipped by the abbot's accomplice, a Bolognese monk. Perplexed, he wonders where he is:

> Ferondo, piangendo e gridando, non faceva altro che domandare: "Dove sono io?"
> A cui il monaco rispose: "Tu se' in Purgatoro."
> "Come?" disse Ferondo "dunque sono io morto?"
> Disse il monaco: "Mai sí." (III.8.40–2)

> [Crying and shouting, Ferondo did nothing but ask: "Where am I?"
> To which the monk responded: "You're in Purgatory."
> "What?" Ferondo said. "So I'm dead?"
> "Most definitely," said the monk.]

Ferondo evidently does not feel dead, but he understands from the man who is beating him that he must be dead since he is in Purgatory. He is all the more surprised when his captor brings him something to drink and eat, which provokes him to ask the quite logical question: "O mangiano i morti?" [Do the dead eat?]. When he is told that his wife brought them as offerings for him, he initially praises her ("Domine dalle il buono anno!") and becomes sentimental about their shared physical intimacy ("io me la teneva tutta nocte in braccio"), until he tastes the poor quality of the wine, which leads him to damn the woman he has just praised ("Domine falla trista!").

The detailed representation that arises out of this dialogue defines the world of Purgatory in a way that pointedly reverses Dante's in several particulars: it is dark, not light; it is inhabited by material bodies that consume food rather than aerial ones; it allows for no progress and brings its subject to terrestrial, rather than eternal, life. When he discovers that his jealousy of his wife has caused him to be located in Purgatory, he praises his wife once more and describes her as if she were a piece of food "piú melata che 'l confetto" [sweeter than a sugarplum] but expresses surprise that jealousy is a sin. The monk suggests that if he ever returns to life, he should change his behaviour. Told that he might be able to return, he declares that he will be "il miglior marito del mondo; mai non la batterò, mai non le dirò villania, se non del vino che ella ci ha mandato stamane" [the best husband in the world. I won't beat her or say bad things to her except about the wine that she sent us this morning]. Even as the extraordinary possibility of a return to life is offered to him, he remains fixated on the "culinary" issue of the poor wine and laments the fact that she has not provided any candles by which he might eat his meal; he learns that they have been burned at the mass.[30]

While Ferondo serves his time in Purgatory, the abbot visits Ferondo's wife in the clothes of her putatively dead husband. The exchange of clothing is the external sign of their changed positions. Observed by the villagers, the abbot's visitations give rise to stories that seek to explain his appearances:

> da alcuni e nello andare e nel tornare alcuna volta essendo scontrato, fu creduto che fosse Ferondo che andasse per quella contrada penitenza faccendo; e poi molte novelle tra la gente grossa della villa contatone, e alla moglie ancora, che ben sapeva ciò che era, piú volte fu detto. (III.8.37)
>
> [sometimes he was encountered coming or going and was believed to be Ferondo who went in that place doing penance; and then many tales were recounted among the common people of the village, and they were told to his wife, who knew well enough what it really was.]

Where the abbot's description of the other world has served to excite the wife's desires, and the Bolognese monk's representation of Purgatory has pacified Ferondo's confusion, the townspeople explain the appearance of Ferondo's clothing as his ghost doing penance. They thus understand this ghostly appearance in terms of an old conception of Purgatory found in Gregory the Great, who "situates the place of expiation in this world."[31] While they tell stories among themselves to explain this

30 Sosso, "Le Vilain de Bailluel," 212 notes "le langage tout populaire et 'culinaire' de Ferondo."

31 Le Goff, *The Birth of Purgatory*, 93. Compare the space of punishment in V.8, which also takes place on earth, although it is unclear whether it is Hell or Purgatory.

apparition, Ferondo's wife conceals the truth that the abbot is visiting her in Ferondo's clothes.

While the abbot impersonates Ferondo and his wife vests herself in a widow's garments, Ferondo bears the robes of a monk in a place built for monks to be punished. These reversals come to an end after nearly ten months when Ferondo's wife finds herself pregnant by the abbot. The abbot calls to Ferondo in a disguised voice ("con una voce contraffatta" [III.8.65]), saying:

> "Ferondo, confortati, ché a Dio piace che tu torni al mondo; dove tornato, tu avrai un figliuolo della tua donna, il quale farai che tu nomini Benedetto, per ciò che per gli prieghi del tuo santo abate e della tua donna e per amor di san Benedetto ti fa questa grazia." (III.8.65)

> [Ferondo, be of good cheer for God wants you to return to the world where once you have returned, from your lady you will have a son, whom you will have called Benedict, since this grace is given to you through the prayers of the holy abbot and your lady and through the love of St Benedict.]

In this preposterous parody of Gabriel's annunciation to Zachariah, the abbot reveals the real source of Ferondo's second son, since "through the prayers of the holy abbot and your lady" could well be interpreted as an equivocal term for sexual intercourse, which did, of course, lead to the pregnancy that requires Ferondo's return to the real world.[32] The name that the abbot provides, Benedetto, further parodies both the Annunciation scene and the monastic orders while also continuing the story's concern with speech.

If the Annunciation is about the efficacy of the Word to make (and become) flesh, in this story a simulated death creates a wordsmith. When Ferondo returns from Purgatory he is no longer the "uomo materiale e grosso" of the opening paragraphs, but "quasi savio." Although people are initially scared of his apparent resurrection and run from him, they soon want to hear news from the apparent miracle:

32 This pregnancy is one of two to appear in stories told by Lauretta, as Barolini, "The Wheel of the *Decameron*," notes. She interprets this fact as part of Lauretta's reality. The first son who is mentioned after Ferondo's death could be read as part of this same realism.

> Ma poi che la gente alquanto si fu rassicurata con lui e videro che egli era vivo, domandandolo di molte cose, quasi savio ritornato, a tutti rispondeva e diceva loro novelle dell'anime de' parenti loro, e faceva da sé medesimo le piú belle favole del mondo de' fatti del Purgatoro, e in pien popolo raccontò la revelazione statagli fatta per la bocca del Ragnolo Braghiello avanti che risuscitasse. (III.8.74)
>
> [But once the people were reassured about him and they saw that he was alive, they asked him about many things, and as if he had returned as a wise man, he responded to all of them and told them stories about the souls of their relatives and made up by himself the most lovely fables in the world about features of Purgatory, and in the presence of everyone he recounted the revelation given to him through the mouth of Rangel Bragiel before he was resurrected.]

His purgatorial experiences appear to have taught him that language can create worlds, so he follows in the tradition of verbal artifice that he observed his jailer employing and begins to use it on his fellow townspeople. He tells them stories about relatives he could not have seen and "makes up by himself" facts about his privileged purgatorial experience. The fake purgatory thus has the real effect of curing him of his jealousy and empowering him to act as a visionary.

Ferondo thus becomes a storyteller like Cepperello or Cipolla, both of whom have been associated by critics with Dante.[33] Although the story's rubric emphasizes "la grossezza di Ferondo," it concludes with his narrative triumph. He may not be the father of his own child, but he is able to enjoy a new status among the townspeople. He may not use language to control his world, but he has learned how to use it to construct an other world of which he is in control. In a reversal of the usual turn-about of the trickster tricked, here the tricked Ferondo becomes a trickster.

Carlo Delcorno suggests that Ferondo's storytelling is a "caricatura dei grandi visionari" [caricature of the great visionaries (*Exemplum e letteratura*, 279)], but in light of both the Dantean structures of the storyteller and the day and the explicit allusion to Dante's self-definition of

33 On Cepperello and Cipolla as Dantean figures, see Hollander, "Imitative Distance." For a more detailed analysis of the relationship between Cepperello and Boccaccio's readings of Dante, see Usher, "A 'ser' Cepparello Constructed from Dante Fragments."

his comedy as a truth that has the face of a lie, it seems likely that Dante is the main object of Boccaccio's parody.[34] Where Dante has his character Virgil challenge the poet Virgil's veracity in *Inferno* XX while also defending the truth of his own poem at the height of its unbelievability at the end of *Inferno* XVI, Boccaccio's "truth that has the appearance of a lie" is a causally connected account of a constructed Purgatory, in which a character invents stories about his otherworldly experiences. To challenge Dante's claim to truth, Boccaccio has Lauretta, a storyteller who shows great familiarity with Dante's poem in her other stories, recount a novella about the creation of a fake Purgatory and the fake stories that its only inhabitant tells about it.

3. True Lies

Boccaccio does not challenge Dante's truth claims in the story of Ferondo in order to assert the veracity of his own stories in the *Decameron*, as Dante does with Virgil in the *Comedy*. Instead, he uses the scene of an ignorant storyteller making up tales of the other world to push to its limit the relationship between poet and liar that he also explores in the stories of Cepperello and Cipolla. Boccaccio's experimentation with the association of poets and liars does not, of course, mean that he accepts this definition, which he rejects implicitly in the *Vita di Dante* (I.131–2 and II.85–6) and explicitly in both the *Genealogie* (XIV.7.4) and the *Esposizioni sopra la Comedia* (I.70–1). Boccaccio returns to the scene of an ignorant storyteller making up tales about the other world in his most forceful argument against those who claim that poets are liars and that their works contain no hidden truths in the defence of poetry of the *Genealogie deorum gentilium* (XIV.10). Arguing that "it is a fool's notion that poets convey no meaning beneath the surface of their fictions," he cites Petrarch's *Buccolica* and Dante's *Purgatorio*, as well as his own eclogues, as examples of modern poetry that can contain hidden truths. One might expect such truth from such great men, he continues,

> sed etiam nullam esse usquam tam delirantem aniculam, circa foculum domestici laris una cum vigilantibus hibernis noctibus fabellas orci, seu fatarum, vel Lammiarum, et huiusmodi, ex quibus sepissime inventa conficiunt,

34 Hollander, *Boccaccio's Dante*, 50, makes a similar suggestion regarding Frate Cipolla, whom he regards "as a sort of Dante run amok."

> fingentem atque recitantem, que sub pretextu relatorum non sentiat aliquem iuxta vires sui modici intellectus sensum minime quandoque ridendum, per quem velit aut terrorem incutere parvulis, aut oblectare puellas, aut senes ludere, aut saltem Fortune vires ostendere. (*Genealogie* XIV.10.7)
>
> [but there was never a maundering old woman, sitting with others late of a winter's night at the home fireside, making up tales of Hell, the fates, witches, and the like – much of it pure invention – that she did not feel beneath the surface of her tale, as far as her limited mind allowed, at least some meaning – sometimes ridiculous no doubt – with which she tried to scare the little ones, or divert the young ladies, or amuse the old, or at least show the power of fortune.] (Osgood, *Boccaccio on Poetry*, 54)[35]

In this startling reversal of the Ferondo story, Boccaccio uses the scene of an unlearned person making up stories about the other world to defend the hidden truth content of almost all stories, including what amount to old wives' tales.[36] Boccaccio thus revisits the scene from the story of Ferondo in which he challenged Dante's claim to truth and remakes it into a scene about the hidden truths of all stories. Read from the vantage point of the *Genealogie*, the scene of Ferondo's made-up stories about the other world may indeed have concealed truths. It may be, in other words, "a truth that has the appearance of a lie."

Dante exploits the relationship between truth and lie in the Geryon scene in the *Inferno* to proclaim the truth of his poem. Boccaccio adapts the same phrase used to describe Geryon to preface a story that challenges Dante's claim to truth. He creates an unlearned character who

---

35 I have revised Osgood's "ghosts" to "witches."

36 This chapter revises, as Osgood notes, the apparent dismissal of "old wives' tales" in the previous chapter, where Boccaccio's classification of the four ways of composing fiction appears to discard old wives' tales (XIV.9). Zaccaria (in Boccaccio, *Genealogie*, 176) notes that this chapter (XIV.10) is "non preceduto in riscontri diretti con Petrarca" and therefore constitutes one of Boccaccio's most original contributions to the definition. This concession to old wives' tales is equally a concession to Boccaccio's own past literary productions. Philosophical poetry is clearly not personification allegory alone. The change in gender may well be determined by the old woman who tells the story of Cupid and Psyche in Apuleius's *Metamorphoses*, which had been mentioned in the previous chapter of the *De genealogia*. Marcus suggests that the anecdote is "a kind of limiting case for the allegorical nature of all fictions" ("The Accommodating Frate Alberto," 5).

makes up stories about the other world to comically deconstruct the epistemological bases for the *Commedia*. In the *Genealogie*, Boccaccio revisits the same scene of unlearned storytelling to make a contrasting point about the potential truth of those same stories and thus applies Dante's definition of his poem as a truth that has the face of a lie to all stories. "In our intellectual tradition," Carlo Ginzburg writes, "a consciousness of the mendacious nature of myths, and by extension of poetry, has accompanied like a shadow, the conviction that they contain a hidden truth" (*Wooden Eyes*, 37). It is in the pleasurable shadow of that in-between that Boccaccio engages Dante, creating both a challenge to Dante's truth claims and a justification for all poetry.

The Tale of Giletta di Narbona (III.9)

ANTHONY CASSELL

With its abbreviated yet intensely complicated plot line that combines folklore topoi, medical theory, sketchy characters, and an elusive narratological pattern connecting it to several other tales in the *Decameron*, the reception of Boccaccio's novella of Giletta di Narbona, *Decameron* III.9, has been chequered at best.[1] Historically, it has not received as much attention from critics as many other tales; editors conventionally omit it from anthologies; modern critics most often list III.9 amid a row of numbers telling us what the narrative contains in common with several other stories. On the other hand, the tale has, ironically, enjoyed a greater history of artistic adaptation than most of its peers. Shakespeare's version for the stage obviously cannot be ignored, since for Boccaccisti, his play will always be the elephant in the drawing room. As we can tell even from his title, *All's Well That Ends Well* – surely reflecting the problematic persuasiveness and final impression of the *Decameron* story – the great playwright admired Boccaccio's cleverness, wondered at the tale's effect outside the structure of the Hundred Tales, and took up its subject matter as a challenge. The Bard's alterations point to his perception of flaws or holes in the original plot; his re-treatment is in part an attempt at resolving the intractable difficulties and ambiguities of motivation and verisimilitude that Boccaccio purposely glossed over in the *Decameron* story. In fact, we might observe that Shakespeare ironically weakens both main characters and makes the believability and acceptability of

1 This essay first appeared in *MLN* with the title "Pilgrim Wombs, Physicke and Bed-Tricks: Intellectual Brilliance, Attenuation and Elision in *Decameron* III.9" *MLN* 121.1 (2006): 53–101.

the plot even harder to swallow. *AWW* is for Shakespeareans the premier "problem" play – but most of its major "problems" are already in Boccaccio as part of the careful rhetorical and narrative strategy of the *Decameron*. Shakespeare only tried to solve them, although somewhat unsuccessfully, with his ingenious alterations and additions. In striving to give the plot more verve and a convincing *lieto fine* by inventing brilliant characters of his own – the Fool Lavatch, the Countess, Diana, and Parolles, plus a panoply of supporting royal courtiers – he almost made things worse for what he must have seen as the story's pale mechanics. For our purposes here I believe that we need to treat and refer to Shakespeare only cursorily as a critic of great acumen who reflected on his famous predecessor's work with a writer's insight. Despite the English Bard's brilliance in trying to improve these supposed, folkloresque "faults," he meets with only limited success, and, though somewhat more popular than Boccaccio's original, his own version has seen only a desultory and disappointing record of modern stage performances.[2] Bernardo Accolti, better known by his sobriquet, "L'Unico Aretino," had already adapted the plot of *Decameron* III.9 for his play, *Verginia*, which formed the major entertainment for the wedding celebration of the magnate Antonio Spanocchi in Siena in January 1494.[3] Boccaccio's tale has played a part in modern film: most recently, the Belgian director Marie-Christine Questerbert adapted the story in her French-language screen version entitled *La chambre obscure*, released in 2000.[4] We thus see

2 As we note above, since Shakespeare most likely read the tale in Painter's or some other bowdlerized version where the structure of the *Decameron* disappears, especially with the omission of tale III.10, the Bard of Avon probably could not have known of Boccaccio's delicate narrative collocation strategies. On the perfunctory and fitful number of performances of *AWW* in the last century from 1916 to 1981, see J.L. Styan, *All's Well That Ends Well*. See also Price, in *The Unfortunate Comedy*, 75–86, who traces negative criticism and rare performances back to the seventeenth century. The rarity of performance is of major concern to most Shakespearian scholars dealing with the play.

3 See Accolti, *Verginia. Comedia di M. Bernardo Accolti Aretino intitolata la Verginia, con un capitolo della Madonna, nuovamente corretta, & con somma diligentia ristampata. MDXXXV*. This 1535 copy is found in the Marvin T. Herrick Renaissance Drama Collection in the Rare Book Room of the University of Illinois, Urbana-Champaign.

4 See the *recensioni* of Marie-Christine Questerbert's *La Chambre obscure* by Donatella Massara, "*La Chambre oscure* [sic]," url.it/donnestoria/film/lachambre.htm, consulted 11 November 2004; and by Ron Holloway, "La Chambre Obscure," film festivalspro.com/cannes_2000/parllel/directors-c... Both *Boccaccio 70* and Pasolini's *Decameron* had ignored the tale.

a curious paradox: the fascination of artists who admire the tale deeply enough to adopt its plot, yet, who along with the critics and editors of Boccaccio, regret its sketch-like qualities and go beyond those critics in their desire to fill it out or "restore," if that is the word, the plot's archetypical potential as entertainment.

Boccaccio's own placing of this tale, which is done with a supremely careful strategy, has, I believe, caused this dichotomy in the "fortune" of Giletta's adventure. Clearly the writer wanted the tale to seem somewhat bland to a reader only bent on entertainment, despite the fact that the writer, at once, actually endowed the story with a most intricate structure and an interwoven symbolic-allegory to the delight of any closer readers, more intense, and more involved. Boccaccio could have rendered the tale's elements, the themes of the abandoned wife, adulterous love, bed-tricks, and coup-de scène revelations, immediately far more gripping and far more uproariously comical had his collocational intentions been different. Clearly the author wanted to create a foil so that the brilliance of the flanking stories would shine more brightly with their witty sexuality, licence, and, in the case of Alibech's adventures in III.10, satiric hagiography barely wearing the scanty net stockings of pornography. For Giletta, then, Boccaccio mutes his strings and plays in a minor key; he purposely skips and syncopates his narrative, omitting what could be the juiciest and naughtiest bits, muting the affective and the outrageous. The bed-trick episode of III.9, usually a topos of lubricious, winking mischief and one made so much of in earlier tales of Day Three, he merely glosses over with an elision. The male protagonist, Beltramo Rossiglione, for all his peculiarity, his snobbish adamance, his whoring life as a *condottiere*, the writer reduces to a merely functional, and, at first glance, shadowy, two-dimensional character. Finally Boccaccio reduces his heroine's great, industrious adventures to a matter-of-fact synopsis, giving us only the major pointers for what could have been one of the most admirable adventures of the most well-rounded and brilliant woman of his whole opus. In the following pages I will explore these diverse but related topics, exposing the manner in which Boccaccio both richly suggests and carefully dampens, while contrasting his strategic muting to the clever, outrageous sparks, both pornographic and intellectual, with which he endows the surrounding tales. Boccaccio avoids letting tale III.9 be overtly remarkable, saving his fireworks for the two flanking narratives and for his pseudo-apology for the whole work in his subversive Introduction to Day Four.

We can see Boccaccio's strategy at work at the beginning of III.9, where he has the queen for the day, Neifile, praise the story that Lauretta has just told and express her fear that it may already, in advance, have eclipsed her own:

> Chi dirà novella omai che bella paia, avendo quella di Lauretta udita? Certo vantaggio ne fu che ella non fu la primiera, ché poche poi dell'altre ne sarebbon piaciute: *e cosí spero che averrà di quelle che per questa giornata sono a raccontare.* Ma pure, chente che sia, quella che alla proposta materia m'occorre vi conterò. (III.9.3; emphasis mine)
>
> [How is anyone now going to tell a tale that could in any way seem engaging now that we have heard Lauretta's? It was certainly a good thing for us that hers didn't come first, for otherwise we would have got very little fun out of the rest of them; and so I *have no hope but that this will happen with the [two] stories that are still to be told today.* But, still, whatever the case may be, I shall tell you a story just as the proposed topic requires of me.][5]

Thus, from the beginning, Neifile herself expresses misgivings and reservations about her story's effect and its ability to please. And, we note, Boccaccio has her pair her tale strategically with Dioneo's naughty frolic of Alibech (yet to be told) for consideration and comparison. In the critical history of the *Decameron*, III.9 has been one of the *least* popular of its stories, and this lack of enthusiasm not only harks back to its unpopular source in Terence but also extends to its unfavoured *fortuna* in the works in Italian and English that it has inspired. As far as I can discover, Boccaccio's III.9 tale has itself, as of this writing, not received an individual critical treatment for over twenty years, not since Pamela Stewart's minor essay entitled "How to Get a Happy Ending" of 1991 that dealt mostly with Shakespeare, and not even a partial book treatment since Howard C. Cole's *The All's Well That Ends Well Story from Boccaccio to Shakespeare* of 1981, which actually contained only one chapter centring on the *Decameron* and was totally marred by several serious

5 All references to the *Decameron* are to Vittore Branca's third edition of the *Decameron* (Turin: Einaudi, 1980), here, 429; all translations and synopses are my own. "Spero" has a negative significance in the citation, meaning "mi aspetto che … non" or "temo che … non."

incomprehensions and misinterpretations of Boccaccio's original language.[6] In the following pages I shall evaluate a number of factors in Boccaccio's text concerning his muffling of its verve and genius; the collocation and external context he gives it within the Hundred Tales indelibly colour our appreciation of its internal content and meaning.

1. An Opal amidst Diamonds

What renders III.9 so unremarkable in comparison, like an opal amidst diamonds? Our first impression is that the motivations of the main personages are fundamentally inexplicable, that the action lacks real excitement, that Beltramo is merely a shallow, callow character, and that Giletta's determination to have him fully as a partner seems at first little more than an *idée fixe*. We discover no enchanting romance there, and the Bakhtinian-style carnival frolic that runs from the tale of Masetto (III.1) up to Ferondo and the abbott (III.8) and that bursts forth thereafter in Rustico and Alibech appears itself to take a vacation in Neifile's rather earnest effort.[7] The narrator does not beguile us with a good yarn

---

6 See Stewart, "How to Get a Happy Ending," and Cole, *The All's Well Story*. Among other writers on Day Three, Cottino-Jones ("Desire and the Fantastic") dismisses III.9 in half a line as "an unusual marriage story" (4). Pamela Stewart argues that the "happy ending," in large part, lies in the contentment of the audience and its demonstration by applause to the gratified group of players putting on the show. Stewart derives her arguments from the ending of *All's Well*. Terence's comedy *Hecyra* (Greek, "mother-in-law") was known to the Bard of Avon; Boccaccio had been well acquainted with Terence's play as well, although I find no direct verbal echoes in III.9. Terence tells us in his Prologue that, at its first performance, the audience had abandoned *Hecyra*, leaving it ignored and outshone by a fascinating dancing tightrope walker in the street outside. In the second production, he informs us: "Act one went well until a rumor mentioned gladiators." The audience again scurried out. After these two dismal flops, the final version begins with the wonderfully named producer, Ambivius Turpio (!), pleading with the audience for a third hearing – if the audience accepts the performance of the young and talented players, it will be a success and the theatre will benefit – but the comedy ends with the orchestra leader having to order the audience in the last line to clap their hands: "Audience, applaud!" Stewart does not point out that the plea for the audience's approval that we find at the end of *AWW* predates Shakespeare. The topos of the husband refusing to bed his newly married wife seems to have remained a rather friendless and jinxed theme throughout literary history.

7 Beside the various editions and studies of Charles S. Singleton of Florentine Carnival songs, Mikhail Bakhtin's *Rabelais and His World* remains a classical work on carnival humour.

but, rather, seems bent on reciting an objective chronicle. The setting deals with feudal courts and kings, but there is no courtly love. The heroine's obsession and determination is stolid, but no caressing passion is expressed. Neifile recounts a tale of enamourment, courtship, and marriage, but she tells us no love story. In short, in Neifile's tale of *Decameron* III.9, Boccaccio tells seduction but does not seduce us. He distracts his audience, especially in their first casual reading, from the care that he actually lavishes upon the narrative structure.

That III.9 bears much in common with the last far more popular and controversial story of the Hundred Tales (X.10) is by no means a new observation.[8] In III.9, the beleaguered role of the impoverished Griselda is taken instead by an upper-bourgeoise Giletta, while the pitiless and proud, god-challenging Gualtieri is replaced by the caddish Beltramo. The parallels between the tales are obvious in the depiction both of male domination of the female and in the effects of class snobbery. But in this narrative precedent in the third day, we also have a lower-born wife who bears her spouse two children; through class distinction, she is cruelly discarded by him, and is finally, with her offspring, then reunited with her husband – while her cruel and irrational spouse at last relents in his rejection, accepting his wife for her industry or for her patience. Both men have their wives reclothed in fine vestments, give them a promissory kiss amid joyous celebration – and, of course, the couples are supposed to live blissfully ever after. A pattern of word-parallels affirm X.10 as a retelling.[9]

---

8 Surdich (*Boccaccio*, 137) comments that in the typology of Giletta's tale, Beltramo is such as "quasi ad anticipare la figura del marchese di Saluzzo." On Griselda, see Kirkham, "The Last Tale." The bibliography on the last tale is huge and beyond our scope here, but a good sample may be consulted in the volumes edited by Raffaele Morabito, *La Circolazione* and *La Storia di Griselda in Europa*.

9 The word parallels make it more than obvious: "E [Beltramo] fattala di vestimenti a lei convenevole rivestire" [and (Beltramo) having had her dressed in clothing fitting for her (442)]; "trattale i suoi pannicelli d'una nobile roba delle sue la rivestirono" [and taking off (Griselda's) rags, they dressed her in one of her noble robes (X.10.67)]; "E in piè fece levar la contessa e lei abbracciò e basciò" [Raising the Countess (Giletta) to her feet, (Beltramo) kissed and embraced her (442)]; "E cosí detto l'abbracciò e basciò" [And saying this, (Gualtieri) embraced and kissed (Griselda) (X.10.67)]; "E da quel dí innanzi lei sempre come sua sposa e moglie onorando, l'amò e sommamente ebbe cara" [And from that day forth honouring her always as his bride and wife, he loved her and cherished her most highly (442)]; "Con Griselda, onorandola sempre quanto si potea, lungamente e consolato visse" [with Griselda did (Gualtieri) live long and contentedly, honouring her to the best of his ability (X.10.67)].

After both novelle, we, as reader-audience, and, in the case of the more memorable Griselda, the internal audience of the *brigata*, are all left questioning, quite reasonably, what possible happiness a wife could ever truly experience henceforth with such a husband, who has shown himself capable of such "matta bestialità," or heartless cruelty and neglect. Yet while Boccaccio places X.10 to crown the Hundred Tales in ambiguous discussion and controversy, he leaves the atrocious sufferings inflicted in III.9 in total silence after the tale's end.

Victoria Kirkham has well observed that the Paradise gained in the framework Introduction to Day Three, the delightful garden of the second villa, descends to a Purgatory in *Decameron* III.8, and is finally lost in Alibech's bawdy "ninferno" of III.10. Boccacio tells us initially: "se Paradiso si potesse in terra fare, non sapevano conoscere che altra forma che quella di quel giardino gli si potesse dare, né pensare, oltre a questo, qual bellezza gli si potesse agiugnere" [If one could make Paradise on earth, they could not tell what form anyone could give it except for the form of that garden, nor could they think of any kind of beauty that anyone could add to it (III.Intro.11)]. The metaphor continues into III.1 with its walled *ortus conclusus* of the virginal convent turned into a parody of *huri* heaven. To continue Kirkham's insightful "descent to the inferno" theme, one can readily concede that III.9 ends without any paradisaical enchantment, with the main characters' bald and sudden reconciliation ambiguously clouded with presaging doubts and anxious undertones. One can easily imagine that despite those final feastings at Beltramo's court, Giletta's life "from that time forth" with a Count Rossiglione, as with the "bestia" Marchese Gualtieri di Saluzzo, would probably relapse into a living hell.[10] That we do not engage in the same endless discussions of the ending of the first of these two similar tales results from Boccaccio's careful planning.

10 A.P. Rossiter observes, "*All's Well* does not end very well." See his chapter, "All's Well That Ends Well," in *Angel with Horns*, 104. See as well Richard A. Levin, "All's Well That Ends Well, and 'All Seems Well,'" who similarly doubts the happy ending of *AWW*, taking sides "with the more cynical account of the play" (141); see also Stewart, "How to Get a Happy Ending," 341. Victoria Kirkham's essay on Alibech is most useful: "Love's Labors Rewarded," now chapter 6 in *The Sign of Reason in Boccaccio's Fiction*, 199–214.

2. More than a Twofold Plot

Critics have generally identified two separate, "folkloristic" episodes in the plot, first Giletta's initial, expert herbal curing of the French king's pulmonary abscess that had confounded all other medical doctors, and second, her amazing ruse of going to bed, *incognita*, with her own husband to bear twin sons.[11] Both episodes, thus isolated, seem mechanical contrivances and functional fantasies of the kind collected by Stith Thompson.[12] There are, of course, other fundamental plot lines that link all these lesser forces and elements together, the major ones being the more central themes of Giletta's obsessive enamourment and the fulfilment of her medical knowledge, threads that give purpose and unity to the subordinate actions and sub-plots.

Boccaccio's tale recounted by a member of his most elegant, upper-middle-class Florentine *brigata* has indeed elements of popular fable involving diverse conventions that ignore verisimilitude. For these sequences scholars have listed several possible oriental sources, but I quite believe Boccaccio when he has Fiammetta (in regard to the Minutolo tale, III.6) say "la nostra città ... come d'ogni altra cosa è copiosa – cosí è d'essempli a ogni materia" [our city ... is filled with exempla for all kinds of stories].[13] Among others from Eastern literature,

11 Boccaccisti and especially Shakespeare scholars note the problem of the bifold plot in *Decameron* III.9 and in *All's Well*. Muriel Bradbrook, for example, remarks that "*All's Well That Ends Well* might have as its title 'Two Plays in One'"; see *Muriel Bradbrook on Shakespeare*, 84. David Haley observes that "These two scenes [of Helena's meeting and curing the king] build upon the folkloric motif of the virgin['s] healing the king, an ancient idea Shakespeare found unadorned in Boccaccio's novella and greatly elaborated it in his play" (*Shakespeare's Courtly Mirror*, 88).

12 Antti Aarne, *The Types of the Folktale*, 306. Stith Thompson, *Motif-Index of Folk-Literature*, item H361, "Hero will marry girl possessing certain ring or jewel," vol. 3; H 36, T67.2, "Marriage to prince as a reward for cure," vol. 6; K1814, "wife in disguise wooed by her faithless husband," vol. 6. See the folklore paradigm in Vladimir Propp, *The Morphology of the Folktale*. See Marcus Landau, *Die Quellen des Dekameron*, 140–1. W.W. Lawrence, in his influential essay *Shakespeare's Problem Comedies*, identifies "the fulfilment of the tasks" and the "substitute bride" (39–49); see also Susan Snyder, "Introduction," 8–24, and Carol Neely, *Broken Nuptials*, 78.

13 Gaston Paris, review of "Über die altfranzösische Vorstufe des Shakespeare'schen Lustspiels *Ende gut, alles gut*" and his "Une version orientale du thème de *All's Well That Ends Well*," 98. See also Landau, *Die Quellen des Dekameron*, esp. 105, 140; A. Collinwood Lee, *The Decameron*. But see *Decameron*, III.6.3.

critics have identified first a Western precedent for the wife-abandoned-after-marriage episode in Terence's classical play *Hecyra* [Greek: "The Mother-in-Law"], and also in a possible medieval forerunner, in the *Le livre du très chevalereux Comte d'Artois et de sa femme.*[14] Further, for the theme of the ill-treated wife, some scholars, and I believe in this case, totally unconvincingly, also point to the anonymous Middle High German poem *Daz Bloch* [*Das Block: The Wooden Block*].[15]

---

14 See Philip d'Artois, *Le livre du Très chevalereux Comte d'Artois et de sa femme.* I here offer a résumé of the story for comparison: the Comte d'Artois adores and weds a young and beautiful wife, but she bears him no children. Worried that his name and line will die out, the count decides to wander the earth in search of adventure and vows never to return to his estate or to see his wife again until she fulfils three impossible tasks: first, that she must bear his child without his knowledge; second, that he should give her his finest diamond without his knowing he had done so; and third, that he must present her with his finest steed under the same conditions. He departs, but within a short time his wife pursues him, aiming to change his mind. She catches up with the count in Spain and enters his household in male disguise under the name of Philippot. As "varlet de chambre" she becomes his confidant(e), and one day he explains his grief over his love for the daughter of the king of Castille; he enlists "Philippot's" help, promising to grant whatever she may ask. She then contrives to become the confidante of the king's daughter's nurse, and, borrowing a large ring familiar to the count, she plans to substitute herself for the princess in an assignation with him. She proceeds thus for a while without the count's realizing the ruse, and finally becomes pregnant by him, thus fulfilling the first condition. As Philippot, she is subsequently rewarded for her devoted service by being granted her choice of his gems: she selects his rarest diamond; lastly, upon pretending to return home as his valet, she is given the count's finest horse. With the three conditions fulfilled, the couple is reconciled. Although the count is portrayed as worthy, the reader still feels that the foreshadowings of a Beltramo-Bertram fall upon him: his whimsical abandonment (quite against medieval canon law), despite his "love" for his wife, and his cruel challenges to her cast him in a negative light and leave us doubting the ending's bliss.

15 I translate Branca's note (*Decameron*, 429n2): "The theme of this novella … was fairly widespread in the East; we have only to think of the Indian drama *Sakuntala di Kalidasa*; and compare, besides, the *Dasakumara Caritra*: P. W. Jacob, *Hindoo tales*, 274. But in the West as well we can descry a classical precedent in the Hecyra of Terence; and then in the Middle Ages in *Le chevalereux Comte d'Artois* … For the popularity of the theme see: J. Bolte and J. Polívka, IV, 254; Thompson and Rotunda, H 1187, K 1814 e 1843.2, L 162, T 67 and 72.2. Compare the substitution of the beloved lady in … III, 6." See J. Bolte and J. Polívka, *Anmerkungen*; D.P. Rotunda, *Motif Index.* In the *Hecyra*, 1.2.137–8, Parmeno says, "Well, they were married … He never took her though; call her his wife [if you like], but she's still a virgin" (trans. Carrier in *Terence: The Comedies*, trans. Palmer Bovie, Carrier, and Parker, 363). Branca also points to the short narrative poem that he cites erroneously,

What critics have not emphasized are the obvious sources from the Bible. Giletta's audience before the king of France, as we will later examine, is reminiscent of various Jewish prophets before foreign tyrants, and the sex-trick closely follows Judah's fornication with his daughter-in-law Tamar, a story that takes up the whole of Genesis' chapter 38. The widowed Tamar, rejected by Onan (whom, as we will never forget, God slays for spilling his seed upon the ground), fearing that she will

---

and perhaps second-hand, as *Der Tod*: but the Middle High German verses, under the title *Daz Bloch* [*The Block*], are actually found in Hans Lambel's edition of *Erzählungen und Schwänke*, 104–22. I again print my synopsis of the supposed source here for the reader's convenience: *Daz Bloch* recounts the tale of a peasant farmer (Bauer) who excessively abuses his wife out of some groundless loathing. Her neighbour and friend (Gevatterin: her "God-mother," or, better, English "gossip," or Italian "comare"), observing the married woman's parlous situation, promises her that if she will follow her advice she as neighbour will make her husband fond of her in a way the latter could only dream of. The neighbour advises the wife that when her husband returns from the fields she is to take to her bed as if she were ill, and to tell him that she is about to die within two days. The neighbour promises to tell the same to the husband as well: "ich wil in ouch gesprechen ê / und wil im waerlĩche sagen / das ir in disen zwéin tágen / vil gwislĩche sterbet" [I will also speak to him and will truly say to him that you will surely die within these two days (vv. 110–12)]. The farmer at first thinks the neighbour is joking, but then he becomes so frightened about the news that he does not want to go home at all to see if his wife is still alive. He begs the neighbour to look after the funeral arrangements and vows that he is ready to reward her for that in any way. The neighbour now leads the wife, together with her clothes and valuables (about which the farmer is totally unaware), secretly to her own house, and then goes to the wife's courtyard, dresses up a block of wood in clothes, and declares it to be the wife's dead body. She immediately repairs to the priest and persuades him to carry out the burial service in great haste, and, when it is over, she sends news to the husband. In reward she exacts the promise from him that if he is to marry again he will ask for and obey her advice in choosing a wife. The peasant willingly swears to it, and after barely five weeks, he returns to her with his request to find someone he can marry. After a few difficulties the neighbour manages to bring him together with his wife, whom she has so spruced and dressed up that her husband does not recognize her. In fact, he finds her so delightful that he refuses evermore to be separated from her. The wife then reveals herself (in a classic lapalissade "ich'n stárp niht, ich lebe noch" [I didn't die; I'm still alive]), but no matter how many times she begs him to keep the story quiet, within twelve days the silly scandal has gone around the neighbourhood, making him the butt of everyone's scorn ("er waere der liute spot gewesen" [he became the people's laughing-stock]). But henceforth the wife enjoys perfect peace with him. We can see that the rejected wife and the bed-trick themes are indeed present, but the German poem has really nothing in common with the second half of the plot of *Decameron* III.9.

never be given the new husband falsely promised by her father-in-law, Judah, puts off her widow's weeds, veils herself as a harlot, and displays herself in the street at the city gate;[16] Judah, taking her for a cult or temple prostitute, lies with her and, upon her request, gives her the pledge of his signet ring, his cord, and his staff. When she bears twin sons she presents these tokens to exculpate herself and prove both Judah's shame and his paternity. By the inclusion of these strong and sombre biblical echoes surely familiar to his fourteenth-century audience, Boccaccio gives his tale a certain seriousness that successfully points up the frivolity of its flanking tales in Day Three.[17] Besides the earlier cases of Bartolomea of II.10 and the nuns in III.1, there is the unnamed lady bedded by the gentleman in III.3 and the example of another nameless lady in IV.10; Caterina in V.4; the wife and the hamper in V.10; Madonna Filippa's legal excogitations in VI.7; Gianni Lotteringhi's wife in VII.1; the mare's tale in IX.10; the whole collection of naughty, scurrilous wives from Day Seven; Peronella and the tub in VII.2; the Stone in the Well in VII.4; the Foiled Husband Disguised as Priest of VII.5; Leonetto, Messer Lambertuccio, and Isabella of VII.6; the String on the Toe in VII.8; and Lydia of VII.9, who makes love to Pyrrhus while Nicostrato actually looks on. In VII.3, the wife is abetted by Friar Rinaldo, who "performs" the charms that convince the husband. Indeed, the exceptional tragic ones are, notably, Ghismonda in IV.1 and the wife of Guglielmo Rossiglione in IV.9.

William Lawrence has pointed out influentially in the case of Shakespeare's problem play, *All's Well*[18] and its Boccaccian source, that

---

16 I use the Douay-Rheims spelling for the names and combine the differing translated details of the Douay Bible with those of the AV and RSV.

17 Besides the social success won by Tamar, the structure and themes of the *Decameron* itself lead us to expect Giletta's triumph because of the preponderance of cases in the Hundred Tales.

18 Lawrence, *Shakespeare's Problem Comedies*. It is fair, if unfortunate, to say that the presence of Shakespeare's problematic adaptation eclipses the Boccaccio tale in the history of literature; Shakespearian scholars mainly see the great Florentine as merely a "source." See Rossiter's comparison of *AWW* with a reprint of its Boccaccian source translated by William Painter (*Angel with Horns*, 82–107), which observes the audience's uneasiness with the contradictions between a *Märchen*-like plotting and the violations of normal human psychology. Sir Arthur Quiller-Couch commented that Shakespeare's play "has no atmosphere save that of the stage" ("New Shakespeare," in Shakespeare, *Works*, ed. Quiller-Couch and Dover Wilson, xxxiv). Joseph G. Price views the Shakespearian adaptation as a "tightly knit" combination of "seemingly jarring worlds" (*The Unfortunate Comedy*, 136). We must hasten

reality and fable collide.[19] But I disagree with him and others that the plot in the *Decameron* can be qualified as a child's fairy-tale,[20] as if it were innocent and apolitical; instead, what we have here is truly a tale for the merchant class and "for mature audiences only." The biblical resonances, the overwhelming and precocious masculine "virtù" of the heroine (*fatti maschi*!),[21] the male-dominated feudal courts, and the inevitable *ragion di mercatura*, as well as (as we will see) the medical implications, all govern the sexually "adult" polemic tenor of III.9. Boccaccio calques the first sequence, "the curing of the monarch" motif, in terms of a commercial bargain: if health be restored to the king, then a noble husband will be the recompense;[22] for the second sequence, the abandonment and reconciliation tale, Boccaccio has the noble (but most ignoble) Beltramo descend to a sarcasm of bourgeois values in setting the dastardly conditions of the contract Giletta must fulfil to win him back: "'Faccia ella il piacer suo; io per me vi tornerò allora a esser con lei che

---

to add that critics who have evaluated *AWW* positively do so mainly because of Shakespeare's alterations in plot and personalities and for the additions of new events and, especially, characters – the Fool, Lafew, Parolles. George Bernard Shaw admired, particularly, the addition of the gracious Countess of Roussillon. Nicholas Brooke insists that *AWW*'s plot is a "consistently naturalistic presentation of traditional romance magic" ("All's Well That Ends Well," 168) – but then, very oddly, Brooke views Shakespeare's exquisite preciosity of language as "blunt and unadorned"! Indeed Shakespeare's "improvements" attempt to give reason to the relative lack of motivation in the tale as told mutedly by Boccaccio. Lawrence, in *Shakespeare's Problem Comedies*, blames modern audiences' puzzlement at *AWW* on the public's unwillingness to acquiesce in folkloric fiction; as Clifford Leech repeats, "We find it difficult to credit the ready Elizabethan acceptance of folktale plotting" ("The Theme of Ambition," 17). Here, as with so much in Shakespearean criticism, we see that this is really a problem in Boccaccio, not merely in Elizabethan literature.

19 Just as Shakespeare has his First French Lord famously observe in the play: "The web of our life is of a mingled yarn" (*AWW* 4.3.60). But this tale of Boccaccio *does not have a yarn-like quality*. The Lord's statement may indicate that Shakespeare felt Boccaccio's two plots did not meld well.

20 I agree with B.J. Layman, who believes that Boccaccio and Shakespeare are here more enamoured of the themes of deceit than of folklore or myth, as W.W. Lawrence and Northrop Frye held: "It [Giletta's tale] is emphatically not simple, and it is not a tale for children" ("Shakespeare's Helena," 42).

21 Isidore of Seville famously pointed out that man was called *vir* because of his *vis*, his strength and force, while *mulier* came from *mollier*, "softer." Isidore, *Etymologiarum sive originum libri XX*, ed. Lindsay, 11:2:17–20.

22 Giletta's bold offer to forfeit her life ("fammi brusciare") is an open expression of her own supreme self-confidence in her medical learning.

ella questo anello avrà in dito e in braccio figliuolo di me acquistato.' Egli avea l'anello assai caro ne mai da sé il partiva per alcuna virtù che stato gli era dato a intendere ch'egli avea" ["Let her do what she likes. As for me, I will come back to live with her when she has this ring on her finger and a son of mine in her arms." He held his ring most dear and would never be separated from it because of a certain virtue that he had been led to believe it possessed (III.9.31)].[23]

The middle-class Giletta succeeds in both obtaining his ring and delivering him not just one son, but twin boys who are his spitting image. Her industrious, earthly "virtù" beats any "virtù" contained in Beltramo's ring – or in his mind and body. These intractable mechanics of the original plot dictate the quality of the "fable" ("fabula") in the *Decameron* and are intended to prove the value of "industria," a term laden with ethical and theological complications, one which Boccaccio had found particularly striking in St Thomas Aquinas's Latin, and that meant "diligence and assiduity, purpose, intention, premeditation, adroitness and skill."[24] For St Thomas, *peccare ex industria* meant to "sin with *intention*."[25] The implacable *intention* of Giletta for socially ordained matrimony, if not love, is the moving force of the whole tale.[26]

---

23 Neely evaluates the contracts added by Shakespeare in *All's Well*; see *Broken Nuptials*, 82.

24 Roy J. Deferrari, *A Latin-English Dictionary*, 515. See St Thomas Aquinas on intention and sin in *Summa Theologica*, art. 1, I, 902; a. 8, I, 908 (excess and deceit in cheating); a. 4, obj. 1 II, 2556 (*Summa Theologica*, trans. *Fathers of the English Dominican Province*, ad loc.).

25 Deferrari, *A Latin-English Dictionary*, 770. While bed-tricks seem to be most commonly successful in fiction, I am not sure of their true record in real life. It is difficult to clarify Boccaccio's intention as to any moral of the tale, not to speak of his idea of his actual comic achievement, by attending to his definition of *fabula* [fiction] in the *Genealogiae deorum gentilium* 14 (cited in Osgood's *Boccaccio on Poetry*, 48–9): "Fiction is a form of discourse, which, *under guise of invention, illustrates or proves an idea*; and as its superficial aspect is removed, *the meaning of the author is clear*." Of the four modes of fiction Boccaccio then lists, Giletta's adventures fit most closely yet uncomfortably into the third type, which the author classifies as "more history than fiction," used by Terence and Plautus in their comedies: "If the events they describe have not actually taken place, yet since they are common, they *could have* occurred." Giletta's tale is in the tradition of Terence's comedy *Hecyra*. But what can the moral be? That women are strong? That marriage is right? Most problematically, Boccaccio insists that this third form is also the parable, the type of fiction used by Christ.

26 "But my intents are fixed and will not leave me," as Shakespeare has Helena put it (*AWW*, 1.1.235).

We recall that the queen for the third day, Neifile, proposes that the *brigata* change locale, and after the move and the siesta, that they tell tales "di chi alcuna cosa molto desiderata *con industria* acquistasse o la perduta recuperasse" [about those who *through their assiduity* have obtained a thing they greatly desired or recovered a thing previously lost (II.Concl.9)]. Boccaccio hints that at the point of her proposal Neifile must already have had the tale of Giletta and Beltramo in mind;[27] and modest as she has revealed herself to be so far (her name signifies "new love" or "new to love"), she waits until her – by now canonical – ninth turn to tell it.[28] Within her story Giletta strives to gain "the thing" she greatly desires by her miraculous curing of the king and thereby winning Beltramo by the monarch's royal command. The heroine then fulfils the second part of Neifile's proposed topic by recovering the lost Beltramo through her tireless, feigned pilgrimage and guile. We note especially that the *brigata* narrows Neifile's rather general suggestion of subject matter immediately into a narrative series of sexual romps: "la cosa," "the thing" lost or regained in this day's tales, is never, for example, a valued gem, a fortune, lost virtue, or true faith, but always a reified lover as sexual object.[29] By the time Neifile comes to tell her own

27 The verb "occorrere" signifies "to need, to be needful or necessary, to be required" in Italian. I note with some dismay that Frances Winwar completely mistranslates "mi occorre" (actually meaning "I must" or "it is required of me") at this point as if it were equivalent to the English "it occurs to me": she renders the sentence with the solecism: "I shall tell you the first story that *comes to my mind* [i.e. the first story that *occurs to me*]" (*The Decameron of Giovanni Boccaccio*, 203). This error misleads Howard Cole to conclude, quite mistakenly, that Neifile is feigning an *extemporary* tale and thus exhibiting a precocious, Trecento "sprezzatura" (*The All's Well Story*, 25). On the contrary, Neifile is portrayed as planning the tale right from the start of the day as she announces the theme and obeys the *brigata*'s set rules.

28 Neifile timidly follows the pattern set by Filomena in Day Two in telling her tale as the ninth story. We can italicize the irregularities in the list to show the pattern: *Pampinea, the queen of Day One, tells the tenth tale and has Elissa tell the ninth;* Filomena, queen of *Day Two*, tells the ninth tale and *Dioneo's privilege is established with the tenth;* Neifile, queen of Day Three, tells the ninth story; Filostrato, king of Day Four, tells the ninth; Fiammetta, queen of Day Five, tells the ninth; Elissa, queen of Day Six, tells the ninth; *Dioneo, king of Day Seven, tells the tenth story, while Filostrato tells the ninth tale;* Lauretta queen of Day Eight, tells the ninth; Emilia, queen of Day Nine, tells the ninth; *and Filostrato, king of Day Ten, as is now the "norm," tells the ninth.* Thus the queen and king tell the ninth story of each day except for Day One (when Dioneo's rule has not yet been set) and Day Seven (when Dioneo, though king, must, according to his rule, come tenth).

29 Cole notes that "the third Day's deceptions are always sexually motivated and usually religiously rationalized" (*The All's Well Story*, 9).

tale, at least eight of her nine companions have not failed to read her unspecified order correctly: like theirs, her pre-planned story too turns upon sexuality.

3. Salaciousness and Elegance

The stories of the third day, along with those of the seventh and those final tales told by the privileged and lubricious Dioneo that conclude Days Two to Nine, are, according to popular repute, among the most shameless and salacious of the book: no editor has ever, to my knowledge, yet included a tale from Day Three in an Italian school textbook. Yet Neifile gives us not a bawdy jest but a comparatively discreet account of how a lawful wife, though risking scandal, secretly gulls her recalcitrant husband into performing his wedded duties; she herself reveals her plot at the end when it is late enough for all opprobrium to fall solely upon Beltramo. Yet with all its relative discretion (and I stress the word "relative" in comparison with the other Day Three tales!), the tale makes no pretension to believability or didacticism: it holds our attention for the first instance of reading as pure pastime, solace, and entertainment; later hermeneutic considerations reveal deeper currents.

Boccaccio even hints at a sign of divine intervention. We earlier noted the resonances of "biblical-prophets-before-alien-monarchs" in the French king's initial rejection of Giletta and his reconsideration of her as perhaps a messenger sent by God:

> Monsignore, voi schifate la mia arte perché giovane e femina sono, ma io vi ricordo che io non medico con la mia scienza, *anzi con l'aiuto di Dio* ... Il re allora disse seco: "Forse m'è costei mandata da Dio; perché non pruovo ciò che ella sa fare?" (III.9.12–13, emphasis mine)

> [Sire, you reject my art because I am young and am a woman; but I remind you that I am not a physician because of my learning but *rather by the aid of God* ... The king then said to himself: "Perhaps she has been sent me by God. Why don't I test out what she knows how to do?"]

Giletta does not attribute her powers to God in a topos of modesty (I don't think we can credit Giletta with modesty); rather her words imitate those of the patriarch, Joseph, the hero of faith (cf. Hebrews 11:22) before the Pharaoh in Genesis 41:16: "*Without me, God* shall give Pharaoh a prosperous answer." And they echo the words of the prophet Daniel before Nebuchadnezzar, king of Babylon: "There is a *God in Heaven* that revealeth mysteries" (Daniel 2:28; Douay-Rheims); "To me this secret is revealed, *not by any wisdom that I have*" (Daniel 2:30). Notably, however, Giletta is not as selfless as her biblical predecessors: she adds also the worldly possession of a deep medical knowledge, "la scienza del maestro Gerardo nerbonese, il quale *mio padre fu e famoso medico* mentre visse" [the learning of Master Gerardo di Narbona, who was *my father and a famous physician* while he lived (III.9.12; emphasis mine)].

For a while, then, this episode places Giletta on the holy side of righteousness. It gives her a temporary super-terrestrial aura that appears to buoy her in her dealings with the king and with the folk of Rossiglione County, but which fades immediately as she begins her ironic and clandestine pilgrimage to obtain Beltramo's fleshly embraces.[30] Before that, all patriarchal and phallic power descends upon her executive head. The king amply rewards her, and it is the "buoni *uomini*" [the good *men*] of her fiefdom who will weep at her departure from Rossiglione (III.9.34). She cunningly deceives her loving subjects about devoting her life henceforth to pilgrimages and works of mercy for the salvation of her soul, only secretly to wend her way in disguise to Florence where she becomes a calculating *voyeuse* watching and spying on Beltramo, who she finds has turned into a wenching mercenary (III.9.36, 58). Her arrangements with the Florentine widow reveal her as a schemer, no matter how charitable her plans are to aid the destitute woman and provide a dowry for her daughter. Giletta is no longer the little girl whose hopeless enamourment aroused our sympathy. Her mature self-confidence, her plans of deception, her secrecy, and her flirting with meretriciousness immediately disorient and disconnect the reader from the Giletta they thought they knew.

4. The Bed-Trick

Bed-tricks are a common enough topos in literature of all kinds, sacred and profane. In the Old Testament, Lot's daughters, one after the other,

30 Cole sees a parodic strategy in the third day, where Boccaccio's characters use different forms of bogus religious practice to contrive their sexual ends. Some of these, he says, lend additional doubt and unbelievability to Giletta's righteousness; see especially his second chapter, passim.

beget children with their intoxicated father (Genesis 19:30–8).[31] Jacob, the trickster who has stolen his father's blessing, is astonished to find Leah in his bridal bed instead of the promised Rachel (Genesis 29:1–30), and, as we have mentioned as a direct antecedent of our tale, Judah takes his daughter-in-law, Tamar, for a prostitute and, as in the Giletta tale, begets twin boys with her (Genesis 38:26). In classical mythology, tales of sex-in-disguise are too many to list here: Zeus visits Danaë as a shower of golden rain, rapes Europa as a bull, and substitutes for Amphytrion in Alcmena's bed to beget Hercules; and Dante also recalls how Ovid's Myrrha lay hell-bent with her drunken father Cinyras.[32] The trick of the sexual tryst in disguise appears in several *Decameron* tales as an element of the narratological vocabulary of the *grammaire du Décameron*. The reader greets the convention usually with a smiling, incredulous acquiescence so that the momentum of the tale not suffer any hindrance. In *Decameron* III.2, Pampinea tells how Agilulfo's groom contrives to impersonate the king and bed the queen while cleverly escaping discovery. In III.6, Fiammetta takes pains to recount how Ricciardo Minutolo substitutes himself for Catella's husband. Some of us are left with suspicious doubts about Queen Teodolinda's bland naïveté in tale III.2. And in III.6 Elissa must reassure us that the Ricciardo Minutolo–Catella Sighinolfo tale is a historical story – and our editor, Vittore Branca, convinces us that it is, at least, about real people (228).[33] The bed-trick in Neifile's later tale of VII.8 is most convincing, since there is no need for

---

31 If a drunkard commits adultery he does not sin, since wine impairs his reason – according to William of Ockham. Alatiel would thus also be innocent because her intention is "pure." See Joan M. Ferrante, "Politics, Finance, and Feminism," 173.

32 I must emphasize that the ruse, most casually announced, is an ellipsis of action in Boccaccio's tale III.9. Snyder stresses that Shakespeare makes the bed-trick "not just a device but a dramatic experience" in *AWW* ("Introduction," 10, and n3). For biblical examples of bed-substitutions, see Zvi Jagendorf, "'In the Morning, Behold, It Was Leah.'" For the bed-trick in four of Shakespeare's plays, see William R. Bowden, "The Bed-Trick," 112–23. See also Raymond B. Waddington, "Entertaining the Offered Phallacy," 121–32; Marliss Carolyn Desens, who equates bed-tricks with rape in "Strange Bedfellows," 3234A, now revised and published as Desens, *The Bed-Trick in English Renaissance Drama*; David Chandler, "The 'Bed-Trick' in *Measure for Measure*," 320–21; Julia Briggs, "Shakespeare's Bed-Tricks"; Eileen Z. Cohen, "'Virtue Is Bold'"; E.A.J. Honigmann, "Shakespeare's Mingled Yarn"; A.D. Nuttall, "Measure for Measure." A recent study is by Wendy Doniger, *The Bedtrick*.

33 On Catella Sighinolfo, who also appeared in the *Caccia di Diana* 10:20, 14:50, on Filippello Sighinolfo at the court of Naples, and on Ricciardo Minutolo as counsellor to King Robert and Queen Giovanna, see Branca's notes, *Decameron*, 378nn2, 4, and 5.

its sexual consummation and the olfactory, the tactile, the aural, and the visual play no part. There the cuckolded husband, temporarily too enraged to notice the difference in the maidservant's voice from his wife's and foiled by his wife's substitution, beats his maidservant black and blue; he brands the unfortunate girl in the same way as King Agilulfo tries to identify his randy groom in III.2, by cutting off her hair.

Although alcoholic and narcotic amnesia, unidentified rapists, and anonymous sex are everyday grist for newspapers, we always balk, quite reasonably, at having to accept the verisimilitude of any such sexual substitution among literary, sober partners already well known to each other.[34] The smoothing of such obvious impediments, in fact, plays a central role in Boccaccio and in his sources, and especially in Terence's most unpopular (!) play, *Hecyra*. There the husband, Pamphilus, anonymously and drunkenly violates his wife, Philumena, before the marriage and leaves her pregnant; only when Philumena's mother, Myrrina, finally recognizes her daughter's ring on the finger of Pamphilus's paramour, Bacchis, do all realize that it was Philumena's own drunken husband who robbed and raped her; Philumena is pregnant with her own husband's child.[35]

Even theologians such as Hugh of St Victor consider bed-tricks in marriage. In his *De sacramentis* he warns that if they are played to gull an innocent party into a false betrothal (the fourteenth-century betrothal or "ringing" took place first in bed) with an unknown, the marriage would be invalid:

> **Chapter XVIII.** ***Whether the ruse called substitution dissolves marriage.*** We have heard that sometimes, when certain men betroth women unknown in appearance, certain other worthless persons were substituted by trickery, in which case indeed, if afterwards those who suffered the trick,

---

34 Northrop Frye subsumes the convention of the bed-trick ("the substitution of one girl for another in the dark"; "lovers ... exchanged in the dark") into "the stock device of the impenetrable disguise"; see *A Natural Perspective*, 76. Boccaccio's literary descriptions of the detailed preparations for bed-tricks are themselves, of course, winking comedy; his device for leaving the ruse *un*elaborated and *un*problematic in III.9 appears all the more intended.

35 Terence, *Terence: The Comedies*, 355–98. Palmer Bovie tells us, "*Her Husband's Mother [Hecyra]* has always been one of the least popular of Terence's comedies" (355); millennial unpopularity dogs both the sources and the fortune of the III.9 tale. See also Terence, *Terence with an English Translation*, trans. John Sargeaunt, 121–211.

> since they did not do what was done intentionally, should not wish to offer their assent, by no means do we believe that the marriage should be valid. For it is established that it was done according to intention, nor can they be constrained to carry out what they neither intended when they did it, nor wished when they knew it.[36]

This is not the case in *Decameron* III.9, but traditional theology burdens the reader with yet another aspect of doubt and ambiguity.

In literature bed-tricks usually require extraordinary strategies on the part of both the protagonists and their authors. Boccaccio assures us that King Agilulfo's smelly groom (III.2) takes advantage of the dark of night and has a good hot bath to rid his body of the stench of dung so that the queen will remain blissfully unaware of the ruse: "prima in una stufa lavatosi bene acciò *che non forse l'odor del letame la reina noiasse* o la facesse accorgere dello inganno" [III.2.13; emphasis mine]. Imitating the king, he knocks loftily on the bedchamber door with a staff, and he also refrains from speaking. In the Ricciardo Minutolo tale (III.6), the author dwells upon overcoming several similar obstacles: the room at the bathhouse is windowless, and, as we are told twice, "exceedingly dark" ("la camera era oscurissima"); the jealous and willing Catella, believing Minutolo to be her philandering husband, is heavily veiled like Tamar in the Bible; both partners at first refrain from speaking (III.6.32). Most remarkably, however, in our tale III.9, Boccaccio feels no need to give us hot baths, darkness, silence, or even disguises. And he cheekily tells us that Giletta's ruse does not have to work just once, as in previous tales, but *many times* to the complete gulling of Beltramo.[37]

We must, of course, keep in mind that we are not dealing here with a previously *consummated* marriage, nor with any earlier habitual fornication with a paramour whom Beltramo already knew intimately. Both women, Giletta and the widow's daughter, are *virgines intactae*, and Beltramo is a soldier urgently needing to satisfy his bodily lust. But he has had at least *social* congress with Giletta since early childhood.

---

36 Hugh of St Victor, *De Sacramentis* 2:11:18, in *On the Sacraments of the Christian faith*, trans. Roy J. Deferrari, 369. Beltramo, by going through with the marriage ritual, has already given his intent and consent to its validity.

37 The repetition is stressed (*Decameron*, 439). Agilulfo's groom (III.2) wisely does not risk the trick again; Ricciardo Minutolo (III.6) drops his ruse during the first encounter and enjoys Catella thereafter; ironically, it is Catella, like the biblical Tamar, who takes care to disguise herself, not he.

Beyond sight, the senses of hearing, touch, and smell would come into sexual play here again, yet in III.9 the author never entertains his usual cautions about the plausibility of the bed-trick. Verisimilitude seems of no concern. Boccaccio's intentional ellipses leave open ambiguities that beggar the readers' ready acceptance and outrageously taunt their suspension of disbelief.[38]

5. Beltramo's Nightingale Connections

The personage of Beltramo must itself be classified as "problematic." While in Boccaccio's classical source, Terence's *Hecyra*, the husband Pamphilus is misguided, he is otherwise – at least when he's not blind drunk – a warm, well-behaved, and somewhat engaging character. The caddishness of Beltramo's personality on the other hand is as repellent in the *Decameron* as in all subsequent versions of the tale, Painter's, Bernardo Accolti's play *Verginia*, Antoine Le Maçon's French version (Paris, 1545, and in many printings thereafter), and Shakespeare's.[39] In none of the later adaptations does Beltramo-Bertram have redeeming features: "handsome is as handsome does *not*" obtains in them all.[40] Beltramo first acts petulantly and immaturely, disobeying the command of his king to take Giletta to wife (a childish petulance that the hopeful

38 In contrast, we reflect that two centuries later the realist Niccolò Machiavelli, giving us a variation on the Ricciardo Minutolo story, will twist the convention a little more believably in his very Boccaccian comedy *La Mandragola*, where Lucrezia, the unfulfilled wife of the foolish cuckold Messer Nicia, *knows* that the disguised man by whom she is about to be bedded is *not* her husband; Callimaco drops his "garzone" disguise, with false nose and twisted face, and has no more need either for darkness or silence as he confesses his love.

39 Compare Snyder's comments on Shakespeare's version: "Bertram is portrayed more harshly than his prototype Beltramo: as a callow snob with Helen, as an eager but crass seducer with Diana [the widow's daughter], as a dupe lacking even ordinary discernment with the tinsel Paroles whom everyone quickly sees through. There is no counterpart in Boccaccio for Bertram's repellent lies and cowardly evasions in the play's last scene" ("Introduction," 5). On various publications of Le Maçon's French version, see Mirella Ferrari, "Dal Boccacio illustrato al Boccaccio censurato," esp. 128–30. We recall that Philumena, the wife – Giletta's counterpart – never appears on stage at all in Terence's *Hecyra*.

40 The observation is Rossiter's in his chapter on *AWW*, in *Angel with Horns*, 82–107, here 87. See Boccaccio's possible source in J. Barrois's edition of d'Artois's *Le livre du Très chevalereux Comte d'Artois et de sa femme*.

Shakespeare emphasizes and elaborates to add realistic motivation);[41] Beltramo then submits, passive-aggressively, to a wedding, which he, in his narrow class consciousness, finds abhorrent. Finally, in revenge upon king and wife, he becomes a thorough churl: refusing to go home to Rossiglione, and abandoning his marriage unconsummated in France, he departs instead for far-off Florence to fight as a mercenary in its wars against Siena. By way of three knights he sends his wife a perverse missive setting out what he believes are impossible conditions for any reconciliation with her: he will return to her when she can obtain the ring from his finger and when she delivers him a son of his loins. Even more reprehensibly, he becomes willing to engage in fornication with a penniless girl of even baser station than the talented physician-now-countess whom he has wedded and shunned. Despite the efforts of certain critics to view him as having some psychologically valid motives,[42] his unprepared turnaround at the end – hardly a conversion – to the acceptance of Giletta leaves most readers feeling uneasy logically, literarily, and psychologically. Beltramo has violated all the precepts of marriage that St Paul set down in the seventh chapter of 1 Corinthians: "Let the husband render the debt to his wife" (7:3, Douay-Rheims); "The husband hath not power of his own body, but the wife" (7:4); "Let not the husband put away his wife" (7:11); "Art thou bound to a wife? Seek not to be loosed" (7:27). And Beltramo disregards the traditional teaching as expressed by Hugh of St Victor: "Marriage is an agreement between male and female that preserves their association in life."[43] And, of course, any second copulation with another is illicit.[44] St Thomas Aquinas avers that the husband must pay his wife the marital debt – even though she might not ask for it.[45]

---

41 Shakespeare grappled with Bertram's motivation in *AWW*, making him far more childish and callow than in Boccaccio. In *AWW* he has the king and other characters address the young Bertram as "boy"; Parolles terms Bertram "a foolish, idle boy, but for all that very ruttish" (4:3:278–9). Rossiter (*Angel with Horns*, 88–96) deals with the problem of the negativity of Bertram's character in Shakespeare's adaptation.

42 See Haley, *Shakespeare's Courtly Mirror*, 17–51.

43 Hugh of St Victor, *De Sacramentis* 2:2:4; *On the Sacraments*, 327.

44 Hugh of St Victor, *De Sacramentis* 2:2:5; *On the Sacraments*, 330. In chapter 6, Hugh deals with some interesting problems concerning concealed marriage and the Church's dilemma over what to hold as proven (333–4).

45 The marriage debt must be paid. See *Summa Theologica*, Supplement, qu. 64, art. 1: "The Marriage Debt": "The husband is bound to pay the debt to his wife although she ask not for it." *Summa Theologica*, 2801.

Beltramo's deeds are unacceptable under any form of moral code and his insolence and superficial snobbishness are simply abhorrent. The fact that Boccaccio does not explicitly describe his mysterious motivations leaves us with a nagging, unsolved problem. We might better approach the enigma of Beltramo in the *Decameron* as a functional construct governed both by a narrative strategy and by a subtext of myth and leitmotif.

We are quite familiar with Boccaccio's habit of classifying characters by their family, "schiatta," or clan in the *Decameron*. We have only to think of Michele Scalza's proof of the ancient nobility of the ugly Baronci clan of VI.6, who are so misshapen and of such great antiquity "as all philosophers agree" that, perforce, "quando Domenidio gli fece … apparve a dipignere" [when the Lord God made them, he was still learning to paint (VI.6.15)]. Beltramo too, as we shall become more aware, belongs to a family of repulsive characteristics. His name, "nightingale," "Rossiglione" (French "rossignol"; and in Boccaccio's language "rusignuolo," "usignuolo"), connects him and this tale not only to the "guiding song" of the nightingale introduced in and accompanying the third day, but also to the tangle of connected tales, jolly and tragic, in the collection – each of which bears thematic and structural interrelations to others in the *Decameron* (as Millicent Marcus has pointed out to us).[46]

On the first page of Day Three, at the very point when the *brigata* begin their move to the enchanted garden of the second villa, there appears the very first mention of the nightingale and its musical accompaniment in the *Decameron*: "La reina … *alla guida del canto di forse venti usignuoli* … prese il cammino" [The queen … *guided by a score or so of nightingales* … took her way (III.Intro.3)]. Thus, Neifile, the queen and *racconteuse*, led by the nightingale from the day's beginning, has introduced the bivalent and baleful myth of Procne and Philomela and the nightingale's ironically sweet music that mythically bears witness (Ovid's "testari") to Tereus's raping of Philomela, to his cutting out her tongue to keep her silent, and to Procne's blood-curdling revenge. Boccaccio repeats the "Philomena-Procne theme" as a leitmotif not only

46 For brief comments on nightingale metaphors in *Decameron* V.4, see Cesare Segre, "Da Boccaccio a Lope de Vega," 234–5. Viktor Šklovskij offers only a mention of the image in *La lettura del "Decameron"*, 217. See especially Millicent Joy Marcus, "Tragedy as Trespass," chapter 3 in *An Allegory of Form*. See also Judy Rawson's "Filomena et le rossignol dans le *Décameron*," which follows Marcus's work often *pedissequamente* with no credit at all in the notes.

through III.9 but also through several other related tales of the *Decameron* where spouses and other family members inflict unspeakable cruelties upon one another. The legend works as a powerful subtext and motivates, at least at the potential, mythic level, the transgressions of Beltramo Nightingale.

I must caution, however, that this understanding works by a process of progressive-retrogressive narrative revelation that as attentive readers we must *read back* into III.9. While Dante used a type of retrogressive revelation in imitation of the prefiguration-fulfilment patterns of the Old and New Testaments, as Charles Singleton showed so elegantly, Boccaccio was primarily aware of his earthly reception among the merchant middle class: his are twice-told, more than thrice-read tales. He knew that his merchant-readers would, and indeed did, dote on his collection, copying his tales in their cursive, business long-hand and passing copies among themselves to be reread again and again, down through generations in reappreciation and reinterpretation.

In the set of novelle following in Day Four, the unhappiness of love becomes central: the king, Filostrato, will order a theme counter to the whole consolatory plan of the *brigata* in their storytelling: "Fiera materia di ragionare n'ha il nostro re data" [Cruel is the subject for discussion given us by our king (IV.1.2)].[47] Filostrato selfishly claims the privilege of living up to the pseudonym-nickname that the author and his fictional society have bestowed on him, meaning "unhappy, or vanquished in love": "E per ciò non d'altra materia domane me piace che si ragioni se non di quello che a' miei fatti è piú conforme, cioè di coloro li cui amori ebbero infelice fine" [And so I prefer no other subject tomorrow other than that which most conforms to my interests, that is, of those whose love affairs had unhappy endings (III.Concl.6)]. Then for *Decameron* IV.1, Filostrato orders Fiammetta to tell the first sad and tragic story, and, torn and distressed, she obliges with the tale of Tancredi, prince of Salerno, and his mature and widowed daughter, Ghismonda.

Thus this next tale-but-one repeats the "infatuated woman and the obstructing male" themes of III.9, but with considerable variation. Ghismonda adores the humble Guiscardo for his virtue. Prince Tancredi, her crypto-incestuous and effeminate father, rejects the suitor because

47 See Marcus, *An Allegory of Form*, 54.

of his lack of noble birth.[48] Neglecting his princely and paternal obligations, thwarting his lonely daughter's needs, and destroying her love affair, the prince sends Guiscardo's heart to her in a large goblet, whereupon she pours poison over it and drinks, committing suicide.

In *Decameron* IV.5, Filomena is called upon: she recounts the similar "Pot of Basil" story, in which Lisa, after the ghostly apparition of her beloved – who reveals the whereabouts of his corpse – plants the disinterred head of her beloved – who has been killed by her brothers as an unfit, lowborn marital match – in a flowerpot. The narrator's name, the usual contemporary variant of Philomela, reminds the reader of Boccaccio's retelling of Ovid's savage myth in the earlier *Teseida* 4:54. Procne, given by her father in an arranged, loveless marriage to the unfaithful Tereus, to avenge the rape and outrage he has committed upon her sister, feeds the cooked flesh of her own son Itys to her husband in several enticing courses. In the *Teseida,* Boccaccio makes the avian transformations absolutely explicit: Procne metamorphosed into a swallow, while her sister Philomela (Filomena) became the nightingale, the literary bird of night: "Progne diventò rondine e Filomela usignuolo."[49]

In *Decameron* IV.9, the king, Filostrato, instigator of the *brigata*'s anger and depression with his tragic topic for the day, pours yet more salt into their wounds as he insists on reworking the gruesome ending of the Ghismonda tale yet again in the ninth story of the fourth day concerning one of Beltramo Rossiglione's brutal relatives, this time, Guglielmo Rossiglione ("William Nightingale"). Procne-like, this member of the wretched clan as heartless husband tricks his wife into eating, to the very last bite, the heart of his former friend and her clandestine lover, minced, cooked, and served up in a silver tureen. Guglielmo sneers his wicked

48 We must note that in Painter's *Palace of Pleasure* the tale of "Tancred of Salerne" (the nearby Ghismonda tale in *Decameron* IV.1) follows *directly* upon the tale of "Gilette" and Bertram. Bertram expresses the same sentiments concerning class-unworthiness in Shakespeare's *All's Well* as Tancred does in Boccaccio's *Decameron* and Painter's English version.

49 Ovid, *Metamorphoses* 6.668. Giovanni Boccaccio, *Tutte le opere*, vol. 2, *Teseida delle nozze di Emilia*, ed. Alberto Limentani, 370, and see esp. n. 1. Completing the avian transformations, Tereus becomes a hoopoe, the "becchipuzzola" or "upupa," the bird of corpses and cemeteries; the little, cannibalized and roasted, Itys turns into an old-world robin, a "pettirosso" (6.671ff). See also Rawson, "Filomena et le rossignol dans le *Décameron*," 161–71.

revelation as if he were Vincent Price in a film by Roger Corman, "[Non] me ne maraviglio se morto v'è piaciuto ciò che vivo piú che altra cosa vi piacque" [I am not surprised that you liked it dead, for when it lived you liked it better than anything else (IV.9.20)]. His cruelty causes his wife to hurl herself from a window to her death; Boccaccio emphasizes "tutta si disfece" [she totally destroyed herself]. This Rossiglione, as does his kinsman Beltramo, then simply flees the scene of his dastardly treachery. Again here, as in the tale of Prince Tancredi of Salerno ("ammenduni in un medesimo sepolcro gli fè sepellire" [IV.1.62]), the lovers' bodies are placed in a single tomb ("in una medesima sepultura fur posti" [IV.9.25]).

In the tenth, following, tale of the day, Dioneo tells us that "Le miserie degl'infelici amori raccontate ... a me hanno già contristati gli occhi e'l petto, per che io sommamente disiderato ho che a capo se ne venisse. Ora, lodato sia Iddio, che finite sono" [These wretched tales of unhappy love affairs ... have brought so much sadness to my eyes and heart that I have most greatly wished that they would come to an end. Praise be to God that they are now over and done with (IV.10.3)]. As Millicent Marcus observed, Boccaccio will have Filostrato later make amends for twice so distressing the framework *brigata* by recounting the famous "catching nightingales" tale of V.4 (*An Allegory of Form*, 55–6). Filostrato there reworks the Ghismonda-Tancredi tale as the joyous nuptial story of Caterina, her lover Ricciardo Mainardi, and her approving father Lizio da Valbona, giving them all a happy ending of wise acceptance, celebration, and reintegration – the very thing, we must add, that Giletta most desires and manages to contrive for herself.

For lovers, the nightingale accompanies and signifies sexual revel and consummation *in bono*: Boccaccio's Caterina Valbona (whose tale in *Decameron* V:4 bears eleven mentions of the bird) catches phallic nightingales of sexual love.[50] The nightingale, however, recalls, *in malo*, outrage, blood, murder, and tragedy. Beltramo hails from a most cowardly and murderous clan indeed and has inherited a name of mythical gore; the actions of this youthful scion bear out his kinsmen's cruel and brutal

---

50 We think immediately of Shakespeare's wonderful nuptial scene in *Romeo and Juliet*, the very culmination of the "alba" or "dawn" poetic tradition where the nightingale plays a central role. There are three other uses of "usignuolo" in the tales of the *Decameron*: one in III.9, with which we deal here, one in VI.10 and one in the Introduction to Day Seven. See Alfredo Barbina, ed., *Concordanze del "Decameron,"* 2:2059. The Rossiglione family appears in III.9 and IV.9. See also Louise O. Vasvari, "L'usignuolo in gabbia," 224–51.

traits. He smacks more of the impious Tereus and of the butcherly Procne than of the family man he is supposed to become at the end of the tale; his conversion to connubial and paternal duties simply comes too suddenly and too late.

Boccaccio reveals Beltramo's miscreance in other ways. We can, I believe, leave aside those who have seen him as a "victim of the establishment," and especially of the king (something developed in Shakespeare's adaptation): social norms of nobility and royalty demanded more often an arranged marriage than one entered into by choice and love of the betrothed. Giletta, the daughter of a famous and wealthy physician, who Beltramo admits is most beautiful, is after all not quite so far down in the social scale as he pretends, and it lies within the powers and privileges of the king of France to ennoble whomsoever he wishes. Although Boccaccio's friend Francesco Petrarch famously denigrates physicians in his *Invective contra medicum*, writers on medicine and teachers at universities were academically trained men in the learned Hippocratic-Galenic tradition who, as here, enjoyed great social prestige and admiration, becoming physicians to Church prelates and nobility, popes and kings: a university doctorate, or "master's" degree, was in important ways considered equal to a knighthood. Many who engaged in the medical profession did so licitly and successfully through long apprenticeship, and this is the case, officially or unofficially, with Giletta and her father: "la scienza del maestro Gerardo nerbonese" (III.9.12), "dal padre aveva assai cose apprese" [she had learned a lot from her father (III.9.8)].[51]

Beltramo has the loutish audacity even to flout Aristotle's definition of nobility. In the first book of the *Politics* the Philosopher himself had declared that nobility (or "good birth") proceeded socially "from virtue and ancient *riches*," while Juvenal in *Satire* 8:20 had reasserted the old saw that virtue alone was its source: "'Nobility [of mind] is the one and

51 Historically, many advances in medical knowledge in the fourteenth century did in fact come from practical, empirical experience. See Nancy G. Siraisi, "Practitioners and Conditions of Practice." At Montpellier University in the Languedoc in 1239, Henry of Mondeville gained great fame by writing on, practising, and teaching surgery there in the first decades of the fourteenth century. On the other hand, quacks and those among the lowest classes who provided medical treatment *without* official training and licence, even successfully, were prosecuted and fined. See Michael McVaugh, "The History of Medicine." For Shakespeare, see Alban H.G. Doran, "Medicine."

only virtue."[52] If we may take Dante's citation of these two diverse classical opinions in his *Monarchia*, Book 2, as a synopsis of fourteenth-century understanding of what constituted nobility, we must conclude that Beltramo is aberrant in snobbishly misjudging Giletta on both counts: first, her considerable riches inherited from her father are the major social restraint that causes her to be so carefully watched and restricted in the noble court of Rossiglione;[53] and secondly, Beltramo ignores her obvious personal virtues (her "virtù") and is blind to her accomplishments until the very last page, when, after the moment of her

52 The young *dolcestilnovista* Dante in the *Convivio* quite misunderstood the origin of the concepts of nobility, but the mature political poet in the second book of the *Monarchia* outlines it clearly. "As the Philosopher says in his *Politics*, "Nobility is virtue and ancient riches"; and according to Juvenal: "Nobility of mind is the one and only virtue." These differing opinions yield two kinds of nobility: that is to say, one's own and that of one's ancestors (*Monarchia* 2.3.4). Dante is probably citing from memory. Aristotle had actually said "*a good birth* is wealth plus virtue going back to one's forbears." Moerbeke, in the widely distributed first Latin translation, used by both Dante and St Thomas Aquinas, had rendered "good birth" as "ingenuitas," not "nobilitas": "*Ingenuitas* enim est virtus et divitiæ antiquæ" [being well-born is virtue and ancient riches (*Politics* IV, 7, 1294a22–3)]. See Aquinas, *In politicorum, Lectio* VII, *Textus Aristotelis 470*, ed. Raymundi M. Spiazzi, 211; Aristotle, *The Politics*, trans. T.A. Sinclair, rev. Trevor J. Saunders, 260. H. Rackham (*Politics* IV, 6: 1294a22–3) translates "nobility means ancient worth and virtue." *Aristotle in Twenty Three Volumes*, 319. Dante had conflated "good birth" with St Thomas's "nobilitas." "Nobility of mind is the one and only virtue." "Nobilitas animi sola est atque unica virtus." Dante also seems to be citing Juvenal's *Satire* 8:20 from memory, adding the word "animi" ["of mind"] that he had found in the twelfth-century *Moralium dogma philosophorum* compiled by William of Conches (or, perhaps, Walter of Châtillon), which gives the sentence better sense; see the edition of the *Moralium* by John Holmberg, 54; see also the version in J.-P. Migne, *Patrologia latina* 171:1073. Dante cites Juvenal's satire on ancestral pride in *Convivio* 4:29:4; there Dante also closely follows Brunetto Latini, *Tresor* 2:114, where Brunetto cites the *Moralium* as he affirms the idea of virtue's constituting nobility (see *Li livres dou Tresor*, ed. F. Carmody, 2:114); however, Brunetto attributes the "virtue alone" thesis solely to Horace instead of Juvenal (see C.T. Davis, *Dante's Italy*, 180–1). We might also consider nobility as presented in Guido Guinizelli's "Al cor gentil rempaira sempre amore." Dante encapsulates these inherited views of the fourteenth century, and Boccaccio's understanding conforms to them. Shakespeare refers to the twinned concepts in 1.1.64–5: "Thy blood and virtue contend for empire in thee." See also Bradbrook, *Muriel Bradbrook on Shakespeare*, 84–98.

53 Painter was quite wrong in adding an arbitrary adjective here in his translation: "A *poor* physician's daughter my wife." The heiress Giletta is kept closely guarded because of her great wealth.

revelations, an ebullition of affection finally overwhelms him. Giletta is the power that forces the immature Beltramo to recognize his own male, phallic powers of begetting and that re-masculinizes him into accepting his place as patriarch.

6. Giletta

The misogynist narrator of the *Corbaccio* gives a vivid list of the incredible dangers faced and feats accomplished by women in the satisfaction of their lusts that reflects the many tricks played by women in the *Decameron*, many of them effected in the tales of Day Seven.

> What will they not dare to satisfy this bestial appetite of theirs? … However, they lend great courage to the shameful things they want to do. How many in the past have gone and go up yet to the tops of houses, palaces, or towers, called and awaited by their lovers? How many in the past have dared and dare every day to hide their lovers from their husbands' eyes under either hampers or chests? How many have had them enter silently into the same bed with their husbands? How many are constantly found following the one who performs best, alone, at night and amidst armies, even across the sea, and through church cemeteries … ?[54]

Giletta's industrious prowess and guile are common and even typical in the literary genres of misogyny, *fabliaux*, and encomiums of women,[55] and hers is obviously not the unique case in which Boccaccio reversed antifeminist charges as praise. Giletta succeeds where her famous and tragic forerunner, the mythical Penthesilea of the *De claris mulieribus*, chapter 32, does not: passionately falling in love with Hector, sight unseen, and desiring an illustrious child by him, Penthesilea journeys to Troy with her great body of troops to demonstrate her manly virtues to

54 Giovanni Boccaccio, *The Corbaccio*, trans. Anthony K. Cassell, 27–8. Compare the tales in the *Decameron* where such exploits are put into practice, such as II.10 (crossing seas), IV.10 (chests), V.10 (hampers), VII.9 (though their husbands are looking), and so on.

55 Hans Robert Jauss's historicist theories, for example, are impossible if the theory of genres be excluded; deconstruction has at long last fairly eliminated Benedetto Croce's aesthetics, those notions that so hobbled literary criticism into the twentieth century; Croce was against such classifying because he held that the individual work of art was a product of unique intuition.

Hector and bed the hero; but, when she arrives, Hector is already slain and embalmed, and Pyrrhus slays her in a subsequent battle.[56] For Sulpicia's successful travels to find her worthy husband, Lentulus, in chapter 85, Boccaccio draws on both the *Corbaccio* and the *Decameron* for details:

> True love … eludes all sentinels. Sulpicia seized the right moment, dressed herself in slave's clothing, and tricked her mother and her other guards. Accompanied only by two little servant girls and two slaves … to follow her husband's faint trail in secret flight through raging seas and over the mountains of Italy to look for him in unknown regions until she found him and took her place by his side. (*De claris mulieribus/Famous Women*, chapter 85, 350)

Quite similar in such antifeminist reversals as well are Madonna Filippa's comically twisted legal excogitations in *Decameron* VI.7. Chaucer later takes up this world-upside-down trick in the prologue of the Wife of Bath, turning the scurrilous into boast.[57] To a great extent, Giletta's travels and deeds adhere to this pattern of reversing misogynist slander, leaving a cloud that colours her heroics in the plot.

Immediately upon the ending of III.9, Boccaccio's "autore" has the tale of Alibech then immediately "prove" the urgency, implacability, and inevitability of both female and male lust, and, after telling of Filippo Balducci's incorrigible son in the Introduction to Day Four, he feigns apologies for his ribald tales, saying that he indeed strives too much to please the ladies:

> Dicono adunque alquanti de' miei riprensori che io fo male, o giovani donne, troppo ingegnandomi di piacervi, e che voi troppo piacete a me. Le quali cose io apertissimamente confesso, cioè che voi mi piacete e che io m'ingegno di piacere a voi: e domandogli se di questo essi si maravigliano … quando colui che nudrito, allevato, accresciuto sopra un monte salvatico e solitario, infra li termini d'una piccola cella, *senza altra compagnia che*

56 See *De claris mulieribus/Famous Women*, ed. and trans. Virginia Brown, 130–1. Christine de Pisan repeats the tale in *La Cité des dames* 1:18; see *The Book of the City of the Ladies*, trans. Rosalind Brown-Grant, 43–6.

57 Geoffrey Chaucer, "The Prologue of the Wyves Tale of Bathe," in *The Complete Poetry and Prose of Geoffrey Chaucer*, 107–20.

> *del padre*, come vi vide, sole da lui disiderate foste, sole adomandate, sole con l'affezion seguitate. (IV.Intro.30–1; emphasis mine)
>
> [Some of my detractors say that I do ill, O youthful Ladies, striving too much to please you and that you please me too much. I openly confess to these charges: that is that you please me and that I strive to please you. And I ask them why they find anything surprising about this … when, after all, even a young man who had been nurtured and bred within the confines of a tiny cell on a bleak and wild mountainside, *with only his father for company*, no sooner caught a glimpse of you than you and you alone became his whole desire, his whole yearning, and the whole bent of his affection.]

Without the clause referring to the father, could we really tell whether that cell was Rustico's or Filippo Balducci's? Boccaccio thus stresses his double send-up of Christian asceticism that *comes immediately after our already-fading reading of the III.9 tale*. The author has made sure that his envious critics have indeed found a bone not only "surprising" but quite shocking to distract them. And he adds for the puzzle-loving reader a spicy tidbit that is even more religiously subversive. *Pace* all editors who have dutifully repeated for centuries the simply tiresome and quite unhelpful footnote that Filippo Balducci's cave on Mount Asinaio is "Monte Senario: a mountain near Florence." Let us note, once and for all, that "Asinaio" is not only *prima facie* "asin-ine," but that it contains an even more irreverent joke: "A-*Sinai*-O." That very "-Sinai-" (of St Catherine's hermitage and of Great-Circle pilgrimage fame, the very Mountain where God traditionally gave the Ten Commandments to Moses) is itself book-ended here with the familiar "alpha-omega" ["α-ω"/A-Ω] topos of theology in art and literature – just as in the traditional Christogram, the Chi-Rho, flanked by alpha and omega, signifying Christ's Resurrection and his divinity as "*Arbiter Omnipotens.*" At the end of the *Letter to Can Grande della Scala*, Dante tells his patron and all his future readers that the Pilgrim of the *Commedia* has reached the vision of all truth at the last canto: "And since, having reached the beginning and first cause which is God, there is nothing further to seek, he being Alpha and Omega, or the first and the last (as he designated in John's vision in Revelation 1:8; 21:6, 22:13), the treatise [that is, the *Divine Comedy*] comes to an end in God himself, who is blessed in the world without end" (*Epistle* XIII.90). But Boccaccio's Filippo Balducci, having climbed and dwelt on Monte A-Sinai-O, has to descend and see his son seek something else: the earthly and the sexual. In the *Decameron*, "alpha and omega" becomes a composite pun yielding a totally opposite, comic and parodic effect.[58] Once again let us note here that Boccaccio saves not only his broad, slapstick pornography but also this elegant, intellectual conundrum "A-Sinai-O" pun for the one and a half tales that *follow* the Giletta tale; only when III.9 has passed are we manipulated into pausing in the moment, to laugh, and then to ponder the intensity and cleverness of Boccaccio's comic, satiric, and joyful naughtiness and his writing's utter defencelessness in any Christian, authoritarian context.

Millicent Marcus in her wonderful book, *An Allegory of Form* (perhaps in the archetypal wake of Hans Robert Jauss's *Rezeptions Aesthetik* and Jauss's theory of the "horizon of expectation" anticipated by a literary work's contemporary readers), shows that the myriad differing genres that Boccaccio combines in the *Decameron* govern the behaviour and actions of the characters; the women, like the men, may not *behave as real people* but *as they are expected to* in the genre in which they appear; conflicting genres present discordant characters.[59]

Griselda, for example, does not fit the biblical Job, nor the Marian tradition, nor even the wooden characters of hagiography, despite

---

58 Christ in the Apocalypse says, "I am the alpha and the omega, the beginning and the end" (Revelation 1:8; see also 21:6; 22:13). In art, the first and last letters of the Greek alphabet flank the Chi Rho, representations of the Cross, of Christ in Majesty, of his Transfiguration, and of the Crucifixion as a sign of his eternity and his Resurrection. For the "alpha-omega" topos as used in theology, see F. Châtillon, "*Arbiter omnipotens* et le symbole de l'Alpha et de l'Omega." See also Leslie Brubaker, "Alpha and Omega." On Mount Sinai as an inspiration for Dante, see John Demaray, *Dante and the Book of the Cosmos*, especially 18–19, 26–9; the volume contains striking illustrations. Relations between the Orthodox monks of St Catherine's Monastery and the Papacy were strong in the first half of the fourteenth century, especially under Pope John XXII; in the tenth and eleventh centuries, Greek anchorites from Mount Sinai had come to Italy and stimulated the Camaldolese movement. See Heinz Skobucha, in *Sinai*, 88–9; Demaray, *Dante and the Book of the Cosmos*, 26. For the Letter to Can Grande, see Robert S. Haller, *The Literary Criticism of Dante Alighieri*, 113, and *Dantis Alaghieri Epistolae: The Letters of Dante Alighieri*, 2nd ed., ed. Paget Toynbee, rev. Colin Hardie, 160–211.

59 Marcus, *An Allegory of Form*, 54–6. Marcus does not, however, list Jauss in her bibliography, although much of her independent thought is parallel to his; see Hans Robert Jauss, *Toward an Aesthetic of Reception*, 144–7, and see also his *Aesthetic Experience and Literary Hermeneutics*. "Boccaccio is constituting a new order of genre as he goes along," comments F. Regina Psaki, "Genres," in her "Women in the *Decameron*," 81–2. See also Lucia Battaglia Ricci, "*Decameron*: Interferenze di modelli."

Boccaccio's teasing misleads; her example mainly serves, in the *brigata*'s final comments, to lampoon such saintly moralizings. Ser Ciappelletto's life spoofs the whole tradition of exempla, and of saints' legends, yet Dioneo supposes that prayers addressed to the wicked notary for intercession are actually granted by God. We cannot pigeonhole the type of tale that III.9 is at all: is it adventure, *fabliau*, or romance? None of these three quite fit. The tale lacks any effective sense of magic or of the fantastic; too short to be a *gest*, it is certainly not an aristocratic *lai*, nor a vision, sermon, *motto*, confession, antifeminist diatribe, hagiography, or exemplum – modern readers cannot make it fit any of the traditional genres comfortably.

Notwithstanding, let us attempt, as an experiment, to see III.9 as a pious *fabula* and examine the exegetical consequences. We do not undertake this exercise capriciously, since Boccaccio himself conceived *both* Christ's parables *and* Terence's plots as his third category of *fabula* in the *Genealogiae deorum gentilium*, 14:9 and 14:18. Not only does Boccaccio derive his second plot from Terence's *Hecyra* but Christ himself, he tells us, actually cited Terence against the stricken Paul: "It is hard for thee to kick against the pricks."[60] Let us for a moment, then, give Giletta the benefit of our doubts, and, instead of attributing her actions to a rather ruthless willingness to descend even to near-whoredom to gain her own sexual ends,[61] view the deception of her subjects and her later sexual *inganno* as a *holy* deceit, an "*onesto fine*" (as the widow rather grudgingly and belatedly observes in self-exculpation [III.9.48]),[62] a respectable, righteous goal, acceptable not only to set right her own status as wife but also to fulfil the twofold Marriage Sacrament of the Holy Roman Catholic and Apostolic Church.[63] Marriage's sacramental

60 See Osgood, *Boccaccio on Poetry*, 87.

61 Hugh of St Victor, in the *De Sacramentis* 2:11:8, declares that there are "Three blessings that accompany marriage, namely, faith, hope of progeny and sacrament. In faith care is taken that there be no lying with another woman or with another man outside of the conjugal bond." Progeny are to be duly cared for spiritually and bodily, and sacramentally divorce must not occur, nor can one partner be joined to yet another for progeny (*On the Sacraments*, 339).

62 The penniless, déclassée Florentine widow considers Countess Giletta's objective as worthy and quite proper (*Decameron*, 439).

63 In marriage "a *twofold* sacrament exists: one in carnal intermingling, the sacrament of that association which exists between Christ and Church; the other in conjugal association, the sacrament of that association which exists between God and soul." *De Sacramentis* 2:11:8; *On the Sacraments*, 341. We must remark that all seven

benefits are indeed effected here according to the theology of marriage: the final consummation technically removes the sinfulness of Beltramo's sexual lust; it fulfils the joining of the flesh in the image of the union of Christ with his Church, and it produces children as Genesis 1:22 and 1:28 command.[64] Indeed, for the Body of Christ which is his Church there is much benefit. The estimable, Presbyterian, Northrop Frye (*The Myth of Deliverance*, 55) even saw in Giletta-Helena's ascendancy in social station in *All's Well* a solemn echo of Mary's Magnificat: "Deposuit potentes de sede et *exaltavit humiles*" [He has put down the mighty from their seats, and hath *exalted the humble* (Vulgate and Douay-Rheims, Luke 1:46–55)].

But Boccaccio's overwhelming carnival irony allows us to entertain such ideas only fleetingly: he avoids any direct pious, biblical, theological, or legal references in the text – although we know that as a learned canonist, the writer was quite able to have provided them had he wished.[65] Boccaccio simply does not dwell on the religiosity he misdirects us to, for such emphasis would detract from the intentional superficiality and the worldly amusement of his telling. Instead, he shows us that his earthly, rather proto-Machiavellian and determined Giletta believes firmly that her ends allow her to use all means at her disposal, disregarding any trammel of patriarchal justice. If any religious motive has governed Giletta, her own fleshly abandon and the boisterous

---

sacraments probably also obtain in Shakespeare's post-Reformation *All's Well That Ends Well*. In 1.3.94–6, the (most probably Anglican) Fool mentions that Church of England ministers had to wear a surplice when officiating, and he mocks Puritan reformers who, wishing "to do no hurt" or offence, pulled a surplice over their black gowns, "though honesty be no Puritan"! See Folger Library ed., 31 and 223; we recall that in *Hamlet*, the hero has no time for "churlish" – that is Roman Catholic – priests.

64 See Hugh of St Victor, *De Sacramentis* 2:11:3; *On the Sacraments*, 325. Concerning the Alatiel tale (*Decameron* II:7), Ferrante (173) cites William of Ockham's *Commentary on Peter Lombard's Sentences*: "William Ockham goes even further, saying that the act of virginity is to abstain from a man for [the sake of] God, in the manner in which God wishes me to abstain. If I wish to abstain, but God wants or orders me to have a man [husband], wishing to have the man since God wants it, I acquire conjugal chastity but nonetheless retain virginity, since I always have the will to abstain 'volendo tunc habere virum quia Deus vult hoc, adquiro castitatem coniugalem et nihilominus retineo virginitatem', *Quaestiones in librum tertium sententiarum, Reportatio*, Bk III, q. xii)."

65 He might very well have had in mind something like Dante's dictum in the *Monarchia* 2:2 that "whatever is pursued righteously has righteousness for its end" and decided to play with it ironically.

sexuality of the surrounding tales immediately eclipses it. Her tale ends with consummation and feasting, and the carnival of sex-and-food finds its way into the following day.[66] I must point out that Alibech's *ali*-mentary "-*bech*" name is not only a joke in itself[67] but also puns on and heralds the feeding-the-poultry metaphors in the conversation between the hermit Filippo Balducci and his hermit son in the next "half" tale – the 101st of the *Decameron*: "Elle si chiamano papere"; "Padre mio, io vi priego che voi facciate che io abbia una di quelle papere ... Deh! Se vi cal di me, fate che noi ci ne meniamo una colà sú di queste papere, e io le darò [da] *becc*are ... "; "Non sai donde elle s'im*becc*ano" [They're called ducklings; Daddy, I beg you, do let me have one of those ducklings! ... Oh, if you care about me, let's take one of them up there with us and I'll give it stuff to peck on; You've no idea what they peck on].[68] Our *fantasia impura* is tickled into paroxysms as Ali-bech's "ninferno" along with the vaginas of the girlish wedding guests become metaphorically the duck's beak, and the phallic "devil" shrivels to bird-food.[69]

---

66 In fact Boccaccio customarily joins metaphors of food, fasting, and feasting when speaking of sexual intercourse. Compare Fiordaliso's erotic sweetmeats and wine as she pretends to seduce poor Andreuccio, or the fasting and feasting of Isabetta, who is yoked to the abstentious tertiary Friar Puccio in *Decameron* III.4: "Faceva molto spesso troppo più lunghe diete che voluto non avrebbe" [She was continually having to diet more than she would have wanted (III.4.6)]. "E parendo molto bene stare alla donna, s'avezzò a' cibi del monaco, che, essendo dal marito lungamente stata tenuta in dieta, ancora che la penitenzia di frate Puccio si consumasse, modo trovò di cibarsi in altra parte con lui e con discrezione lungamente ne prese il suo piacere" [And when Friar Puccio's penance was all done, since the lady felt so on top of the world, she became addicted to the monk's food; so that having been kept on a diet so long by her husband, she found ways to dine with the monk elsewhere and indulge herself with him both at her leisure and discreetly (III.4.32)] .

67 Latin *alimentum*: food; Latin *beccus* and Italian *becco*, from Gallic, signifying "beak" or "bill." "ALI-BEC" could easily be a modern brand of bird food!

68 A note on translating "papere": "anatra" (or "anitra") is "duck" on an Italian menu, while Disney's Donald Duck in the cartoons is Paperino; a "paperina" conjures the image of a fuzzy yellow and brown baby duck, as in the child's song "Papaveri e papere," made so famous by Beniamino Gigli. While "duckling" is found in farmyards and roasted on menus in English-speaking countries, I have yet to encounter "gosling" roasted on any Anglo-Saxon menu anywhere – the term is certainly not current among children in the USA, Australia, Canada, or Britain, while Paperino or Donald Duck is recognizable worldwide.

69 We must note also, parenthetically, that this half story in the Introduction is the naughty *eleventh* tale of Day Four: and eleven was, after all, the "number of all sin," for St Gregory the Great. Eleven was one less than twelve (one short of totality,

At all events, as readers we must observe that the lubricious concerns of the *Decameron* have by now been so radically and immediately charged after III.9 that *the puns and sexual exploits of Alibech have already completely overshadowed, if not totally obliterated from our minds, the adventures of Giletta and Beltramo.*

In both III.9 and III.10, it turns out that the men are bested by the strength of women's industrious lust. Alibech's insatiability eventually saps the health and spirituality of the heretofore ascetic, fasting young hermit. Rustico, at first the eager instigator and partner, is almost the reverse of Beltramo in every way; the cad who is by Christian law obliged to fulfil *licit* sex contrasts with the till-now decent ascetic who can only indulge in sex sinfully.[70] The giddy Alibech journeys for religious solace in "the service of God," much as Giletta feigns she does: "intendeva di consumare il rimanente della sua vita in pellegrinaggi e in servigi misericordiosi per salute dell'anima sua" [she intended to spend the rest of her life making pilgrimages and in works of charity for the salvation of her soul (III.9.33)]. Alibech's religious dedication leads her unexpectedly to discovering and fulfilling her own lust too with her new-found partner. No *terzo incomodo* or jealousy comes to disturb either couple,[71] and implacable sexual desire conquers all. Thus Dioneo's tenth tale of Alibech in fact bawdily parodies Neifile's (*comparatively* chaste!) tale of Giletta's quest and conquest (truly, in III.9, *il tacere è bello*).

Later in the Conclusion, when Dioneo jokingly complains of the chastity of the ladies of the *brigata* and praises their extrovert leadership in the first three days with "You have not been behaving like sheep," Neifile again ironically asserts the woman as the predatory partner, allying herself with the forward nuns in the salacious tale of Masetto da Lamporecchio of *Decameron* III.1: "Odi Filostrato: voi avreste, volendo a noi insegnare, *potuto apparar senno come apparò Masetto da Lamporecchio*

---

abundance, and fullness) and exceeded ten, the number of perfection. Alibech's tale may owe much to a *fabliau* by Rutebeuf (fl. 1248–77), "De Frère Denise," who, like Héloise, is seduced by lessons; see R. Howard Bloch, *The Scandal of the Fabliaux*, 44. Neither Bloch nor Lee (*The Decameron*) notes III.9's similarities to the Alibech tale.

70 See St Paul's dicta in 1 Corinthians 7, in the text below.

71 Stavros Delighiorgis, "Neifile's Reign," chapter 3 in *Narrative Intellection in the Decameron*, 68. The love triangle indeed plays a role in Day Three. We think of Filostrato's blasphemous first tale where Masetto lends Christ a set of cuckold's horns (echoing Dante's *tenzone* with Forese), but the last two tales do not employ it. On lust triangles in the third day, see Maria Gabriella Stassi, "Amore e industria: III Giornata."

dalle monache a riaver la favella a tale ora che l'ossa senza maestro avrebbono apparato a sufolare" [Listen, Filostrato: if you men intended to teach us (anything of the sort), *you would have learned some sense [from us], as Masetto did from the nuns*, and regained the use of your speech when your bones were rattling from exhaustion (III.Concl.3)].

In fact, something out-of-kilter, something emotionally and physically askew always seems to dog Giletta's adoration of Beltramo in the story. Even when her passion is first presented, it is both precocious and excessive. "Giletta, la quale *infinito* amore e *oltre al convenevole della tenera età* fervente pose a questo Beltramo" [Giletta, who bore this Beltramo infinite love, quite *beyond what was seemly* for her tender years" (III.9.27; emphasis mine)].[72] She loves him "more than herself" (III.9.27), not for his virtues but for his exceeding bodily good looks, a fact that is hyperdetermined by the author: "Beltramo, il quale era bellissimo e piacevole"; "Ora avvenne che, ardendo ella d'amor di Beltramo piú che mai, per ciò che bellissimo giovane udiva ch'era divenuto" [Beltramo, who was handsome and attractive; Now it happened that, she, burning with love for Beltramo more than ever, since she heard he had grown up to be a handsome youth (III.9.7)]. She insists on possessing him even though he rejects her outright and immediately. Does her wilful and excessive desire to manipulate and dominate, backed by royal command, spell true love for another? We must respond in the negative, for Neifile's heroine attempts to *earn* what should be love psychologically and theologically freely given: as the king says: "Damigella, voi avete ben *guadagnato* il marito" [Young lady, you have well *earned* a husband (III.9.17)]. Giletta's "love" is pure *eros* and *aphrodisia*, not Christian *agape*.[73] Belying her pilgrim's cloak, her virtues are all thoroughly political, not spiritual. The orphaned Giletta really knows nothing of true, unselfish, unmotivated, and unmerited human love on the pattern of the Christian God's love for mankind, a grace freely given, a love gratuitous beyond merit and understanding. She follows instead a more heathen quest to complete her full, even orgiastic, initiation into womanhood: cut off from intimate contact, isolated and blocked by the court and obstructed by her husband, an orphan whose mother is never present or even

---

72 Painter freely translated: "[She] fervently fell in love with Beltramo, more than was meet for a maiden of her age." Lope de Vega uses the Caterina-Nightingale tale in *El ruiseñor de Sevilla*; see Segre, "Da Boccaccio a Lope de Vega," 231, 234–5.

73 For transporting desire and *aphrodisia* and its devaluation in Christianity, see Michel Foucault, *The Use of Pleasure*, vol. 2, 42–3, et passim.

mentioned, she chooses alone to complete her own secret initiation passage from maidenhood by achieving childbirth.[74]

But let us move now from these religious and ritualistic observations to examine Giletta's much more applicable medical and psychological motives.

Giletta pursues her goal avidly from beginning to end; critics who see merely a collision of two plot commonplaces have failed to see that a medical theme strongly unites the two parts of the tale, just as medical considerations govern the whole framework and action of the Hundred Tales' narrators; the *Decameron* is, as we all recognize, a prophylaxis from the plague:

> Quanti valorosi uomini, quantte belle donne, quanti leggiadri giovani, li quali non che altri, ma Galieno, Ipocrate o Euscalapio avrieno giudicati sanissimi, la mattina desinarono co' lor parenti, compagni e amici, che poi la sera vegnente appresso nell'altro mondo cenaron con li lor passati! (I.Intro.48)
>
> [How many valiant gentlemen, how many fair ladies and sprightly youths, whom Galen, Hippocrates, and Aesculapius (to say nothing of others) would have judged hale and hearty, having breakfasted in the morning with their kinsfolk, acquaintances, and friends, supped later that very evening with their dead ancestors in the next world!][75]

Hippocrates and Galen: we may not have emphasized enough the implication of Giletta's being a student of her famous father Gerardo: "dal padre aveva assai cose apprese" [she had learned many things from her father (III.9.8)]. As a young woman who is truly not only "bella" but

74 See Mircea Eliade, "Degrees in Female Initiations," in *Rites and Symbols of Initiation*, 44–7, et passim. He examines initiation rites from Australia's aborigines to European modern societies.

75 If it were not clear before, the "Author" here is obviously *not* Boccaccio, the composer of the *Genealogiae deorum gentilium*, who knew very well that Asclepius-Aesculapius, son of Apollo and pupil of Chiron, was the ancient god of healing and not a mere physician or writer. Boccaccio is also amusing himself by making the waggish Author ignorant of their order in history: Hippocrates, a contemporary of Socrates, flourished in the fifth century BC, while Galen of Pergamon was born in 129 and died in 199 AD; Aesculapius's cult had been brought to Rome after the plague in 293 BC.

"savia," as the French king protests to Beltramo (III.9.25) – and unlike Shakespeare's comparatively limited Helena in *All's Well*, who is bequeathed merely a few paternal recipes – Giletta has a serious, now proven, knowledge of traditional medicine and has as good and as learned medical reasons for acting as she does in the second, peregrine, part of the tale as she had in the first. Giletta and her father, like their creator Boccaccio, most likely learned about Timaeus of Locri's views on the *hystera*, or womb, from Plato's *Timaeus* 92c:

> In women ... what is called *the uterus* or *womb*, a living thing within them with a desire for child bearing, if it remains long barren after puberty, is distressed and frustrated, and *wandering throughout the body and blocking the breathing passages, by impeding respiration, brings the sufferer to extreme distress* and causes all manner of disorders; until at last the Eros [of the man] of the one and the Desire of the other [the woman] bring the pair together, pluck as it were the fruit from the tree and sow the ploughland of the woman with living creatures [*zoa*] ... by bringing them to the light of day [they] accomplish the birth of the living creature.[76]

According to Hippocrates (469–399 BC) and his followers, the womb, deprived and stifling with heat, became light and dry and rose in the body to absorb moisture from other organs, causing suffocation. The odd theories of the wandering uterus, repeated in Plato, appear again in Aretaeus of Cappadocia's *The Causes and Symptoms of Acute Diseases* of the second century AD: this time, the writer is not dealing with bereft and deprived older widows as was Hippocrates, but with younger women whose habits and judgment are "more mobile, wandering" and whose "[uterus] is ... altogether erratic":

---

76 Plato, *Timaeus*, trans. Francis M. Cornford, 115; translation adapted. The *metaphor* of the womb as a "creature" is rhetorical; see Helen King, "Once upon a Text," 27. Concerning the male, Plato has Timaeus of Locri use the *simile* of the penis likewise as a *zoon* not under the control of *logos* or reason. Compare Aretaeus's rather over-obvious discussion of priapism: "It is said, that women also suffer from this affection; that they have the same impulse to venery, and the other symptoms the same. I believe, indeed, that lust is engendered in women of humid temperament ... but I do not at all believe that they are affected with Satyriasis [priapism], for their nature, being cold, is not adapted to it. But neither, also, has woman the parts necessary for erection ... and neither also are men subject to suffocation from the womb, because men have not a uterus" (*The Extant Work of Aretaeus*, 289).

> In the middle of the flanks of women lies the womb, a female viscus, closely resembling an animal; for it is moved of itself hither and thither, also upwards in a direct line to below the cartilage of the thorax, and also obliquely to the right or left, either to the liver or spleen; and it likewise is subject to prolapsus downwards, and, in a word, it is altogether erratic. It delights, also, in fragrant smells, and advances towards them; and it has an aversion to fetid smells, and flees from them; and, on the whole, the womb is like an animal within an animal. When, therefore, it is suddenly carried upwards, and remains above for a considerable time, and violently compresses the intestines, the woman experiences a choking, after the form of epilepsy, but without convulsions. For the liver, diaphragm, lungs and heart, are quickly squeezed within a narrow space; and therefore loss of breathing and speech seems to be present. And, moreover, the carotids are compressed from sympathy with the heart, and hence there is heaviness of head, loss of sensibility, and deep sleep.[77]

Thus medical writers taught that unsatisfied libido caused stifling of the womb, the *hysterike pnix*, and made it rise and affix itself to various organs, the liver, lungs, spleen, and heart each producing varied suffocating symptoms (such supposed diseases of the womb, of the *hystera*, were far later given the name "hysteria," at least by 1603).[78]

The more influential writers Soranus (98–138 AD) and Galen of Pergamon (129–99 AD) rejected the "errant womb" ideas (dissection had proved that membranes and ligaments bound it solidly in place) and "hysterical suffocation" theories, and gave a different explanation: retaining Hippocrates' doctrine of the four humours, they reasoned

---

77 *The Extant Work of Aretaeus*, 287. Treatments included placing sweet-smelling substances near the uterus and applying foul smells to the nose to force the uterus downward. See Philip R. Slavney, *Perspectives on "Hysteria,"* 14; Verne L. Bullough, "Medieval Medical and Scientific Views of Women," 494; King, "Once upon a Text," 26, 38. Aretaeus knew that the womb was held by membranes but saw them as pulling the womb back into place, thus combining both concepts; see *The Extant Work*, 285–6; womb suffocation was like a grand-mal seizure (244–6). See also Niel Micklem, *The Nature of Hysteria*. Foucault examines the perpetuation of the hysteria theory into the French Classical period of the seventeenth century; see his "Hysteria and Hypochondria," in *Madness and Civilization*, 136–58.

78 Slavney, in his *Perspectives on "Hysteria"* (16), cites Edward Jorden's *A Brief Discourse*.

that, since women were moist and cold as men were hot and dry,[79] if a woman failed to have sexual intercourse, then a feminine "semen," retained seed or menses from the uterus, would coldly corrupt and putrefy her blood.[80] In the treatises ascribed to "Dame Trotula," the *Trotula*, named after the *Practica* of Trota, a twelfth-century woman physician of Palermo,[81] we read:

---

79 "It is generally agreed upon that this disease mostly affects widows, and particularly those who have previously menstruated regularly, had been pregnant and were eager to have intercourse, but were now deprived of all this. Is there a more likely conclusion from these facts than that in these patients the retention of menstrual flow or of semen causes the so-called uterine condition by which some women become apnoic, suffocated or spastic? And possibly, this affliction is made worse by the retention of semen … It became evident to me that a badly composed semen has a greater power to inflict damage to the whole body than does menstrual discharge. Consequently, a widow could have her monthly flow but retention of troublesome and damaging semen can still occur" (Galen, *On the Affected Parts*, trans. Rudolph E. Seigel, 184–5; Slavney, *Perspectives on "Hysteria,"* 15). The causes made engagement in an active sexual life the obvious treatment; alternatively, midwives and physicians could manipulate the affected parts. See Soranus, *Gynecology*, trans. Owsei Temkin. On the question of heat, cold, moisture, and dryness and the parts of sanguineous animals, see also Aristotle in *The Parts of Animals*, 650a8–650b10 (*The Complete Works of Aristotle*, ed. Jonathan Barnes, 1:1011–12). On arguments on women's coldness, see King, "Once upon a Text," 30–2. Hippocrates' followers (and Aristotelians) saw the womb as an oven, thus producing heat; menstruation purged sanguinary heat; some saw menstrual blood not as the hot, healthy form but as cold and corrupt.

80 The existence of the female ovum was unknown. Hippocrates (as opposed to Aristotle later, who saw the womb only as a container for incubation) saw two forms of semen, male and female; see King, "Once upon a Text," 55. King corrects such studies as that of J. Palis, E. Rossopoulos, and L. Triarhou, "The Hippocratic Concept of Hysteria," 226–8. See Micklem, *The Nature of Hysteria*, 30. Galen, interpreted also by Avicenna, saw that both male and female seeds had the coagulative power in pregnancy, though the male's was stronger; see Bullough, "Medieval Medical and Scientific Views," 490. Menstruation cleansed the system, but pregnancy prevented the excretion of poisons in the first place; even hemorrhoids in both sexes were considered a purification that led to longer life; see Gianna Pomata, "Menstruating Men," and Introduction to the volume (*Generation and Degeneration*) by the editors Valeria Finucci and Kevin Brownlee. A disorder of the spleen, normally cold, caused it to be hot and dry and affect the uterus, an ardour connected to unfulfilled amorous ardour. Cf. Foucault, *Madness and Civilization*, 139.

81 John F. Benton believed that there was no reason to hold that the "Trotula" ("Little Trota," Chaucer's "Dame Trot") treatises were actually written by a woman; the "Trotula" is actually a compendium of three totally separate treatises by three anonymous authors: see his "Trotula, Women's Problems," 10; Monica Green took

> Too much spoiled seed abounds in them and it changes to a poisonous character. Especially does this happen to those who have no husbands, widows in particular and those who previously have been accustomed to make use of carnal intercourse. It also *happens in virgins who have come to marriageable years and have not yet husbands,* for in them abounds the seed which nature wished to draw out by means of the male.[82]

The female body was thought to poison itself because the patient's behaviour did not permit the uterus to function normally; thus, the husband, by endowing his wife with moisture in sexual union, would act as the steadying and controlling force over her – a concept quite compatible with St Paul's dictum that the husband was "the head of woman" (1 Corinthians 11:3), as Boccaccio has Elissa confirm in the *Decameron*'s Introduction (I.Intro.76).[83] Although both Soranus and Galen had vehemently denied that the uterus could move, their translators and followers *perversely reinserted* the Hippocratic-Platonic "wandering womb" theory back into their works,[84] and *in practical medical manuals the wandering womb became an accepted commonplace.* Classical and medieval medical traditions, dislocated from the physical uterus and transposed into elaborate nineteenth-century theories of hysteria concerning the brain and nervous system, were, of course, not missed by Sigmund Freud (1856–1939), who built his whole misogynistic theory of psychoanalysis upon them.[85]

---

over Benton's work to produce her excellent new edition, *The Trotula*. Green's work supersedes Trotula, *The Diseases of Women*, trans. Elizabeth Mason-Hohl, which is no longer widely available, and the few libraries who own it will not lend it extramurally. See also Beryl Rowland, "Women's Health Care and Trotula Florilegium," and Lorrayne Y. Baird-Lange, "Trotula's Fourteenth-Century Reputation."

82 See John F. Benton, "Trota and Trotula," 213–14.

83 "Veramente gli uomini sono delle femmine capo": cf. "The head of the woman is the man; and the head of Christ is God," 1 Corinthians 11:3.

84 On the readmission in Soranus, see King, "Once upon a Text," 54; on the reinstatement in Salernian medicine of the theory in Galen, see ibid., 55.

85 Carl Jung (1875–1961) saw that hysteria also had a positive, constructive side, a concept comically anticipated in Giletta's creative *industria*. At the start of the seventeenth century, Jacques Ferrand, in his *Maladie d'amour ou mélancholie érotique*, pondered whether the internal heat caused by hysteria, spreading throughout the whole body, was not related to the amorous ardour in girls looking for husbands and in young widows who had lost theirs (see Foucault, *Madness and Civilization*, 139). See also Bullough, "Medieval Medical and Scientific Views," esp. 495–96; Kenneth Pennington, "A Note to *Decameron* 6.7," 902–5, esp. 905.

We immediately recognize that the passage from the *Timaeus* and the persistence of Hippocrates' errant womb theories sound very much like a comic allegoresis of Boccaccio's tale: Boccaccio's wandering Giletta, a creature yearning to fulfil motherhood (not to speak of others, such as the peregrine Alatiel and Alibech), literalizes and parodies medical concepts while industriously trying to show them in practice. For both its wonderfully informative and comic value I cite Verne Bullough's encapsulation of Hippocratic theory in his essay "Medieval Medical and Scientific Views of Women" to show the simply terrible dangers that Giletta could be running if her errant uterus was not held firmly in place by her husband's marriage debt:

> Some advocates of humoral theory assumed that unless women engaged regularly in sexual intercourse the uterus would dry up and lose weight, and in its search for moisture it would rise towards the hypochondrium – whatever that might be – thus impeding the flow of breath. If the organ came to rest in this position it would cause convulsions similar to those of epilepsy. If it mounted higher and attached itself to the heart, the patient would feel anxiety and oppression and begin to vomit. If it fastened onto her liver, the woman would lose her voice, and grit her teeth, and her complexion would turn ashen. If it lodged in the loins, she would feel a hard ball or lump in her side. If it mounted as high as her head, it would bring pain around her eyes and nose, make the head feel heavy, and cause drowsiness and lethargy to set in.[86]

In popular plastic arts, European examples from the fourteenth century of a vulva dressed as a pilgrim have been preserved for us in lead badges depicting the female pudendum. Satirizing real pilgrim leaden

---

86 Bullough, "Medieval Medical and Scientific Views," 493. In fact, we must spoil Bullough's feigned and comic bafflement here by indicating that the organs of the midriff or abdominal region were those given the collective plural term "hypochondria"; "hypochondrium" in the singular meant, specifically, the spleen itself; "hypochondriasis" meant the suffocation (perhaps, swelling) of the spleen. Later, as it became recognized that (mythical!) "hysteria" occurred also in men, masculine pride and vanity dictated that a new term, "hypochondria," be applied to the male indisposition, and thus later to unexplained or imagined diseases connected to melancholia, the humour "black bile" excreted by the spleen. Hysteria today is a psychological term used, roughly, to describe any number of psychosomatic ailments in both sexes that show the symptoms of physically caused disease. See Micklem, *The Nature of Hysteria*, 12.

badges, they were perhaps used as an *apotropaion* to ward off bad luck or the evil eye, *il malocchio*. Malcolm Jones in his fascinating study on popular art, *The Secret Middle Ages* (256),[87] reproduces a figure of a vulva interestingly accoutred in a pilgrim's hat and penile epaulets, with a rosary and a phallus-tipped *baculum* or pilgrim's staff. It is immediately recognizable as a worthy companion to Boccaccio's metaphoric medical ribaldry in *Decameron* III.9.

Suffering the same syndrome as Giletta, Boccaccio's Caterina Valbona feels the discomfort and danger of her womanly moisture evaporating in *Decameron* V:4. Caterina, thus, is not, after all, *really* lying to her parents: her excessive *caldo* might very well be quenched only just in time by the lucky Ricciardo Manardi! In the twelfth century, even such a person as Hildegard of Bingen warned that if a women felt hot like a man, she would be unable to bear children and sterility would set in as it does in the earth from the baking of the sun (Bullough, "Medieval Medical and Scientific Views," 486). Thus we can say that a real knowledge and wisdom, *saviezza, sapienza* – one not merely ironically transgressive (like that of Peronella or of the widow in the *Corbaccio*) but a serious knowledge absorbed from the world of medical men and from women mystics and physicians – underlies Giletta's wild and dogged pursuit of her husband. She pursues her legal rights of sexual fulfilment *out of medical self-preservation*. Fittingly, then, another topos can be revealed that even Shakespeare seems to have missed: after this physician has healed others, *she must heal herself*.

For us Giletta indeed represents a case of sex-role reversal, and Boccaccio often expresses his certainty that women are every bit as capable as men in all affairs. But in this assertion we can detect also an underlying anti-feminism that bleeds through most medieval praises of women and stains them all. Boccaccio praises women in the Preface of *De claris mulieribus* for forgetting their sex and for acting with the great souls of *men*:

> If we grant that men deserve praise whenever they perform great deeds with the strength bestowed upon them, *how much more should women be extolled* – almost all of whom are endowed by nature with soft, frail bodies and sluggish minds – *when they take on a manly spirit* they show remarkable

---

87 Concerning medieval pilgrim badges see J. Koldeweij, "Iconography of Dutch Misericords and Pilgrim Badges," and S. Stockhurst, "Passionate Pilgrims."

intelligence and bravery and dare to execute deeds that would be extremely difficult even for men? (Emphasis mine)[88]

On the other hand, we remember that Boccaccio has the two male protagonists of the *Corbaccio* each jeeringly censure his overly merry widow because she acts in all respects, threateningly, much too much like a man – from the domination of her household and her total liberation in sex to – the greatest crime of all – the effrontery of writing poetry, the exclusive prerogative of the contemporary Florentine male (*Corbaccio*, trans. Cassell, 18–19).

Marxist critics are not alone in noting that Giletta's bourgeoise nature revolts against her feudal milieu and conquers it. Ironically, she struggles only to lock herself solidly in a feudal marriage at the close. We learn from her industrious *scaltrezza*, however, that she will surely be ultimately the dominant partner.[89] The action of III.9 is fully understandable in the feminist terms borne out in the text: in the first half of the tale, Giletta suffers the inhibiting and watchful male gaze of society – first that of her father, then of the Rossiglione court, later of the king, and finally, at tale's end, of her formerly unrequiting beloved. After her father's death she is closely surveilled and guarded, the female victim of the manners of a court that entrap and restrict her: at home she is "molto guardata" (III.9.5), and at the king's court in Paris, she herself concedes: "Monsignore ... fatemi guardare" [Sire ... keep me under watch (III.9.14)].[90] Early in her girlhood she conceives of a plan to pursue Beltramo by travelling to

88 "Et si extollendi sunt homines dum, concesso sibi robore, magna perfecerint, quanto amplius mulieres, quibus fere omnibus a natura rerum mollities insita et corpus debile ac tardum ingenium datum est, si in virilem evaserint animum et ingenio celebri atque virtute conspicua audeant atque perficiant etiam difficillima viris, extollende sunt?" Giovanni Boccaccio, *De claris mulieribus*, Preface, para 3–4; *Famous Women*, ed. and trans. Virginia Brown, 8–9. Examples could be multiplied: compare Penthesilea, who "through practice ... became much more manly in arms than those born male" (130–1).

89 The Marxist critic Mario Alicata comments that Agilulfo's stablehand "appare quasi il simbolo del vecchio mondo feudale che cede il passo ad un mondo nuovo." Beltramo is "un altro tipico rappresentante ... della vecchia classe feudale" ("La terza giornata del *Decameron*," 250–1). I totally disagree with Mario Baratto that in *Decameron* III.9, "I gesti e i tempi dell'azione obbediscono a un codice cavalleresco di comportamento" [Gestures and time of action follow a chivalric code of conduct (*Realtà e stile*, 143)]. If this can be entertained at all, I must firmly add "only in the breach."

90 We can reflect on the "author's" philogynous opinion on the unfortunate restriction on women's movements in the *Decameron's* Proemio (7–9).

Paris, but she finds her success thwarted by social restrictions on woman's freedom – conventions that must colour the later accomplishment of her adolescent plan: "E non guari appresso essendosi il padre di lei morto, se onesta cagione avesse potuta avere, volentieri a Parigi per vedere Beltramo sarebbe andata; *ma essendo molto guardata*, per ciò che ricca e sola era rimasa, onesta via non vedea" [Hardly had her father died than she would have gladly gone to Paris to see Beltramo, had she been able to find a respectable reason; but, *since she was kept closely watched* because she was now rich and all alone, she could see no proper way (III.9.5; emphasis mine)]. The question of her personal morality does not enter; court society compels her modesty as the commercial and controlled counterpart of her considerable wealth. She dwells in a milieu that rejects her personhood and sees her as a trade commodity, one that evaluates her womanly desires as unfitting and abject; she herself becomes, as is clearly depicted in the novella, "deject."[91] To escape the phallocultural hold, she identifies with a third party now transcendent to the borders of her present situation – ironically, with her by-now-dead father in the beyond – and at first replaces him, embodying his intellectual male presence and learned expertise to cure the king.[92] Then, as Countess of Rossiglione, she supplants her absent husband with her mastery of accounting and in governing the county. Finally, she indulges in what might seem a reversal beyond all rational logic. She both plays the male aggressor and casts herself existentially as abject (refused and rejected) to the tricked embraces of Beltramo; thus she descends masochistically into a ritual maelstrom of what she would most fear and reject (abandoned, abject whoredom) but in so doing gains manipulative and even sadistic mastery over what has made her abject to herself and to others (now personified in the rejecting Beltramo).[93] Giletta's female sublimation follows that of any late male *stil nuovo* or Petrarchan lover: it has no object. Her phantasmal vision of marital bliss

91 For a comparison to *All's Well*, see Mariella Cavalchini, "Giletta-Helena." I am here attempting to cast my own ideas approximately into Julia Kristeva's terms in "The Powers of Horror," 234–6.

92 Helena's learning in *AWW* is much downplayed by Shakespeare, who has her father only leave her a few "receipts" (recipes for herbal potions) on his deathbed; Helena is far too transparent and *far less* accomplished than her mysterious predecessor Giletta, and, thus, I find, far less interesting as a "feminist" heroine.

93 Carol Neely provides an extremely fine and concise synopsis of the situation in *AWW*: "When Bertram flees her, she must, in effect, prostitute herself in the bed-trick, engaging in anonymous sexual encounter and receiving his ring as payment" (chapter 2, "Power and Virginity," in *Broken Nuptials*, 74).

with Beltramo is that of everything that she has missed – a girlhood dream of joy and fascination, one that has no connection whatsoever with the object but which is also absolutely inseparable from what implacably drives her.[94] Giletta is led both by libido and superego. She makes us uncomfortable because she takes on abjection existentially; she dares psychologically and physically what "respectable" male society would not permit her to contemplate. We might, however, suggest, as we leave her, the capital motivation of all of Giletta's exploits: as Giletta has already co-opted the roles held by the males in her life, at the end she achieves the mythical presence of her ever-missing mother by embodying motherhood in her own person.

7. Conclusions

Scholars have long worked on the intimate relations between the framework and the tales, and found that there is a carefully worked out aesthetic in the collocation, or complex *dispositio*, of the Hundred Tales. After Vladímir Propp's examinations of folktales and the collections of themes by Stith Thompson, and through Todorov's exploration of the narrative "grammar" of the *Decameron*, we know that Boccaccio's tales involve a narratological language functioning diacritically, with the sense of each narrative entity emerging from its relation to all others within the system.[95] The interwoven medical subtexts, particularly the "wandering womb" absurdities, the daring and erudite parodies of Christian morality and theology, the exaltation of merchant-class craftiness, the manly wiles of women, the loutish brutality of certain male characters, and other such leitmotifs and myths as the Philomela-nightingale theme all bind this tale to the structured symphonic fabric of the *Decameron*.

My sense is that Boccaccio tempered and placed *Decameron* III.9 with a careful strategy and purpose. He endowed it with a minimum of verve or élan, as Neifile's preamble implies; in fact, I hold that, despite its extreme cleverness (to be admired by the close reader), the author wanted it to appear at first reading as an unremarkable, rather parenthetical or

94 See Kristeva, "The Powers of Horror," 238.

95 Todorov, *Grammaire du Décaméron*; Propp in *The Morphology of the Folktale* examined the constants and variables in the oral tradition of tales of the marvellous (*conte merveilleux*); rarely do we see the functions analysed by Propp unaltered in Boccaccio's literary and problematic writing. See Thompson, *Motif-Index*, 58. See also A. Baudoux-Spinette, "Les motifs flokloriques," and Roland Barthes, "Introduction à l'analyse structurale des récits."

hyphen-like tale of second order to spotlight the tales that he placed immediately before and after it – a kind of tympani-roll before the day's final cymbal clash in III.10. Time proved Boccaccio right. Tale 10's Alibech has always made the biggest salacious splash: her tale is the one that even the most cursory reader remembers best. Its ribaldry has always curdled opinion of the rest of the tales, and it has always been the main subject for expurgation and the primary cause of the *Decameron*'s banning throughout the centuries.[96] Prudish translators refused to render III.10 into English until the second half of the nineteenth century; some earlier versions substituted the 101st Filippo Balducci half-novella or another tale, while other translators, such as J.M. Rigg (still published in the modern Everyman's Library series), priggishly left it in the original Italian.[97] While the *brigata*'s women are many times moved to uproarious

96 Savonarola burned the *Decameron* on his pyramid of vanities in 1497. The whole *Decameron* found itself on Paul IV's first *Index librorum prohibitorum* of 1559: "Boccatii *Decades* seu novellae centum, quae hactenus cum intolerabilibus erroribus impressae sunt, et quae in posterum cum eiusdem erroribus imprimetur" (see Heinrich Reusch, ed., *Die Indices*, 180), and its banning is reiterated again in Pius IV's list of 1564. Three bowdlerized versions appeared in Italy in 1572, 1573, and 1583. In the latter year, too, the General Inquisitor of Spain, Cardinal Archbishop Gásparo a Quiroga, banned the original and permitted only those expurgated versions published after 1572. See Reusch, ed., *Die Indices*, 255, 394. Quiroga admonishes: "Boccaccii, *Decades sive decameron aut novellae centum*, nisi fuerint ex purgatis et impressis ab anno 1572." Clement VIII's of 1596 leaves Boccaccio unmentioned. For Sixtus V's Index in his Bull of 1590 allowing only expurgated versions, see 467. See also Giuseppe Chiecchi and Luciano Troisio, *Il Decameron sequestrato*. Kirkham, in her hugely entertaining and fact-laden article, "John Badmouth," 360, lists the earliest bowdlerized editions: the Vatican "Deputati" *Decameron* of 1573, mainly the responsibility of Vincenzio Borghini; Lionardo Salviati's "rassettato," or, rather, much-mauled Giuntine text of 1572 (at least ten editions until that of 1638), and the text vandalized in 1583 by the Venetian Luigi Groto. The first complete English version was John Payne's fustian translation, privately printed for the Villon Society in 1886, and revised by Charles S. Singleton and printed at the reviser's own private expense by Martino Mardersteig at the Stamperia Valdonega on Manunzia Laid Italian paper in a deluxe three-volume set for the University of California Press in 1982. See also Raul Mordenti's examination of the bowdlerizers' marginal, autonomous texts in "La Griselda della Controriforma italiana." The *Decameron* often suffered banning in the overly modest United States during the first half of the twentieth century (Kirkham, "John Badmouth," 360–3).

97 In Giovanni Boccaccio, *The Decameron*, trans. J.M. Rigg, 220–4, we are left only with the Italian text with the prim, coy, and totally unhelpful footnote: "No apology is needed for leaving, in accordance with precedent, the subsequent detail untranslated." See also the listings in F.S. Stych, *Boccaccio in English*.

laughter, delighted with Dioneo's tenth story of Day Three – "Mille fiate o più aveva la novella di Dioneo a rider mosse l'oneste donne, tali e sí fatte lor parevan le sue parole" [A thousand time or more Dioneo's novella moved the proper women to laughter, so and such a way did his words seem to them (III.Concl.1)] – in absolute contrast, Boccaccio has his framework characters make *no comment at all* upon our ninth story of Giletta. Dioneo, we are told, listens to Neifile attentively as if quietly plotting his smirking parody and impish shock before he pounces. Boccaccio reveals in his following Introduction to Day Four that he foresaw that Dioneo's deliciously witty and pornographic tale would likely be the most outstanding and scandalous of all those in the collection so far, and he wanted not only to keep it from abutting Lauretta's previous, excellent tale (III.8) but especially to avoid having his well-considered III.9 detract in any way from the unforgettable, licentious punch that he had decided, perhaps with a flip of his middle finger, or, more probably, a raised arm brandishing *le corna*, to leave for the end of the third day.

The Tale of Alibech (III.10)

STEVEN GROSSVOGEL

Boccaccio's most notorious novella was virtually ignored by critics until 1929, when D.H. Lawrence published *Pornography and Obscenity*. In this essay Lawrence offers reasons why people respond negatively to erotic literature. According to Lawrence, obscene words have two meanings, an "individual meaning" (the meaning an individual assigns to a word according to his or her own sincere feelings) and a "mob meaning" (the meaning given to the word by public opinion). The latter is the one which inevitably becomes law, because individuals rarely ask if their reaction is individual, or is merely a reaction of their "mob self." According to Lawrence, the individual is manipulated by the "trickster" and the "exploiter," who assume the form of advertising companies, businessmen, clergymen, and professors. Were it not for these people, an individual would probably admit that he or she is "not shocked, not outraged, nor indignant" because his or her apparent indignation is merely part of a "mob-reaction, mob-indignation, and mob-condemnation" (238).

For Lawrence, pornography relies on secrecy and degradation, something he sees in English Victorian novels where sex enticement is accompanied with a "desire to spite the sexual feeling, to humiliate it and degrade it" (*Pornography*, 243). By contrast, however, "the plain and simple excitement, quite open and wholesome, which you find in Boccaccio's stories is not for a minute to be confused with the furtive excitement aroused by rubbing the dirty little secret in all secrecy in modern best sellers … Today Boccaccio should be given to everyone young and old, to read if they like. Only a natural fresh openness about sex will do any good, now [that] we are swamped by secret or semi-secret pornography. And perhaps the Renaissance story tellers, Boccaccio, Lasca and the rest, are the best antidote we can find now, just as more plasters of Puritanism are the most harmful remedy we can resort to" (243).

However we wish to view Lawrence's remarks, they anticipate, by several decades, the position of several Boccaccio scholars on both sides of the Atlantic – Aldo Scaglione (*Nature and Love*, 48–82), Carlo Salinari (*Boccaccio Manzoni*, 55–70), Mario Baratto (*Realtà*, 56–8), and Carlo Muscetta (*Giovanni Boccaccio*, 219–20) – who have seen in this and Boccaccio's other erotic novelle the Author's advocacy for naturalism. Lawrence is also the first in a line of critics to look at these novelle as being divorced from traditional moral strictures and social constructs; and in so doing, Lawrence reveals how most responses to these novelle are more a reflection of the readers' moral prejudices than of the Author's amorality.

It would be several decades, however, before this particular novella received critical analysis. In *The Rhetoric of Fiction* (1961), Wayne Booth looked at the rhetorical strategies used in the novella and concluded, "Even Dioneo, the most lewd of all the ten narrators, must spend a good deal of energy manipulating us into the camp of those who can laugh with a clear conscience at his bawdy and often cruel stories. In the potentially distressing tale of how the holy man, Rustico, debauches the young and innocent Alibech by teaching her how to put the devil in hell (third day, tenth tale), great care is taken with the character and ultimate fate of the simple-minded girl in order to lead us to laugh at conduct that in most worlds, including the world in which Boccaccio lived, would be considered cruel and sacrilegious rather than comic" (14–15).

Booth's astute observation offers another reason for this novella's poor reception over the centuries; but it also prompts us to ask: Why does Boccaccio have Dioneo do this? Is it just for comic effect? Or is it to show how easily rhetoric can alter the value system of those who laugh at what happens in this novella? The moral implications raised by the novella cannot be ignored, and Boccaccio himself would probably have wanted his readers to consider them. After all, unlike other examples of sexual deception perpetrated by Boccaccio's other clerics, the deceit in this novella is perpetrated on an innocent and naïve girl of fourteen, not on a worldly and knowledgable woman; and as Booth suggested, Boccaccio has gone to great lengths to mitigate this sexual abuse so that his readers will view it in a different way. Furthermore, the fact that Boccaccio follows III.10 with a defence against those who allegedly criticized his work thus far suggests that he is well aware of the moral issues raised by this novella.

Five years before Booth's *The Rhetoric of Fiction*, Vittore Branca published the first edition of his seminal work, *Boccaccio medievale* (1956). As Branca pointed out, this and the other erotic novelle in the *Decameron* follow closely medieval models of parody, as seen in the stylistic register that Boccaccio used in order to illustrate a different world from that found in his other novelle (339). Branca is the first to point out that not only the saints' legends, which serve as sources for this novella, but even the religious language is humorously violated through this parody.

Following Branca's lead, in 1972 Carlo Muscetta looked at how Rustico, named after St Rusticus, is converted from the religion of the spirit to that of the flesh through an amphiboly that is not only profane, reminiscent of Apuleius, but also profanely carnivalesque (*Giovanni Boccaccio*, 220). Muscetta also shows how Rustico's deception and Alibech's ingenuousness are mirrored off each other, producing comic witticisms that are quite new for the time (220). Although Muscetta does not see anything edifying in this novella, he does see a moral in the naturalism that this novella advocates.

Three years after Muscetta's observations, Guido Almansi published *The Writer as Liar* (1975), and for the first time in its chequered history, this novella was given more than one page of serious critical attention. In his analysis of the novella, Almansi shows the precise parallelism between erotic ritual and religious ceremony which recalls the analogy of sex to religion, especially mysticism, in the works of Bernardus Silvestris and Jacopone da Todi. According to Almansi, "the whole novella is constructed around the affinity of the obscene and the sacred, and this symbiosis should not be automatically dismissed as implausible or unproductive, even if the subsequent cultural history of Europe will witness an ever-widening gap between these two sections of human experience" (85). Boccaccio's deliberate irony "succeeds in persuading the reader subconsciously to review his automatic assumptions about sexual activity and religious observance." Almansi illustrates the symmetry of the novella's two halves, "which can be traced back to Boccaccio's combinative fondness for exhausting all the variations and organizing a neat geometrical reversal between separate units of a given plot." Besides satisfying the reader's delight in symmetry, the reversal of roles between Rustico and Alibech in the second half of the novella also tones down the impression of sacrilege in what is happening, and "serves to filter out our anguish at a possible outrage in what we are reading" (86). Furthermore, the way in which Boccaccio portrays the sexual activity between Rustico and Alibech, without traces of reticence or prudishness, transforms it "into a unique event rather than a tired pornographic cliché" (88).

A year after Almansi's insightful analysis, Janet Smarr posited a symmetry and balance in the *Decameron* which point to a moral reading of Boccaccio's magnum opus: "Boccaccio had a very special interest in order; and the framework he selected to contain his tales is one which repeatedly emphasized order in moral as well as in aesthetic terms" ("Symmetry and Balance," 174). According to Smarr, this novella was meant "to correct by laughter," and does so by transforming a stern tale narrated by Passavanti in the *Specchio della vera penitenza* and in the *Detti ed esempi contro la tentazione carnale* into a novella which criticizes society, but not in the bitter and gloomy tone of Passavanti (177). "The laughter imposes a distance between the values of the characters and of the narrators. As Dioneo put it, it is those who see their own image in a tale of scandal who cannot be amused by it" (179). As Smarr states, the humour and laughter of the narrators are also a mechanism for dealing with their own sexual feelings. Even Dioneo – the most aggressive of the amorous narrators – never allows his humour to disrupt the orderly society of the *brigata*, but rather makes its continuity possible by allowing a civilized outlet for sexual aggression: "The outlet of sexual tension is also Boccaccio's method for curing his lovesick readers" (179).

Two years after Smarr's article appeared, Alfonso Paolella wrote the first article ("I livelli narrativi") devoted entirely to this novella. In it he compares the narrative structures of the novella with those of the Life of St Mary of Egypt from the *Vita Patruum* to show how Boccaccio uses and deforms the mystical and ascetic culture represented in the saint's life. Paolella breaks down the narrative into several of Propp's basic plot components by way of Greimas's distinction between actors and "actants" and Bremond's narrative network. By breaking down Boccaccio's technique of parody into minimal components, Paolella shows how the Author's profanation of the theological and ascetic culture of the *contemptus mundi* [contempt of the world] becomes an affirmation of "libertà carnevalesca" [carnivalesque freedom (204)].

Three years after Paolella's article, in 1981, Victoria Kirkham wrote the first article in English devoted entirely to this novella. Like Smarr before her, Kirkham sees unifying patterns linking the individual tales of the third day, thereby providing our novella with the edification promised by the Author in the Proemio. Following the example set by Dante, "Boccaccio's fictional lessons are going to take the form of precept both by negative and positive example" ("Love's Labors Rewarded," 206), and the novelle of the third day, according to Kirkham, are designed to teach by negative precept. The adultery and fornication of the third day can either lead to the tragedy and death of the fourth day or to "the life-affirming institution of matrimony" (209) in the fifth day. Marriage "becomes society's way of accommodating the threats posed by our natural sexual instincts" (210). Kirkham shows how, throughout the third day, there is an intricate progression of allusions from Paradise to Purgatory, and finally to Hell. The "hell-bent trajectory of the Third Day" (213) ultimately suggests that illicit love leads to perdition. The fall of Rustico and Alibech, however, is also an ironic commentary on the given theme for Neifile's reign: "Taken individually, the protagonists of these stories all get what they desire ... When judged from the broader perspective of the *Decameron* and the earlier works, however, they all get what they deserve" (214). The moral pattern that Kirkham finds in this and the other novelle of the third day is convincing; however, Boccaccio's moral message may be more than an advocacy of marriage and a cautionary tale of illicit love.

Like Kirkham before him, Wayne Storey devoted an entire article to this novella in 1982. Storey shows in detail the way in which Boccaccio used a significant number of religious sources, antecedents, and traditions to produce an extensive parody that is far greater than what previous critics have shown. Storey illustrates how Boccaccio's linguistic parody underlies the tale's true success in imitating the rhetorical style of its sources and parodying their moral tone. Analysing how Rustico's pride is punished according to the traditional lesson in humility one finds in the lives of the Desert Fathers and in the Gospel, Storey states, "It is precisely the linguistic structure of this moral lesson ... which provides Boccaccio with the central motif of Alibech's tale. At the same time, however, Boccaccio discredits this moral lesson with the very contents of that structure" ("Parodic Structure," 170). Storey also shows how Alibech's response to her sexual experience is parodically patterned after the mystical experience of the *dulcedo Dei*: "With the subsequent 'resurrezione della carne,' Alibech is *maravigliata* as the mystical transfiguration takes place. Through the symbol the mystery is physically manifested. Receiving the monk's benediction ('benedetta sia tu!'), she is then taught 'come starsi dovesse a dovere incarcerare quell maladetto da Dio.' Soon the sweetness, delight and pleasure she dutifully accepts in her devotions to God encourage her to surpass her master in devotional fervor, seeking continually and without sloth sacred ecstasy" (173). Storey concludes that Rustico's "traditional morality and chastity are supplanted by a doctrine of *naturalezza*, in which Love becomes the ultimate *auctoritas*" (175).

Giuseppe Mazzotta sees ambiguity inherent in the language of sexuality and that of the practice of spiritual askesis (*The World at Play*, 117). Analysing key words and phrases in the novella, Mazzotta shows how they "rhetorically organize the text by their overt movement from their original spiritual sense to a physical context, as well as by their concealing the sexual act in the guise of moral allegory. The humor of the story issues from the strident and close union of the spiritual and physical activities, from the ease with which the registers are 'exchanged.'"

Emma Grimaldi looks at the way in which Boccaccio "incarnates" the metaphors of the novella; and like Muscetta and Paolella, she underscores the parodic, carnivalesque element in this novella (*Il privilegio di Dioneo*, 81). For Grimaldi, the novella marks the triumph of "naturalità-istinto" [naturality-instinct] over cultural violence and abuse (83). Grimaldi concludes that Boccaccio establishes a contrast between an empirical reality, which is absolutely impractical, and the reality of the word, which, even in its most transgressive usage, becomes the only reality allowed by the *brigata*.

Along the same lines of Almansi, Storey, and Mazzotta, Paolo Valesio has shown how this novella contains so many different kinds of writing and narrative trends that it is open to diverse interpretations, some diverging, but none of them necessarily exclusive or contradictory ("Sacro," 384). Looking at this novella from an anthropological point of view, Valesio shows how the Hindu figure of the temptress, who comes to disrupt the life of the ascetic, does not alter the nature of the sacred: irony, comedy, and the grotesque easily integrate themselves with the sacred. Valesio downplays Rustico's moral culpability by characterizing his seductive strategy as child-like, and by claiming that the ensuing seduction scene is "innocentemente mattinale" [innocently matinal]. For Valesio, the temptation of Rustico has as much to do with his own ingenuousness as with Alibech's innocence. The sacral dimension of the novella can be seen as an ironic lesson of humility that the divinity inflicts on Rustico for having taken in Alibech "per voler fare della sua fermezza una gran pruova" [wishing to put his resolve to a great test]. Valesio claims that a similar lesson is taught to Alibech for assuming too lightly the vocation of a hermit: "non da ordinato disiderio ma da un cotal fanciullesco appetito" [not by an orderly desire but by a child-like impulse (III.10.6)].

Valesio concludes that it is through the grotesque that the divine is made manifest, as one finds in similar Hindu sources and analogues ("Sacro," 384). For Valesio, however, the sacred is most vividly recalled when Rustico and Alibech undress while kneeling on the ground. The naïve fourteen-year-old is not only portrayed as a *figura Evae* (a figure of Eve, devoid of sexual self-consciousness), but she also evokes a complex tradition of Christian mysticism which at times bordered on the unorthodox. Valesio gives as examples St Francis of Assisi's marriage to Lady Poverty and Angela da Foligno's stripping herself naked before the Cross, in keeping with the topos of following the naked Christ naked. Besides alluding, quite parodically, to mystical practices, Boccaccio is also juxtaposing the two complementary and opposing poles of the mystical experience – the ascetic and the erotic, both of which belong to the sacred. Quoting Schubart, Valesio states, "La persona erotica esce da se stessa, la persona ascetica si ritrae in se stessa, e ognuna delle due chiama la sua via la via della libertà" [the erotic persona comes out of itself, the ascetic persona withdraws into itself, and each one of them calls their way the road of freedom (385)].

More recently, Diane Duyos Vacca shows how this novella "can be read as a pointed, though oblique, commentary on the patristic and scholastic constructions of Christian morality and the understanding of sexuality of Sts Jerome and Augustine" ("Converting Alibech," 208). Like Storey and Valesio, Vacca sees a "deliberate conflation of religious and sexual images which reveals the imbrication of the mystic and the erotic, the scandalous proximity of reverence and blasphemy" (209). Jerome's letter to Rusticus not only establishes ironic parallels to Rustico and his relationship to Alibech but also establishes an analogy between the text and the feminine body. Vacca suggests that Boccaccio is challenging the reader to interpret according to his own desires: either the text may be a "Galeotto" gratifying the reader's prurient interest, as Rustico did with Alibech, or "the reader may instead peek beneath the veil of suggestive ambiguity and discover an unexpected *nuda veritas*" [naked truth] (214). According to Vacca, the novella illustrates St Paul's and St Augustine's contention that the eternal and the spiritual may be comprehended by means of corporeal and temporal things: "Alibech is like Eve before she acquires knowledge of good and evil. She exemplifies Paul's wisdom in Romans 14:14: 'Nothing is impure in itself; only, if a man considers a particular thing impure, then to him it is impure'" (215–16), a point Boccaccio stresses in the *Decameron*'s epilogue. Alibech's ignorance in sexual and religious matters is involuntary and consequently makes her free from sin. Looking at Rustico and Filippo Balducci in relation to their respective pupils, Alibech and Balducci's son, Vacca points out that these "padri" not only use language to deceive rather than to teach their pupils but also pervert the ideal purpose of language, as defined by St Augustine, which is to teach faith (224–5). In terms of a larger edifying moral for the *brigata* and for Boccaccio's contemporary readers, Vacca sees this novella and the novelletta of Filippo Balducci as countering death, disease, and the plague with the promise of regeneration: "Laughter heals body and spirit as it dispels melancholy, and new life results from both spiritual devotion and erotic love … The confluence of *amor* and *caritas* in Alibech's novella suggests that religious devotion and carnal love are not diametrically opposed but rather different aspects of the same emotion" (227). It is not clear, however, where Vacca sees *caritas* in this novella.

In her article, "Beyond Seduction: A Reading of the Tale of Alibech and Rustico," Marilyn Migiel takes issue with some of the aforementioned interpretations of this novella, and focuses instead on how the third day proposes an extended meditation on the nexus of word and deed, and on how this novella "invites the reader to reflect critically on the role that language plays in the creation of desire – indeed, in the role that language plays in the construction of all social reality" (164). Language creates the desiring subject, and the drama of the novella is not that of Alibech and Rustico, but of need, demand, and desire. The indeterminacy of Alibech's "appetite" allows her to be misled. By testing Alibech, Rustico is himself tested by temptation; and the questions he asks her are the sign of his own desire: "'coming to know' that Alibech is unsullied by other male hands is his own desire to 'know' her himself" (167). According to Migiel, Dioneo is showing the reader how, and under what conditions, language precipitates action. From words, Rustico passes to deeds: to understand what he has said, Alibech must imitate his actions: "He tries to assure that Alibech reads bodily signs in strict accord with the symbolic system that he has generated" (168). As Migiel points out, Rustico binds narrative and mimetic action with constant reminders of their verbal exchange; in so doing he attempts to create a subject (Alibech) that will assume a desired role. Migiel concludes: "The *Decameron* remains uncompromisingly focused on language and history as they are constructed by humans, with no transcendent point that grants the system meaning or coherence" (171); she sees this novella "as a self-reflexive meditation about language, subjectivity, and the construction of social reality" (173).

Judging from the novella's critical reception, the issue of whether or not there is an edifying and/or moral message is still open to debate. I would like to suggest a reading of the novella that sides with those critics who feel that such a message exists. Branca (*Decameron* 443)[1] and Paolella have suggested that Alibech's life in the Thebaid is patterned after the saint's life of St Mary of Egypt. Alibech's life, however, seems to have more in common with the life of another desert hermit, also named Mary, the niece of Abraham the Hermit. In fact, Boccaccio's

1 All quotations from *Decameron* are from Branca's edition (Turin: Einaudi, 1980).

novella can be seen as an inversion of the *Life of Maria the Harlot*, written by the Archdeacon Ephraim. When Maria was seven, her father died and her uncle Abraham raised her as a hermit in the desert. After living in the Thebaid for eighteen years, Maria is visited by a monk who seduces her. Ashamed of what has happened to her, she returns to the city and becomes a prostitute. When her uncle finds out, he too returns to the city and convinces her to return with him to the desert. Maria eventually redeems herself in the desert, and dies a saint.

As Benedicta Ward has shown, this saint's legend adopts some of the same elements found in similar tales of repentant prostitutes: St Mary Magdalene, St Mary of the Desert, Pelagia, and Thais (*The Harlots of the Desert*, 85). What strikes us when we read this saint's legend is the sensitive portrayal of uncle and niece. Not only is Maria's shame so great that she leaves her uncle without telling him anything, but she feels so defiled that she identifies herself with the prostitutes in the city and becomes one herself. Aware of his niece's shame, Abraham enters the brothel disguised as a soldier; and in order to speak to her privately, Abraham goes through all the motions a man would ordinarily take in order to gain access to a prostitute's bedroom. Maria does not recognize him and has no fear of him when the two are sitting on her bed. When Abraham removes his disguise and reveals his true identity, he makes a moving appeal to Maria to return to her previous life. Instead of reproaching her for what she has done, he reassures her of her salvation. In his speech Abraham expresses hope, forgiveness, and a great paternal love, all of which reveal his Christological nature. After listening to her uncle and after spending the night with him in tears, Maria agrees to return with him to the desert.

If Boccaccio was familiar with this saint's legend, the way in which he altered it in his novella is significant. Whereas St Abraham conceals his paternal love for his niece with a feigned sexual desire for her, Rustico conceals his purely sexual desire for Alibech with a feigned spiritual and paternal devotion (Rustico addresses her as "figliuola mia" [my daughter] and Alibech addresses him as "padre mio" [my father]). Like Maria, Alibech is seduced by a monk in the desert, but unlike her counterpart, Alibech feels neither shame nor the need to leave the desert and return to the city. Whereas Maria gladly abandons her sexual activities in the city to return with her uncle to the desert, Alibech unwillingly abandons her sexually active life in the desert to return to the city. More importantly, however, Alibech is spared the spiritual and emotional trauma that Maria suffered from her first sexual experience. This may explain why Boccaccio wanted Alibech's response to her sexual experience to be so different from that of her counterpart in the saint's legend: it is a positive and healthy response which actually saves Alibech from the self-destructive life that Maria led in the city. When Dioneo ironically states that women should do what Alibech did because much good can come of it, including the salvation of their souls, what Boccaccio may be saying, at one level, is that Alibech's response to her sexual experience is less dangerous to both her body and soul than the responses that Maria and other "harlots of the desert" had to similar experiences.

Although one may argue, as Migiel has done, that Dioneo's representation of Alibech's sexuality is gendered in order to create an exceedingly willing young girl whose sexual desire, once aroused, is insatiable – all part of Dioneo's strategy of seduction (*A Rhetoric of the "Decameron"*, 72) – Boccaccio the Author, on the other hand, may be asking his readers to seriously reexamine the sexual experience from Alibech's liberating perspective. This is supported by the "novelletta" about Filippo Balducci that immediately follows Dioneo's novella. Alibech and the son of Filippo Balducci are inclined to Eros after coming in contact with a "diavolo" [devil] and "papere" [ducks] respectively. Both interpret sexual attraction as something good, not simply as something desirable, thereby giving it a moral dimension that is consonant with the dynamics of desire and love as expounded by St Thomas Aquinas and Dante, and that Boccaccio incorporates in his works. The most important difference between these two novelle lies in the fact that Filippo Balducci devotes his whole life to keeping his son away from sexual attractions, whereas Rustico is prepared to introduce Alibech to them shortly after she enters his hut. By not giving us an ending to his "novelletta," Boccaccio is forcing the reader to focus on the importance of what he has narrated, namely that no matter what restrictions exist, the adolescent will inevitably feel the attraction of Eros and will undoubtedly view it as something good. In other words, if readers of III.10 are inclined to criticize this novella because of Rustico's role in Alibech's sexual experience, replacing Rustico with a far less permissive "padre" like Filippo Balducci does not change the end result: sooner or later Alibech, like the younger Balducci, would have experienced Eros, and their responses would have probably been the same.[2]

2 As Vacca points out, "Balducci and his son and Rustico and Alibech both dramatize the problems of rhetoric and sexuality in their relationships and their language … These recluses all attempt, with varying degrees of success, to reshape reality with language" ("Converting Alibech," 223–4).

The novella of Alibech and Rustico is about two people who view their common sexual experience in radically different ways. Alibech, the naïve fourteen-year-old, interprets her experience in truly individualistic terms, as D.H. Lawrence would have liked. As Mario Baratto pointed out, the sexual act is captured in its primordial state, the most healthy and natural one possible (*Realtà*, 384). Unlike Maria, Alibech's reaction to her sexual experience is not determined by established social or religious constructs. The only external opinion which comes into play is Rustico's assertion that, by putting his euphemistic devil in Alibech's euphemistic hell, she is ultimately serving God. By redefining their sexual experience as something good, Rustico reinforces Alibech's already positive feelings about it. Whereas Rustico's interpretation of their sexual activity is an act of bad faith, Alibech's interpretation of it is made in good faith. Her sexual conduct, in fact, recalls the sexual innocence St Augustine attributes to Adam and Eve during their prelapsarian state. In the *City of God* (XIV.23–4) Augustine states that if Adam and Eve had not disobeyed God, and had not been expelled from Eden, they would have been able to engage in sexual intercourse without shame or lust:

> And certainly, had not culpable disobedience been visited with penal disobedience [original sin], the marriage of Paradise should have been ignorant of this struggle and rebellion, this quarrel between will and lust, that the will may be satisfied and lust restrained, but those members, like all the rest, should have obeyed the will. The field of generation should have been sown by the organ created for this purpose, as the earth is sown by hand. And whereas now, as we essay to investigate this subject more exactly, modesty hinders us, and compels us to ask pardon of chaste ears, there would have been no cause to do so, but we could have discoursed freely, and without fear of seeming obscene, upon all those points which occur to one who meditates on the subject. (XIV.23)

Augustine's own post-lapsarian inhibitions are characteristic of a reaction to human sexuality that is shared by Rustico, as well as other members of the medieval Church. (It is safe to assume that Rustico would have not deceived Alibech had he viewed human sexuality differently.) This reaction also manifests itself through the laughter of the women of Gafsa, when Alibech tells them about her adventures in the desert, as well as by the *brigata*'s laughter; and it is ultimately shared by the readers who laugh at Alibech's uninhibited behaviour: they all are acknowledging their own post-lapsarian perceptions of and prejudices about Eros.[3]

Alibech, however, never laughs. She is free of shame and inhibitions not only when she has sex with Rustico, but also when she narrates her sexual experiences to the women of Gafsa. In Alibech human sexuality is stripped of all its traditional trappings and connotations of sinfulness, and acquires in her its purest form. As Paolella ("I livelli narrativi," 205) and Vacca ("Converting Alibech," 216) have shown, Boccaccio frees her of any culpability, and consequently, Alibech retains a prelapsarian innocence even after she has lost her virginity.

If Alibech's sexual experience represents the sexual drive divested of all its negative cultural connotations and social constructs, Rustico's sexual conduct evokes many of the negative interpretations given to Eros and the body in the Middle Ages. In contrast to Alibech's prelapsarian sexual experience, Rustico's sexual experience recalls the fall of Adam and Eve. By seducing Alibech with his "diavolo," Rustico falls from the world he created for himself in the Thebaic desert, a world which, like Eden, stood metaphorically between the temporal world of fallen man (the city) and heaven (the City of God). Like the Devil, Rustico deceives his Eve; and by conflating his "diavolo" and Alibech, Rustico parodically reenacts the Temptation of St Anthony, the first Desert Father and role model for subsequent hermits in the Thebaid. Unlike Jesus in the wilderness (a word that is synonymous with the desert), who humbly tells the Devil not to tempt him, Rustico "per volere fare della sua fermezza una gran pruova, non come gli altri la mandò via o più avanti ma seco la ritenne nella sua cella" [wishing to put his resolve to a great test, unlike the others, he did not send her away nor further down the road, but kept her with him in his cell (III.10.9)]. Like Lucifer's sin in heaven and Adam's sin in Eden, Rustico's sin is one of pride before becoming a sin of lust. Like so many words with religious connotations in this novella, Rustico's "fermezza" [literally, "firmness"] has sexual connotations that anticipate both his erotic and moral downfall. The sins of *superbia* (pride) and *lussuria* (lust) are also linked to the pseudo-religious language Rustico uses to align his concupiscible appetite to Alibech's "fanciullesco appetito" [child-like appetite] to serve God. When Rustico and Alibech "gli trassero sí la superbia del capo" [removed his pride from his head] we are reminded of the *cervica superbiae*, or "stiff neck of pride"

3 For a related discussion, see David Wallace (*Giovanni Boccaccio*, 41–7).

in the Book of Genesis.[4] We are also reminded that just as Adam and Eve's lust (often associated with "original sin") was a direct consequence of their pride to "be as gods," Rustico's *lussuria* is a direct consequence of his initial *superbia*. To paraphrase St Augustine, his disobedience to God is punished by the flesh's disobedience to his will. By contrast, however, Alibech's will and "appetito" are in harmony with each other and are both directed towards God, as would have been the will and appetite of Adam and Eve had they not fallen from Eden.

The fact that *superbia*, the deadliest of the seven vices, is juxtaposed to *lussuria*, the least deadly vice, is not without significance. St Gregory's famous dictum, "peccata carnalia sunt minoris culpae et maioris infamiae quam spiritualia" [carnal sins have less culpability and greater infamy than spiritual sins] (Reade, *The Moral System of Dante's "Inferno"*, 207), and his hierarchy of seven deadly vices that makes *lussuria* the least culpable and *superbia* the most culpable of the seven, are reflected in this novella by the way in which *lussuria* commands the reader's attention, as evinced by the novella's critical reception, while *superbia* is almost obscured. The fact that Boccaccio has presented *superbia* and *lussuria* in this manner suggests that the reader should not look at one without considering the other: pride and the self are as intricately tied to desire as the soul is to the body.[5] Just as Alibech is seduced by virtue of her ignorance of Eros, Rustico is also seduced by virtue of his ignorance of himself, of his pride, and of the power of Eros in him and, later, in Alibech.

With the passing of time, Alibech's zeal to serve God runs against Rustico's "ozio" [idleness], a word which not only recalls the Ovidian "otium" [idle life] often associated with lovers, but also the deadly sin of "accidia" [sloth] which often afflicted hermits in the desert, according to St Cassian of Marseilles (Waddell, *The Desert Fathers*, 157). When Rustico fails to adequately respond to Alibech's religious exhortations, "la giovane, non parendole tanto servire a Dio quanto voleva, mormorava anzi che no" [it did not appear to the young girl that she was serving God as much as she wanted, and so she grumbled more often than not (III.10.30)]. Her "mormorare" recalls the Israelites' grumbling in the desert in Exodus 15–17. The Israelites' disappointment with the hardships their liberation brought them, and their recollection of better

---

4 I am grateful to Professor Walter Stephens for bringing this to my attention.

5 For a related discussion, see Francesco Bruni, "'*Historia Calamitatum, Secretum, Corbaccio*.'"

times in bondage, were interpreted by biblical exegetes as an allegory of Christian man's yearnings for temporal things which keep him from reaching God's promised land or heaven (Singleton, "In Exitu Israel de Aegypto," 104–6). Similarly, Alibech's sexual liberation in the desert no longer fulfils what was promised to her.

When Alibech's real father dies in a fire ("il quale nella propria casa arse il padre d'Alibech con quanti figliuoli e altra famiglia avea" [which burned to death Alibech's father with whatever children and other household members he had in his house, III.10.31]), Neerbale enters her life by taking her away from her "desert father," if not her spiritual father, and brings her back to the city in order to marry her. As the third man in her life, Neerbale unwittingly redefines the role Alibech had acquired in the desert from Rustico's concubine to Neerbale's legitimate wife. In so doing, Neerbale unknowingly mitigates the social damage Rustico did to Alibech when he made her unmarriageable.[6] Furthermore, by revealing the significant financial benefits Neerbale will derive from this marriage, Boccaccio also mitigates any emotional and social damage Neerbale may experience when he finds out that Alibech is not a virgin: "avendo in cortesia tutte le sue facultà spese, sentendo costei esser viva, messosi a cercarla e ritrovatala avanti che la corte i beni stati del padre, sí come d'uomo senza erede morto, occupasse, con gran piacere di Rustico e contro a' voler di lei la rimenò in Capsa e per moglie la prese e con lei insieme del gran patrimonio di lei divenne erede" [having spent all his wealth in splendid living, and having heard that she was alive, he went out to look for her, and having found her before the government could confiscate her father's wealth, since he had died without an heir, to Rustico's great pleasure and against her will, he led her back to Gafsa and took her as his wife, and along with her became the heir of her large estate (III.10.32)].[7] Here too Boccaccio goes to great lengths to remove any unpleasant or ambiguous feelings his readers might have about the course of events in this novella, while at the same time inviting us to imagine, in a moment of comic *reticentia* (the rhetorical device of ellipsis), the surprising discoveries each spouse will make on the wedding-night, discoveries that are anticipated by the women of Gafsa when they tell Alibech: "'Non ti dar malinconia, figliuola, no, ché egli si fa bene anche

6 I am grateful to Dr Elizabeth Wells for bringing this to my attention.

7 One could also argue that Neerbale's eventual discovery that Alibech is not a virgin is an appropriate retribution for his greed.

qua; Neerbale ne servirà bene con esso teco Domenedio'" [Don't abandon yourself to melancholy, child, no, for here too one does that well; Neerbale will serve the Lord God with you very well (III.10.34)].

As a result of her new role, Alibech's sexual activities are channelled into a socially accepted context, and Neerbale becomes the new head of her new family, in keeping with the traditional Pauline idea that "vir caput est mulieris" [the husband is the head of the wife (Ephesians 5:23)]. The contrasting and often obscene allusions to a "capo" throughout this novella are finally reconciled with Alibech's marriage to Neerbale. If the salvation, alluded to by Dioneo, is not quite spiritual, it certainly is physical: the flames of her "ninferno" are what actually saved her from the flames that destroyed her family in the city; one more narrative detail that mitigates any discomfort a reader might have about what happened to Alibech in the desert, as well as a parody of the Pauline idea of fire as a saving principle (1 Corinthians 3:13–15).

Alibech's marriage to Neerbale not only restores her Edenic experience from the desert to the city but also places it in a traditional religious context. As Giuseppe Mazzotta has pointed out in a later novella of the *Decameron*, "If the fall is the sin by which man has lost the order of Eden ... marriage is the sacrament that reflects and reenacts the plenitude of the prelapsarian condition" (*The World at Play*, 122). By redirecting her sexual activities within the context of marriage, Alibech in fact serves God by obeying his earliest commandment to "Be fruitful and multiply." Alibech's return to the city changes only the form, not the nature, of her Edenic experience.

By returning to the city and speaking to the women of Gafsa about her experiences in the desert, Alibech parodically follows in the footsteps of women mystics who returned to their cities to make public their religious devotion. Furthermore, the reversal of dominant position that Wayne Storey mentions, when Alibech becomes the pursuer and Rustico the pursued, is parodically analogous to how woman mystics endow themselves with phallic power in a patriarchal society and institution. The fact that Alibech appropriates this power as she learns "il servir a Dio" [to serve God] enables her to bring her private experience into the public realm as other female mystics had done before her. As Luce Irigaray has stated, mysticism is the only place in Western history where woman speaks and acts in such a public way (*Speculum*, 191). By publicly divulging to the women of Gafsa how she served God in the Thebaid, Alibech is combining her private and public selves, while at the same time affirming in the public sphere both the erotic and ascetic poles of the mystical experience. In so doing, she divulges a new way of looking at Eros and the human body. Even though Alibech's voice, like that of many women mystics, is altered by her male scribe (Dioneo), her position on human sexuality compels the reader to examine it carefully, beyond the laughter and reticence that have tried to obscure it. By using religious texts as a subtext for his parodic novella, Boccaccio not only achieves comic effect but also makes a statement about how differently and arbitrarily the human sexual experience can be represented and interpreted by both his characters and his audience.

Rustico, on the other hand, reveals an unconscious yearning for a prelapsarian sexual experience, not just his own, but Dioneo's too. The fact that it is turned upside down suggests that Boccaccio is underscoring the impossibility of sustaining such a fantasy. The Edenic experience described in this novella remains very problematic. While suggesting, on the one hand, that the sexual abuse of a young, naïve teenager does not necessarily have to have traumatic consequences for the victim, it also shows how easily that abuse can be perpetrated and misrepresented. As Wiley Feinstein has shown in Julia Voznesenskaya's rewriting of this novella, women's hell (Alibech's "ninferno") "is redefined quite simply as the experience of sex under patriarchy for women who are abused as a result of the male obsession with triumphant penetration of the woman's body" ("Twentieth-Century Feminist Responses," 117). This may explain why this novella, more than any other in the *Decameron*, has been so disturbing to readers, and why Boccaccio inserted the novelletta of Filippo Balducci where he did, in order to mitigate the implications of Dioneo's novella. Any attempt at creating a prelapsarian state of sex without sin or abuse, as described by Augustine and as enacted by Alibech in the desert, is always tempered by the presence of the city, the tree of the knowledge of good and evil. Since the Edenic experience is predicated on innocence, an absence of sexual self-consciousness, and ignorance, it is eventually undermined by the return to the city, whether it be Alibech's Gafsa or the *brigata*'s Florence, since the social constructs and moral strictures imposed by the city will eventually prevail over any idealized fantasies. The issue of how to fulfil one's desire, a theme that all the novelle of the third day share, concludes with a novella that underscores the inherent difficulties of fulfilling any fantasy. If the Edenic experience of the *brigata* was suggested by the *locus amoenus* where the ten narrators told their stories that day, a place that they themselves compare to "un paradiso in terra" [a paradise on earth], and if all the novelle of the third day reflect the *brigata*'s own desire to fulfil their personal sexual fantasies, as Migiel has indicated, then by concluding the third day with Dioneo's problematic novella, Boccaccio underscores the dangers and difficulties associated with creating any terrestrial paradise. As in the case of most fantasies and utopian dreams, those of the ten narrators are never fulfilled, but are mitigated when projected in speech, in the recounting of their novelle.

Bibliography

Primary Sources

Accolti, Bernardo. *Verginia. Comedia di M. Bernardo Accolti Aretino intitolata la Verginia, con un capitolo della Madonna, nuovamente corretta, & con somma diligentia ristampata. MDXXXV.* This 1535 copy is found in the Marvin T. Herrick Renaissance Drama Collection in the Rare Book Room of the University of Illinois, Urbana-Champaign.

Alighieri, Dante. *Dantis Alaghieri Epistolae: The Letters of Dante Alighieri.* Ed. Paget Toynbee. 2nd ed. rev. by Colin Hardie. Oxford: Oxford University Press, 1966.

– *The Divine Comedy of Dante Alighieri.* Ed. and trans. Allen Mandelbaum. 3 vols. New York: Bantam Books, 1982.

– *La Divina Commedia.* Ed. Bosco Umberto and Giovanni Reggio. Florence: Le Monnier, 1988.

– *La Divina Commedia.* Ed. P. Cataldi and E. Abate. Florence: Le Monnier, 2002.

– *Monarchia.* Ed. Pier Giorgio Ricci. Florence: Società Dantesca Italiana, 1965.

– *Rime giovanili, e della* Vita nuova. Cura, saggio introduttivo e introduzioni alle rime di Teodolinda Barolini. Note di Manuele Gragnolati. Milan: BUR 2009.

Aretaeus. *The Extant Work of Aretaeus.* Trans. Francis Adams. London: Sydenham Society, 1865.

Aristotle. *Aristotle in Twenty Three Volumes.* Loeb Classical Library. Vol. 21. Cambridge, MA: Harvard University Press, 1932. 1990.

– *The Complete Works of Aristotle.* Ed. Jonathan Barnes. Princeton: Princeton University Press, 1984.

– *In libros Politicorum Aristotelis expositio.* Ed. Raymundi M. Spiazzi. Turin: Marietti, 1951.

– *The Politics*. Trans. T.A. Sinclair; rev. Trevor J. Saunders. New York: Penguin Books, 1992.

Augustine, St. *The City of God*. Trans. Marcus Dods. New York: Random House, 1950.

Boccaccio, Giovanni. *The Book of Theseus*. Trans. Bernadette Marie Coy. New York: Medieval Text Association, 1974.

– *The Corbaccio*. Trans. Anthony K. Cassell. Urbana, Chicago, London: University of Illinois Press, 1975; 2nd rev. ed. Binghamton, NY: Medieval and Renaissance Texts and Studies, 1993.

– *The Decameron*. Trans. James Macmullan Rigg. London: Bullan, 1903.

– *The Decameron of Giovanni Boccaccio*. Trans. Frances Winwar. Modern Library. New York: Random House, 1930, 1955.

– *The Decameron of Giovanni Boccaccio*. Trans. John Payne. New York: Random House, 1931.

– *Il Decameron*. Ed. Carlo Salinari. Bari: Laterza, 1963.

– *Decameron*. Ed. Vittore Branca. Florence: Accademia della Crusca, 1976.

– *Decameron*. Trans. John Payne. Ed. Charles S. Singleton. 3 vols. Berkeley: University of California Press, 1982.

– *Decameron*. Trans. M. Musa and P. Bondanella. New York: New American Library, 1982, 2002.

– *Decameron*. Ed. Vittore Branca. Milan: Mondadori – I Meridiani, 1985.

– *Decameron*. Ed. Vittore Branca. Turin: Einaudi, 1980.

– *Decameron*. Ed. Vittore Branca. Turin: Einaudi, 1992.

– *The Decameron*. Trans. G.H. McWilliam. 2nd ed. London: Penguin, 1995.

– *The Decameron*. Ed. Vittore Branca. Milan: Mondadori, 2008.

– *De casibus virorum illustrium*. Ed. Pier Giorgio Ricci and Vittorio Zaccaria. In *Tutte le opere di Giovanni Boccaccio*. Vol. 9. Milan: Mondadori, 1983.

– *De claris mulieribus/Famous Women*. Ed. and trans. Virginia Brown. Cambridge, MA: Harvard University Press, 2001.

– *Diana's Hunt = Caccia Di Diana: Boccaccio's First Fiction*. Ed. Anthony K. Cassell and Victoria Kirkham. Philadelphia: University of Pennsylvania Press, 1991.

– *Elegia di Madonna Fiammetta*. Ed. Francesco Erbani. Milan: Garzanti, 1988.

– *Esposizioni sopra la Comedia di Dante*. Ed. Giorgio Padoan. 2 vols. Milan: Mondadori, 1965.

– *Il Filocolo*. Ed. A.E. Quaglio. In *Tutte le opere di G.B.*, vol. 1. Ed. V. Branca. Milan: Mondadori, 1967.

– *Genealogie deorum gentilium*. In *Tutte le opere di Giovanni Boccaccio*. Ed. Vittorio Zaccaria. Vols. 7–8. Milan: Mondadori, 1998.

– *Opere in versi. Corbaccio. Trattatello in laude di Dante. Prose latine. Epistole*. Ed. Pier Giorgio Ricci. Milan-Naples: Ricciardi, 1965.
– *Tutte le opere*, vol. 2, *Teseida delle nozze di Emilia*. Ed. Alberto Limentani. Milan: Mondadori, 1964.
– *Vita di Petrarca*. Rome: Salerno, 2004.
Brunetto Latini. *Li livres dou Tresor*. Ed. F. Carmody. Berkeley: University of California Press, 1948.
Capellanus, Andreas. *The Art of Courtly Love*. Trans. John Jay Parry. New York: Columbia University Press, 1960, 1990.
– *On Love*. Trans. P.G. Welsh. London: Duckworth, 1982.
Chaucer, Geoffrey. *The Complete Poetry and Prose of Geoffrey Chaucer*. Ed. John F. Fisher. 2nd ed. New York: Holt, Rinehart and Winston, 1989.
Christine de Pisan. *The Book of the City of the Ladies*. Trans. Rosalind Brown-Grant. London: Penguin, 1999.
Comestor, Petrus. *Historia scholastica. Patrologia Latina* 198, Alexandria, VA, 1995.
d'Artois, Philip. *Le livre du Très chevalereux Comte d'Artois et de sa femme*. Ed. J. Barrois. Paris: Crapelet, 1837.
Diaconus, Paulus. *Historia Langobardorum*. Ed. Elio Bartolini. Trans. Amedeo Giacomini. Udine: Casamassima, 1982.
– *History of the Lombards*. Ed. Edward Peters. Trans. William Dudley Foulke. Philadelphia: University of Pennsylvania Press, 1974.
Ephraim, Archdeacon. *Life of Maria the Harlot*. In *The Harlots of the Desert: A Study of Repentance in Early Monastic Sources*. Ed. and trans. Benedicta Ward. Kalamazoo: Cistercian Publications, 1987.
Francesco da Barberino. *Reggimento e costumi di donna*. Rome: Zauli, 1995.
Galen. *On the Affected Parts*. Trans. Rudolph E. Seigel. Basel: S. Karger, 1976.
Hugh of St Victor. *De Sacramentis/On the Sacraments of the Christian Faith*. Trans. Roy J. Deferrari. Cambridge, MA: Mediaeval Academy of America, 1951.
Isidore of Seville. *Etymologiarum sive originum libri XX*. Ed. W.M. Lindsay. Oxford: Clarendon Press, 1911.
Johannes de Capua. *Directorium vitae humanae alias parabolae antiquorum sapientum*. Ed. V. Puntoni. Pisa: Nistria, 1884.
Marie de France. *The Fables of Marie de France*. Ed. Marie Lou Martin. Birmingham: Summa Publications, 1984.
Migne, Jacques-Paul. *Patrologia Latina*. Paris: Garnier, 1844–92.
Il Novellino. Intro. Giorgio Manganelli. Milan: Rizzoli, 1989.
Il Novellino. Ed. Alberto Conte. Rome: Salerno, 2001.

The Novellino or One Hundred Ancient Tales. An Edition and Translation based on the 1525 Gualteruzzi editio princeps. Ed. Joseph P. Consoli. New York and London: Garland Publishing, 1997.

Petrarca, Francesco. *Le Familiari = Familiarium rerum libri*. Ed. Umberto Bosco and Vittorio Rossi; trans. Ugo Dotti. 5 vols. Racconigi: Aragno, 2004.

– *Invective contra medicum: Testo latino e volgarizzamento di Ser Domenico Silvestri*. Ed. Pier Giorgio Ricci and Bortolo Martinelli, new ed. Rome: Ed. di storia e letteratura, 1978.

Plato. *Timaeus*. Trans. Francis M. Cornford. Library of Liberal Arts. Indianapolis and New York: Bobbs-Merrill, 1959.

Seneca, Lucius Annaeus. *Ad Lucilium Epistulae morales*. Trans. Richard M. Gummere. 3 vols. New York: G.P. Putnam's Sons, 1917–25.

Shakespeare, William. All's Well That Ends Well. Folger Library edition: http://www.worldcat.org/title/alls-well-that-ends-well/oclc/46987986&referer=brief_results

– *Works*. Ed. Arthur Thomas Quiller-Couch and John Dover Wilson. Cambridge: Cambridge University Press, 1929.

Terence, Publius Afer. *Terence: The Comedies*. Trans. Smith Palmer Bovie, Constance Carrier, and Douglass Parker. Ed. Palmer Bovie. Baltimore: Johns Hopkins University Press, 1992.

– *Terence with an English Translation*. Trans. John Sargeaunt. Loeb Classical Library. Vol. 2. Cambridge, MA: Harvard University Press, 1912, 1947.

Thomas Aquinas. *In libros Politicorum Aristotelis expositio*. Ed. Raymundi M. Spiazzi. Turin: Marietti, 1952.

– *Summa Theologica*. Trans. *Fathers of the English Dominican Province*. 3 vols. New York: Benziger Brothers, 1948.

William IX of Aquitaine. *The Poetry of William VII, Count of Poitiers, IX Duke of Aquitaine*. Ed. and trans. Gerald A. Bond. New York: Garland, 1982.

William, of Conches. *Moralium*. Ed. John Holmberg. Uppsala: Holmquist & Wiksells, 1929.

Secondary Sources

Aarne, Antti. *The Types of the Folktale: A Classification and Bibliography*. Trans. and enlarged by Stith Thompson. 2nd ed. Folklore Fellows Communications 184. Helsinki: Suomalainen Tiedeakademia, 1961.

Albers, Irene. "The Passions of the Body in Boccaccio's *Decameron*." *MLN* 125 (2010): 26–53.

Alicata, Mario. "La terza giornata del *Decameron*." In *Scritti letterari*. Milan: Il Saggiatore, 1968. 248–53.

Allen, Peter L. *The Art of Love: Amatory Fiction from Ovid to the Romance of the Rose.* Philadelphia: University of Pennsylvania Press, 1992.

Almansi, Guido. "Un nuovo codice attribuibile a Boccaccio? Un manoscritto d'autore." *Medioevo Romanzo* 29 (2005): 275–313.

– *The Writer as Liar: Narrative Technique in the "Decameron".* London: Routledge & Kegan Paul, 1975.

Art and Love in Renaissance Italy. Catalogue edited by A. Bayer. New Haven: Yale University Press, 2008.

Ascoli, Albert Russell. "Boccaccio's Auerbach: Holding the Mirror University Press to Mimesis." *Studi sul Boccaccio* 20 (1991–2): 377–97.

Auerbach, Erich. *Mimesis: The Representation of Reality in Western Literature.* Trans. Willard R. Trask. Princeton: Princeton University Press, 1953, 2003.

Baird-Lange, Lorrayne Y. "Trotula's Fourteenth-Century Reputation, Jankyn's Book, and Chaucer's Trot." *Studies in the Age of Chaucer: The Yearbook of the New Chaucer Society* 1 (1985): 245–56.

Bakhtin, Mikhail. *Rabelais and His World.* Trans. Helene Iswolsky. Bloomington: Indiana University Press, 1984.

Baldassarri, Guido, and Giorgio Varanini, eds. *Racconti esemplari di predicatori del Due e Trecento.* Rome: Salerno, 1990.

Baldassarri, Stefano Ugo. "*Adfluit incautis insidiosus amor*: La precettistica ovidiana nel *Filostrato* di Boccaccio." *Rivista di studi italiani* 14 (1996): 20–42.

Baratto, Mario. *La commedia del Cinquecento.* Vicenza: Neri Pozza, 1977.

– *Realtà e stile nel "Decameron".* Vicenza: Neri Pozza, 1970; Rome: Editori riuniti, 1996.

Barbero, Alessandro. "Storia e politica fiorentina nella Cronaca di Giovanni Villani." In *Il Villani illustrato: Firenze e l'Italia medievale nelle 253 immagini del ms. Chigiano L VIII 296 della Biblioteca Vaticana.* Ed. Chiara Frugoni. Biblioteca Apostolica Vaticana, Florence: Le Lettere, 2005. 13–22.

Barbiellini Amedei, Beatrice. *Libro d'Amore attribuibile a Giovanni Boccaccio.* Florence: Accademia della Crusca, 2013.

– "La novella di Gualtieri e Griselda e il 'Libro di Gualtieri.'" *Filologia e critica* 30 (2005): 3–33.

Barbina, Alfredo, ed. *Concordanze del "Decameron".* Accademia della Crusca. 2 vols. Florence: Giunti/Barbera, 1969.

Barolini, Teodolinda. *Dante's Poets: Textuality and Truth in the Comedy.* Princeton: Princeton University Press, 1984.

– "'Le parole son femmine e i fatti sono maschi': Toward a Sexual Poetics of the *Decameron* (*Decameron* II 10)." *Studi sul Boccaccio* 21 (1993): 175–97.

– *The Undivine Comedy: Detheologizing Dante.* Princeton: Princeton University Press, 1992.

– "The Wheel of the *Decameron*." *Romance Philology* 36 (1983): 521–39.

Barsella, Susanna. "I marginalia di Boccaccio all'*Etica Nicomachea* di Aristotele. (Milano, Biblioteca Ambrosiana A 204 Inf.)." In *Boccaccio in America: Proceedings of the 2010 International Boccaccio Conference at The University of Massachusetts Amherst*, ed. M. Papio and E. Filosa. Ravenna: Longo 2012. 143–86.

Barthes, Roland. "Introduction à l'analyse structurale des récits." *Communications* 8 (1966): 1–27.

Battaglia, Salvatore. *Dizionario storico*, vol. 3, and *Tesoro della lingua italiana delle origini*: http://tlio.ovi.cnr.it/TLIO/ricindex.html.

Battaglia Ricci, Lucia. "*Decameron*: Interferenze di modelli." In *Autori e lettori di Boccaccio: Atti del Convegno internazionale di Certaldo (20–22 settembre 2001)*. Ed. Michelangelo Picone. Florence: Franco Cesati, 2002. 179–94.

Battistini, Andrea. "Retorica." In *Lessico critico decameroniano*, ed. Renzo Bragantini and Pier Massimo Forni. Turin: Bollati Boringhieri, 1995. 320–43

Baudoux-Spinette, Alberte. "Les motifs flokloriques dans le *Décameron*." In *Boccaccio in Europe: Proceedings of the Boccaccio Conference, Louvain, December 1975*, ed. Gilbert Tournoy. Louvain: Leuven University Press, 1977.

Bauman, Zygmut. *The Individualized Society*. Cambridge: Polity Press, 2001.

– *Liquid Modernity*. Cambridge: Polity Press, 2000.

Baumgartner, Emmanuèle. "Des femmes et des chiens." *De l'histoire de Troie au livre du Graal*. Orléans: Paradigme, 1994.

Baxmann, Emil. *Middletons Lustspiel "The Widow" und Boccaccios "Il Decamerone" III, 3 und II, 2*. Dissertation. Köthe: Halle, 1904.

Bayer, Andrea. *Art and Love in Renaissance Italy*. New Haven: Yale University Press, 2008.

Bellomo, Saverio. "Il sorriso di Ilario e la prima redazione in latino della *Commedia*." *Studi sul Boccaccio* 32 (2004): 201–35.

Benson, Larry D., and Theodore Anderson, eds. *The Literary Context of Chaucer's Fabliaux: Texts and Translations*. Indianapolis: Bobbs-Merrill, 1971.

Benton, John F. "Trota and Trotula." In *Dictionary of the Middle Ages*, vol. 12. New York: Scribner, 1989. 213–14.

– "Trotula, Women's Problems, and the Professionalization of Medicine in the Middle Ages." *Bulletin of the History of Medicine* 59 (1985): 30–53.

Berlioz, Jacques, and Marie Anne Polo de Beaulieu. *Les "Exempla" Médiévaux: Introduction à la Recherche, Suivi Des Tables Critiques de l'*Index Exemplorum *de Federic C. Tubach*. Carcassonne: Garae/Hesiode, 1992.

Bettinzoli, Attilio. "Occasioni dantesche nel *Decameron*." In *Dante e Boccaccio: Lectura dantis scaligera 2004–2005*, ed. Ennio Sandal. Rome and Padua: Antenore, 2006. 55–85.

– "Per una definizione delle presenze dantesche nel Decameron I. I registri 'ideologici', lirici, drammatici." *Studi sul Boccaccio* 13 (1981–2): 267–326.

– "Per una definizione delle presenze dantesche nel Decameron II. Ironizzazione e espressivismo antifrastico-deformatorio." *Studi sul Boccaccio* 14 (1983–4): 209–40.

Billanovich, Giuseppe. *Restauri boccacceschi.* Rome: Edizioni di Storia e letteratura, 1947.

Bloch, R. Howard. *The Scandal of the Fabliaux.* Chicago: University of Chicago Press, 1986.

Block, Elaine C., and Malcom Jones, eds. *Profane Imagery in Marginal Arts of the Middle Ages.* Turnhout: Brepols, 2009.

Boitani, Piero. *Il trecento italiano: Chaucer e la lunga durata, Letteratura italiana e vita intellettuale.* Ed. F. Bruni. Turin: UTET, 1993.

Boli, Todd. "Boccaccio's *Trattatello in laude di Dante,* Or *Dante resartus.*" *Renaissance Quarterly* 41 (1988): 389–412.

Bolte, Johannes, and Jiří Polívka. *Anmerkungen zu den Kinder-und Hausmärchen der Bruder Grimm.* Helsinki: Suomalainen Tiedeakademia, 1932.

Bond, Gerald A. *The Loving Subject: Desire, Eloquence, and Power in Romanesque France.* Philadelphia: University of Pennsylvania Press, 1995.

Booth, Wayne C. *The Rhetoric of Fiction.* Chicago: University of Chicago Press, 1961.

– *A Rhetoric of Irony.* Chicago: University of Chicago Press, 1975.

Bowden, William R. "The Bed-Trick, 1603–1642: Its Mechanics, Ethics, and Effects." *Shakespeare Studies: An Annual Gathering of Research, Criticism and Reviews* 5 (1969; actually published 1970): 112–23.

Bradbrook, Muriel. *Muriel Bradbrook on Shakespeare.* Brighton, Sussex: Harvester Press, 1984.

Bragantini, Renzo, and Pier Massimo Forni, eds. *Lessico critico decameroniano.* Turin: Bollati Boringhieri, 1995.

Bramanti, Vanni. "Il 'Purgatorio' di Ferondo (*Decameron,* III, 8)." *Studi sul Boccaccio* 7 (1973): 178–87.

Brambilla Ageno, Franca. "Riboboli trecenteschi." *Studi di filologia italiana* 10 (1952): 422.

Branca, Vittore. *Boccaccio: The Man and His Works.* Trans. Richard Monges. New York: New York University Press, 1976.

– *Boccaccio medievale.* Florence: Sansoni, 1956.

– *Boccaccio medievale e nuovi studi sul Decamerone.* Florence: Sansoni Editore, 1981.

– *Giovanni Boccaccio: Profilo biografico.* Florence: Sansoni, 1997.

Branca, Vittore, and Chiara Degani. "Studi sugli 'Exempla' e il 'Decameron.'" *Studi sul Boccaccio* 14 (1983–4): 178–207.

Bremmer, Jan N. *The Rise and Fall of the Afterlife: The 1995 Read-Tuckwell Lectures at the University of Bristol.* London: Routledge, 2002.

Brémond, Claude, Jacques Le Goff, and Jean-Claude Schmitt. *L'Exemplum*. Turnhout: Brepols, 1982.

Briggs, Julia. "Shakespeare's Bed-Tricks." *Essays in Criticism* 44.4 (October 1994): 293–314.

Briggs, Richard S. *Words in Action: Speech Act Theory and Biblical Interpretation: Toward a Hermeneutic of Self-Involvement*. Edinburgh: T&T Clark, 2001.

Brooke, Nicholas. "All's Well That Ends Well." *Shakespeare Survey* 30 (1977): 73–84.

Brown, Peter. "The Decline of the Empire of God: Amnesty, Penance, and the Afterlife from Late Antiquity to the Middle Ages." In *Last Things: Death and Apocalypse in the Middle Ages*, ed. Caroline Walker Bynum and Paul H. Freedman. Philadelphia: University of Pennsylvania Press, 2000. 41–59.

– *The Rise of Western Christendom*. Oxford: Blackwell, 1996.

Brownlee, Kevin, and Valeria Finucci, eds. *Generation and Degeneration: Tropes of Reproduction in Literature and History from Antiquity through Early Modern Europe*. Durham, NC: Duke University Press, 2001.

Brubaker, Leslie. "Alpha and Omega." In *Dictionary of the Middle Ages*, ed. Joseph Strayer. Vol. 1. New York: Charles Scribner's Sons, 1982. 204.

Brundage, James A. *Law, Sex, and Christian Society in Medieval Europe*. Chicago: University of Chicago Press, 1987.

Brunnemann, Martha. *Decamerone III 3 im englischen Drama*. Rostock: Hinstorffs, 1910.

Bruni, Francesco. *Boccaccio: L'invenzione della letteratura mezzana*. Bologna: Il Mulino, 1990.

– "'Historia Calamitatum, Secretum, Corbaccio': tre posizioni su luxuria (- amor) e superbia (- gloria)." In *Boccaccio in Europe: Proceedings of the Boccaccio Conference, Louvain, December 1975*, ed. Gilbert Tournoy. Louvain: Leuven University Press, 1977. 23–52.

– "Prove di arcaismo cortese: A proposito di un codice attribuito al Boccaccio (Ricc. 2317)." *Giornale storico della letteratura italiana* 184 (2007): 1–11.

Bruno Pagnamenta, Roberta. *"Il Decameron": L'ambiguità come strategia narrativa*. Ravenna: Longo, 1999.

Brusegan, Rosanna, ed. *Fabliaux, Racconti francesi medievali*. Turin: Einaudi, 1980. 224–41

Bullough, Verne L. "Medieval Medical and Scientific Views of Women." *Viator* 4 (1973): 485–501.

Calabrese, Michael. "Male Piety and Sexuality in Boccaccio's *Decameron*." *Philological Quarterly* 82.3 (Summer 2003): 257–76.

Cardini, Franco. *Le cento novelle contro la morte*. Rome: Salerno, 2007.

Casini, Tommaso. "Notizie e documenti per la storia della poesia italiana nei secoli XIII e XIV." *Il Propugnatore* new series, 2 (1889).

Cassell, Anthony Kimber. *Dante Alighieri's Monarchia, Guido Vernani's Refutation of the Monarchia composed by Dante and Pope John XXII's bull, Si fratrum*, Washington, DC: Catholic University of America Press, 2004.

– "Pilgrim Wombs, Physicke and Bed-Tricks: Intellectual Brilliance, Attenuation and Elision in *Decameron* III:9." *Modern Language Notes* 121.1 (2006): 53–101.

Cavalchini, Mariella. "Giletta-Helena: Uno Studio Comparativo." *Italica* 40 (1963): 320–3.

Cazalé-Bérard, Claude. "L'*Exemplum* Est-Il un Genre Littéraire? II L'*Exemplum* et la Nouvelle." In *Les "Exempla" Médiévaux: Nouvelles Perspectives*, ed. Jacques Berlioz and Marie Anne Polo de Beaulieu. Paris: Honoré Champion, 1998. 29–42.

Chandler, David. "The 'Bed-Trick' in *Measure for Measure*: A Source Suggestion." *Notes & Queries* 42.3 (September 1995): 320–1.

Châtillon, François. "*Arbiter omnipotens* et le symbole de l'Alpha et de l'Omega." *Revue du Moyen Âge Latin* 11.3–4 (1955): 1–46.

Cherchi, Paolo. *Andreas and the Ambiguity of Courtly Love*. Toronto: University of Toronto Press, 1995.

– "From '*controversia*' to '*novella*.'" In *Genèse, codification et rayonnament d'un genre medieval: la nouvelle: Actes du Colloque International de Montréal (McGill University, 14–16 Oct. 1982)*, ed. M. Picone, G. Di Stefano, and P. Stewart. Montreal: Plato Academic Press, 1982. 89–99. Republished in *L'alambicco in biblioteca: distillati rari*, ed. G. Guardiani and E. Speciale. Ravenna: Longo, 2000. 119–32.

Chiappelli, Fredi. "Discorso o progetto per uno studio del *Decameron*." In *Studi di italianistica in onore di Giovanni Cecchetti*. AA.VV. Ravenna: Longo, 1988. 105–11.

Chiecchi, Giuseppe. *"Dolcemente dissimulando": Cartelle laurenziane e "Decameron" censurato (1573)*. Padua: Antenore, 1992.

Chiecchi, Giuseppe, ed. *Le annotazioni e i discorsi sul Decameron del 1573 dei deputati fiorentini*. Padua: Antenore, 2001.

Chiecchi, Giuseppe, and Luciano Troisio. *Il Decameron sequestrato: Le tre edizioni censurate del Cinquecento*. Milan: Unicopli, 1984.

Ciabattoni, Francesco. "Musica sacra e musica profana nel *Decameron*." In *Boccaccio in America: Proceedings of the 2010 International Boccaccio Conference at The University of Massachusetts Amherst*, ed. M. Papio and E. Filosa. Ravenna: Longo, 2012. 67–77.

Close, Anthony J. "Seemly Pranks: The Palace Episodes in *Don Quixote* Part II." In *Art and Literature in Spain: 1600–1800. Studies in Honour of Nigel Glendinning*. Madrid: Támesis, 1993. 69–87.

Cohen, Eileen Z. "'Virtue Is Bold': The Bed-Trick and Characterization in *All's Well That Ends Well* and *Measure for Measure.*" *Philological Quarterly* 65.2 (Spring 1986): 171–86.

Cole, Howard C. *The All's Well That Ends Well Story from Boccaccio to Shakespeare*. Urbana: University of Illinois Press, 1981.

Constantine the African. *De coitu*. Quoted in J.A. Brundage, *Law, Sex, and Christian Society*. Chicago: University of Chicago Press, 1987.

Costantini, Aldo Maria. "Studi sullo Zibaldone Magliabechiano. II. Il Florilegio senechiano." *Studi sul Boccaccio* 8 (1974): 79–126.

Cottino-Jones, Marga. "Desire and the Fantastic in the *Decameron*: The Third Day." *Italica* 70 (1993): 1–18.

– *Order from Chaos: Social and Aesthetic Harmonies in Boccaccio's "Decameron"*. Washington, DC: University Press of America, 1982.

D'Andrea, Antonio. "Le rubriche del *Decameron*." In *Il nome della storia*. Naples: Liguori, 1982. 98–119.

Davis, Charles Till. *Dante's Italy*. Philadelphia: University of Pennsylvania Press, 1984.

De Coste, Mary-Michelle. "Filomena, Dioneo, and an Ass." *Heliotropia* 2.1 (2004).

Deferrari, Roy J. *A Latin-English Dictionary of St. Thomas Aquinas Based on the Summa Theologica*. Boston: St Paul Editions, 1960.

Delcorno, Carlo. *Exemplum e letteratura: Tra medioevo e rinascimento*. Bologna: Mulino, 1989.

– "L''exemplum' nella predicazione medievale in volgare." In *Concetto, Storia, Miti e Immagini del Medio Evo*, ed. Vittore Branca. Florence: Sansoni, 1973. 393–408.

– *Giordano da Pisa e l'antica predicazione volgare.* Florence: Olschki, 1975.

– "Ironia/parodia." In *Lessico critico decameroniano*, ed. Renzo Bragantini and Pier Massimo Forni. Turin: Bollati Boringhieri, 1995.

– "Modelli agiografici e modelli novellistici: Tra Cavalca e Boccaccio." In *La novella italiana*. Rome: Salerno, 1989. 337–63.

– "La 'predica' di Tedaldo." *Studi sul Boccaccio* 27 (1999): 55–75.

Delcorno Branca, Daniela. "Tradizione arturiana in Boccaccio." *Lettere italiane* 37.4 (1985): 425–52.

Delighiorgis, Stavros. *Narrative Intellection in the Decameron*. Iowa City: University of Iowa Press, 1975.

de Man, Paul. *Theory and History of Literature*. Minneapolis: University of Minnesota Press, 1982.

Demaray, John. *Dante and the Book of the Cosmos*. Transactions of the American Philosophical Society 77, part 5. Philadelphia: American Philosophical Society, 1987.

De Matteis, C. Maria. *Tractatus de bono communi*. Bologna: Pàtron, 1977.
De Sanctis, Francesco. *Storia della letteratura italiana*. 3rd ed. Vol. 1. Naples: Morano, 1879.
Desens, Marliss Carolyn. *The Bed-Trick in English Renaissance Drama: Explorations in Gender, Sexuality, and Power*. Newark and London: University of Delaware Press, Associated University Press, 1994.
– "Strange Bedfellows: The Bed-Trick in English Renaissance Drama." Dissertation, University of California, Los Angeles. *Dissertation Abstracts International* (April 1990).
Doniger, Wendy. *The Bedtrick: Tales of Sex and Masquerade*. Chicago: University of Chicago Press, 2000.
Doran, Alban H.G. "Medicine." In *Shakespeare's England*, ed. C.T. Onions et al. Vol. 1. Oxford: Oxford University Press, 1916. 413–43.
Duranti, Alessandro. "Le novelle di Dioneo." In *Studi di filologia offerti dagli allievi a Lanfranco Caretti*, AA.VV., 2 vols. Rome: Salerno, 1985. 1–38.
Edwards, G.R. "Purgatory: 'Birth' or Evolution?" *Journal of Ecclesiastical History* 36 (1985): 634–46.
Eliade, Mircea. "Degrees in Female Initiations." In *Rites and Symbols of Initiation: The Mysteries of Birth and Rebirth*. New York: Harper & Row, 1958.
Falvo, Joseph. "Ritual and Ceremony in Boccaccio's *Decameron*." *MLN* 114 (1999): 143–56.
Falvo Heffernan, Carol. "Chaucer's Miller's Tale and Reeve's Tale, Boccaccio's *Decameron*, and the French Fabliaux." *Italica* 81.3 (2004): 310–21.
Feinstein, Wiley. "Twentieth-Century Feminist Responses to Boccaccio's Alibech Story." *Romance Languages Annual* 1 (1989): 116–20.
Ferrand, Jacques. *Maladie d'amour ou mélancholie érotique*. Paris: Moreau, 1623.
Ferrante, Joan. "The Frame Characters of the *Decameron*: A Progression of Virtues." *Romance Philology* 19 (1965): 212–26.
– "Politics, Finance, and Feminism in *Decameron*, II, 7." *Studi sul Boccaccio* 20 (1993): 151–74.
Ferrari, Mirella. "Dal Boccaccio illustrato al Boccaccio censurato." In *Boccaccio in Europe: Proceedings of the Boccaccio Conference, Louvain, 1975*, ed. Gilbert Tournoy. Louvain: University of Louvain Press, 1977. 111–33.
Ferreri, Rosario. "La novella di frate Puccio." *Studi sul Boccaccio* 20 (1991): 73–83.
Ferroni, Giulio. "Eros e obliquità nella terza giornata del *Decameron*." In *Studi di filologia e letteratura italiana in onore di Gianvito Resta*, ed. Vitilio Masiello. Vol. 1. Rome: Salerno, 2000. 235–48.
Fido, Franco. "Dante personaggio." In *Il regime delle simmetrie imperfette*. Milan: Franco Angeli, 1988.

– "Dante personaggio mancato nel *Decameron*." In *Boccaccio: Secoli di vita (Atti del Congresso Internazionale, 17–19 Ottobre 1975)*, ed. Marga Cottino-Jones and Edward F. Tuttle. Ravenna: Longo, 1977. 177–89.

– "Silenzi e cavalli nell'eros del 'Decameron.'" *Belfagor* 38.1 (1983): 79–84.

Flasch, Kurt. *Poesia Dopo la Peste: Saggio su Boccaccio*. Bari: Laterza, 1995.

Forni, Pier Massimo. *Adventures in Speech: Rhetoric and Narration in Boccaccio's Decameron*. Philadelphia: University of Pennsylvania Press, 1996.

– *Forme complesse del "Decameron"*. Florence: Olschki, 1992.

– "Realtà/verità." In *Lessico critico decameroniano*, a cura di R. Bragantini e P. M. Forni. Turin: Bollati Boringhieri, 1995. 300–19.

– "Retorica del reale nel 'Decameron.'" *Studi sul Boccaccio* 17 (1988): 183–202.

– "The Tale of the King of Cyprus and the Lady of Guascony." In *The Decameron: First Day in Perspective*, ed. Elissa B. Weaver. University of Toronto Press: Toronto, 2003: 207–21.

– "Zima sermocinante (*Decameron*, III, 5)." *Giornale storico della letteratura italiana* 163 (1986): 63–74.

Forni, Pier Massimo, and Renzo Bragantini, eds. *Lessico critico decameronano*. Turin: Bollati Boringhieri, 1995.

Foster Gittes, Tobias. *Boccaccio's Naked Muse: Eros, Culture, and the Mythopoeic Imagination*. Toronto: University of Toronto Press, 2008.

Foucault, Michel. "Hysteria and Hypochondria." In *Madness and Civilization: A History of Madness in the Age of Reason*. Trans. Richard Howard. New York: Random House, 1988.

– *The Use of Pleasure: The History of Sexuality*. Vol. 2. New York: Random House, 1985, 1990.

Franceschetti, Antonio. "Dall'amore cortese all'adulterio tranquillo: lettura della novella di Tedaldo degli Elisei." In *Boccaccio e dintorni: Miscellanea di studi in onore di Vittore Branca*, ed. V. Branca and A. Balduino. Florence: Olschki, 1983. 147–60.

Frank, Martina. *Giardini Dipinti: Il Giardino nella Pittura Europea dal Medioevo al Primo Novecento*. Verona: Banco popolare di Verona, 2008.

Frojmovič, Eva. "Giotto's Allegories of Justice and the Commune in the Palazzo della Ragione in Padua: A Reconstruction." *Journal of the Warburg and Courtauld Institutes* 59 (1996): 24–47.

Frugoni, Chiara, ed. *Il Villani illustrato: Firenze e l'Italia medievale nelle 253 immagini del ms. Chigiano L VIII 296 della Biblioteca Vaticana*. Florence: Le Lettere, 2005.

Frye, Northrop. *The Myth of Deliverance: Reflections on Shakespeare's Problem Comedies*. Toronto: University of Toronto Press, 1983.

– *A Natural Perspective*. New York: Columbia University Press, 1965.

Garin, Eugenio. *Medioevo e Rinascimento: Studi e ricerche*. Bari: Laterza, 1954.

Gerard of Berry. *Notule (Glosule) super Viaticum*. In *Lovesickness in the Middle Ages*, ed. M. Wack. Philadelphia: University of Pennsylvania Press, 1990.

Getto, Giovanni. *Vita di forme, forme di vita nel Decamerone*. Turin: Einaudi, 1958.

Giannetto, Nella. "Madonna Filippa tra *casus* e *controversia*: Lettura della *novella* VI 7 del *Decameron*." *Studi sul Boccaccio* 32 (2004): 81–100.

Ginzburg, Carlo. *Wooden Eyes: Nine Reflections on Distance*. Trans. Martin Ryle and Kate Soper. London: Verso, 2002.

Godzich, Wlad. *Theory and History of Literature*. Minneapolis: University of Minnesota Press, 1982.

Gousset, Marie-Thérèse. *Eden: le jardin médiéval à travers l'enluminure, XIIIe–XVIe siècle*. Paris: Albin Michel, Bibliothèque nationale de France, 2001.

Grabher, Carlo. "Particolari influssi di Andrea Capellano sul Boccaccio." *Annali della Facoltà di Lettere e Filosofia e Magistero dell'Università di Cagliari* 21 (1953): 69–88.

Grassi, Ernesto. "La priorità del pensiero metaforico." In *Umanesimo e retorica: Il problema della follia*, ed. Ernesto Grassi and Maristella Lorch. Modena: Mucchi, 1988. 11–30.

Grimaldi, Emma. *Il privilegio di Dioneo: L'eccezione e la regola nel sistema "Decameron"*. Naples: Edizioni Scientifiche Italiane, 1987.

– "Il silenzio di Agilulf." *Misure critiche* 12 (1982): 5–22.

Haley, David. *Shakespeare's Courtly Mirror: Reflexivity and Prudence in "All's Well That Ends Well"*. Newark: University of Delaware Press, 1993.

Haller, Robert S. *The Literary Criticism of Dante Alighieri*. Lincoln: University of Nebraska Press, 1973.

Hanning, W. Robert. *The Individual in Twelfth-Century Romance*. New Haven: Yale University Press, 1977.

Havely, Nick. "Chaucer, Boccaccio and the Friars." In *Chaucer and the Italian Trecento*, ed. P. Boitani. Cambridge: Cambridge University Press, 1985. 249–68

Hillers, Delbert R. "Two Notes on the 'Decameron' (III vii 42–43 and VIII vii 64, IX v 48)." *MLN* 113.1, Italian issue (January 1998): 186–91.

Hollander, Robert. "Boccaccio's Dante." *Italica* 63.3 (Autumn 1986): 278–89.

– *Boccaccio's Dante and the Shaping Force of Satire*. Ann Arbor: University of Michigan Press, 1997.

– "Boccaccio's Dante, Imitative Distance." *Studi sul Boccaccio* 13 (1982): 25–54.

– *Boccaccio's Two Venuses*. New York: Columbia University Press, 1977.

– "*Decameron*: The Sun Rises in Dante." *Studi sul Boccaccio* 14 (1983–4): 241–55.

– "The Struggle for Control among the *novellatori* of the *Decameron* and the Motivation for the Return to Florence." Forthcoming.

Honigmann, E.A.J. "Shakespeare's Mingled Yarn and *Measure for Measure.*" *Proceedings of the British Academy* 67 (1981): 101–21.

Irigaray, Luce. *Speculum of the Other Woman*. Trans. Gillian C. Gill. Ithaca, NY: Cornell University Press, 1985.

Jacob, Philip Whittington. *Hindoo tales*. London: Strahan & Co., 1873.

Jagendorf, Zvi. "'In the Morning, Behold, It Was Leah': Genesis and the Reversal of Sexual Knowledge." In *Biblical Patterns in Modern Literature*, ed. David H. Hirsch and Nehama Aschkenasy. *Brown Judaic Studies* 77 (1984): 51–60.

Jauss, Hans Robert. *Aesthetic Experience and Literary Hermeneutics*. Trans. Michael Shaw. Minneapolis: University of Minnesota Press, 1982.

– *Toward an Aesthetic of Reception*. Trans. Timothy Bahti. Minneapolis: University of Minnesota Press, 1982.

Jeanroy, Alfred. *Poésies de Guillame IX*. Toulouse: Edouard Privat, 1905.

Jewers, A. Caroline. *Chivalric Fiction and the History of the Novel*. Gainesville: University of Florida Press, 2000.

Jones, Malcolm. *The Secret Middle Ages: Discovering the Real Medieval World*. Stroud: Sutton, 2002.

Jorden, Edward. *A Brief Discourse of the Disease Called the Suffocation of the Mother*. 1603; rpt. New York: Da Capo Press, 1971.

King, Helen. "Once upon a Text: Hysteria from Hippocrates." In *Hysteria Beyond Freud*, ed. S.L. Gilman et al. Berkeley: University of California Press, 1993. 3–90.

Kirkham, Victoria. "An Allegorically Tempered *Decameron*." *Italica* 62.1 (1985): 1–23.

– "John Badmouth: Fortunes of the Poet's Image." In *Boccaccio 1990: The Poet and His Renaissance Reception*, ed. Kevin Brownlee and Victoria Kirkham. *Studi sul Boccaccio* 20 (1991–2): 355–76.

– "The Last Tale of the *Decameron*." *Mediaevalia* 12 (1986): 205–23.

– "Love's Labors Rewarded and Paradise Lost: *Decameron* III.10." *Romanic Review* 72 (1981): 79–93; now chapter 6 in *The Sign of Reason in Boccaccio's Fiction*. Florence: Olschki, 1993. 199–214.

– "Morale." In *Lessico Critico Decameroniano*, ed. R. Bragantini and P.M. Forni. Turin: Bollati Boringhieri, 1995. 249–68.

– *The Sign of Reason in Boccaccio's Fiction*. Florence: Olschki, 1993.

– "The Tale of Guglielmo Borsiere." In *Lectura Boccaccii*, ed. Elissa Weaver. University of Toronto Press, 2003. 179–206.

– "The Word, the Flesh, and the *Decameron*." *Romance Philology* 41.2 (1987): 127–49.

Knight, George Wilson. *The Sovereign Flower*. London: Routledge, 2002.

Koldeweij, Jos. "Iconography of Dutch Misericords and Pilgrim Badges." In *Profane Imagery in Marginal Arts of the Middle Ages*, ed. E.C. Block and Malcolm Jones. Turnhout: Brepols, 2009.

Kristeva, Julia. "The Powers of Horror." In *The Portable Kristeva*, ed. Kelly Oliver. New York: Columbia University Press, 2002. 234–6.

Lambel, Hans. *Erzählungen und Schwänke*. Leipzig: Brockhaus, 1872.

Landau, Marcus. *Die Quellen des Dekameron*. Niederwalluf: Martin Sändlig, 1971.

Lausberg, Heinrich. *Elementi di retorica*. Bologna: Il Mulino, 1969.

Lawrence, D.H. *Pornography and Obscenity* (1929). In *The Cambridge Edition of the Letters and Works of D.H. Lawrence: Late Essays and Articles*, ed. James T. Boulton. Cambridge: Cambridge University Press, 2004. 236–53.

Lawrence, William Witherle. *Shakespeare's Problem Comedies*. New York: Macmillan, 1931; rpt. New York: Ungar, 1960.

Layman, B.J. "Shakespeare's Helena, Boccaccio's Giletta and the Riddles of 'Skill' and 'Honesty.'" *English Miscellany* 23 (1972): 39–53.

Lee, Alfred Collinwood. *The Decameron: Its Sources and Analogues*. London: Nutt, 1909; rpt. New York: Haskell House, 1966.

Lee, Charmaine. *Auberée*. Ed. C. Lee. Parma: Pratiche, 1994.

Leech, Clifford. "The Theme of Ambition in *All's Well That Ends Well*." *ELH* 21 (1954): 17–29.

Le Goff, Jacques. *The Birth of Purgatory*. Trans. Arthur Goldhammer. Chicago: University of Chicago Press, 1984.

– *Pour un autre Moyen Âge*. Paris: Gallimard, 1977.

Levin, Richard A. "All's Well That Ends Well, and 'All Seems Well.'" *Shakespeare Studies* 13 (1980): 131–44.

Lewis, Clive Staples. *The Allegory of Love: A Study in Medieval Tradition*. London: Oxford University Press, 1953.

Limoli, Howard. "Boccaccio's Masetto (*Decameron* III, 1)." *Romanische Forschungen* 77 (1965): 281–92.

Loxley, James. *Performativity*. New York: Routledge, 2007.

Makowski, Elizabeth. "The Conjugal Debt and Medieval Canon Law." *Journal of Medieval History* 3.2 (1977): 99–114.

Mancini, Mario. "Antitesi e deviazione in Bernart de Ventadorn." In *Metafora feudale:Per una storia dei trovatori*. Bologna: Il Mulino, 1993. 63–86.

Marchesi, Simone. *Stratigrafie decameroniane*. Florence: Olschki, 2004.

Marcozzi, Luca. "*Passio* e *ratio* tra Andrea Capellano e Boccaccio: la novella dello scolare e della vedova (*Decameron*, VIII 7) e i castighi del *De Amore*." *Italianistica* 30 (2001): 9–32.

Marcus, Millicent. "The Accommodating Frate Alberto: A Gloss on *Decameron* IV, 2." *Italica* 56 (1979): 3–21.

– *An Allegory of Form: Literary Self-Consciousness in the Decameron*. Saratoga: Anma Libri, 1979.

– "Seduction by Silence: A Gloss on the Tale of Masetto." In *An Allegory of Form: Literary Self-consciousness in the "Decameron"*. Saratoga: Anma Libri, 1979.

– "The Sweet New Style Reconsidered: A Gloss on the Tale of Cimone (*Decameron* V.1)." *Italian Quarterly* 81 (1980): 5–16.

Martin, June Hall. *Love's Fools: Aucassin, Troilus, Calisto and the Parody of the Courtly Lover*. London: Tamesis Books, 1972.

Martinez, Ronald L. "Calandrino and the Powers of the Stone: Rhetoric, Belief, and the Progress of Ingegno in *Decameron* VIII.3." *Heliotropia* 1.1 (2003).

Mathes, Hamilton A. "*Decameron*, III, 3, and a *Canzone a ballo* of Lorenzo de' Medici." *Modern Philology* 48 (1950–1): 82–5.

Mazza, Antonia. "L'inventario della 'Parva libraria' di Santo Spirito e la biblioteca del Boccac cio." *Italia medievale e umanistica* 9 (1966): 1–74.

Mazzacurati, Giancarlo. *All'ombra di Dioneo: Tipologie e percorsi della novella da Boccaccio a Bandello*. Florence: La Nuova Italia, 1996.

Mazzotta, Giuseppe. "The *Decameron*: The Marginality of Literature." *University of Toronto Quarterly* 42 (1972): 64–81.

– *The World at Play in Boccaccio's "Decameron"*. Princeton: Princeton University Press, 1986.

McGregor, James H., ed. *Approaches to Teaching Boccaccio's "Decameron"*. New York: Modern Language Association of America, 2000.

McVaugh, Michael. "The History of Medicine." In *Dictionary of the Middle Ages*, ed. Joseph Strayer. Vol. 8. 247–54.

Medri, Litta Maria. "Le architetture vegetali nelle rappresentazioni pittoriche." In *Giardini celesti, giardini terrestri: Un modello culturale per il giardino della Casa di Giovanni Boccaccio. Atti del Convegno: Certaldo Alto, 29 maggio 2004*, ed. Paolo Santagati. Florence: Ente Nazionale Giovanni Boccaccio, 2006.

Micklem, Niel. *The Nature of Hysteria*. London and New York: Routledge, 1996.

Migiel, Marilyn. "Beyond Seduction: A Reading of the Tale of Alibech and Rustico (*Decameron* III.10)." *Italica* 75.2 (1998): 161–77.

– *A Rhetoric of the "Decameron"*. Toronto: University of Toronto Press, 2003.

Minghelli, Giuliana. "Il ritorno di Efigenia, la statua, i silenzi e la discreta retorica." *Italian Culture* 8 (1990): 265–78.

Morabito, Raffaele, ed. *La Circolazione dei temi e degli intrecci narrativi: il caso Griselda (Atti del convegno di studi, L'Aquila, 3–4 dicembre 1986)*. L'Aquila: Japadre, 1988.

– ed. *La Storia di Griselda in Europa (Atti del Convegno: Modi dell'intertestualità: la storia di Griselda in Europa, l'Aquila, 12–14 maggio 1988)*. L'Aquila and Rome: Japadre, 1990.

Moravia, Alberto. *Man as an End: A Defence of Humanism; Literary, Social, and Political Essays.* Trans. Bernard Wall. New York: Farrar, Straus & Giroux, 1966.

Mordenti, Raul. "La Griselda della Controriforma italiana." In *La Circolazione dei temi e degli intrecci narrativi: il caso Griselda*, ed. Raffaele Morabito. L'Aquila: Japadre, 1988. 67–74.

Morosini, Roberta. *"Per difetto rintegrare": Una lettura del Filocolo di G.Boccaccio.* Ravenna: Longo, 2004.

Muscetta, Carlo. *Giovanni Boccaccio.* Bari: Laterza, 1972.

Neely, Carol. *Broken Nuptials in Shakespeare's Plays.* Urbana and Chicago: University of Illinois Press, 1993.

Nuttall, A.D. "*Measure for Measure*: The Bed-Trick." *Shakespeare Survey: An Annual Survey of Shakespearian Study and Production* 28 (1975): 51–6.

Ó Cuilleanáin, Cormac. *Religion and the Clergy in Boccaccio's "Decameron".* Rome: Edizioni di Storia e Letteratura, 1984.

Olson, M. Kristina. "Resurrecting Dante's Florence: Figural Realism in the *Decameron* and the *Esposizioni.*" *MLN* 124.1 (2009): 45–65.

Onions, Charles Talbut. *Shakespeare's England.* Vol. 1. Oxford: Oxford University Press, 1916.

Orlandi, Stefano. *"Necrologio" di S. Maria Novella.* Florence: Olschki, 1955.

Osgood, Charles G. *Boccaccio on Poetry.* Princeton: Princeton University Press, 1930; rpt. New York: Liberal Arts Press, 1956.

Palis, James, Evangelos Rossopoulos, and Lazaros Triarhou. "The Hippocratic Concept of Hysteria: A Translation of the Original Texts." *Integrative Psychiatry* 3.3 (1985): 226–8.

Panella, Emilio. "Dal bene comune al bene del comune: I trattati politici di Remigio dei Girolami nella Firenze dei Bianchi-Neri." *Memorie Domenicane* 16 (1985): 1–198.

– "Nuova cronologia Remigiana." *Archivium Fratrum Praedicatorum* 60 (1990): 145–311.

Pani, Laura. "*Propriis manibus ipse transcripsit.* Il manoscritto London, British Library, Harley 5383." *Scrineum rivista* 9 (2012): 305–25.

Paolella, Alfonso. "I livelli narrativi nella novella di Rustico ed Alibech 'romita' del *Decameron.*" *Revue Romane* 13 (1978): 189–205.

Paris, Gaston. Review of "Über die altfranzösische Vorstufe des Shakespeare'schen Lustspiels *Ende gut, alles gut,*" by H. von Hagen. *Romania* 8 (1879): 636.

– "Une version orientale du thème de *All's Well That Ends Well.*" *Romania* 16 (1887): 98–100.

Pasquini, Emilio. *Dante e le figure del vero: La fabbrica della Commedia.* Milan: Bruno Mondadori, 2001.

Pellegrini, Letizia. *I manoscritti dei predicatori*. Rome: Istituto Storico Domenicano, 1999.

Pennington, Kenneth. "A Note to *Decameron* 6.7: The Wit of Madonna Filippa." *Speculum* 52.4 (October 1977): 902–5.

Pernicone, Vincenzo. "La novella del marchese di Saluzzo." *La cultura* 9 (1930): 961–74.

Perrus, Claude. "Le *Décaméron* de Boccace." In *La Nouvelle: Boccace, Marguerite de Navarre, Cervantes*, ed. Bessier Jean and Philippe Daros. Paris: Champion, 1996. 49–68.

Petrey, Sandy. *Speech Acts and Literary Theory*. New York: Routledge, 1990.

Petrocchi, Giorgio. *La Commedia secondo l'antica vulgata*. Florence: Le lettere, 1994.

Picone, Michelangelo. "Gioco e/o letteratura." In *Boccaccio e la codificazione della novella. Letture del Decameron*, ed. N. Coderey, C. Genswein, and R. Pittorino. Ravenna: Longo, 2008.

– "La vergine e l'eremita: Una letteratura intertestuale della novella di Alibech (*Decameron* III.10)." *Vox Romanica* 57 (1998): 85–100.

– "The Tale of Bergamino." In *The "Decameron" First Day in Perspective*, ed. Elissa Weaver. Toronto: University of Toronto Press 2004. 160–78.

Picone, Michelangelo, ed. *Autori e lettori di Boccaccio: Atti del Convegno internazionale di Certaldo (20–22 settembre 2001)*. Florence: Franco Cesati, 2002.

– ed. *La letteratura cavalleresca dalle Chanson de geste alla Gerusalemme Liberata*. In *Atti del Convegno Internazionale di Studi, Certaldo Alto, 21–23 giugno 2007*. Pisa: Pacini, 2008.

Plaisance, Michel. "La structure de la *beffa* dans les *Cene* d'Antonfrancesco Grazzini." In *Formes et significations de la "Beffa" dans la littérature italienne de la Renaissance*, ed. André Rachon. Paris: Université de la Sorbonne Nouvelle, 1972. 45–97.

Pomata, Gianna. "Menstruating Men: Similarity and Difference in Early Modern Medicine." In *Generation and Degeneration: Tropes of Reproduction in Literature and History from Antiquity through Early Modern Europe*, ed. and intro. Valeria Finucci, ed. Kevin Brownlee. Durham, NC: Duke University Press, 2001. 109–52.

Porcelli, Bruno. "L'*Amorosa Visione* del Boccaccio e Andrea Capellano." *Studi e Problemi di Critica Testuale* 49 (1994): 81–95.

Potter, Joy Hambuechen. *Five Frames for the "Decameron": Communication and Social Systems in the "Cornice"*. Princeton: Princeton University Press, 1982.

Price, Joseph G. *The Unfortunate Comedy: A Study of "All's Well That Ends Well" and Its Critics*. Toronto: University of Toronto Press, 1968.

Propp, Vladimir. *The Morphology of the Folktale*. Trans. Laurence Scott. 2nd ed. Publications of the American Folklore Society, Bibliographical and Special Series 9. Austin: University of Texas Press, 1968.
– *Le radici storiche dei racconti di fate*. Turin: Bollati-Boringhieri, 1972.
– *Theory and History of Folklore*. Ed. Anatoly Liberman. Minneapolis: University of Minnesota Press, 1984.
Psaki, F. Regina. "Women in the *Decameron*." In *Approaches to Teaching Boccaccio's Decameron*, ed. James H. McGregor. New York: Modern Language Association of America, 2000. 79–86.
Rackham, Harris. *Aristotle in Twenty Three Volumes*. Loeb Classical Library. Cambridge, MA, and London: Harvard University Press, 1932, 1990.
Rawson, Judy. "Filomena et le rossignol dans le *Décameron*." In *Le monde animal au temps de la Renaissance*. Centre de Recherches sur la Renaissance 15. Paris: Jean Touzot, 1990. 161–71.
Reade, William Henry Vincent. *The Moral System of Dante's "Inferno"*. Port Washington, NY: Kennikat Press, 1969.
Reedy, Jeremiah. *Boccaccio in Defence of Poetry: Genealogia deorum gentilium liber XIV*. Toronto: Pontifical Institute of Mediaeval Studies, 1978.
Reusch, Heinrich, ed. *Die Indices Librorum Prohibitorum des sechszehten Jahrhunderts*. Tübingen: Turnholt, 1886.
Romanelli, Claudia. "La novella di Tedaldo degli Elisei e la revitalizzazione della precettistica medievale nel *Decameron*." *Carte italiane* 2.5 (2009): 1–22.
Rossi, Aldo. "Dante, Boccaccio e la laurea poetica." *Paragone* 13 (1962): 3–41.
Rossi, Luciano. "Ironia e parodia nel *Decameron*: da Ciappelletto a Griselda." In *La Novella Italiana, Atti del Convegno di Caprarola (19–24 settembre 1988)*. 2 vols. Rome: Salerno, 1989. 365–405.
Rossiter, Arthur Percival. *Angel with Horns and Other Shakespearian Lectures*. Ed. Graham Storey. London: Longmans, Green, 1961.
Rotunda, Dominic Peter. *Motif Index of the Italian Novella in Prose*. Bloomington: Indiana University Press, 1942.
Rowland, Beryl. "Women's Health Care and Trotula Florilegium." *Carleton University Papers on Late Antiquity and the Middle Ages* 8 (1986): 56–70.
Rubinstein, Nicolai. "Marsilio Ficino and Italian Political Thought." In *Europe in the Late Middle Ages*, ed. J.R. Hale, Beryl Smalley, and J.R.L. Highfield. London: Faber and Faber, 1965. 54–5.
Russo, Luigi. "Griselda e il marchese di Saluzzo." In *Letture critiche del Decameron*. Bari: Laterza, 1973. 315–28.
Saccone, Eduardo. "Azione." In *Lessico critico decameroniano*, ed. R. Bragantini and P.M. Forni. Turin: Bollati Boringhieri, 1995. 60–72.

Salinari, Carlo. *Boccaccio Manzoni Pirandello*. Ed. Nino Borsellino and Enrico Ghidetti. Rome: Editori Riuniti, 1979. The chapter "Introduzione al *Decameron*" is a reprint of Salinari's introduction to Boccaccio in his edition of the *Decameron*.

Santagati, Paolo, ed. *Giardini celesti, giardini terrestri: Un modello culturale per il giardino della Casa di Giovanni Boccaccio. Atti del Convegno: Certaldo Alto, 29 maggio 2004*. Florence: Ente Nazionale Giovanni Boccaccio, 2006.

Scaglione, Aldo. *Nature and Love in the Late Middle Ages*. Berkeley: University of California Press, 1963.

– *Knights at Court: Courtliness, Chivalry and Courtesy from Ottonian Germany to the Italian Renaissance*. Berkeley: University of California Press, 1991.

Schneyer, J.B. *Repertorium der Lateinischen Sermones Des Mittelaters Für di Zeit von 1150–1350*. Münster: W. Aschendorff, 1969–80.

Scordilis Brownlee, Marina. "'Wolves and Sheep': Symmetrical Undermining in Day III of the *Decameron*." *Romance Notes* 24 (1984): 262–6.

Segre, Cesare. "Da Boccaccio a Lope de Vega." In *Boccaccio: Secoli di vita, Atti del Congresso Internazionale, Boccaccio, 1975*, ed. Marga Cottino-Jones and Edward F. Tuttle. Ravenna: Longo, 1977. 234–5.

Serafini-Sauli, Judith. "The Pleasures of Reading: Boccaccio's *Decameron* and Female Literacy." *MLN* 126 (2011): 29–46.

Shahar, Galili. "Auerbach's Scars: Judaism and the Question of Literature." *Jewish Quarterly Review* 101 (2011): 604–30

Singleton, Charles S. "In Exitu Israel de Aegypto." In *Dante: A Collection of Critical Essays*, ed. John Freccero. Englewood Cliffs, NJ: Prentice Hall, 1965. 102–21.

Sinicropi, Giovanni. "Chastity and Love in the *Decameron*." In *The Olde Daunce*, ed. Robert R. Edwards and Stephen Spector. Stonybrook: State University of New York Press, 1991. 104–20.

Siraisi, Nancy G. "Practitioners and Conditions of Practice." In *Medieval and Early Renaissance Medicine: An Introduction to Knowledge and Practice*. Chicago: University of Chicago Press, 1990.

Skinner, Quentin. *The Foundations of Modern Political Thought*. Cambridge: Cambridge University Press, 1978.

Šklovskij, Viktor. *La lettura del "Decameron": Dal romanzo d'avventura al romanzo di carattere*. Trans. Alassandro Ivanov. Bologna: Il Mulino, 1969.

Skobucha, Heinz. *Sinai*. Toronto: University of Toronto Press, 1966.

Slavney, Philip R. *Perspectives on "Hysteria."* Baltimore: Johns Hopkins University Press, 1990.

Smarr, Janet Levarie. *Boccaccio and Fiammetta*. Chicago: University of Illinois Press, 1986.

– "Ovid and Boccaccio: A Note on Self-Defense." *Mediaevalia* 13 (1987): 247–55.
– "Symmetry and Balance in the *Decameron*." *Mediaevalia* 2 (1976): 158–87.
Snyder, Susan. "Introduction" to her edition of *All's Well That Ends Well*. Oxford: Clarendon Press, 1993.
Soranus. *Gynecology*. Trans. Owsei Temkin. Baltimore: Johns Hopkins University Press, 1956.
Sosso, Paola. "Le Vilain de Bailluel et la nouvelle de Ferondo." *Studi francesci* 39 (1995): 201–12.
Stassi, Maria Gabriella. "Amore e industria: III Giornata." In *Prospettive sul Decameron*, ed. G. Barberi Squarotti. Turin: Tirrenia Stampatori, 1989. 39–58.
Stewart, Pamela. "How to Get a Happy Ending: *Decameron* III:9 and Shakespeare's *All's Well*." *Studi sul Boccaccio* 20 (1991–2): 325–44.
Stillinger, Thomas C. "The Place of the Title (*Decameron*, Day One, Introduction)." In *The "Decameron" First Day in Perspective*, ed. Elissa B. Weaver. Toronto: University of Toronto Press, 2004. 29–56.
Stockhurst, Stefanie. "Passionate Pilgrims: The Forms and Functions of Late Medieval Lead Badges." In *Profane Imagery in Marginal Arts of the Middle Ages*, ed. E.C. Block and M. Jones. Turnhout: Brepols, 2009.
Storey, Harry Wayne. "Parodic Structure in 'Alibech and Rustico': Antecedents and Traditions." *Canadian Journal of Italian Studies* 5.3 (1982): 163–76.
– "The Utility of Fragments and Fragmentation." In *L'ornato parlare: Studi di filologia e letterature romanze per Furio Brugnolo*. Padua: Esedra, 2008. 509–32.
Strayer, Joseph, ed. *Dictionary of the Middle Ages*. New York: Scribner, 1982.
Styan, John Louis. *All's Well That Ends Well*. Shakespeare in Performance Series. Manchester: Manchester University Press, 1984.
Stych, Franklin Samuel. *Boccaccio in English: A Bibliography of Editions, Adaptations, and Criticism*. Westport: Greenwood, 1995.
Surdich, Luigi. *Boccaccio*. Bari: Laterza, 2001.
– "La 'varietà delle cose' e le 'frondi di quercia': la nona giornata." In *Introduzione al Decameron*, ed. M. Picone and M. Mesirca. Florence: Cesati, 2004. 227–6.
Thompson, N.S. *Chaucer, Boccaccio, and the Debate of Love*. Oxford: Clarendon Press, 1996.
Thompson, Stith. *Motif-Index of Folk-Literature*. Bloomington: Indiana University Press, 1955–8, 1966.
Todorov, Tzvetan. *Grammaire du Décaméron*. The Hague and Paris: Mouton, 1969.
Todorović, Jelena. "Nota sulla *Vita Nova* di Giovanni Boccaccio." In *Boccaccio in America: Proceedings of the 2010 International Boccaccio Conference at The*

University of Massachusetts Amherst, ed. M. Papio and E. Filosa. Ravenna: Longo 2012. 105–12.

Toscano, Antonio. "*Decameron*: Cimone's Metamorphosis." *Italian Quarterly* 29.114 (1988): 25–35.

Trotula. *The Diseases of Women*. Trans. Elizabeth Mason-Hohl. Los Angeles: Ward Ritchie, 1940.

– *The Trotula: An English Translation of the Medieval Compendium of Women's Medicine*. Ed. and trans. Monica H. Green. Middle Ages Series. Philadelphia: University of Pennsylvania Press: 2002.

Tsohatzidis, Savas L., ed., *Foundations of Speech Act Theory: Philosophical and Linguistic Perspectives*. London: Routledge, 1994.

Tubach, Federic C. *Index Exemplorum*. Helsinki: Suomalainen Tiedeakatemia, 1969.

Usher, Jonathan. "A 'ser' Cepparello Constructed from Dante fragments (*Decameron* I, 1)." *Italianist* 23 (2003): 181–93.

– "Boccaccio, Cavalcanti's Canzone *Donna me prega* and Dino's Glosses." *Heliotropia* 2.1 (2004).

– "Courtly Allusions and the Unraveling of Metaphor in the Novella of Simona and Pasquino (*Decameron* IV.7)." *Italianist* 9 (1989): 52–65.

– "Discorsi d'oltretomba nel *Decameron*." *Paragone* 36 (1985): 48–57.

– "Industria e acquisto erotico: La terza giornata." In *Introduzione al Decameron*, ed. Michelangelo Picone and Margherita Mesirca. Florence: Cesati, 2004. 99–114.

Vacca, Diane Duyos. "Converting Alibech: 'Nunc spiritu copuleris.'" *Journal of Medieval and Renaissance Studies* 25.1 (1995): 207–28.

Valesio, Paolo. *Ascoltare il silenzio. La retorica come teoria*. Bologna: Il Mulino, 1986.

– "Sacro." In *Lessico Critico Decameroniano*, ed. R. Brigantini and P.M. Forni. Turin: Bollati Boringhieri, 1995. 372–418.

Van Den Hoven, Birgit. *Work in Ancient and Medieval Thought*. Amsterdam: J.C. Gieben, 1996.

Vasvari, Louise O. "L'usignuolo in gabbia: Popular Tradition and Pornographic Parody in the *Decameron*." *Forum Italicum* 28.2 (Fall 1995): 224–51.

Velli, Giuseppe. *Petrarca e Boccaccio: Tradizione – Memoria – Scrittura*. Padua: Antenore, 1979.

– "Seneca nel *Decameron*." *Giornale storico della letteratura italiana* 168 (1991): 321–34.

Wack, Mary Frances. *Lovesickness in the Middle Ages*. Philadelphia: University of Pennsylvania Press, 1990.

Waddell, Helen. *The Desert Fathers*. Ann Arbor: University of Michigan Press, 1957. 156–62.

Waddington, Raymond B. "Entertaining the Offered Phallacy: Male Bed Tricks in Shakespeare." In *Shakespeare's Universe: Renaissance Ideas and Conventions*, ed. John M. Mucciolo, Steven J. Doloff, and Edward A. Rauchut. Hants, England: Scolar, 1996. 121–32.

Wallace, David. *Giovanni Boccaccio: Decameron*. Cambridge: Cambridge University Press, 1991.

Ward, Benedicta, ed. and trans. *The Harlots of the Desert: A Study of Repentance in Early Monastic Sources*. Kalamazoo: Cistercian Publications, 1987.

Weaver, Elissa B., ed. *The "Decameron" First Day in Perspective*. Toronto: University of Toronto Press, 2004.

Welter, J. Th. *L'"Exemplum" dans la Littérature Religieuse et Didactique Du Moyen Âge*. Paris: Guitard, 1927.

Wettstein, Jacques. *Mezura: L'Idéal des troubadours, son essence et ses aspects*. Zürich: Leenman, 1944.

Wheelock, James T.S. "The Rhetoric of Polarity in *Decameron* III, 3." *Lingua e stile* 9 (1974): 257–74.

White, Jonathan. *Italy: The Enduring Culture*. London: Continuum International, 2001.

Wright, Herbert G. "The Indebtedness of Painter's Translations from Boccaccio in *The Palace of Pleasure* to the French Version of Le Maçon." *Modern Language Review* 46 (1951): 421–35.

– "How Did Shakespeare Come to Know the *Decameron*?" *Modern Language Review* 50 (1955): 45–8.

Zanni, Raffaella. "La poesia del *Decameron*: Le ballate e l'intertesto lirico." *Linguistica e letteratura* 1 (2005): 59–142.

Index

www.ingramcontent.com/pod-product-compliance
Lightning Source LLC
Chambersburg PA
CBHW030403180625
28310CB00013B/82/J

* 9 7 8 1 4 4 2 6 4 8 2 4 1 *